THE ROMAN FAMILY IN ITALY

This book is one in a publishing series established by Oxford University Press in conjunction with the Humanities Research Centre of the Australian National University, Canberra. The OUP/HRC series includes single-author volumes by members of the HRC, past and present, and composite volumes deriving from the HRC conferences. Volumes with a specifically Australian content are produced in Melbourne; other titles are handled through their Oxford headquarters. The General Editor of the series is the Director of the HRC.

Scene of funerary meal for P. Caecilius Vallianus, an equestrian military officer ('a militis') who died aged 64. He reclines on a *kline* (couch) while slaves serve food, entertainers play musical instruments, and two children and a dog play in front of the couch; 3rd century AD. The inscription and the sculpture indicate Vallianus' high status. He is surrounded by members of his *familia* in the expansive space of his own house.

The Roman Family in Italy
Status, Sentiment, Space

EDITED BY
BERYL RAWSON AND PAUL WEAVER

HUMANITIES RESEARCH CENTRE · CANBERRA
CLARENDON PRESS · OXFORD

OXFORD

UNIVERSITY PRESS

Great Clarendon Street, Oxford OX2 6DP

Oxford University Press is a department of the University of Oxford.
It furthers the University's objective of excellence in research, scholarship,
and education by publishing worldwide in

Oxford New York

Athens Auckland Bangkok Bogotá Buenos Aires Calcutta
Cape Town Chennai Dar es Salaam Delhi Florence Hong Kong Istanbul
Karachi Kuala Lumpur Madrid Melbourne Mexico City Mumbai
Nairobi Paris São Paulo Singapore Taipei Tokyo Toronto Warsaw

with associated companies in Berlin Ibadan

Oxford is a registered trade mark of Oxford University Press
in the UK and certain other countries

Published in the United States
by Oxford University Press Inc., New York

British Library Cataloguing in Publication Data

Data available

Library of Congress Cataloging in Publication Data

The Roman family in Italy : status, sentiment, space
edited by Beryl Rawson and Paul Weaver.
Includes bibliographical references and index.
1. Family—Rome—History. 2. Rome—Social life and customs.
I. Rawson, Beryl. II. Weaver, P. R. C. (Paul Richard Carey)
III. Series, OUP/HRC (Series)
HQ511,R65 1997 306.85'0945'632—DC 21 96-45146
ISBN 0-19-815283-3

1 3 5 7 9 10 8 6 4 2

Typeset by Graphicraft Ltd., Hong Kong
Printed in Great Britain
on acid-free paper by
Bookcraft (Bath) Ltd., Midsomer Norton

Preface and Acknowledgements

THIS volume is aimed at a wide readership. In order to make it as accessible as possible to non-specialists, we have explained or translated most technical terms and quotations in Latin and Greek.

The period covered herein is approximately five centuries, from the first century BC to the fourth century AD. The focus is particularly on the first century BC and the first two centuries AD, but there is a greater extension into the Christian periods than in previous volumes. (See pp. v–vi of Rawson 1991 for more chronological detail.) For most of the late Republic and early Empire, nomenclature was a fairly reliable indicator of status and personal relations: see p. vi of Rawson (1991), which includes the connection between nomenclature and Roman legislation.

Nomenclature is an important focus of the major research project sponsored by the University of Tasmania (at Hobart) and the Australian National University (at Canberra), funded in part by the Australian Research Council. It has so far produced a database of all Italian inscriptions relevant to 'the family', which will eventually be made available to the scholarly community (as the Hobart database).

Thanks are due to a number of organizations and individuals. The Humanities Research Centre at the Australian National University sponsored the conference in 1994 out of which grew the contributions to this volume. Respondents and other participants at that conference played a valuable role in discussion. In addition to acknowledgements made in individual chapters, particular mention should be made of Professor Jean Andreau (École des Hautes Études en Sciences Sociales, Paris), whose paper on 'Adoption and Status in Roman Society' is planned for publication elsewhere, and Dr Lesley Devereaux (Anthropology, Faculty of Arts, Australian National University), who opened discussion on Richard Saller's paper.

The Faculty of Arts at the Australian National University made possible the visits of Peter Garnsey and Lisa Nevett. The Australian Research Council has funded research for all the Australian contributors to this volume. Edyth Binkowski has continued to provide much-valued research assistance to Beryl Rawson, and Zeta Hall has provided administrative support at many stages of this project.

We are grateful for the comments of OUP's readers and for the skilled assistance of OUP editors in preparing the text for publication. Finally, we thank the museums from whose holdings we have drawn the illustrations for the photographs and permission which they have granted. Particular thanks are due to the J. Paul Getty Museum in Malibu, California, and Associate Curator of Antiquities, Dr Marit Jentoft-Nilsen for hospitality and professional assistance.

B. R. and P. R. C. W.

Contents

List of Contributors   ix
List of Figures   xi
List of Tables   xiii
Abbreviations   xv

Introduction   1
Beryl Rawson and Paul Weaver

1. Roman Kinship: Structure and Sentiment   7
   Richard P. Saller

2. Legal Stumbling-Blocks for Lower-Class Families in Rome   35
   Jane F. Gardner

3. Children of Junian Latins   55
   Paul Weaver

4. Rome and the Outside World: Senatorial Families and the World They Lived In   73
   Werner Eck

5. Sons, Slaves—and Christians   101
   Peter Garnsey

6. Out of Sight, Out of Mind: Elderly Members of the Roman Family   123
   Tim Parkin

7. Conflict in the Roman Family   149
   Suzanne Dixon

8. Interpreting Epithets in Roman Epitaphs   169
   Hanne Sigismund Nielsen

9. The Iconography of Roman Childhood   205
   Beryl Rawson
   Iconography: Another Perspective   233
   Janet Huskinson

10. Familial Structures in Roman Italy: A Regional Approach   239
    Paul Gallivan and Peter Wilkins

Contents

11. Perceptions of Domestic Space in Roman Italy   281
       Lisa Nevett

12. Repopulating the Roman House   299
       Michele George

13. Artefact Distribution and Spatial Function in
    Pompeian Houses
       Penelope Allison   321

References   355
Index   373

List of Contributors

PENELOPE ALLISON, Australian Research Council Post-Doctoral Research Fellow, University of Sydney, Australia

SUZANNE DIXON, Reader in Classics and Ancient History, University of Queensland, Australia

WERNER ECK, Professor of Ancient History, Institut für Altertumskunde, University of Cologne, Germany

PAUL GALLIVAN, Senior Lecturer in Classics, University of Tasmania, Australia

JANE F. GARDNER, Professor of Ancient History, University of Reading, United Kingdom

PETER GARNSEY, Fellow of Jesus College and Reader in Ancient History, Cambridge, United Kingdom

MICHELE GEORGE, Assistant Professor of Classics, McMaster University, Canada

JANET HUSKINSON, Lecturer, The Open University, United Kingdom

LISA NEVETT, Lecturer, The Open University, United Kingdom

HANNE SIGISMUND NIELSEN, Research Fellow, Aarhus University, Denmark

TIM PARKIN, Senior Lecturer in Classics, Victoria University of Wellington, New Zealand

BERYL RAWSON, Professor of Classics, Australian National University, Canberra

RICHARD P. SALLER, Professor of History and Classics, University of Chicago, United States

PAUL WEAVER, Emeritus Professor, University of Tasmania, and Visiting Fellow in Classics, Australian National University, Canberra

PETER WILKINS, Research Fellow in Classics, University of Tasmania, Australia

List of Figures

Frontispiece: Sarcophagus of P. Caecilius Vallianus. 3rd
cent. AD. Musei Vaticani, Museo Gregoriano Profano. DAI
Rome Neg. 90.413

4.1	Tomb of the Plautii, Tibur. Photo: W. Eck	80
8.1	Age distribution, *CIL* 6	173
8.2	Age distribution, *bene merens*	184
8.3	Age distribution, *carissimus*	191
8.4	Age distribution, *dulcissimus*	192
8.5	Age distribution, *pientissimus/piissimus*	198
9.1	Relief of Seruilii family, Rome, 30–20 BC. Musei Vaticani, Museo Gregoriano Profano (inv. 10491). *CIL* 6.26410	212
9.2	Roman coin (denarius) of Julius Caesar, 47/46 BC. Aeneas fleeing from Troy, carrying father Anchises on left shoulder. British Museum, *BMC* East 31. Australian National University Classics Department Museum no. 74.06. M. H. Crawford, *Roman Republican Coinage* (1974) 458/1	214
9.3	Roman coin (denarius) of Augustus, 13 BC. Julia with sons Gaius and Lucius. British Museum, *BMC* 106. *RIC* 1². 72 nos. 404, 405	215
9.4	Roman coin (denarius) of Augustus, 2 BC. Gaius and Lucius as *principes iuuentutis*, 'leaders of youth'. British Museum, *BMC* 533. *RIC* 1². 55–6 nos. 205, 212	215
9.5	Marble relief of child and two adults, Rome, 13 BC–AD 5. Villa Doria Pamphili, Rome. DAI Rome, 62. 641. Kleiner (1977 no. 66)	218
9.6	Roman coin (sestertius) of Drusus, AD 23. Twins emerging from cornucopiae. British Museum, *BMC* Tiberius 95. Australian National University Classics Department Museum no. 74.10	219
9.7	Tondos of a boy and a girl, on walls of doorway in House of M. Lucretius Fronto, Pompeii, AD 45–79. J. R. Clarke (1991: 161, figs. 81, 82). Photo: Michael Larvey	220
9.8	Altar of A. Egrilius Magnus, aged 5 years, Ostia,	

AD 50–60. Ostia Museum, inv. 1375. *CIL* 14. 4899. Kleiner (1987 cat. no. 12). Photo: DAI Rome, 88. 342   221

9.9 Altar of Q. Sulpicius Maximus, aged about 11 years, Rome, AD 94–5. Palazzo dei Conservatori, Rome. DAI Rome, 71. 1964. *CIL* 6. 33976. Kleiner (1987 cat. no. 45)   222

9.10 Roman coin (aureus) of Antoninus Pius, AD 141–61. Distribution scene, PVELLAE FAVSTINIANAE. British Museum, *BMC* 324. *RIC* 3.74–5 nos. 397–9   226

9.11 Relief, Rome, AD 164–80. Procession of girls (*puellae Faustinianae*) approaching empresses. Villa Albani, Rome. Photo: Fratelli Alinari, Rome   226

9.12 Bust of slave boy, Rome, 2nd cent. AD. J. Paul Getty Museum, Malibu, 85. AA. 352   228

9.13 Sarcophagus, Rome, late 2nd cent. AD. Scenes of infant's first bath, education, funeral, and apotheosis. Museo Torlonia, Rome. DAI Rome, 33. 11. Kampen (1981: 53–4)   230

9.14 Sarcophagus of boy aged about 10 years, *c*.AD 120–30. Bust of boy held by Erotes; griffins. J. Paul Getty Museum, Malibu, 74. AA. 25   231

12.1 House of the Labyrinth, Pompeii   304
12.2 House of the Faun, Pompeii   308
12.3 House of the Vettii, Pompeii   309
12.4 House of the Gold Coins, Volubilis   312
12.5 House of the Large Pilasters, Volubilis   313

13.1 Plan of Pompeii, showing distribution of houses in sample   327

13.2 Luxury domestic material. From near south wall of room B, Casa del Menandro, Pompeii (inv. nos. 4685, 4686, 4689, 4722, 4730)   330

13.3 Utilitarian domestic material. From south-east corner of courtyard 41, Casa del Menandro, Pompeii (inv. nos. 4973, 4972, 4977, 4978, 4979, 4980, 4981)   330

13.4 Personal/private material. From room 37, Casa del Menandro, Pompeii (inv. nos. 4918, 4919, 4921, 4923, 4924)   331

13.5 Commercial/industrial material. From centre and north-east corner of room 43, Casa del Menandro, Pompeii (inv. nos. 5028, 5031A–F)   331

List of Tables

8.1   Distribution of relationships   172
8.2   Distribution of age indications by relationship
      group   174
8.3   Common epithets   176
8.4   Distribution of commemorated with at least
      one epithet   177
8.5   Distribution of epithets by relationship group   178
8.6   Distribution of single epithet inscriptions   180
10.1 Families with children (1–10)   258
10.2 Families with multiple children (2+)   259
10.3 Families with children of one sex   260
10.4 Families with children of both sexes   261
10.5 Comparison of Tables 10.3 and 10.4   262–3
10.6 Gender of parents   264
10.7 Parents of single children   265
10.8 Parents of multiple children (2+)   266
10.9 All grandchildren and great-grandchildren   267
10.10 Epitaphs involving only grandparents and
      grandchildren   268
10.11 Stepchildren   269
10.12 *Alumni*   270
10.13 Siblings   271

Abbreviations

AE	*L'Année épigraphique*, Paris.
Att.	Cicero, *Epistulae ad Atticum*, ed. D. R. Shackleton Bailey (Cicero's *Letters to Atticus*), 7 vols. (Cambridge, 1965–70).
BGU	*Ägyptische Urkunden aus den Staatlichen Museen zu Berlin, Griechische Urkunden* (Berlin, 1895–).
BMC	British Museum Catalogue
Bull. Comm.	*Bullettino della Commissione Archeologica Comunale di Roma*, Rome.
C.	*Codex Iustinianus*, ed. P. Krueger (Zurich, 1880).
C.Th.	*Codex Theodosianus*, ed. T. Mommsen and P. M. Meyer (Zurich, 1904–5; repr. 1970–1).
CAH	*Cambridge Ancient History* (Cambridge, 1923–).
CCL	*Corpus Christianorum. Series Latina* (Turnhout, 1954–65).
CIL	*Corpus Inscriptionum Latinarum* (Berlin, 1876–).
CSEL	*Corpus Scriptorum Ecclesiasticorum Latinorum* (Vindobona, 1866–).
D.	*Digesta Iustiniani*, ed. T. Mommsen (1877), in *The Digest of Justinian*, ed. A. Watson. 4 vols. (Philadelphia, 1985).
En. Ps.	*Enarrationes in Psalmos.*
Fam.	Cicero, *Epistulae ad familiares*, ed. D. R. Shackleton Bailey. 2 vols. (Cambridge, 1977).
FIRA	*Fontes Iuris Romani Anteiustiniani*, ed. S. Riccobono *et al.* 3 vols. 2nd edn. (Florence, 1968–9). Includes:
	Gaius, *Institutes* (Gaius)
	Paulus, *Sententiae* (Paulus, *Sent.*)
	Fragmenta Vaticani (*FV*)
	Ulpian, *Tituli/Regulae* (Ulpian, *Reg.*)
	Fragmentum incerti auctoris quod vulgo Dositheanum dicitur (*Frag. Dosith.*)
	Gnomon of the Idios Logos.
HT	*Tabulae Herculanenses*, ed. G. Pugliese Carratelli. *Parola del Passato* 1 (1945), 3 (1948), 9 (1954), 10 (1955), 16 (1961).
I.Eph.	*Die Inschriften von Ephesos*, vols. 13–17 of

Inschriften griechischer Städte aus Kleinasien
(Bonn, 1981–4).
I.It.   *Inscriptiones Italiae* (Rome, 1981–).
IG   *Inscriptiones Graecae* (Berlin, 1873–).
ILLRP   *Inscriptiones Latinae liberae rei publicae,*
                ed. A. Degrassi (Florence, 1958–63).
ILS   *Inscriptiones Latinae Selectae,* ed. H. Dessau.
                3 vols. in 5. 2nd edn. (Berlin, 1954–5).
Inst.   The *Institutes* of Justinian.
NS   *Notizie degli Scavi di Antichità* (Rome).
Pergamon *Altertümer von Pergamon,* 8. 3: *Die Inschriften*
                des Asklepieions, ed. C. Habicht (Berlin, 1969).
*PIR, PIR*² *Prosopographia Imperii Romani.* 3 vols. (Berlin,
                1897–8; 2nd edn. 1933–).
P.Oxy.   *The Oxyrhynchus Papyri* (London, 1898–).
PL   *Patrologiae cursus completus . . . ,* ed. J. P. Migne
                (Paris). *Patrologia Latina,* i.e. series [Latina] prima
                (1844–).
Q.fr.   Cicero, *Epistulae ad Quintum fratrem,* ed. D. R.
                Shackleton Bailey (Stuttgart, 1988).
RAC   *Reallexikon für Antike und Christentum*
                (Stuttgart, 1950–).
RE   *Paulys Realencyclopädie der classischen*
                Altertumswissenschaft, 34 vols. in 77 (Stuttgart,
                1893–1967; repr. 1958–67).
RIC   *The Roman Imperial Coinage,* ed. H. Mattingly
                et al. 10 vols. in 13 (London, 1923–94).
RIT   *Die römischen Inschriften von Tarraco,*
                ed. G. Alföldy (Berlin, 1975).
SHA   Scriptores Historiae Augustae.
TLL   *Thesaurus Linguae Latinae* (Leipzig, 1900–58;
                then Harvard).
ZSS-R   *Zeitschrift der Savigny-Stiftung für*
                Rechtsgeschichte. Romanistische Abteilung (Graz).

Papyri editions: see list in any standard papyrological textbook, e.g.
E. G. Turner, *Greek Papyri: An Introduction* (Oxford, 1968).

Introduction

BERYL RAWSON and PAUL WEAVER

The concept of the 'Roman family' is of strategic importance in the study of Roman society. This applies whether the focus is on social structure, or the legal framework of Roman institutions, or cultural, moral, and emotional sensibilities, or quantitative economic questions. This importance is reflected in the vast expansion of scholarship devoted to the field and in the increase in serious attention to 'the family' over the last two decades. The field has expanded to embrace areas of study as diverse as the Roman aristocracy, municipal élites, the familial roles of women and children and slaves and freedmen, and housing. There have also been fertile contributions from cognate disciplines such as anthropology, sociology, archaeology, art history, and legal scholarship.

What is 'the Roman family'? What are its distinguishing and specifically Roman features? The three international conferences on The Roman Family which have been held in Canberra since 1981 have helped develop answers to these questions. The volume which resulted from the first conference, *The Family in Ancient Rome: New Perspectives* (Croom Helm and Cornell University Press 1986, Routledge paperback 1992), argued that there was so little material readily available on the topic that a book was needed 'to guide scholars in other fields and students to what has already been done, to give examples of specialised current research which illuminates the subject, and to point the way to future research'. The present volume still has the same aims but there is now a wealth of new work on which to draw. It is also possible now to have a more coherent and nuanced view of 'the Roman family' as a result of the work done in the last fifteen years or so.

Not that this claims to be a definitive study: perhaps there will never be a definitive work on the family in any society, because there will always be diverse perceptions of the evidence. This volume is partly about perceptions, but it also presents a wide range of evidence on which to base perceptions, arguments, and future discussion. We draw on literary and legal texts, inscriptions, art and architecture, and on a variety of disciplines. Most chapters focus on one of the volume's themes of 'status, sentiment, and space' but many have implications for the whole range of themes, illustrating their interrelationship. Most deal particularly with the sub-élite classes, where there is still scope for much new work, but there are also discussions which bear on the upper classes, providing an opportunity to see the workings and interactions of a whole society. Whereas the first volume, and then the second (*Marriage, Divorce, and Children in Ancient Rome*, Oxford University Press 1991, and OUP paperback 1995), focused on the city of Rome, aware of the importance of regional variation and the dangers of generalizing over a wide geographical and cultural area, this volume explicitly and systematically moves to a study of the whole of Roman Italy. It also ventures beyond the boundaries of the previous volumes in that it discusses the society of the provinces and of a later, Christian period. These are new directions, and they may well flag the route for future research.

The growing recognition of the importance of visual and physical evidence is reflected here. The publisher has made possible a good range of illustrations, which have been integrated into the text. The last three chapters, the ones most explicitly on 'space', make extensive use of house-plans and artefacts to try to reconstruct room use and domestic behaviour. It is no coincidence that these chapters come from young scholars, all familiar with current work in prehistoric archaeology. It is in fact one of the most encouraging aspects of this volume that many of its authors are younger scholars: this augurs well for the future of studies in ancient society and, in particular, for new directions in family studies.

Richard Saller's study of structure and sentiment sets the framework for much of what follows. His chapter has much to say to other disciplines, especially anthropology, about the misinformation which has been based on claims about Roman society. He raises the important question of the relationship between social behaviour on the one hand and formal law and linguistic terminology on the other. What correlation is there between linguistic categories and social roles? His systematic empirical study of the language and behaviour of Romans leads him to the view that there was considerable flexibility in kinship terms and their implications. Rather than formal obligations attaching to specific kin, it was the household, the *domus*, which had overriding importance for the formation of a Roman's identity. His meticulous, systematic testing of the evidence, especially funerary dedications, refutes some of the claims which have been made about commemoration preferences. He finds no special pattern of sentimental or property ties to paternal or maternal kin. Saller also draws on his previous demographic work to stress 'how incomplete the kinship universe must have been for most Romans' and thus the unlikelihood of kinship roles being tightly defined and delimited.

Although Saller shows the dangers of reading legal rules as sociology, and Gardner warns (n. 26) that law should not be confused with accepted morality, that does not mean that the legal rules are unimportant. Gardner and Weaver show that there were undeniable consequences of such rules and one's status. Gardner's treatment of 'anomalous' families, however, reveals considerable flexibility and generosity in the authorities' application of the law when dealing with such families. Weaver takes one status category of lower-class families, the Junian Latins, who may well turn out to be numerically very important and who occupy the space between citizenship and slavery. He examines the anomalies between parents' and children's status when one or both parents have been freed informally. Legislation which improved opportunities for slaves (making them Junian Latins) may well have discriminated against their children.

Like Weaver, Eck makes extensive use of inscriptions, this time for the upper end of the social scale. He finds that it is essential to examine the inscriptions in their archaeological context. This enables him to assess the function and role of these monuments in senatorial families' self-representation and display. His evidence of monuments near Rome, in other parts of Italy, and in the provinces reflects something of the broadening base of the Roman senate in the imperial period. Senators from a widening geographical area had commitments to the city of Rome and might have spent long periods there, perhaps with family members; but a sense of place, of geographical origin, had continuing importance in a family's history and identity. It had emotional value for such people and provided a point of reference for them.

Status is important for Garnsey's study too, and he takes forward some aspects of Saller's chapter in the 1991 volume, on sons and slaves. But he turns to the Christian and biblical world of later antiquity to see what difference Christianity made to views about slavery and consequent action. He reveals the wealth of evidence for the study of interpersonal relationships in the family context in new or little used sources, such as Lactantius and Augustine. The texts which he makes more accessible than heretofore include recently discovered sermons of Augustine. He discusses the use of metaphor from the household (*familia*), which encompasses sons and slaves, and the tendency in theological argument to collapse the father–son distinction; but there was no aim to collapse such distinctions in the actual world, in real social interactions.

Parkin's chapter takes us from the young (sons) to the elderly (parents), and to the potential power of offspring over aged parents with consequent dependence of parents on children. In contrast with earlier Athenian law, Roman law made no provision for this. Care of the elderly in Roman society was a private rather than a public matter. Those with means may have had some protection. Some reliance could be placed on children or spouse, but there should be no romanticized notion of support from an extended family. Demographic data and techniques—so ably presented by Parkin himself in his 1992 book and by Saller in articles of 1986 and 1987—can be effectively used to reveal unsuspected social facts about the life-cycle of families that help put the legal rules in more realistic perspective.

Generational difficulties are not the only ones in a family, and Dixon extends the areas of possible conflict. She draws on modern theoretical perspectives, including Marxism and feminism, to show that conflict of various kinds is to be expected in family dynamics. She shows also, however, how families unite against external threats to provide material and emotional support. There is thus tension between competition and solidarity. She discusses various ways of mediating this: it is notable that the powers of the *paterfamilias* do not figure largely here.

Roman funerary evidence, especially that of epitaphs, has long been a rich source for sub-élite family history. Sigismund Nielsen takes such studies further by considering each of a large number of epitaphs as a whole, with all their interrelating data about age, gender, status, relationships, and epithets. She shows that there is more discrimination in a dedicator's choice of epithets than previously supposed and provides another tool for differentiating different relationships. Rawson and Huskinson focus on the figurative representations associated largely with funerary commemoration. Iconographic material has great potential value for family studies. It was the foundation of Ariès' seminal 1960 study, but has not been extensively exploited for the Roman family. Its interpretation is sometimes difficult, and two perspectives are presented in Chapter 9. This chapter reveals increasing attention paid to children, and points to the role of children in Roman families as a subject of future research.

Gallivan and Wilkins take up the funerary inscriptions of Italy more comprehensively and systematically than any previous study, giving first-fruits of a major research project. When their database becomes available to other scholars it will allow a variety of analyses of the copious data. Their own pioneering work, though necessarily tentative on some points, is suggestive, offering new light on family formation, bonds, and sentiment and revealing signs of notable regional differentiation. The regionality of Italy has long been recognized in political and economic spheres, but this phenomenon can now be extended to the world of sentiment and personal interrelations. It goes beyond 'family' matters to the structure of Roman Italian society more generally.

The three final chapters move us from place to space, using archaeological evidence—especially architecture—to try to reconstruct patterns of domestic activity. This builds on the work of Andrew Wallace-Hadrill, including his contribution to the previous volume, *Marriage, Divorce, and Children in Ancient Rome*. They warn against populating the Roman house with twentieth-century people and activities. It is no coincidence that these three are younger scholars: they use new evidence and new approaches to take the study of the family in new directions. They do not, however, discard the solid body of literary evidence which has long been known: they use it extensively and critically but do not let it dominate or distort what the material evidence might tell us. They try to discover what relationships there might be between the two bodies of evidence. It is encouraging that each of these authors (Nevett, George, Allison) has been supported by post-doctoral research fellowships or grants by peak bodies in their respective countries (from the British Academy, the Social Sciences and Humanities Research Council of Canada, and the Australian Research Council). The final chapter takes up one of the points of the first: our responsibility to other disciplines to guide them into drawing appropriate conclusions from the evidence.

'Space' will be one aspect of future Roman family studies offering further challenges and opportunities. The question of regional differentiation has been opened up in this volume and can gradually be extended to other areas of the Roman empire, offering new insights into Romanization and acculturation. Further interaction between classical studies and studies of early Christianity will provide the opportunity to look at the intersection of Roman, Greek, and Near-Eastern cultural traditions. This should illuminate the role of religion and cult in the lives of families and their societies.

Any regional extension in future Roman family studies is bound to reveal much greater diversity than suggested here for Roman Italy. It will raise difficult questions of definition, and perhaps a reformulation of our opening questions above about the nature of 'the Roman family'. The nature of the evidence will probably require a different perspective, integrating 'the family' more closely with other cultural evidence.

I

Roman Kinship: Structure and Sentiment

RICHARD P. SALLER

In the absence of developed impersonal institutions in the Roman world, individual social relationships had a special value and have a special importance in our understanding of Roman society. Over the past decade, historians have devoted their time to research of intimate family relationships on the one hand and patron–client and master–slave bonds on the other. Less attention has been given to bonds of extended kinship—that is, relationships with those who are related but live outside the household, particularly aunts, uncles, and cousins. This paper aims to analyse how Roman culture conceptualized the kinship universe and what social obligations kinship entailed.

The subject of Roman kinship holds special interest because of the central role it has had in the development of the discipline of anthropology and the formulation of social theory. Robin Fox (1967: 16–17) noted that at the beginning of anthropology in the mid-nineteenth century the interest in kinship arose from lawyers who founded the discipline: 'That is why the study of kinship today is replete with legal terminology and concepts: rights, claims, obligations, *patria potestas*, contract, agnation, corporate, etc.' These lawyers, in comparing systems of family law, 'were constantly referring back to Roman law, the source of most of their ideas'. In pre-state societies kinship was believed to provide the key to understanding social organization. In the absence of civic hierarchies and roles, individuals took their place in a web of obligations defined by their kinship roles. Rome served as paradigm of early society for nineteenth-century scholars, who were educated in the law, language, and legendary history of early Rome. As Fustel de Coulanges (1980: 3) wrote: 'in our system of education, we live from infancy in the midst of the Greeks and Romans, and become accustomed continually to

I wish to thank Jane Bestor, David Cohen, and Paul Friedrich for their helpful suggestions, and Leslie Devereaux, as discussant, for her stimulating critique.

compare them with ourselves'. Intellectual historians of the discipline
of anthropology have recognized the influence of classical learning
on the founders of anthropology, but they have not appreciated
how partial a view of Roman kinship scholars such as Henry Maine
and Lewis Morgan gathered from the legal evidence. Their partial
understanding has come back to haunt classical studies, in so far as
anthropology has influenced recent treatments of Roman kinship.

The most extensive recent study of Roman kinship beyond the
immediate family is Maurizio Bettini's *Anthropology and Roman
Culture: Kinship, Time, Images of the Soul.* As a starting-point, I
want to lay out his treatment of the subject. I do this, not to engage
in an *ad hominem* attack, but because his book illustrates a wider
understanding of Roman kinship in *structural terms* as embodied in
language, and in *jural terms* as embodied in the law. His aim (1991:
1) is to examine 'legendary, religious, and linguistic' models to establish 'attitudes'—that is, 'particular patterns of behavior which are
expected to govern the personal relations that define one's role in a
family'. Bettini observes that the Latin language presents an unusually
highly differentiated set of kinships terms. 'We can therefore expect,
and verify by analysis, that a culture which uses different names for
various aunts and uncles will also differentiate the relations to be
observed with each and assign to each a sphere of activity' (ibid. 3).
Notice here the presumption of a close correlation between linguistic
categories and social roles.

Bettini's chapters on the *patruus*, the *auunculus*, the *matertera*,
and the *amita* develop his structural theme. The *patruus*, or father's
brother, takes on a role similar to the father, characterized in much
the same way. Through a process of extension of sentiments towards
the father, the *patruus* is a detached, severe figure in Roman society.
By contrast, the *auunculus* (mother's brother) has 'a role of greater
moderation and indulgence than *patruus*' (ibid. 38). The avunculate
is defined both by structural opposition to *patruus* and by extension
of the nurturing sentiments of the mother. To validate this interpretation, Bettini invokes the anthropological study of Radcliffe-Brown:
'That the two relationships complement each other has been known
since Radcliffe-Brown: when fathers are severe, [maternal] uncles are
usually affectionate and permissive' (ibid. 46). In accepting the structural approach of Radcliffe-Brown (to which I will return), Bettini
is following the lead of Jan Bremmer (1976: 72).[1]

---

[1] The tone of Beekes's invocation of Radcliffe-Brown is typical: 'It is well known that
in a patrilineal society authority is vested in the father while Mo[ther's] Br[other] has the
position of friendly counsellor. This situation was described by A. R. Radcliffe-Brown' (Beekes
1976: 59).

The roles of aunts developed similarly from the extension of contrasting sentiments along maternal/paternal lines. The *matertera* (mother's sister), a role 'particularly marked in Roman society', was 'almost another mother', in Bettini's view (1991: 68). As another mother, 'maternal aunts perhaps had the task of rearing and supporting children who had lost one or both of their parents'. *Materterae* took the omen for their nieces' marriages and nursed their nephews at the festival of Mater Matuta. By contrast, the *amita* (father's sister) assumed a stern, paternal role. In general, 'the system of attitudes . . . seems sufficiently clear. The father's side and the mother's side are differentiated from each other according to a consistent pattern: it contrasts the detached severity of the former (*pater*, *patruus*, perhaps *amita*) with the intimacy and affection of the latter (*auunculus*, *matertera*)' (ibid. 106).

I present Bettini's interpretation at some length, because it raises the complex methodological and substantive issues that I wish to pursue. To underwrite their structural interpretation, Bettini and Bremmer invoke anthropology, and particularly Radcliffe-Brown and Lévi-Strauss. To be sure, anthropology is the place to go for sophisticated approaches to kinship, yet there is no acknowledgement that these two are part of a massive tradition of critical debate, which has left behind the structural-functionalism of Radcliffe-Brown. By presenting a somewhat deeper and more expansive archaeology of the anthropological discipline of kinship studies, I intend to offer a two-pronged critique. First, because Radcliffe-Brown and Lévi-Strauss stand in an intellectual tradition rooted in the study of Roman law and the Latin language, their conclusions do not necessarily provide independent confirmation of structural principles of kinship; to use their work for this purpose may be to indulge in circular argument. Rather than invoking a few anthropologists to validate a particular approach to Roman kinship, we ought to ask whether the Roman evidence really supports the uses of the Roman paradigm by anthropologists in their theories of society and its evolution. For instance, because Radcliffe-Brown uses a Latin derivative, 'avunculate', to describe a certain pattern of social relations, we should not assume without systematic empirical study that the pattern has any applicability to Rome. The label may be merely an artefact of the standard classical education of the past century. Secondly, anthropologists themselves are engaged in debate about the very concept of kinship and how to study it. To cite a couple of great anthropologists as authoritative is to ignore much of what the discipline has to teach us, especially about the weaknesses of a structural-functional approach.

After briefly examining the anthropological tradition of kinship studies for the influence of classical learning, I wish to turn to an examination of the empirical bases for interpretations of Roman kinship. A systematic study of language and behaviour of the Romans, I will argue, does not suggest highly differentiated roles based on opposition of sentiments towards paternal and maternal kin, except in certain limited circumstances. On the contrary, fine distinctions of kinship were commonly elided by Romans, whose identity was based above all on the symbols and hierarchical social relations of the *domus*.

THE ANTHROPOLOGICAL TRADITION OF KINSHIP STUDY

The discipline of anthropology emerged in the mid-nineteenth century. The 1860s were a decade of remarkable creativity in social thought. Sir Henry Maine published his *Ancient Law* in 1861; Fustel de Coulanges his *La Cité Antique* in 1864, and in 1868 Lewis Morgan finished writing his *Systems of Consanguinity and Affinity of the Human Family*, a work that served as the basis for his more general *Ancient Society* published in 1877. These three men, who established the subject of kinship as a central concern of anthropology, were educated in classics and knew Roman law. As a result, they formulated their concepts and theories with reference to Roman law. Maine in his *Ancient Law* reflected on the influence of the discipline of Roman law (1931: 283): 'Of the subjects which have whetted the intellectual appetite of the moderns, there is scarcely one, except Physics, which has not been filtered through Roman jurisprudence.' Maine was thinking about the law's influence on moral and political philosophy and the nature of obligations, but today we would say that he and the other founding figures in anthropology illustrate that influence as much as those in any other subject—an influence that, as Fox noted, is evident in the terminology used in contemporary kinship studies.

The common project of these three men was to understand the evolution of human social organization as a means of ordering the diversity of human societies, with their Europe as the highest point of development (Burrow 1966). The theories of Maine, Fustel, and Morgan differed, but shared certain basic features: (1) they attempted to reconstruct social evolution on an empirical basis rather than from a priori assumptions about the nature of man; (2) they posited that the earliest stages of human society were based on family and kinship; (3) classical Greece and Rome figured importantly, though differently, in their evolutionary schemes.

Today, Greece and Rome figure less overtly, perhaps, but the first two features are still very much with us. As Trautmann (1987: 180) noted in his study of Lewis Morgan, 'Every anthropological investigation of kinship sets out from one variant or another of the idea that kinship is somehow more important to the working of simple societies than of complex ones, and that in the course of their development complex societies have substituted something else for kinship.' It is easy to chuckle at the quaint statements of the nineteenth-century theorists about 'savages', but the evolutionary assumptions have not died.

I want to sketch the main elements of the evolutionary schemes of Maine, Fustel, and Morgan, with special attention to their use of Graeco-Roman society. Sir Henry Maine held a chair in Roman law and used his expertise in legal history to criticize the view of moral philosophers that the natural state of man was one of unattached individuals. Rather, early societies were 'an aggregation of families'. 'The contrast', he wrote, 'may be most forcibly expressed by saying that the unit of an ancient society was the Family, of modern society the Individual' (1931: 104). To form a larger society, 'the aggregation of Families forms the Gens or House. The aggregation of Houses makes the Tribe. The aggregation of Tribes constitutes the Commonwealth' (ibid. 106). Maine was adamant that family and kinship were not defined biologically but culturally through law: 'In truth, in the primitive view, Relationship is exactly limited by Patria Potestas. Where Potestas begins, kinship begins; and therefore adoptive relatives are among the kindred. Where the Potestas ends, Kinship ends; so that a son emancipated by his father loses all rights of Agnation' (ibid. 123). Here is the essence of Maine's *Patriarchal* Theory, in contrast to Bachofen's *Das Mutterrecht*. Maine suggested that this legal construct of kinship was always in tension with 'natural affection' (ibid. 185), rather than positing some harmonious past era when law, language, and social relations were all congruent. In Maine's story of social evolution, 'the movement of the progressive societies has been uniform in one respect. Through all its course it has been distinguished by the general dissolution of the family dependency and the growth of individual obligation in its place. The Individual is steadily substituted for the Family, as the unit of which civil laws take account'—this is the famous development from Status to Contract (ibid. 139). To trace this evolution, Maine acknowledged 'the necessity of taking Roman law as a typical system' (ibid. p. v). For my purposes, the important points are: (1) that Maine's evolution is one from society organized by family and kinship to individualism, and (2) that the evidence for early social structure comes from the Roman legal rules of *patria potestas* and agnation (Kuper 1985).

In his *Ancient City*, Fustel de Coulanges presented views similar in important respects to those of Maine. From Graeco-Roman materials, Fustel argued that the basic unit of early society was the family, but a larger family than in historical times. He too denaturalized the family: 'The ancient family was a religious rather than a natural association. Religion, it is true, did not create the family; but certainly it gave the family its rules; and hence the constitution of the ancient family was so different from what it would have been if it had owed its foundation to natural affection' (1980: 34).[2] Before law, Fustel emphasized religion, particularly household ancestor cult, as the defining principle of the family, but law remained central to his interpretation:

What we have seen of the family—its domestic religion, the gods which it had created for itself, the laws that it had established, the right of primogeniture on which it had been founded, its unity, its development from age to age until the formation of the gens, its justice, its priesthood, its internal government—carries us forcibly in thought, towards a primitive epoch, when the family was independent of all superior power, and when the city did not yet exist. (ibid. 104)

Here Fustel sees the family as providing the framework of law regulating social relations prior to the emergence of the state.

The American Lewis Morgan, a practising lawyer and traveller among American Indian societies, took a major step in the study of kinship by breaking out of the classical straitjacket both in chronology and geography. Greece and Rome remained a fundamental reference point for him, even though he placed them in a much larger scheme. Trautmann's study of Morgan stresses the influence of the developments in geological studies that suddenly required human development to be understood on a scale, not of several thousand years, but of hundreds of thousands of years (1987: 3). Relatively speaking, archaic Greece and Rome no longer represented the distant beginning, but the recent past. Morgan's *Ancient Society* posited three great stages of social evolution, each subdivided into three: savagery, followed by barbarism, culminating in civilization. Early Greece and Rome, Maine's and Fustel's starting-points, were fixed by Morgan as the highest point of the barbarism stage, ready for the transition

---

[2] On this issue, Schneider (1984: 53) is wrong to claim that 'at first kinship was taken to be a purely biological relationship deriving from the facts of human sexual reproduction'. Schneider perhaps does not appreciate how dependent the views of Maine and Fustel de Coulanges were on a particular, legalistic reading of Roman culture.

to civilization. To fill in the earlier stages, Morgan collected a vast quantity of ethnographic data from non-European societies around the world.

He was especially interested in kinship terminology as a guide to the development of social organization.

Throughout the latter part of the period of savagery, and the entire period of barbarism, mankind in general were organized in gentes, phratries, and tribes. . . . In like manner, the family has passed through successive forms, and created great systems of consanguinity and affinity which have remained to the present time. These systems, which record the relationships existing in the family of the period, when each system respectively was formed, contain an instructive record of the experience of mankind while the family was advancing from the consanguine, through the intermediate forms, to the monogamian.   (1878: p. vi)

Morgan summarized his view of social evolution as the development from Person to Territory, similar to Maine's Status to Contract. Early society was organized according to kinship, and with the passage of time kinship bonds loosened to liberate the individual to act independently within the state.

Though his vision was broader, Morgan went back to Rome and its law for several critical points. To characterize the Patriarchal Family associated with the upper level of barbarism, he turned to the Roman family and *patria potestas*: 'In the patriarchal family of the Roman type, paternal authority passed beyond the bounds of reason into an excess of domination' (ibid. 466). More fundamentally, he relied on the system of Roman kinship terminology. Early savage societies practised brother–sister marriage, yielding a kinship terminology that did not differentiate maternal from paternal kin, because husbands would have had the same parents as their wives. In the next stage, group marriage of brothers and sisters yielded a kinship terminology that collapsed collateral lines, as all brothers and sisters were fathers and mothers to all their collective children. Such systems Morgan labelled 'classificatory'. With social development came higher family forms and increasing differentiation of kin in terms of maternal and paternal lines and collaterals. In the Roman nomenclature, with its distinctions between paternal and maternal aunts, uncles, and cousins, Morgan found the paradigmatic differentiated system, which he labelled 'descriptive' in contrast to 'classificatory': 'the Roman is the most perfect and scientific system of consanguinity under monogamy which has yet appeared' (ibid. 485). For Morgan, the evolution from savage to civilized was marked by the development from a classificatory kinship system to a descriptive system, as embodied in Roman law. It was Roman law that made the descriptive system the basis of European—i.e. civilized—kinship.

To summarize, for Maine, Fustel, and Morgan, Roman kinship was fundamental to the formulation of their theories of social evolution. Maine's view was based on Roman law, Morgan's on Roman law and terminology as presented by the jurists. Fustel's views, which have been criticized by Momigliano and Humphreys for their doubtful evidential base,[3] incorporated legal and antiquarian information on religious cult. All three men claimed to be writing about social organization and behaviour, but on the basis of unattested assumptions about the correspondence between language and law on the one hand, and social behaviour on the other. None of them attempted a thorough or systematic study of daily usages and social practices related to kinship in Rome. Their focus on legal and linguistic evidence produced interpretations of kinship that were rule-oriented and emphasized kin types.

This linguistically based, rule-oriented approach to kinship left a powerful legacy in the twentieth century. Radcliffe-Brown, a formative figure in British social anthropology from the 1920s to the 1950s, was contemptuous of Morgan's evolutionary 'conjectural history', but accepted and elaborated the view of social roles based on kinship classification. His classic 1924 paper, 'The Mother's Brother in South Africa', with its structural-functionalist approach, has exercised a strong influence, as it has been repeatedly invoked by classicists working on Roman kinship. His approach is structural-functional in the sense that he closely identifies social behaviour with position in a kinship structure: 'In most primitive societies the social relations of individuals are very largely regulated on the basis of kinship. This is brought about by the formation of fixed and more or less definite patterns of behaviour for each of the recognized kinds of relationships' (1952: 18). Behaviour is guided by ideal structures: 'In a system of father-right . . . a man is largely dependent on his patrilineal lineage and therefore on his father and his father's brothers, who exercise authority and control over him, while it is to them that he has to look for protection and for inheritance. Father-right is represented by the system of *patria potestas* of ancient Rome.' The mother and her relatives then stand in structural opposition to paternal kin: 'Since it is from his mother that he expects care and indulgence, he looks for the same sort of treatment from the people of his mother's group, i.e. from all his maternal kin. On the other hand, it is to his paternal kin that he owes obedience and respect'

[3] Fustel de Coulanges (1980: pp. xx–xxiii).

(ibid. 25). Consequently, the relationship with mother's brother, the *auunculus*, is marked by a warm, 'privileged familiarity' (ibid. 13).[4] Here the structure of kinship roles is defined through the principle of extension of sentiments: that is, a child tends to extend its feelings about closest kin to more distant kin related through them. Notice that Radcliffe-Brown, like his predecessors, found Roman legal terminology and nomenclature congenial to the delineation of kinship structures, which in turn has made their conclusions apparently neatly transferable back to ancient Rome. But before transferring this structural interpretation, we need to realize that it has been criticized by other anthropologists.[5]

While the neatness and symmetry of such a delineation may give it an intuitive appeal, Malinowski, a contemporary of Radcliffe-Brown, found in his fieldwork that real life and behaviour did not conform to ideal structures. He emphasized the discrepancies between what his Trobrianders did, what they said they ought to do, and what they thought. Individualism was not the monopoly of complex, developed societies; individuals in simpler societies did not have their behaviour *determined* by rules fixed in accordance with kinship roles. Rather, they, like their modern counterparts, adapted and manipulated customs and rules, with the result that those customs and rules are not a mirror of practice. So we should not assume a simple fit between kinship system, as represented in language and law, and behaviour in any society. Malinowski wrote of 'the ill-omened kinship nomenclatures—a subject so widely over-discussed, so often exaggerated in records of field-work, that one is sometimes led to suspect that it is nothing but an avenue to anthropological insanity' (1932: p. xx).

Yet, individual pursuit of interest could not explain differences between societies or cultural systems. Meyer Fortes, a student of Malinowski's but critical of his devaluation of ideal structure, reflected on the relation of structure to behaviour, and the lack of direct correspondence of one to the other. 'When we describe structure we are already dealing with general principles far removed from the complicated skein of behaviour, feelings, beliefs, etc., that constitute the tissue of actual social life. We are, as it were, in the realm of grammar and syntax, not of the spoken word. We discern structure in the "concrete reality" of social events only by virtue of

---

[4] The structural opposition between patriarchal authority and the benevolent avunculate has been emphasized again and again by contemporary anthropologists such as Friedrich (1979: 202).

[5] I have depended on Kuper (1983) for a professional account of the debate among anthropologists.

having first established structure by abstraction from "concrete reality"' (Fortes 1970: 56). Even Fortes's less rigid approach to kinship structure led him, in his widely cited essay on *pietas*, to misinterpret Roman society by overstating the structural distinction between paternal and maternal (see below).

In an effort to understand the relation between ideal structures and daily behaviour, Edmund Leach argued in the 1950s for a political approach which views societies as constituted of competing individuals from whose actions the anthropologist abstracts the structure, which is the anthropologist's interpretative construct. Rather than standing out as a clear system of rules, the anthropologist's abstraction of social structure, including kinship, is expressed ambiguously, even contradictorily, thus leaving the way open to manipulation through interpretation in changing circumstances. Therefore, it is necessary to distinguish three levels of analysis: (1) actual individual behaviour (what one uncle did); (2) the statistically average behaviour, called the norm (what most uncles do); and (3) the ideal (what uncles are supposed to do). Kuper notes that Leach 'never believed that the structure of the ideal system was congruent with the structure of the statistical pattern which emerged as the sum of individual choices in a dynamic and ecological context' (1983: 164). In this, Leach differed from Lévi-Strauss, who wrote in terms of the 'social rule' regulating kinship and saw a close correspondence between the manifestations of the structure in linguistic categories and in behaviour (Lévi-Strauss 1969: ch. 3, esp. p. 29).

From the continuing debate about the relation between cultural structure and individual behaviour, I want to single out a more recent essay that develops Leach's position and comments on the significance of choices of terminology and behaviour. Maurice Bloch in a paper entitled 'The Moral and Tactical Meaning of Kinship Terms', based on his fieldwork in Madagascar, wrote that 'while the kinship terminology is, with minor variation, uniform throughout [Madagascar], the social organization and the kinship systems which employ these terms vary to an extreme degree. . . . Despite these extreme variations in kinship organization, however, all these people speak the same language and use virtually the same system of kinship terminology, thus apparently denying all connection between terminology and social organization' (1971: 79). Rather than trying to abstract a social structure from the system of kinship terms we would do better to look at them: '(1) in terms of the place they hold in the system of values; and (2) from the point of view of which tactical uses they can serve—in other words what transformation in the social situation they can achieve. Kinship terms do not denote kinship roles;

rather, they are part of the process of defining a role relation between speaker and hearer . . .' (ibid. 80). Bloch found that this approach helped to explain two phenomena: the use of vague kinship terms in place of highly specific ones, and metaphorical extensions of kinship terms.

A decade ago David Schneider presented a controversial critique of the whole enterprise of anthropological kinship studies as fundamentally Eurocentric. He asked:

Why has kinship been defined in terms of the relations that arise out of the processes of human sexual reproduction? . . . It is simply that so much of what passes for science in the social sciences, including anthropology, derives directly and recognizably from the commonsense notions, the everyday premises of the culture in which and by which the scientist lives. These postulates of European culture are simply taken over and put in a form that is customary for rational scientific discourse, appropriately qualified and made slightly more explicit in places and served up as something special, sometimes even in Latin. That is, the study of kinship derives directly and practically unaltered from the ethnoepistemology of European culture.

(1984: 175)

Without having done fieldwork in non-European societies, I am not in a position to judge the value of the concept of kinship for the study of those cultures. But having studied Roman kinship, I would press Schneider's critique further: that is to say, what anthropologists assumed they knew about the organization of societies in the European past goes back to a very partial and misleading reading of the evidence from Rome and some unwarranted assumptions about law, language, and practice.

Our brief archaeology of the tradition of kinship studies has suggested the following conclusions. First, from Morgan to Radcliffe-Brown and some more recent anthropologists (Friedrich 1979: 201, 221), it has been assumed that there was a close correspondence between the linguistic structure of kinship terminology and the organization of social roles. Not only has the assumption not been systematically tested for Rome, but anthropologists (and classicists invoking them) have not undertaken a comprehensive study of how and in what contexts the terminology was actually used. Instead of a thoroughgoing empirical survey, anthropologists have repeatedly referred to the Roman paradigm, which is in fact a stereotype based on selected legal rules and the highly elaborated system of Latin kinship terms.[6]

---

[6] Friedrich (1979: 222), e.g. continues the reliance on Roman law to characterize proto-Indo-European kinship with the term 'strong patripotestality' and to cite the Roman father's power of life and death over his children, on which see Saller 1994: 114–17.

Secondly, within the discipline of anthropology structural approaches to kinship have provoked critiques and debate by those attempting to understand how ideal structures can be identified and how they are used by individuals. When classical scholars cite Radcliffe-Brown or Lévi-Strauss as if their work were unproblematic, much of what is most suggestive from anthropology is lost. Moreover, by uncritical invocation classicists forfeit the contribution that we can make to the critique. When Fox notes that the understanding of kinship relations has had a jural quality from the time that Maine and Morgan founded the field of study, we may add that that understanding by men trained in civil law has been distorted by its legalistic formulation. Not only do kinship relations not function according to a system of jural obligations today, but I shall argue that the non-legal evidence does not support a predominantly jural or structural interpretation of kinship relations in ancient Rome, at least as far back as the evidence goes.

ROMAN KINSHIP

How satisfactory is the linguistically based, rule-oriented approach to kinship that is the legacy of the legally trained founders of anthropology? The debate in anthropology suggests that we should distinguish several levels of understanding. First, what was the cultural paradigm or system of kinship in Roman society, regardless of whether individual behaviour conformed to the ideals or types? The second issue is one of social identity: what part did kinship beyond the immediate family play in the Romans' placement of themselves in the social hierarchy and in webs of power relationships? The third level of analysis is behavioural: was the performance of duties by Romans for one another patterned along the lines of kinship structure? Did certain kinship roles regularly cause Romans to act in particular ways?

The linguistic-structural approach to Roman kinship, with its near-perfect system of terminology, may appear to be the best avenue to understanding the cultural paradigm. The third-century AD jurist Paul enumerated the system of 448 types of kin out to the sixth degree. Surely, the social historian ought to be able to make something of this magnificent structure, which distinguished paternal from maternal kin. But there are several reasons not to assume that the linguistic system reflects a structure of social roles and obligations.

First, much of the linguistic interpretation amounts to etymological games with speculation about derivations that cannot be fixed

in time. It may be reasonable to assume that at their origins the terminological distinctions had some social significance, but kinship
terms may continue to be used long after the social distinctions have
ceased to be meaningful. The truth is that we cannot pin-point the
origins of words in most cases, and so studies of prehistoric proto-
Indo-European society based on kinship terms float uselessly in time.[7]

The methodological difficulties may be illustrated by the etymological explanations of the *auunculus–nepos* relationship, so central
to interpretations of Roman or proto-Indo-European social structure.[8] What was the social significance of calling the mother's brother
'auunculus'? Is the ending a diminutive? And, if so, what would it
mean to be a 'little grandfather'? And is the grandfather paternal or
maternal or both? Since no good case can be made for thinking that
the term *auus* was specific to the maternal or paternal line (Beekes
1976: 60), how can we explain the association between the 'little
grandfather' with his alleged benevolence and the paternal *auus* who
would have been *paterfamilias* and characteristically severe?[9] To cite
Festus for an authoritative explanation of a prehistoric linguistic
development is to indulge in wishful thinking, since Festus had no
more authentic information than we have.[10] Even if these questions
could be decisively answered, we would still be unable to place the
social role of 'little grandfather' in time or social context. Here Bloch's
conclusion is crucial: since various social structures can be associated
with the same terminology, there are no logical grounds for arguing
back from kinship terminology alone to social structure.

The danger of arguing from kinship term to social role is evident
in the etymological speculation concerning the use of *nepos* to mean
'nephew' and also 'wastrel'. The meaning of *nepos* is especially interesting, because its development occurs in the historical era when we

---

[7] The lack of firm historical grounding is evident in Friedrich's use of the Roman *nomen*
(1979: 230) as evidence of patrilineality in proto-Indo-European society, apparently without
realizing that use of the *nomen gentile* was a specific historical development of the archaic
period in Italy that did not go back to Indo-European society (see Momigliano 1989: 81).
This is an especially good example of the pitfalls of generalizing from early Rome to early
society or early Indo-European society.   [8] See above.

[9] Bettini (1991: 54) tries to reconcile the two roles, but unconvincingly in my view; see
below.

[10] Beekes (1976: 59) argues for the genuineness of Festus' explanation on the grounds that
Festus picked out protection of the sister's *daughter* as the special duty of the *auunculus*
'quod aui locum optineat'. Why, Beekes asks, name the *filia sororis* in particular, unless there
were authentic grounds to support the statement? But Beekes fails to indicate how Festus
could possibly have acquired authentic information of this sort from a prehistoric age.
Neither Beekes nor Bettini (1991: 64) acknowledges the problem that Festus presents for their
structural explanation of the *auunculus*' role: if we take the passage seriously, then it must
be admitted that Festus writes only of the relationship with the niece and noticeably omits
any reference to a special relationship between *auunculus* and nephew.

have some evidence for social relations. Benveniste explained the meaning of 'wastrel' as a development from the *auunculus*'s typical benevolence toward his indulged *nepos*. The problem with this explanation is that the earliest attested use of *nepos* to mean 'nephew' in the second century after Christ is much later than the late-Republican occurrences of *nepos* as 'wastrel' (Beekes 1976: 49).[11] Acknowledging this chronological obstacle to an etymology that would suit his structural interpretation of kinship, Bettini turns the explanation around and argues that *nepos* came to mean 'nephew' and much earlier *auunculus* was called a 'little grandfather', because the *auus–nepos* bond and the *auunculus–nepos* bond were characterized by indulgence 'set over against a stern father'. '[S]uch intimate relations were impossible with the father or his brother' (1991: 56). But this reasoning is difficult to reconcile with the linguistic reality that when *nepos* came to mean 'nephew' in the imperial era, it was with respect to both the maternal uncle and the (allegedly stern) paternal uncle. This difficulty could perhaps be explained away by arguing that the *patruus* had lost much of his severity by the second century, but the fact remains that the neat case of structural similarities and contrasts to explain etymologies simply does not work at any one point in time.

In the historical era, the Roman system of kinship terminology in its full form was a legal construct. The jurist Paul is quite explicit that these terms constituted a specialist knowledge needed by lawyers in special circumstances—notably, inheritance, *tutela*, and exemption from giving testimony in court. Even within the legal sphere, in other matters the descriptive precision was not as thorough as Morgan thought. For instance, the jurists point out that *filius* could be taken to include *nepos*, just as *pater* could cover *auus* (D. 50. 16. 201, Iulianus); and *socer/socrus* (i.e. father-in-law and mother-in-law) included grandparents' spouses (D. 50. 16. 146, Terentius). The commonly used term *parens* was ambiguous, sometimes referring to father, but potentially including all direct paternal and maternal ascendants (D. 50. 16. 51, Gaius). In other words, outside a few important matters such as inheritance where precise degree of kinship mattered, even legal usage could collapse generations and blur the paternal/maternal distinction. This is an awkward problem for such structural interpretations as Bettini's that interpret descending generations as alternating between relations of authority between fathers and sons and bonds of affection between grandfathers and

---

[11] There are many late-Republican contexts in which *nepos* could have been used to mean nephew, but the phrase *filius sororis/fratris* appears instead.

grandsons.[12] This simply is not evident in a terminological syste__ that conflates generations and may alternatively call the same elderly household head either (stern) *paterfamilias* or (indulgent) *auus*.

If linguistic categories are to yield insights into the cultural order and the social structure, then we must look at how the terms were put to use. Paul indicated that the full vocabulary was needed in cases of inheritance and guardianship, but daily social discourse, as far as it can be detected, was a different matter. Arguably, the letters of Cicero and Pliny offer us the best insight into the social lives of the Roman élite. What is most striking to my mind about specific kinship terms is their rarity in those letters. Cicero's letters contain not a single use of *amita*, *matertera*, or *patruelis*; *auunculus*, *consobrinus*, and *patruus* together occur about a dozen times.[13] The rarity of specific terms stands in contrast to the frequency (60 occurrences) of the vague terms *necessarius* and *propinquus*, which refer to someone near or related but do not discriminate kin from friend or dependent. Pliny uses specific terms such as *amita* and *auunculus* about 20 times in his letters, as compared with 30 uses of *necessarius* and *propinquus*. When Cicero praised the virtue of *pietas* in his *Republic* (6. 16), he identified *parentes* and *propinqui* as the objects of this respect, thus choosing words that gave no sharp structural definition to this core family virtue (see below).

It has been suggested to me that the works of Cicero and Pliny are relatively late in Roman history, and that the structural significance in the terminology of kinship is clearer in the plays of Plautus from the early second century BC. This argument is of some importance because of claims about historical development, which I want to address at the end of the chapter. Suffice it to say here that *amita* does not appear in Plautus' plays; *matertera* only once in a *non sequitur* that may be corrupt. *Auunculus* does occur 5 times, but all in a single play, the *Aulularia*. Plautus uses *patruus* numerous times, but all except one are in the *Poenulus* and describe a Carthaginian uncle rather than a Roman. *Consobrinus* is absent from the extant plays, and *patruelis* occurs only in the *Poenulus*, along with *patruus*.

---

[12] Nor did Roman terminology separate paternal from maternal kin as clearly as Bettini believes, since, as Modestinus reminds us (*D.* 38. 7. 5. pr.), *agnati* and *cognati* were not mutually exclusive categories: *agnati* were a subset of *cognati*.

[13] Bradley (1991: 140–3) lays out the Latin system of kin terminology and argues that 'the inference is possible from the lexical evidence that in many moments in an individual's life the "family" embraced a much broader constituency than that nuclear model implies'. I would accept this conclusion, because it does not place a strong emphasis on a structure of kin roles. Indeed, it is noteworthy that in the two extended passages quoted by Bradley from Persius and Cicero paternal kin, maternal kin, and affines are run together in a way that suggests no strong structural oppositions.

The plays of Plautus give no warrant at all for supposing that in middle-Republican Rome the classificatory terminology structured social relations more powerfully than in the Ciceronian age.

If the usage of kinship terms in non-legal contexts suggests anything about social relations, it is that we ask not how the *patruus* and *amita* were differentiated from the *auunculus* and *matertera*. Rather, it may be more germane to ask: what is the social significance of the infrequency of specific kinship terms by comparison with vaguer terms in certain spheres of discourse? Why did Romans favour words that blurred distinctions among kin types and between kin and non-kin? I will suggest an answer later. A related, corroborating aspect of linguistic usage is worth noting: in the classical prose authors, as far as I can see, the specific terms for extended kin underwent no metaphorical extension to non-blood relations of the kind that terms for the immediate family—father, brother, and so on— underwent in social relations and religion.[14] Thus, there is no reason to believe that the extended kinship system presented a set of meanings that were significant in ordering Roman thought about the cultural or social universe.

Of course, it could be argued that word counts will not provide insights into cultural systems. What, then, is the evidence that the Romans organized their social world in a system divided along severe paternal/indulgent maternal lines? It is necessary to insist on the methodological point that single examples of an *auunculus* doing one thing or a *patruus* doing another are not adequate evidence for a cultural type or system. Bettini makes much of the legendary example of Brutus' sons joining their *auunculus* in a conspiracy to overthrow the newly founded Republic. This is taken to show the special relationship between *auunculus* and nephew. But Livy does not say or imply that the particular type of relationship provided special motivation, and this example can be countered by that of Tarquinius Superbus' execution of his sister's son (who was Brutus' brother—Livy 1. 56. 7).

For evidence of cultural types or systems, we need direct statements of kinship types, or indirect evidence of stereotypes, or patterns of behaviour.[15] The clearest and most familiar is the evidence for the stereotype of the severe *patruus*—a stereotype which has its

---

[14] On metaphorical extension, see Pitt-Rivers in Goody (1973: 89–105).

[15] Lévi-Strauss (1969: p. xxxiii) distinguishes between a prescriptive and a preferential system of marriage, which would be demonstrated by prescriptive statements and patterns of behaviour, respectively. To get a sense of what would constitute clear evidence of structure, I find comparison helpful. Comaroff and Roberts (1981: 46) offer the following description of kinship structure in southern Africa: 'Tswana distinguish sharply between the normative

roots in the specific social obligation of guardianship (see below). In his defence speech Cicero likened Caelius' prosecutor, L. Herennius, to a *pertristis patruus* in order to belittle Herennius' exaggerated moral criticism (*Pro Caelio* 25). Similarly, in response to heavy-handed moralizing, Horace's satirical persona protests: 'don't be a *patruus* to me' (*Sermones* 2. 3. 88; also 2. 2. 94–8). And Manilius writes of the *patrui rigor* (*Astronomica* 5. 450). Yet, this stereotype did not dominate the associations with *patruus* in Roman culture and may have been more a stock joke than a reflection of social role. In Plautus' *Poenulus* and *Aulularia* it is impossible to find the opposition between the severe *patruus* and the warm *auunculus*. The *patruus* of the *Poenulus*, Hanno, is a warm, concerned figure, whose benevolence draws from the nephew the ecstatic exclamation: *O patrue mi patruissime* (1197).[16]

In contrast to the evidence for stereotyping of the *patruus*, I know of no direct statements or stereotyping to support the claim that the Roman *auunculus* was specially regarded as a warm, indulgent type. The only direct statement comes from Tacitus' *Germania* and describes German mores, not Roman. Tacitus reports that among the Germans the bond between *auunculus* and *sororum filii* was more sacred and tighter than the bond between father and son. As a result, Germans preferred nephews as hostages (*Germania* 20). It may be that Tacitus comments on this as another of the curiosities of German society that distinguished it from Roman customs. Of course, there are individual examples of Roman *auunculi* favouring their nephews, gathered by Bettini (1991: ch. 3), but these do not add up to a type or kinship system. Cicero attests to the love and concern of Atticus for young Quintus, his sister's son, but along with Atticus' love Cicero writes of his own love as *patruus* for the boy (*Att.* 10. 4. 6).[17]

content of agnation and matrilineality. The opposition between them is expressed, in a variety of forms, as one between the values of rivalry-conflict and support-alliance—between material and political antagonism, on the one hand, and moral and social protagonism, on the other. The essentially hostile agnatic universe, beyond the confines of the house, is the scene of individual management, competitive activity, and the negotiation of power relations. In contrast, the matrilateral domain is characterized by a non-negotiable moral unity that is constantly affirmed in ritual, symbolic, and structural terms. "A man and his mother's brother *never* fight", the Tswana say.' I know of no comparable proverbs from Rome regarding any paternal or maternal kin, and no statement of a general opposition of domains.

[16] It is true that Tacitus (*Annales* 1. 33) refers to the hostility of *patruus* Tiberius towards his nephew Germanicus, but it is not clear that Tacitus meant that the hostility derived from Tiberius' being a *patruus*, since Tacitus also noted the hostility of *auia* Livia towards Germanicus, and no one would use this passage to deduce that *auiae* were generally severe towards their grandchildren.

[17] On these relationships in Cicero's family, see Bradley (1991: ch. 8).

The opposition between paternal and maternal aunts finds no direct support in the Roman sources. The 'good evidence' for the role of the *matertera* to which Bettini refers (1991: 68) is entirely inference from a very few examples. In fact, the word *matertera* occurs only twice in the works of Cicero, Sallust, Livy, Seneca, Pliny, Tacitus, and Suetonius taken together—hardly evidence of a role 'particularly marked in Roman society'.[18] On the other side, not only is there no evidence for the stern *amita*, but Pliny (4. 19. 1) refers to the *adfectus amitae* in a way to suggest that affection was associated with the father's sister.

In sum, there is evidence that the *patruus* was occasionally stereotyped as a stern figure, but nothing to support the idea of some broader cultural structure organized by the opposition between severe paternal kin and warm, indulgent maternal kin. Furthermore, Radcliffe-Brown's explanation of the avunculate in South Africa should not lead us to expect such a structure in Rome. Only a blinkered reading of the Roman evidence has led anthropologists and classicists to find an analogy. Radcliffe-Brown explicated a sweeping structural dichotomy for South Africa based on father-right: that is, authority and property on the father's side as against affection and nurturing on the mother's side. At first glance there might appear to be a basis for this dichotomy in Roman society in the father's authority, exemplified by *patria potestas* and underwritten by filial *pietas*, and in agnatic rights of inheritance. According to Radcliffe-Brown, the concentration of property and authority on the paternal side left relationships with *auunculi* and other maternal kin free and easy.

Closer consideration, however, suggests that in Rome the grounds for the dichotomy are weaker than they first appear. The fundamental opposition between paternal authority and maternal indulgence is not so marked in Roman culture. Both parents were owed *pietas* and *obsequium*—affectionate duty and respectful obedience (Saller 1988; 1994: ch. 5). Despite Meyer Fortes' elegant theory and cross-cultural comparisons in regard to *pietas*, the truth is that, strictly speaking, it was not a patrilineal virtue placing special value on agnatic relatives, and it was not a virtue of filial obedience. The lack of distinction between paternal and maternal ancestors, evident in

---

[18] Beyond individual examples, Bettini makes much of the role of the *matertera* in the festival to honour Mater Matuta. He argues that in this rite *materterae* prayed for their sisters' children, but at 268 n. 24 he concedes that nothing in the language of the sources identifies precisely *materterae* rather than *amitae*. His ultimate justification for his interpretation—'In any case, a sister's concern for her sister's children fits perfectly into the functions of the *matertera* as sketched thus far'—illustrates the circularity of argument based on inference from too little evidence.

the vocabulary of *auus* and *auia*, was replicated in certain rituals. For instance, the law of *parricidium* punished with death the murder of a relative, but added the horrible ritual punishment of the sack for particularly heinous cases. The law defines the heinous cases as the murder of *auus* or *auia* 'in addition to mother and father' (*praeter matrem et patrem*, D. 48. 9. 9.1, Modestinus). The crucial distinction in defining the especially heinous crime here is between direct ascendants and collaterals, not between paternal and maternal.

Moreover, the whole structural argument is based on a dubious argument of extension of sentiments from father or mother to kin related through each. It is by no means clear that the Romans saw a strong polarity between paternal severity and maternal indulgence. As Suzanne Dixon (1988) has shown, the Roman mother was associated with discipline. I have argued that Roman fathers were expected to display towards their children *pietas* or dutiful affection: Roman fathers were expected to be authority figures, but not generally severe or detached.[19] Doubts about the structural opposition are suggested by one of the very examples Bettini relies on. During the civil war Brutus wrote to Cicero to plead on behalf of his sister's children, fathered by Lepidus, the opponent of Cicero. The letter does illustrate the commitment of an *auunculus* to his sister's children, but any structural interpretation based on a paternal/maternal dichotomy is wholly belied by Brutus' plea that Cicero think of Brutus as acting in the role of father ('in patris locum successisse': *Ad M. Brutum* 1. 13. 1). Cicero responded to Brutus by acknowledging the harshness of punishing Lepidus' children for the wrongs of Lepidus, but he nevertheless justified the means by the ends, contending that such punishment would restrain parents from wrongdoing on account of *caritas liberorum* (*Ad M. Brutum* 1. 12). Cicero's reasoning is based on the premiss that paternal (and maternal) affection for children is a fundamental force in society. If the principle of extension of sentiments had influenced kin relationships, the Romans would not have distinguished paternal kin from maternal on the basis of the warmth and love of the bond.

Perhaps most fundamentally, Radcliffe-Brown's description of the implications of father-right for property transmission does not correspond to Roman law and practice in important ways. By the historical period both Roman fathers and mothers passed on estates to their children by written wills, which gave them great flexibility to determine who should benefit. The absence of a genuine father-right

[19] 1994: ch. 5. The paradigmatic stories about paternal severity concerned discipline in defence of the state, not the imposition of authority within the family.

system at this time is illustrated by the terminology used in Cicero's *Pro Cluentio* 21, where a *uterine* half-brother is called simply *frater* and instituted heir. Even in the time of the XII Tables property was not passed down solely along patrilineal lines: the primary heirs were the *sui heredes*, including a man's unmarried daughters as well as his sons. The logic of Radcliffe-Brown's explanation of the opposition between the *patruus* and the *auunculus* is that a young man shared property interests (and the consequent potential for conflict) with his paternal uncle but had no such common interests or conflicts with his maternal uncle. As will be shown below, Romans did inherit from their maternal relatives and so did not expect a disinterested relationship with them. I am not suggesting that father and mother, or paternal and maternal relatives, were indistinguishable on these counts, but that their roles were not defined as clear structural oppositions.

My second level of analysis concerns the way in which Romans placed themselves in society. To what extent did they consider their position and power to be the outcome of a structure of kin relations? When Cicero spoke in court on behalf of a client or Pliny wrote a recommendation on behalf of a protégé, how were ties of kinship (as opposed, say, to friendships or civic rank) deployed? In such situations, we might assume, the Romans would emphasize agnatic kin, as the *nomen* was passed along male lines. The honour and position of agnatically related men who carried the same *nomen* reinforced each other. There is certainly something to this, especially during the Republic, but again there was no simple, clear-cut structural principle. In locating individuals in society, Romans regularly noted the honour or infamy of both their paternal and maternal connections. Speaking on behalf of M. Aemilius Scaurus in 54 BC, Cicero invoked the fame of Scaurus' maternal *auus*, as well as his paternal kin (*Pro Scauro* 46; see also *Pro Sestio* 101). Later, Cicero placed the famous Gracchan brothers among the nobility as sons of Tiberius Gracchus and grandsons of Scipio Africanus, their mother's father (*De officiis* 2. 80). I have argued elsewhere (1984) that under the emperors the stress on agnatic *nomen* weakened. In his recommendations written around AD 100 Pliny regularly placed the recommended by reference to his kin, listing indiscriminately paternal and maternal grandparents and uncles; just like *patrui*, *auunculi* are described as serious, not indulgent or familiar (1. 14. 6; 2. 9. 4; 4. 4. 2). In the same period Tacitus identified the social position of Junia, who died in AD 22, on the basis of her links to Cato as her *auunculus*, Cassius as her husband, and Brutus as her brother (*Annales* 3. 76). In narrating the ill fate of the loser Libo Drusus,

Tacitus pointed out the foolishness of his continually dwelling on his dreams about his famous kin, his (maternal) *proauus* Pompey, Scribonia his *amita*, and Agrippina his *sobrina prior* (*Annales* 2. 27). Altogether, kin ties were regularly invoked to establish the identity of Romans in high society, but they were often elaborated without sharp distinction between paternal and maternal lines, and placed alongside friendships as evidence of social respectability.

The absence of a strong boundary between agnatic and other kin is evident in the religious rituals and festivals that contributed to a Roman's sense of place in society. The household cult of the *genius*, emphasized by Fustel de Coulanges, did sanctify lineage through males, but only direct ascendants and descendants. I know of no religious festival that celebrated or marked off the group of collateral agnatic kin. On the other hand, the festival called the Caristia honoured 'dear cognatic kin' (*cara cognatio*). Ovid's *Fasti* (2. 617) describes the festival as one in which *propinqua turba* ('a crowd of relatives') shows up at the house to pay homage *ad socios deos* ('to related gods'). Here again, the vague term *propinqua* is used, and Ovid's subsequent description makes it clear that paternal, maternal, and affinal kin are included (Scullard 1981: 75–6).

The third level of inquiry concerns behaviour: what did kin do for one another in Rome, and what were they expected to do? As a social historian, I am inclined to agree with Malinowski about the 'insanity' of fixations on kinship nomenclature, if it causes us to lose sight of behavioural manifestations of social relationships. In analysing the importance of kinship in defining social relationships, I want to separate two questions: (1) What obligations did kin fulfil? (2) To what extent can the expectations and performance of kin obligations be explained in structural terms? That is, to what extent and in what contexts were social roles defined and behaviour influenced by oppositions between, say, *patruus* and *auunculus*?

The methodological problems involved in answering these behavioural questions are considerable, even for anthropologists able to observe living populations. I have pointed to the pitfalls of generalizing from individual examples of a kinsman's behaviour, and we have little data suitable to quantitative analysis, although I cannot resist offering a few tombstone counts, if only to counter some obviously false claims about preferences for commemoration of certain relatives.

A survey of those few kinsmen we happen to hear about does not reveal a general behavioural pattern of severity by paternal kinsmen as opposed to affection from maternal kinsmen. For instance, Cicero's letters reveal that both he, as paternal uncle of young Quintus, and

Atticus, as maternal uncle, were expected to love their nephew, but both in fact had a complex, vacillating relationship with the awkward young man (Bradley 1991: ch. 8). In Pliny's letters we find on the paternal side the loose-living grandmother, Ummidia Quadratilla (7. 24), and the affectionate aunt, Calpurnia Hispulla (4. 19; 8. 11), and on the maternal side the severe grandmother of Minicius Acilianus (1. 14). The sweeping structural characterizations find little support in attested examples, and probably we should not expect corroboration.

It is more useful to consider kinship in specific social contexts. Kinsmen came to the fore in cases where a child lost his parent before adulthood (Saller 1994: ch. 8). The child who had lost his father and required a *tutor* (guardian) to manage his inheritance was quite common—perhaps one-third of Roman children lost their fathers before coming of age. In this situation, the law and custom structured expectations. The *tutor legitimus*, the guardian specified by law in the absence of one designated in the father's will, was the child's closest adult agnate, most often the *patruus*. Legal and literary texts show that the father's brother clearly was an expected choice as *tutor*,[20] but other types of kin were expected to serve too. The agnatic principle in the selection of *tutores* was weakened by the facts that: (1) Roman fathers had the power to name others as *tutores* in their wills—a discretion noted as peculiarly Roman by the jurists; and (2) multiple *tutores* were common, with the result that the *patruus* would not usually be the sole tutor, but one of an assortment of kin and friends. Nevertheless, the *patruus* was stereotyped as severe in Roman literature, and the reason lies in the *patruus*'s role as *tutor* responsible for restraining the expenditures for his ward. As Bettini (1991: 17) rightly notes, *patrui* were regarded as the watchdogs against luxurious waste.[21]

In law and in practice, the tasks of raising the fatherless child and of managing the estate were separated. The child-rearing was commonly left to the mother, or, in her absence, to other relatives. Bettini (ibid. 76) suggests that the *matertera* as 'other mother' was the culturally preferred relative for this responsibility.[22] In fact, no Latin text attests to this role, and no pattern emerges from our meagre

[20] The paternal uncle was the expected choice to such a degree that, according to Scaevola, a *tutor* appointed by will had legitimate grounds for being excused if a *patruus* was available (D. 27. 1. 37. pr., Scaevola).

[21] Both the examples of stereotyping from Horace's *Satires* cited above concerned restraint on lavish expenditure.

[22] Bremmer (1976) claims that maternal uncles had a special role in fosterage, but does not provide a single example from Rome.

sources: among the handful of examples, both Nero and Vespasian were taken into the homes of their *paternal* aunts to be raised (Suetonius, *Nero* 6. 3; *Vespasianus* 2. 1).

Similarly, it is hard to find patterns in choice of spouses based on kinship. Brent Shaw and I (1984*b*) argued ten years ago that cousin marriage, though permitted, was infrequent in Roman society. Since then, critics have pointed out instances of cross-cousin marriage that we missed (Corbier 1991). These examples do not change the basic facts that we have no general prescriptive statements from Romans revealing a preference for paternal or maternal, parallel- or cross-cousins as spouses, and no statistical pattern of cousin marriage has been demonstrated. In connection with marriage, Bettini argued that the *matertera* had a special role in taking the omen before her niece's marriage. However, a close reading of the only example, described in Cicero's *De diuinatione* (1. 104), suggests that it was the shrine where the omen was taken, rather than the *matertera*'s involvement, that was customary (Bettini 1991: 88).[23]

The law of inheritance, more than anything else, has provided the basis for structural analyses of Roman kinship. I have suggested that even the system of intestate inheritance of early Rome does not correspond with Radcliffe-Brown's concept of father-right, because daughters as well as sons inherited an equal share of the patrimony.[24] For Rome of the historical period (and also of the XII Tables) testators were given the flexibility to make a will, and in practice by the second century BC wills were used to transfer property well beyond the bounds of the agnatic kin group. The Praetor's Edict was developed to give cognates a claim after agnates. Although agnation remained significant in the devolution of property, it was not nearly so clear-cut or dominant as in Radcliffe-Brown's description of father-right. As a result, the principle that a man had no property interest in common with his maternal kin simply does not hold true of Rome. Some of the best-known and most important successions in Roman history were from *auunculus* to nephew: dour old Caecilius to Atticus, Julius Caesar to grand-nephew Octavius, later Augustus, and the elder Pliny to the younger Pliny.[25]

---

[23] At 272 n. 55, Bettini acknowledges that Cicero and Valerius Maximus (1. 5. 4) do not indicate explicitly that the taking of this omen was generally part of a *matertera*'s role, but he nevertheless generalizes on the basis of his confidence in the structural model.

[24] Goody (1990: ch. 14) rightly emphasizes the property rights of Roman women, even in early Rome.

[25] It is true that in these cases the nephew-heir was adopted, but only posthumously: the adoption does not alter the fact that property was very much a consideration in relationships between *auunculi* and sister's sons during the lifetime of the *auunculus*.

Inheritance relationships are indirectly and imperfectly reflected in funerary commemorations, because heirs were morally responsible to take care of the burial and commemoration of the deceased testator.[26] The funerary commemorations are the only quantifiable documents extant from the western empire. Dedications by or to *materterae* and *auunculi* have been adduced by Bettini and Bremmer as evidence of an especially affectionate relationship with maternal kin (Bettini 1991: 72–6; Bremmer 1976: 68). But selective citation is misleading here. In fact, the index for *CIL* 6 reveals 7 dedications involving *amitae*, precisely the number for *materterae*. The number of *auunculus* commemorations (6) is only about half that of *patruus* commemorations (11). A wider survey of the dedications from all the Latin-speaking provinces yields only a few to kinsmen beyond the immediate family, and those few are scattered evenly between paternal and maternal kin.[27] Funerary inscriptions reveal no special pattern of sentimental or property ties to paternal or maternal kin.

Altogether, except for a few specific contexts, I find little evidence that the system of Latin kinship terms, whose richness so dazzled Lewis Morgan, denoted specific social roles or constituted a structure in any strong sense. Why should this be so? I doubt that it is possible to give a sufficient answer, but let me suggest three points. First, it is not clear that we should expect clearly defined roles. The anthropological theories that depicted early society in terms of systems structured by such roles were rooted ultimately in Roman law and a nomenclature enumerated by lawyers. John Crook's statement of twenty-seven years ago (1967: 114) deserves repetition here: 'The Romans in law not only . . . pushed things to the limit of logic, so that, given that *paterfamilias* had certain roles, their implications were rigorously drawn; they also kept law sharply apart from religion and morals, so that the legal character of *patria potestas* stands out in sociologically misleading clarity.'[28] It is a mistake to read

[26] The link between inheritance and commemoration is not as direct as Meyer (1990) suggests; see Saller (1994: 99).

[27] Drawn from the study in Saller and Shaw (1984a). In this survey we found the following: Latium: 1 paternal *auus*, 1 paternal *auia*, 1 maternal *auia*, 1 *patruus*, 9 *alumnus*; Italy Regio XI: 3 paternal *auus*, 2 maternal *auus*, 1 maternal *auia*, 1 *patruus*, 1 *auunculus*; Southern Italy: 1 *auia*, 2 *alumnus*; Gallia Narbonensis: 1 paternal *auus*, 1 maternal *auus*, 1 paternal *auia*, 1 maternal *auia*, 2 *patruus*, 1 *auunculus*, 11 *alumnus*; Spain: 2 *auunculus*; Danubian region: 4 *auus*, 1 *auia*, 2 *auunculus*, 6 *alumnus*. The only clear pattern to emerge from these numbers is the rarity of funerary dedications from extended kin, and the comparative numerousness of dedications to foster-children (*alumni*)—a fact which supports my point below about the centrality of the house.

[28] Goody (1990: 411) similarly recommends caution in interpreting legal codes and rules.

legal rules as sociology or to generalize from legal rules to cultural system, as Maine, Morgan, and Radcliffe-Brown did. Their legacy has been a jural approach to kinship relations that has provided only a partial understanding of certain aspects, and a misunderstanding of the whole.

Secondly, what I see as a relative lack of stress on kin in practical matters of obligation may be related to the fundamental Roman emphasis on bonds within the household. Cicero described social evolution as beginning with the bond between husband and wife, then between parents and children, and then bonds within the household including dependents and slaves; then followed in Cicero's scheme links to collateral kin (*De officiis* 1. 54). In practical terms, propertied Romans did not normally rely on kin for daily support and services in so far as they utilized slaves, freedmen, and other dependants. In terms of their perception of their place in the world, they symbolized their leading position in society, not by representing themselves as head of a clan or family—Roman kinship relations were not hierarchical in this sense (Crook 1967: 116)—but by representing themselves as lords (*domini*) of wealthy and powerful houses (*domus*). This is manifested, I would suggest, in the frequency, noted earlier, of ambiguous words such as *necessarius* or *mei* ('my people') encompassing kin and dependents, and of words denoting bonds of dependency within the household, such as *patronus* and *libertus*. For instance, *patronus* occurs 24 times in Cicero's letters in contrast to a mere 4 occurrences of *patruus*. This comparison may be discounted as mechanical counting, but I would suggest that it is related to the relative significance of these relationships in daily social life and in the symbols of social position and power. In the funerary commemorations collected in *CIL* 6, dedications involving a *patronus* outnumber those with a *patruus* by more than 100 to 1. Since commemoration was an important symbol and sacred duty of an intimate social bond, this ratio says something significant about which relationships were represented as central to a Roman's social experience. To move to a different sphere of discourse, in the *Digest*, if we exclude from the count Paul's elaborate kinship table, the word *patronus* occurs ten times as often as *patruus*. Needless to say, that does not demonstrate that the *patronus* was ten times as important as the *patruus*—whatever that would mean. But the numbers provide one measure of which relationships preoccupied Romans in thinking about social obligations. For instance, when the jurists defined who was legally obligated to help an impoverished relative *ex aequitate caritateque sanguinis* ('from justice and affection of blood-kin'), they included direct ascendants and descendants, paternal and maternal, and also freedmen's responsibility for their *patroni*. But collateral kin were not part of the welfare net of mutual obligation as defined in juristic texts. One hypothesis for the lack of metaphorical extension of words for uncles, aunts, and cousins in Roman culture is precisely that they lacked the power to create strong bonds of obligation.

Finally, I want to suggest briefly that a computer simulation may cast light on how ideals of kinship obligation were manifested in practice. An intricately elaborated system of kinship with clearly differentiated roles may serve the individual who has a full set of kin. In reality, however, most Romans had to make do with a very incomplete set of living kin. The contrast between father's brother and mother's brother may be intuitively appealing, but how many Roman children would have had both to perform complementary obligations? In the absence of empirical data to answer this question, a simulation developed by James Smith of the Cambridge Group for the History of Population and Social Structure can provide a rough guide (Smith and Oeppen 1993). The computer generates a model population by taking invented individuals through their lives month by month and having them marry, bear children, and die in accordance with the probabilities fed into the computer. Those probabilities come in part from Roman evidence and in part from best guesses that are unlikely to be far wrong, to judge by comparative evidence. Once the model population is created, it can be analysed, and we can ask how many of what kinds of relatives would have been alive for individuals at certain times of life.[29]

The results of the simulation are striking in that they show how incomplete the kinship universe must have been for most Romans. Suppose, for example, that a Roman lost his father by age 10, as perhaps 25 per cent of Roman children did. Only 4 per cent of those fatherless 10-year-olds would have had a paternal grandfather alive as *paterfamilias*. Consequently, a *tutor* would have been needed. Only 1 per cent would have had a brother old enough to fill that role, and only a little more than one-third would have had a *patruus* (Saller 1994: 197). The simulation gives substance to Bloch's observation that too precise a denotation of social roles of kin may be counterproductive. To the extent that a particular obligation or role is defined specifically for one type of kin, then the binary operation of definition means that it is not part of the role for other types. If

---

[29] For a fuller explanation and defence of the simulation, see Saller (1994: chs. 2–3).

tutela had been the exclusive responsibility of the *patruus*, then a majority of orphans would have been without one for demographic reasons. How useful could the complementarity of *patruus* and *auunculus* have been in practice, when only one out of six orphans had both types of uncle between which to choose? Given an incomplete kinship universe, there was pragmatic value in not constructing fine structural distinctions, but defining roles loosely, vaguely, hence interchangeably. Even if there had been systematic distinctions in kinship roles (and generally the evidence does not show even significant preferences), we would still expect to find both paternal and maternal aunts taking in orphans, both paternal and maternal kin dedicating funerary monuments in the absence of parents, *patrui*, but also other kinsmen and friends, serving as *tutores*.

This chapter has been aimed at two audiences (and may satisfy neither). For anthropologists aware of the roots of their own tradition of kinship studies, my intention has been to suggest that Roman kinship as a paradigm of father-right has been constructed by anthropologists from Maine and Morgan to Radcliffe-Brown and Fortes out of a very limited reading of Roman texts. Maine and Morgan started a jural approach to the study of kinship because they were steeped in civil law, not because the Romans themselves interpreted the role of the father and his kin primarily in legal terms as stern figures endowed with absolute powers. In certain legal contexts, to be sure, the distinction between agnatic kin and maternal kin came into play. In particular, the father's brother's responsibility to act as guardian of the estate of his brother's orphans gave substance to the stereotype of the *patruus* as a figure of moral restraint. But more generally, all older kin—father, mother, *patruus*, *auunculus*, and so on—were expected to show loving concern, *pietas*, and younger Romans owed obedience to maternal and paternal ascendants alike. The evidence for actual performance of obligations does not reveal a general pattern of oppositions between paternal and maternal kin. The characteristics of Radcliffe-Brown's 'father-right' and 'avunculate' simply do not correspond to Roman practices.

For the classical audience, my intention has been to show why we should stop the uncritical invocation of Radcliffe-Brown to substantiate an interpretation of Roman kinship that emphasizes structure. Since Radcliffe-Brown's essay on the avunculate, published seventy years ago, anthropologists have largely abandoned his structural-functional approach. I have suggested that the complexities of the classical evidence may be better understood through some of the

recent approaches that de-emphasize the structure of kinship terminology and roles, and focus on the individual making choices among
a peculiar, changing set of alternatives, and more often manipulat-
ing vague, elastic terms of familiarity rather than specific classificatory
labels.[30]

---

[30] It has been suggested to me that my argument is based on a chronological sleight-of-
hand in using classical evidence to critique claims made about primitive or archaic Rome. To
this criticism I would offer several responses. (1) In using the XII Tables and Roman comedy,
I have gone as far back as the evidence goes and found no strong kinship *system* in society.
(2) Attention to the classical evidence shows the potential for divergence between law and
terminology, on the one hand, and social relations, on the other; if such divergence was possible in the 1st cent. BC, why should we believe, without evidence, that such divergences were
not common in earlier eras? (3) Even if we suppose that some earlier primitive era of conver-
gence of law, language, and behaviour existed, when would we place this era? Already by the
time of the XII Tables, Rome was one of the major cities of the Mediterranean, with written
legal documents available to supersede customary rules of kinship. In truth, if there ever was
in Rome a period of a *system* based on true father-right, as described by Radcliffe-Brown,
it was a period for which we have no evidence whatever.

2

Legal Stumbling-Blocks for Lower-Class Families in Rome

JANE F. GARDNER

INTRODUCTION: FAMILY AND *FAMILIA*

The nuclear family of parents and children is not an institution of Roman civil law. It exists before and beyond the law, in the realm of instinct, what the Romans called *ius naturale*, natural law. Natural law, said Ulpian (*D*. 1. 1. 1. 3), was common to all living creatures, on land, in the sea, in the air. From it came the joining together of male and female, 'which we call *matrimonium*', and the procreation and rearing of children.

It is only in *ius ciuile*, and specifically in Roman civil law, that we find the *familia*, a legal construct the existence of which (together with the operation of its two main functions, control over persons and property) depended entirely on status. Citizenship and *conubium* were essential for a family group to constitute a *familia*. The group defined by the term *familia* included some of the groups in Roman society which constituted families according to natural law, but by no means all of them, and it might include besides various extraneous persons. The basic *familia* consisted of a father and his legitimate children and sons' or grandsons' children. Mothers, though legally necessary as lawful wives and parents of legitimate children, and biologically related to children in the *familia*, were, with the decline of *manus* marriage, legally extraneous to it. On the other hand, persons not biologically related could be brought within the *familia* by adoption.

Human emotions, including family feelings (*pietas*), such as proper dutifulness towards one's parents and parental duties towards children, belonged to *ius gentium*, those institutions found in all human societies (*D*. 1. 1. 1 *fin*–5). Their existence within the *familia* was given some limited recognition in civil law. Legal interpretation accepted, for instance, concern for the material welfare of a legitimate child as adequate basis for rejecting the imputation that a *paterfamilias* acted with fraudulent intent (*D*. 38. 5. 1. 10, Ulpian,

below). Praetorian law protected children whose parents' testamentary dispositions showed insufficient parental feeling—the *querela inofficiosi testamenti* ('complaint of an unduteous will').[1] The wider
social importance of observation of *pietas* in familial relationships is
expressed by Ulpian (*D.* 37. 15. 1. 2): abuse of parents is a *delictum
ad publicam pietatem pertinens*, an offence affecting the proper relations of respect that should exist in society at large. This view helps
to explain the extension of legal recognition of the moral obligation
of *pietas* to legal, as well as biological, relationships in the *familia*.
Within the *familia*, since the natural father (or grandfather) also
normally had *potestas* over the legitimate child, the idea of *pietas*
was reasonably held to apply to the legal relationship of the *pater*
and those within his *potestas*. It was applied to those brought within
his *potestas* by adoption (but not on their part towards his wife)
and the persons adopted nevertheless retained that relationship with
their original parents. It was also extended to persons released from
potestas by emancipation or manumission, and was important in the
rationale of patron's rights. Law also recognized obligations of *pietas*
between certain persons biologically related but in different *familiae*
if they were connected by lawful marriage.[2] The closest relationship
was that between mother and child, and the absence of *potestas*
probably made it easier for legal interpretation eventually to recognize illegitimate children as having a duty of *pietas* towards their
mothers, but not, however, towards their fathers.[3] Paternity of illegitimate children was not legally recognized (except for considerations such as the avoidance of incest).

The *familia* was devised for Roman citizens, joined in lawful matrimony and producing legitimate children, and (usually) with some
property to transmit by inheritance. Paternal inheritance was tied to
membership of the *familia*. Inheritance rights between mothers and
children were a relatively late development, and gradually improved.
Mechanisms existed for moving persons out of the *familia* (by emancipation) or into another (by adoption—until Justinian),[4] and these

---

[1] Gardner (1986a: 183–90 and refs. at 202 n. 39).

[2] *D.* 3. 1. 1. 11, Ulpian. Persons with criminal convictions were banned from prosecuting
on behalf of others, with certain exceptions: parents, children, wives, siblings, and certain
connections by marriage: in-laws, stepparents, and stepchildren.

[3] *D.* 2. 4. 4. 4, Ulpian; 5, Paul. Paul gives a reason: 'quia semper certa est, etiam si uulgo
conceperit; pater uero is est, quem nuptiae demonstrant' ('because it is always certain who
the mother is, even if she had an illegitimate child; but the *pater* is the person shown to be
such by lawful marriage').

[4] *C.* 8. 47 (48). 10 (AD 530): adoptive children, adopted by anyone other than a natural
male ascendant, would in future acquire only rights of intestacy in the adoptive family (without losing those in the family of origin), and would not pass into the *familia* and *potestas*
of the adopter.

might be employed by a *pater* looking, for example, for ways to benefit himself or his children financially within his own lifetime. The means were cumbrous, and resulted in the partial transfer of one *familia* into another, or its splitting up into one or more *familiae*, all legally distinct; but although the legal relationships were dissolved, what these activities often show is members of families in a consensus to exploit the legal rules for their benefit. The frequency of such practices is indicated, e.g. by (1) the development of the law of inheritance to allow children technically no longer members of the *familia* to retain, in certain circumstances, some inheritance rights, (2) the strategic use of a combination of emancipation and readoption to restructure priority of inheritance claims within the *familia* itself, and (3) practices such as serial giving of the same person in adoption, or readoption of someone already given in adoption (commented on already by Labeo in the late Republic: *D.* 1. 7. 34).[5] Families, that is, were exploiting the *familia* to suit themselves.

Many families in Roman society, however, were unable to avail themselves of the opportunities afforded in Roman law, because they did not or could not fit into the standard pattern, usually because one or more of the family members had been a slave. This chapter will go on to examine some of the legal and practical obstacles in the way of establishing the appropriate legal relationships to constitute a *familia*, as well as the advantages and disadvantages of doing so, and some of the ways in which Roman law developed in such a way as to, and in part perhaps in order to, take account of the special situation of anomalous families.

THE COMPOSITION OF LOWER-CLASS FAMILIES

Families in Roman society in which one or more member was or had been a slave present a wide range of possible variations in status and in composition. At one end of the spectrum, and nearest to the *familia* as constructed in Roman law, were the families in which both parents were Roman citizens, legitimately married, and with legitimate offspring, i.e. freeborn *and* born after the marriage of their parents. Even for these, however, the ex-slave status of one or other parent could affect their economic situation and the prospects of their children.

Some families in which the parents were Roman citizens might

---

[5] For these practices, see Gardner (forthcoming).

have children born before the parents were legitimately married.[6] The children might themselves be ex-slaves, born while the mother or both parents were still in slavery, or freeborn, but to a father who had at the time still been a slave. The latter began as one-parent families, and sometimes were obliged to remain so. One-parent families in the modern sense (that is, with no father present in the household) also arose from other situations, e.g. a slave-woman freed before bearing her patron's child, but not subsequently married by him.

Then there were mixed-status families, where parents cohabited but were not able to marry, e.g. a peregrine man or Junian Latin man, who did not succeed in attaining citizenship, and a Roman woman, or a Roman man and a Junian Latin woman. The status of the children in these instances would differ. Only the child of the Junian man and Roman woman would be Roman, and that only from Hadrian onwards; before then there was argument about the status of the child. Legal opinion, as reported by Gaius 1. 80, seems to have been divided. He reports, as the view of one side, that the child of a union between a Latin man and a Roman woman whose matrimonial intent was attested before seven citizen witnesses (as provided in the *lex Aelia Sentia*: Gaius 1. 29) was a Latin, while the child of concubinate cohabitation was a Roman. These are in fact two separate judgements, resting on two separate opinions, separately applied: (1) that in the former case the *lex Aelia Sentia* and *lex Iunia* gave *conubium* for the matrimony (so Gaius 1. 80); and (2) that in the latter case the *lex Minicia*, which provided that the offspring of a Roman and a peregrine not enjoying *conubium* should be a peregrine, did not apply (this follows from 1. 79). Gaius does not state what other views were held. Cherry (1990: 255) says: 'Other jurists believed that children born to the marriage of a Junian Latin and a Roman woman took their mother's status whether or not their parents had married in the manner prescribed by the *lex Aelia Sentia*. This was the opinion which eventually prevailed.'

As the last sentence shows, Cherry's basis for saying this is the Hadrianic *senatusconsultum* itself, which resolved matters to the

---

[6] Free parents might have slave children. In *ILS* 7479 = *CIL* 3. 14206 (nr. Philippi, Macedonia), a father—whether himself freeborn or freed is not known—commemorates his slave son, a *uerna* (so the mother was also owned by the father) who, until his death at the age of 17, was managing his father's roadhouse. Though, as 'good cause' could be shown on two counts under the *lex Aelia Sentia*, there was no legal bar to manumitting him, from a business point of view there was, as it happens, no legal advantage in doing so (rather a disadvantage: Gardner 1993: 59–60). Whether that consideration prevented it, or simply the practical difficulty of getting access to an appropriate official, we do not know. Had he lived long enough, he could have been freed and made heir in his father's will.

advantage of the children: in all cases (i.e. whether the parents were married in accordance with the *lex Aelia Sentia* or not) the child of a Latin man and a Roman woman would be born a Roman citizen. The matter, however, was more problematic than appears from Gaius or is noted by Cherry. On the view Gaius cites, the curious situation emerges that the child of a matrimonial union was denied Roman citizenship, while the offspring of concubinage received it. If the Hadrianic settlement does in fact represent an alternative view that in all circumstances the child was Roman, what were the original grounds for that view? Presumably that the Minician law did not apply, and that *in addition* the 'marriage' was not one because there was no *conubium*. There was another possibility: if the Minician law applied, then, whether there was *conubium* or not, in both cases the children were Latins. Neither this nor the preceding view (the one that makes the children Roman in both cases) draws any distinction between matrimony and concubinage. Clearly the situation needed clarification. The Hadrianic solution was simply to treat this as a special case, to the advantage of the freeborn children of Roman mothers. The citizen or non-citizen status of the children had never been the central concern of the *lex Aelia Sentia* and *lex Iunia*, but rather the eligibility of the fathers to become Roman citizens, from which other consequences followed—legitimation of existing children (and consequent acquisition of *potestas* over them[7]) and the possibility of having other legitimate children in *matrimonium iustum*—which affected patronal rights.

Those families to whom Roman family law, i.e. the law concerning the Roman *familia,* had least direct application were entirely of

---

[7] *Potestas* over existing children was acquired along with citizenship by *anniculi probatio* (Gaius 1. 29, 65–6), but probably not initially by iteration of manumission; according to Ulpian, *Reg.* 3. 4, a later *senatusconsultum* allowed (sc. Latin) children to become citizens on iteration of their father's manumission. It is not stated that any of the special methods of earning citizenship subsequently introduced (Gaius 1. 32b–4) had any effect upon the status of existing members of the family. Gaius 1. 66 gives, as an example of children not under *potestas* at birth but subsequently brought under it, only the child of a Latin married under the *lex Aelia Sentia*, who obtained citizenship by *anniculi probatio*. Whether the various kinds of public service mentioned by Gaius earned not only citizenship but *potestas* over existing children is doubtful. The evidence of the Spanish charters of communities with Latin rights sheds no light on the question, since, as pointed out by Sherwin-White (1973: 378) and González (1986: 148), *potestas* already existed within these communities (naturally, since, as we learn from clause 93 of the *lex Irnitana*, the inhabitants were to adopt the institutions of Roman law in their dealings with each other: cf. Gardner (1993: 188–91)). If such public service won citizenship only for the individual, then there was no *conubium* if his wife was Latin. If she was Roman, they could *then* begin lawful marriage; only children subsequently born would be *in potestate*. Children (initially only males) previously born could be adopted, but as we have seen this was not necessarily advisable, if patron's inheritance rights were still active.

non-citizens. Junian Latins were probably the largest single group. They were dismissed as numerically insignificant by Buckland (1966: 94): 'It is impossible to say how far [the children of Junian Latins] were subject to the disabilities of Junian Latins ... but for reasons now to be stated the class affected would not be numerous'; and again (ibid. 380, on inheritance): 'The Latin's children had no claim. It was however so easy for a Latin so to arrange his marriage that he and his family should be *ciues* that the case would be rare.' Weaver (1990) has shown, on the contrary, that the practical difficulties of doing all that was necessary to attain citizenship were such that comparatively few Junians are likely to have succeeded in doing so.

FAMILIA OR FAMILY? POSSIBILITIES AND PROBLEMS

Fathers with freeborn but illegitimate[8] children could transform their families into *familiae*, it might seem, simply by the adoption of these children and the consequent acquisition of *potestas* over them. There could be advantages for all concerned. Adoption would unite families in name, and create legally recognized claims of *pietas*, and also inheritance rights, not only between fathers and children, but between these children and their freeborn, legitimate siblings.

However, for citizens as well as for mixed-status families, adoption was not always possible, and sometimes it was possible but disadvantageous. The ex-slave status of the adopter or the person being adopted could create problems. Adoption by an ex-slave father, especially, was not always a wise move, if the material interests of the children were considered.

In families in which either parent or child had the status of a Junian Latin while the other was a Roman citizen, adoption was not legally possible at all. Adoption in Roman law was possible only between citizens. Ulpian (*Reg.* 10. 3) states categorically: 'a *peregrinus* cannot hold a Roman citizen *in potestate*, nor a Roman citizen a *peregrinus*'[9]. If both were citizens, adoption was possible, but since illegitimate children were legally fatherless, the adoption had to be by adrogation, the rules for which (since it entailed the extinction of a *familia*) were fairly stringent.[10] Legal interpretation,

---

[8] On the absence of stigma attached to illegitimacy, see Rawson 1989.

[9] Though the procedure of *mancipatio* could be conducted between Romans and Junians, at least for the transfer of property and the witnessing of wills, according to Ulpian, *Reg.* 19. 4 and 20. 8, this appears to be a later development; Gaius 1. 119 says that the procedure is exclusive to Roman citizens. See also Gardner (1996: n. 14).

[10] For detailed discussion of what follows, see Gardner 1989.

however, suggests that some of these could be waived for freedmen and their families, at least under the empire. Adoption of illegitimate daughters was not possible by the older procedure of adrogation before a token assembly of the *comitia curiata*, which was not finally replaced by imperial rescript until the late third century AD (C. 8. 47. 6, AD 293). Adrogation of the freedmen of others was not normally allowed, nor the adrogation of minors, nor was adrogation normally allowed to someone who already had, or was still capable of having, children (*D. 1. 7. 15. 2*, Ulpian). However, sympathetic consideration appears to have been given to requests for adrogation of one's own natural children (*D. 1. 7. 17. 1, 2*, Ulpian), and direct appeal to the emperor in individual cases was possible in some circumstances (for those able to avail themselves of it) earlier than the third century, and possibly even as early as the Augustan marriage legislation.[11]

Where adoption was legally possible, it was not always in the best interests of the family of a freedman. The situation changed over time. Under the empire especially, much depended on how prosperous a freedman was or expected to be. For fathers to acquire *potestas* over their children, and thereby control over their present property and future acquisitions, could benefit the less well-off and their families. However, in doing so the better-off freedmen would be taking a chance, and risking damaging the inheritance prospects of their children, unless their patron was already dead and/or childless[12] when they themselves died.

The rights of patrons and their families to inherit from freedmen developed in three main stages (summarized in Gaius 3. 39–42).[13] First, under the law of the XII Tables, the patron inherited only if the freedman left no will, and if he had no *sui heredes* (immediate heirs on intestacy). These included not only his own natural children but also adoptive children and his wife, if she was in *manus*. Gaius (3. 40), explaining the shift to the second stage, remarks: 'if it was an adoptive son or daughter or a wife who was in *manus* that was *suus* or *sua heres*, it was obviously unjust that no right should remain to the patron'. This perhaps admits of the suspicion that some childless freedmen may deliberately have been adopting strangers, or

---

[11] *D. 1. 7. 46* comes from Ulpian's commentary on the *lex Iulia et Papia*.

[12] Extraneous heirs did not have a claim on a citizen freedman's estate, as they did for Junian Latins: Gaius 3. 58, 64.

[13] See Gardner (1993: 21–3). The situation of freedwomen was different. Since a patron was a *tutor legitimus*, it was in his power to prevent his freedwoman making a will; this changed only after the Augustan marriage legislation, and then only for freedwomen who managed to qualify for the *ius liberorum* (see below).

marrying with *manus*, to try to exclude the patron. However, the only way they could make their own illegitimate children *sui heredes* was to adopt them. The second stage was the introduction of a modification of the rules in the praetor's edict, probably towards the end of the second century BC, and the result was that freedmen, whether they left a will or not, could benefit fully only their legitimate freeborn children. Adopted children received only half under a will and nothing at all on intestacy. In the third stage, by the *lex Papia Poppaea* (AD 9), patrons could claim a share of the estates of wealthier freedmen—those leaving over 100,000 sesterces—even against legitimate natural children. It took three children to exclude the patron entirely, and each child's share was correspondingly less. Even an only child would get no more than half. In such a situation it made no sense at all for a successful freedman to adopt his illegitimate children. He risked leaving them destitute. It could even be positively advantageous for him to emancipate his legitimate children (see below).

Freedmen appear frequently to have tried to forestall the possibility of patronal inroads on their estates by trying to dispose of much of their property in their lifetime, before their death should enable the patron to lay claim to it. By the early second century, two separate legal actions, the *actio Fabiana* and the *actio Caluisiana*, were available against tactics of this kind. The former applied where the freedman had left a will, the latter where he had not. The *Digest* title on these actions (38. 5) indicates some of the tactics employed. Ulpian characterizes these (1. pr.) as intended to prevent from receiving their due portion of the estate some one of those persons who could claim possession against a will—though the prime case he has in mind, as emerges a little later (1. 3), is the patron. Among typical devices mentioned is, first, alienation of property. If it was claimed to be a simple alienation, the onus was on the complainant to prove that it was done with intent to defraud the patron. If fraudulent intent was proven, then, whether or not it was then alleged to be a gift *mortis causa* (in anticipation of death), patron's rights took precedence. However, a freedman could, in legal opinion (Julian and Ulpian), neglect with impunity the chance to acquire property, e.g. an inheritance, legacy, or gift (*D.* 38. 5. 1. 6, Ulpian)—since it never had been his. Other devices are mentioned. For instance, a freedman might sell, let out, or exchange property at a ridiculously low valuation; the sale, etc. was not directly rescinded, since the freedman had a perfect right to sell what was his, but the purchaser or leaser was given the option of either paying a fair price or taking his money back and giving up the property. Similarly, the freedman might buy at an exaggeratedly high valuation; the seller who benefited was then given the option of dropping the price or cancelling the sale.

Lines must be drawn somewhere, however. Ulpian's discussion of the *actio Fabiana* (D. 38. 5. 1. 15) considers possible—or perhaps actual—objections made by patrons to disposal of property, on such grounds as that the place was conveniently nearby, or had a pleasant climate, or had sentimental associations because the patron was reared there, or because his parents were buried there. That, Ulpian declares roundly, does not make the disposal fraud on the freedman's part—only pecuniary loss to the patron is relevant.

The beneficiary of these sales or purchases is identified only as the purchaser or vendor, but it is a fair presumption that in most cases he or she will have been the freedman's wife, or a biological child, who was not subject to his *potestas*, either because illegitimate or—and this is an interesting possibility, not mentioned by Ulpian—a legitimate, freeborn child deliberately emancipated.[14]

We find emancipation used in Roman society for a variety of purposes, usually to enable the emancipated to benefit materially or financially in some way (Gardner 1993: 67–71); that is, the *familia* was broken up for the sake of the welfare of members of the family. We ought to be prepared, I think, to entertain at least the possibility (not directly discussed in our legal sources, nor one which would be revealed in epigraphic evidence) that a freedman under the empire whose property exceeded the crucial 100,000 sesterces, and who had a full-blown *familia*, complete with legitimate children (but only one or two), freeborn to him in lawful matrimony, might actually think it advisable to break up the *familia* by emancipating his children; otherwise any acquisitions they made would be swallowed up in his property and liable to be shared with the patron. Once emancipated, not only were they free to keep their acquisitions, but he might succeed in conveying some of his property to them in ways that escaped the operation of the two *actiones*.

There are some indications, both in relation to what were regarded as acceptable dispositions of property which escaped these *actiones*, and also more generally, that legal interpretation under the empire was inclined to attach weight to family affection (*pietas*) and biological

---

[14] An interesting variation, both of method and of immediate recipient, appears in D. 38. 5. 6, Julian, *xxvi digestorum*. A freedman, to cheat his patron, might lend money to a *filiusfamilias* (i.e. the son, still *in patria potestate*, of someone else) in contravention of the *senatusconsultum Macedonianum*, which made such loans irrecoverable. (Julian held that this should be held to constitute a gift with intent to defraud the patron, rather than a loan.) The *filiusfamilias*, of course, might be the freeborn son of the freedman's own biological son or daughter, or of a relative.

relationship in the absence of a legal familial relationship.[15] The same terminology was sometimes applied to both types of relationship. Scaevola's decision on a hypothetical conflict of claims between two wills (*D.* 31. 88. 12) turned on the interpretation of *filius*, and is explained by Claudius: *quia creditur appellatione filiorum et naturales liberos, id est, in seruitute susceptos contineri* ('because the term *filii* is believed to include also natural children, i.e. those born in slavery').

Parents were naturally anxious to provide as well as they could for their children, freeborn, legitimate, or otherwise, and in some texts I think we can also detect a rather unreasonable resentment of such provision on the part of patrons, and observe lawyers siding with parents. So, for instance, the creation for a daughter of a dowry (*D.* 38. 5. 1. 10, Ulpian), which of course became the legal property of an *extraneus*, her husband, for the duration of their marriage, was held not to be a fraud upon the patron, 'since a father's *pietas* is not to be censured'. The likelihood of the dowry returning to the father was small. Whether or not the daughter was legitimate, if she was still married when her father died, the dowry was lost to the patron. The only circumstance in which the dowry might return was if it was given for a legitimate daughter, who died before her father. In terms of the legal opinion cited by Claudius (above), however, *filia* might be intended to refer also to an illegitimate daughter— in which case, the dowry was lost to the patron for good. As her father was not her *pater*, the dowry was *dos aduenticia*[16] and would not return to the father should his daughter predecease him.

Both legitimate and illegitimate children may also be referred to in praetorian law, reported by Ulpian (*D.* 38. 5. 1. 2), that a gift *mortis causa* (in anticipation of death)[17] was not revocable on grounds of fraud on patron if made to a son or daughter. Ulpian says in justification, rather strangely:[18] 'Someone who was free to leave to

---

[15] This is only one area—the law of inheritance is another—in which I believe some of the developments in the law are the result of an awareness of the large numbers of illegitimate children in ancient society. In the texts in the *Codex Iustinianus* the status of those consulting the emperor is seldom indicated, but perhaps we should not rule out the possibility that some were in families that were not technically *familiae*.

[16] Gardner (1986a: 105 n. 22 and refs. there).

[17] For *donationes mortis causa*, see Buckland (1966: 257–8); Kaser (1971: 763–5).

[18] I say 'strangely', with reference to the phrase 'whatever amount he wanted to', because under the *lex Papia*, if the patron had a claim, then only one-half or at most two-thirds of the property was in fact available to the freedman to dispose of by will, either to heirs or as legacies, as he wished (Gaius 3. 42), and in any case, since the *lex Falcidia* of 40 BC, no more than three-quarters of a total estate could be left away from the heir(s) as legacies. The oddity disappears, though, if we take Ulpian as treating *donatio* and legacy as alternative methods of transferring the same legally permissible amount. *Donationes* were by successive enactments (see text above) brought under the same regulations as legacies.

his *filius* as a legacy whatever amount he wanted to, does not appear to have defrauded his patron by making a gift.' He has already clearly stated that fraudulent intent (*dolus malus*) is not held to apply either to gifts *mortis causa* or to legacies in general, and we are not told anything relevant to explain why a gift, or indeed a legacy, to a *filius* is mentioned as a separate case. This text of Ulpian, it is important to remember, is from a commentary on the praetor's edict, so he may in fact be telling us that in the edict itself these manifestations of family *pietas* were explicitly mentioned. Perhaps we have here echoes of controversies from before the reign of Hadrian.

In relation to gifts *mortis causa*, it might seem as if in practice an enormous loophole was left allowing freedmen[19] to dispose of much of their property before death, and independently of any will, to the benefit of their children and to the detriment of the patron, so in effect nullifying both the patrons' privileges under Republican legislation and the clause of the *lex Papia Poppaea* mentioned above. However, there were restraints. Such gifts, to whomever made, were, from an early date, subject to the same restrictions on amount as were legacies under the *lex Furia* of uncertain date and the *lex Voconia* of 169 BC, although the *lex Falcidia* of 40 BC was first applied to them only by Septimius Severus.[20] However, by a *senatus-consultum* dating between the reigns of Vespasian and Hadrian (Talbert 1984: 451, no. 148) the loophole was effectively closed, when these gifts were subjected to the same regulations as those on inheritances imposed by the Augustan marriage laws. This meant in effect that the amount given as a gift *mortis causa* to a legitimate child could not exceed what could be left to that child by will (while illegitimate children could benefit, as *extranei*, only if they were qualified by marriages and children of their own). In this perspective, the sympathy of jurists is perhaps less striking, since the loss to patrons was limited.

Where, however, it was a matter of enabling ex-slaves and their families to benefit from the generosity of others (and in particular of their patrons), some lawyers, by the end of the second century AD at any rate, were prepared to interpret in their favour. Ulpian expresses qualified approval (*D*. 36. 1. 18 (17). 4) of a decision of his predecessor and former senior colleague Papinian. Where a landed estate had been left to a number of freedmen, with the provision that the share of any who died childless (*sine liberis*—strictly, without legitimate children) should go to the others, Papinian (*D*. 31.

---

[19] Or freedwomen with four (legitimate) children and the *ius liberorum* (Gaius 3. 44).
[20] Kaser 1971: 764; Gaius 2. 225; *D*. 39. 6. 42. 1, Papinian.

77. 13) said that someone who was the son and fellow-freedman of one of the beneficiaries should count as a 'child'. This I take as a recognition of the fact that for many or most ex-slaves, their family, not through their own choice, would include illegitimate children, and these children it was not always possible to turn into *liberi*, i.e. children *in potestate*, by adoption. However, Ulpian adds cautiously that the important thing is to establish the intention of the testator, and for that his status and rank are relevant factors. Some patrons would concern themselves less about such matters than others. A great lord, leaving a block bequest, in general terms, to 'his freedmen', whomever that term might at the time of his death cover, would not be supposed to have been concerning himself about the precise details of their family situations; a patron of lower status, perhaps himself a freedman, personally familiar with and even biologically related to the beneficiaries, might.

HUSBAND AND WIFE

For freed parents, even if the integration of their children into a legal *familia* was impossible or inadvisable, there would be some advantage for the couple themselves to enter into *matrimonium iustum*, as this would remove some of their incapacities to benefit under wills, under the Augustan marriage legislation. For Junian Latins also, becoming citizens and able to enter *matrimonium iustum* would be an advantage, allowing spouses to inherit from each other. Latins could not take from Romans, nor could they make wills, so the couple could not make bequests to each other, nor to their children.

In the case of a mixed marriage, i.e. Latin husband, Roman wife, not only were possibilities of provision for the surviving spouse limited, but also inheritance prospects generally. The Roman wife could not take from anyone else, save close relatives, under the rules of the *lex Papia Poppaea*, since she was not lawfully married in *matrimonium iustum*; and if she was not herself freeborn she had no close relatives. She could still receive nothing from her husband, and if she had given him anything as a dowry she lost it at his death. At her death, she could convey something to the husband via a *fideicommissum*—that is, if she herself were capable of making a will. For that, she would need her tutor's consent, unless she had the *ius liberorum*; and if she were a freedwoman herself with a living patron, the tutor was *legitimus* and could not be forced to consent. The children born from her cohabitation with the Latin were illegitimate. Illegitimate children until the latter part of the second century AD are not attested as qualifying their mother for the *ius liberorum;* and they had no claim to inherit on intestacy from her—the patron took precedence.

MOTHERS AND CHILDREN

That was the situation for the whole of the first century AD and well into the second, when the prospects for Roman mothers and children were improved—at least potentially. At some time probably in the first half of the second century AD freeborn illegitimate children were accepted as qualifying a mother for the *ius liberorum* (Gardner 1986a: 198, and refs. at n. 56). By then the rules of intestate succession under the edict had already been modified[21] to allow mothers and their illegitimate children, and the latter and their brothers and sisters, to inherit from each other as cognates (*D.* 38. 8. 2, Gaius; 4, Ulpian); previously, legitimate children and their mothers had had mutual rights at this level, legitimate brothers and sisters at a higher level, as agnates. The step was not a great one; as Ulpian points out, *spurii* had in law no agnates or *consanguinei* to inherit from them. Mothers and children would inherit from each other only if there were no one eligible to inherit at a higher level (such as patrons). Besides, all this could apply only to relationships with freeborn children (see next paragraph).

Under Hadrian, the *senatusconsultum Tertullianum* gave mothers with the *ius liberorum* a right of succession to their (legitimate) children ahead of cognates. By the latter half of the second century, legal interpretation (*D.* 38. 17. 2. 1, Julian, cited by Ulpian) extended this to mothers of illegitimate children. This was consistent, since these mothers already had *ius liberorum* under the edict, and it injured no other claims, since *illegitimi* had no agnates or cognates. However, as Julian properly pointed out (ibid. 2, 3), this applied only to freeborn children (properly, since, apart from considerations of avoiding incest, servile biological relationships are not recognized in Roman law).[22] The motive for maintaining the requirement of *ius*

---

[21] Possibly by Hadrian; cf. his concession allowing the children of soldiers to inherit from their fathers (*FIRA* 1. 428–30, no. 78). However, there was no general extension of this concession to inheritance from civilian fathers. Only legitimate children were in their father's *potestas* and in his *familia*, and only legitimate children had succession rights from their father (or, initially at least, and only with a low priority, from their mothers).

[22] On the reasons for the limitation to mothers with *ius liberorum*, see Gardner (1986a: 197–8); these reasons apply particularly to freeborn mothers.

liberorum even for a mother of illegitimate children was, I suspect, fiscal. Illegitimate children qualified her to inherit; but unless she had had at least three (or four for a freedwoman), the estate went to the *fiscus*.

In AD 178 the *senatusconsultum Orphitianum* gave children, including illegitimate children, priority in intestate inheritance to their mothers; before that, they had succeeded merely among cognates (Gardner 1986a: 198–200). The inclusion of illegitimate children makes sense; with the decline of *manus* marriage, mother and child were usually in different *familiae* anyway, and the marital status of a mother made no difference. There could be conflict, however, with patrons' succession rights; how this was resolved is unclear.[23] The *lex Papia Poppaea* apparently still applied to inheritance by legitimate children (Gaius 3. 44), who would share with the patron; perhaps the effect of the *senatusconsultum* was that illegitimate children, who had previously been entirely excluded by a mother's patron, could now also share with him.

Buckland (1966: 374) regards the two *senatusconsulta* as resting on quite different ideas. 'The Tertullian is a late part of the legislation for the encouragement of marriage of which the *leges caducariae* are the best known part. The Orphitian is an early part of that legislation which ultimately superseded the agnatic idea altogether.' The *Tertullianum*, like the *Orphitianum*, should rather be regarded as part of a continuing process, long under way, by which the claims of agnates had been undermined by measures (notably the changes to *tutela*) allowing those of 'family', and especially of the mother–child relationship, to be exercised. As I have argued elsewhere (Gardner 1986a: 197–8), the purpose of the requirement of *ius liberorum* for benefit under the *senatusconsultum Tertullianum* was not to encourage women to breed, but rather to reduce the likelihood of dispersal of patrimonial property outside the children's paternal line. The measure was primarily conceived in terms of freeborn parents; few freedwomen mothers would find it possible to fulfil the requirements.

In theory at least, the change to the rules for *ius liberorum*, allowing freeborn illegitimate children to count, was a benefit for mixed-status families including one or more ex-slaves, and with a Roman

---

[23] They inherited in the same rank as children now did; the latter, at least if legitimate, were apparently given priority over *consanguinei* and agnates (Ulpian, *Reg.* 26. 7); however, the *lex Papia Poppaea* on patron's rights probably still applied (Gaius 3. 44; Ulpian, *Reg.* 29. 3, with which *D.* 38. 17. 1. 9, Ulpian, is not incompatible, since the patron there was sharing with the son, and receives in addition the son's portion when the latter withdraws). The arguments of Meinhart (1967: 69–89) that freedwomen were not originally included are not conclusive.

mother. However, whether in practice many families ever took advantage of this possibility is doubtful; there were still many obstacles in the way. To start with, the family would have to have the necessary legal knowledge. The mother would have to be still capable of having the requisite number of freeborn children; if she were an ex-slave manumitted formally in accordance with the *lex Aelia Sentia* and without 'good cause' shown, she would be at least 30 years old at the start. She would have to have had the foresight to make and, desirably, obtain a record of, witnessed sworn declarations of the birth of each of three or four children, as proof of her entitlement to the *ius liberorum*. She then, probably, had to go to Rome or to the office of the appropriate official in a province to register her claim. (Our only evidence is the Egyptian papyri, but it is probable that this applied elsewhere: Gardner 1986a: 20.)

And even after all that, the benefits to the children and the husband, whether Latin or Roman, were uncertain. If the wife were a freeborn Roman, or a freedwoman with no surviving patron or patron's children, grandchildren and even great-grandchildren in the male line (Gaius 3. 45)—qualifications which would already exclude many—there was no problem. Otherwise, what the Augustan legislation gave with one hand, it took away from the freedwoman with the other, for reasons which, at least on the surface, were not based on social prejudice but on traditional familial (and family) principles about the rights of agnates. The freedwoman mother who had already surmounted all the hurdles was allowed to benefit by her will those children who survived her, but even if all four survived her (or perhaps no matter how many did),[24] a share of her property must go to her quasi-agnate, i.e. her patron, or his[25] family (Gaius 1. 165; 3. 43–4).

Overall, the general tendency of the law on inheritance from an early date in the Republic, both for lawfully married couples and their offspring (the archetypal *familia*) and for nuclear families, was to accord more consideration to biological relationships. From this, the families of ex-slaves could, in favourable circumstances, gain some limited benefits, more from the maternal than the paternal

---

[24] The wording of Gaius 3. 44 is possibly not quite parallel to that of 3. 42, on inheritance from freedmen. Three children, he says, excluded a patron from a freedman's inheritance ('si tres relinquat, repellitur patronus'); four apparently (though the text is defective) still allowed a patron a fifth share of a freedwoman's inheritance ('ex bonis eius quae omnes quattuor incolumes liberos reliquerit, quinta pars patrono debetur'). It is possible that he was never excluded entirely from a freedwoman's inheritance.

[25] Under praetorian rules women patrons had no rights of succession, and only limited rights under the *lex Papia* (Gardner 1986a: 195–6).

relationship. The nature of the changes under the principate suggests that they were actuated at least in part by an awareness of the pervasiveness[26] of illegitimacy, but the way for the changes was already paved by the prevalence of marriage without *manus*, which meant that the wife and mother was an outsider to the *familia* of her husband and children.

Patria potestas, however—power both over persons and over property—remained virtually intact. The practical inconveniences this might occasion for the individual would, for the most part, not be apparent in ordinary life, where the personal status of persons with whom one had dealings tended simply to be assumed and seldom needed to be checked. Many technically illegal transactions must daily have been made, and there was little motive on the part of the law-making classes to encourage legal changes which would diminish patronal rights.

THE EFFECTS OF THE *CONSTITUTIO ANTONINIANA*

The declaration of AD 212 made all free inhabitants of the empire Roman citizens, but the effect for ex-slave families was mainly to create *conubium* for existing mixed-status couples, and so the possibility of *matrimonium iustum* and legitimate children. Other practical difficulties concerning inheritance and patronal rights remained. Owing to the operation of the laws themselves, new Junian Latins and *dediticii* would continue to be created, and citizens to be born illegitimate. In the long term, Caracalla's declaration changed little, beyond perhaps a slight rise in the proportion of freeborn Romans.

CONCLUSION: LAW AND LIFE

As indicated above, in ordinary life people would tend to take each other's status for granted, or even their own—proof was not always

---

[26] For legal reasons, not from rejection of conventional morality, as Moses Finley (1977: 131, in 'The Silent Women of Rome') notoriously hinted: 'A large proportion of the free population, even of the citizen class, was increasingly drawn from ex-slaves and the children of slaves. This alone—and specifically their experience, as females, while they were slaves—would have been enough to give them, and their men, a somewhat different attitude towards the accepted, traditional, upper-class values.' Finley's comments here arose in part from his own awareness of the legacy of slavery in sections of American society; he appears also to have been confusing law and accepted morality, by committing the common error of regarding civil law as mainly prescriptive and therefore evaluative. For a discussion of Roman attitudes to illegitimacy, see Rawson (1989: esp. 18–23).

readily forthcoming, and the rules of legal status could often have been broken without detection.[27] Many of the problems outlined above may never have arisen for mixed-status families, simply because they were unaware that they had them; even patrons may not always have realized the extent of their legal entitlement, specially if they themselves were from the humbler social levels. Since the interests involved were usually private and personal, the pursuit of detected errors would depend on an initiative by someone with something to gain thereby, and there might be no such person.

Understandably, since breach of the rules of private law does not usually carry penalties, but merely renders certain private transactions invalid (a matter of purely private concern), there is evidence to suggest that the authorities of the state were not much concerned to pursue such technical illegalities. They may even perhaps be seen actively condoning them. The possible implications of Gaius 1. 67–75 are worth considering. A *senatusconsultum* of Hadrianic date at latest[28] allowed persons having married, as they thought, in accordance with the *lex Aelia Sentia*, but under a misapprehension about their own status or that of their partner, to claim mistake and, if this was proved, to gain citizenship for themselves and/or partner and *potestas* over the child. Gaius lists the following hypothetical cases: a Roman man marrying a Latin or peregrine woman, thinking her Roman;[29] a Roman woman marrying a peregrine thinking him Roman or Latin; a Latin woman marrying a peregrine thinking him Latin; a Latin man marrying a peregrine woman, thinking her Latin or Roman; a Roman thinking himself Latin and marrying a Latin woman, or thinking himself peregrine and marrying a peregrine woman; and even (though this had been disputed) a peregrine marrying a Roman woman.

All these cases ended up in citizenship for everyone and legitimation of the children, if mistake were proven. But how was a mistake of this kind proved? There had to be witnesses to a marriage under the *lex Aelia Sentia* (Gaius 1. 29), but they were witnesses only to the marital intent of the relationship, not to the status of the parties. There might be evidence obtainable about the manumission of the doubtful party, and so about his or her status, but how would the negative fact, that the spouse was in ignorance of this, be proved? It is hard to resist the suspicion that there was sometimes collusion

---

[27] See Gardner (1986*b*; 1993: 186–91).

[28] Talbert (1984: 452, no. 158); see also Gaius 2. 143.

[29] Or even one classed among the *dediticii*, though she does not become a citizen; nevertheless, the child is legitimated and taken into *potestas*. If a Roman woman marries a *dediticius*, the son, again, becomes Roman, but of course is not *in potestate*.

or complicity on the part of the authorities before whom the case was brought.

As to who brought the matter to light, or why, one possibility is that it was raised by the spouse concerned in the interests of legitimating the child and so repelling a possible patronal claim on property (although it is doubtful how much weight such a motive would carry with the authorities). There are, of course, other possible incentives, some already mentioned, such as escape from the inheritance penalties on the unmarried and childless, inclusion of children in entitlement to paternal estate, or acquisition of eligibility to contract marriage with a Roman citizen.[30] Besides these practical incentives, we may speculate that considerations of personal sentiment or social reputation may sometimes have operated. What is noteworthy, however, is the apparent flexibility and generosity (and perhaps deliberate complicity) of the authorities in extending the private benefits of citizenship to almost any relationship that seemed to constitute a stable nuclear family.

A similar attitude is discernible in the 'statute of limitation' introduced by Nerva and extended by Hadrian.[31] No enquiry was to be made into the status of a person once five years had elapsed since that person's death, nor into that of a living person, if that had a prejudicial effect on the status of the deceased.[32] The accounts given of the persons concerned, in some of the rescripts preserved in the *Codex Iustinianus*, are enlightening as to circumstances and motives for questioning status.

A lawsuit on the property of a deceased freedwoman turns on the status of her patron, allegedly deceased five years before, 'who lived as a Roman citizen until his death' (*qui ciuis Romanus in diem mortis uixit*); this could mean that he was alleged either to have been a slave himself, or a Latin (who could not lawfully manumit). An heir claiming an estate is resisting a counterclaim that the testator's mother (allegedly dead more than five years previously), and

---

[30] Suggested as a motive for Petronia Justa (Gardner 1986a: 224–5). Paternal estate: *illegitimi* could become entitled only by being brought into the *familia*.

[31] *D.* 40. 15. 1. 3, Marcianus; 4, Callistratus; perhaps especially significant, seen in the context of the Hadrianic contribution to the development of Roman family law, through such measures as the *senatusconsultum Tertullianum* (above) and the recognition of the inheritance rights of soldiers' children (*FIRA* 1. 428–30, no. 78), and especially the final codification of the praetorian edict. Already Claudius, according to Callistratus (*D.* 40. 15. 4), had given a rescript forbidding pursuit of a fiscal enquiry which was prejudicial to status.

[32] *D.* 40. 15; *C.* 7.21. Later interpretation allowed enquiry, if it would enhance the status, e.g. if free status was claimed for someone who had died as a slave: *D.* 40. 15. 3, Hermogenianus. Previous interruptions to life as a citizen, or challenges to status, did, however, permit enquiry (*C.* 7. 21. 2, AD 205; 6. 1, AD 260). For this and some other temporal limitations (*praescriptiones temporis*), see Kaser (1966: 386).

therefore the testator himself, was a slave. In a text with overtones of the Petronia Justa case, the enquirer, Polla, is told that if her mother had been commonly accepted as freeborn (*ingenua*), then the daughter could repel the *res publica* (i.e. the fisc) and the *pupilli*, if they should try to open the question of her mother's status.[33] Nothing seems to have happened yet, but Polla apparently thinks that the tutors of certain *impuberes* may try to claim her mother's estate on behalf of their wards, alleging that she was their father's freedwoman, and, even if they do not, that the fisc may claim the estate, once doubt is cast on her status.[34]

From these instances, several things emerge. Not only was it quite possible, as already said, for persons to pass for something that they were not, but the law took a relaxed and tolerant attitude about this. It was not the business of the state to intervene officially to secure the private and personal gain of interested individuals; it was up to the interested parties themselves to intervene, and if they did not do so within a reasonable time (and this applied even to the fisc itself), then they lost their claim. In the ordinary life of families in Roman society, what mattered was not so much the legal status of the people involved, as whether there was anyone in whose interest it was to insist upon the legalities being observed.

[33] C. 7. 21. 1, 2, 6. It must, however, be established that the person had lived as a Roman citizen uninterruptedly (*sine interpellatione*).

[34] What is challenged in C. 7. 21. 6 is whether the mother was freeborn (*ingenua*), not whether she was free; 'communi opinione uixit' seems to preclude a grant of *natalium restitutio*, since consent of patron would have been required, and that would surely be a matter of record.

3
Children of Junian Latins

PAUL WEAVER

The primary purpose of this chapter is to consider the condition
of children belonging to a status group in Roman imperial society
intermediate between slaves and citizens, in the context of the general issues raised by the whole question of Junian Latinity. I have
tried to keep the more complicated legal material to a minimum.[1]

What have children of Junian Latins got to do with the present
context of the Roman family? At one level, they continue earlier
discussions of the status of children in lower-class family groups, in
succession to children of mixed marriages (Weaver 1986) and children of freedmen and freedwomen (Weaver 1991). The latter had
led irresistibly to Junian Latins, whose children serve the invaluable
purpose of providing at least one method of detecting the status of
their parents (Weaver 1990). On another plane, the important contribution of Junian Latinity to the complex fabric of Roman imperial
society demands further investigation and, where possible, elucida-
tion. As a unique social and seemingly elusive demographic phenomenon, it represents a black hole of large but unknown proportions
at the heart of our understanding of that 'slave society'. Here we are
concerned with questions of status as well as numbers. These questions are primarily legal and involve not only the lower-class sections of Roman society at one end, but also the slave-owning classes
at the other. They also involve, potentially, very large numbers of
families, especially those in urban settings in Rome and Italy. Where
the institution of slavery is embedded in the social and economic
structure, questions of status are bound to be a constant concern in
the legal sources, both in the law of persons and the law of property. Junian Latins also raise important social questions in an acute
form. Why were the Romans, who are not known for soft hearted
generosity, unique among slave societies in setting free so early so
many of their slaves? This is better expressed as: in what form,

---

[1] For bibliography before 1924, see the article 'Latini Iuniani' by Steinwenter, *RE* 12.
910–24. For detailed treatment of sources and recent bibliography, see esp. Sirks (1981;
1983); Lopez Baria de Quiroga (1986).

under what conditions, and for what reasons did the Romans manumit slaves? Where are we to look for Junian Latins and once having
become a Junian Latin what was the likelihood of remaining one?
Without underestimating the methodological problems involved, the
most promising approach is through their familial structures and in
particular their children.

I begin with three basic propositions:[2]

1. In personal nomenclature, the Roman *tria nomina* indicate
   only free (non-peregrine) status, that is, there is no essential
   link between use of *tria nomina* and Roman citizenship. *Tria
   nomina* in individual cases, in the absence of evidence to the
   contrary, were regularly used by Latins and, in particular, by
   Junian Latins.
2. Very large numbers of slaves of Roman citizen owners were
   informally freed and acquired the status of Junian Latins.
3. Conversion of Junian Latin status to Roman citizenship status
   (*ciuitas Romana*) was formal, restricted, and even difficult.
   Therefore, there are likely to be large numbers of Junian Latins
   who remained Junian Latins.

JUNIAN LATINS

Who or what are the Junian Latins? At the risk of stating the obvious, but briefly, in Roman law slaves could be set free (manumitted) formally or informally.[3] Formal manumission (*uindicta, censu,
testamento*) required the approval of a Roman magistrate with *imperium*, either the praetor in Rome or the governor in a province
or, in special cases, the emperor. It conferred both freedom (*libertas*)
and Roman citizenship. Under the *lex Aelia Sentia* of AD 4, part of
the Augustan legislation on slavery, a major new condition was
introduced: the slave must be 30 years of age or over (Gaius 1. 18;
Ulpian, *Reg.* 1. 12). A strict set of exceptions required a case to be
proved (*causae probatio*) before a panel (*consilium*) presided over
by the praetor or governor, and these were heavily concentrated on
family and personal relationships within the household, e.g. a natural son or daughter, brother or sister, foster-child, intended marriage, etc. (Gaius 1. 19–21). These restrictions remained in force for
over 500 years till, with characteristic finality, Justinian in 531 abol-
ished the legislation as a whole (C. 7. 6. 6); that is, they survived

---

[2] For further details and basic arguments, see Weaver (1990: 277–81; 1991: 166–90).
[3] For more detailed accounts, see Buckland (1908: 532–44, 714–18); Kaser (1971: i. 294–5).

unimpaired the effects of the *constitutio Antoniniana* of 212, which purported to include the free population of all communities in the empire. As for children, if both parents satisfied the required conditions, those subsequently born were freeborn Roman citizens (*ciues Romani ingenui*).

Informal manumission, on the other hand, e.g. *inter amicos* or of slaves under 30 years of age where a magistrate with *imperium* was not involved, under the *lex Iunia* conferred *libertas* and Latin status (*Latinitas*), but not *ciuitas*, hence the name 'Latini Iuniani' (Gaius 1. 22; 3. 56).[4] The children of Junian Latins, in particular those of a Junian Latin mother, acquired the status of *Latini/Latinae*, i.e. they were *freeborn* Latins[5] and, as with illegitimate children of citizen status, were 'Sp(urii) f(ilii)'. Various procedures were available to convert Junian Latins to Roman citizen status, but all were formal and required the participation of the praetor, governor or emperor; none were easy or short, e.g., for those 30 and over, a repetition of formal manumission (*iteratio*) by the former quiritary owner before a magistrate (*uindicta*) or by will (*testamento*);[6] and, for those under 30, the complicated *anniculi probatio* procedure (proof of a 1-year-old child). All these procedures at some point under the early empire also included the freeborn Latin children (Gaius 1. 29–32; Ulpian, *Reg.* 3. 3–4).

The main effect and the most serious defect of informal manumission at the personal level was that Junian Latins had no right of inheritance, either to make a will or take under a will (except by *fideicommissum*) or be appointed *tutor* under a will (Gaius 1. 23–4; 2. 275–6). Thus during their lifetime they enjoyed *libertas* and *commercium*, which otherwise included full rights of owning property, conducting business transactions, contracts, etc. as if they were Roman citizens (*ex iure Quiritium*), and having access to the Roman courts. But after death, by a special clause in the *lex Iunia*, they were treated as if they had been *slaves* all along, 'just as if the law had not been passed' (*proinde . . . ac si lex lata non esset*)! Their whole estate went by right of slave ownership (*iure peculii*) to their patron who had manumitted them informally, and *not* to the deceased's

---

[4] For formal manumission to effect citizenship, quiritary ownership of the slave was a necessary precondition (Gaius 1. 17). If the owner had bonitary possession only, even formal manumission procedures still resulted in informal manumission.

[5] Even if the wife of a Junian Latin was a *ciuis Romana*, it was uncertain whether their children were Latins or Roman citizens, until the 2nd cent. when Hadrian legislated in favour of the latter (Gaius 1. 30, 80; Ulpian, *Reg.* 3. 3).

[6] Not available, of course, to those whom their quiritary owner had previously freed informally by will.

children, who were totally excluded (Gaius 3. 56)[7]—a situation expressed later with epigrammatic force by Salvian (*Ad ecclesiam* 3. 7. 31) as 'living as if born free and dying as slaves'.[8] This must be one of the most extraordinary caveats in Roman law. The children of Junian Latin parents were thus the most obvious losers. It is easier to explain how this came about than why. A brief diversion into chronology is called for.

Did the *lex Iunia*, from which the Junian Latins derived their status and name, precede or follow the *lex Aelia Sentia* of AD 4? The question figures prominently in most discussions on Junian Latins. It is a source problem of keen interest to Romanist legal historians and to writers on the social policies of Augustus. Both groups are faced with seemingly intractable difficulties. The range of dates is limited— by the need to have a Junius as consul—to either 17 BC at one end or AD 15 or, more usually, 19 at the other, that is, either twenty years before the *lex Aelia Sentia* or eleven to fifteen years after.[9]

Much hinges on the use of the phrases 'Latinus ex lege Aelia Sentia (factus)' and 'matrimonium/conubium ex lege Aelia Sentia'.[10] Instead of being in the previous position of those protected in a state of freedom by the praetor (e.g. Gaius 3. 56: 'quos praetor in libertate tuebatur') but in civil law still effectively *serui*, at some point in the reign of Augustus informally manumitted slaves had their legal status clarified and immeasurably improved by being equated with *Latini coloniarii*; they were not Roman citizens, but possessed substantial civil law rights (see above). Did this happen as a result of the *lex Aelia Sentia* in AD 4? The phrase 'Latinus ex lege Aelia Sentia', which occurs in the principal source, Gaius, several times over, might seem to imply that this was the case. That law, while imposing the age restriction for formal manumission to 30 years and over, also made provision for such 'Latini' to acquire full

---

[7] 'Legis itaque Iuniae lator ... necessarium existimauit, ne beneficium istis datum in iniuriam patronorum conuerteretur, cauere ut bona eorum proinde ad manumissores pertinerent *ac si lex lata non esset.* itaque iure quodammodo peculii bona Latinorum ad manumissores ea lege pertinent.'

[8] 'Ut uiuant scilicet quasi ingenui et moriantur ut serui.' Cf. Tacitus, *Annales* 13. 27: 'quos uindicta patronus non liberauerit, uelut uinclo seruitutis attineri'; and even, with uncharacteristic feeling, in Justinian, *Inst.* 3. 7. 4: 'cum Latinorum legitimae successiones nullae penitus erant, qui licet ut liberi uitam suam peragebant, attamen ipso ultimo spiritu simul animam atque libertatem amittebant'.

[9] The literature is considerable and fertile. The best statement of the case for 17 BC is still H. M. Last, *CAH* 10[1] (1934), 888–90; cf. Sirks (1981: 250), where the earlier date is taken for granted. For the later date, see Steinwenter, *RE* 12. 910–14; A. Wilinski, 'Zur Frage von Latinern ex lege Aelia Sentia', *ZSS-R* 80 (1963), 378–92, in an ingenious and sometimes over-cautious discussion of the sources; Sherwin-White (1973: 332–4).

[10] The passages in question are: Gaius 1. 29, 31, 66, 68, 70, 71, 80; 3. 73. Ulpian, *Reg.* 1. 12; 7. 4.

citizen status under prescribed conditions, such as *apud consilium* and *anniculi causae probatio*. If so, why are they called *Latini Iuniani* and not *Latini Aeliani* or *Sentiani*, and why, if the *lex Iunia* was not till AD 19, did it take more than a decade to protect the financial interests of Roman citizen patrons from the apparently unforeseen and unintended consequences of the *Aelia Sentia* by introducing in particular the discriminatory amendment 'proinde . . . ac si lex lata non esset' mentioned above? That, one might think, was a bit late, was surely obvious at the time, and should have been anticipated. It was awkward enough to introduce it at the same time as the class of Junian Latins was created,[11] but to have to declare much later that the law was null and void in one key respect—inheritance— would be, to say the least, thoroughly confusing. That would not be characteristic of Augustan legislation. The protection of owners' financial interests was much more likely to have been one of the main purposes of the law in the first place. Our best source, Gaius, who picks his way carefully between the provisions of the two laws, states unequivocally that former slaves who were under the protec- tion of the praetor got their freedom as Latins under the *lex Iunia* (Gaius 1. 22).[12] Along with their status as free Latins went the legal recognition of their marriages, although they did not have the *ius conubii*, which required both partners to be Roman citizens.

The problematic phrases mentioned above are perhaps to be interpreted in the following light. Some twenty years after the *lex Iunia*, as part of the Augustan social legislation, came the *lex Aelia Sentia* restricting formal manumission to those over 30 and thus adding a major new category, those informally freed under 30, to the already existing *Latini Iuniani*. These would be the 'Latini ex lege Aelia Sentia'. In providing for exceptions leading to full Roman citizenship, that law instituted among others the *anniculi probatio* procedure which required specific action by couples at the time of marriage in the form of a declaration of their intent to have children in order to qualify for future citizenship. This would be at least one category of 'matrimonium ex lege Aelia Sentia'.[13] In some cases,

---

[11] See esp. Gaius 3. 56. Other passages in which the *lex Iunia / Latini Iuniani* are men- tioned are: Gaius 1. 22–4, 167; Ulpian, *Reg.* 1. 5, 10; 19. 3; 20. 8, 14; *Fragmentum Dositheanum* 6, 7, 8, 12.

[12] 'Iuniani . . . quia per legem Iuniam libertatem acceperunt, cum olim serui uiderentur esse.'; 3. 56: 'eos qui nunc Latini Iuniani dicuntur olim ex iure Quiritium seruos fuisse, sed auxilio praetoris in libertatis forma seruari solitos; . . . Latinos quia lex eos liberos . . . esse uoluit'.

[13] Other passages referring to (Junian) Latins, but which do not bear on the argument, are: Gaius 1. 15–17, 32c–5; Ulpian, *Reg.* 3. 1, 2, 4–6; *Fragmenta Vaticana* 221; *Fragmentum Dositheanum* 11, 13, 16. There is a distinct lack of interest in Junian Latins in the civil law compilations of the Justinianic period.

however, it does appear that these phrases are also used simply as an alternative to the term 'Latini Iuniani'.

The puzzle is why Junian Latin couples should be encouraged to have children—or at least one child—in order to qualify for citizenship by *anniculi probatio*, while at the same time provisions were left in place that discriminated against the many more children of Latins who were unlikely ever to progress to citizenship. The routes to citizenship for Junian Latins outside Rome were not easy and hardly selective on grounds of social or moral value, even where family or marriage ties between citizen patrons and under-age slaves (i.e. under 30) were involved or contemplated. Various political, financial, and ethical grounds for the Augustan social legislation and for its timing have been canvassed. The most thorough recent discussion of the purpose of the *lex Iunia* connects the measure closely with the investment strategies of the élite which were designed to secure the return of capital (and profits therefrom) outlaid in the hands of their informally manumitted freedmen (Sirks 1981: esp. 257–74).[14] This may not have been the full story, but financial considerations are undoubtedly prominent. Certainly it cannot have given citizen slave-owners in general any incentive to proceed with early *formal* manumission of their slaves, even deserving ones; indeed, by setting the minimum age at 30, the *lex Aelia Sentia* made this much more difficult than before. That age level, representing at least fifteen years of service, was a very long span in the lifetime of the average Roman urban slave. On the other hand, the *lex Iunia*, with its creation of the status category of Junian Latins, represented a significant step forward in ameliorating the practice of Roman slavery by offering slaves at any age the prospect of obtaining their freedom and secure legal rights for whatever reason it pleased their masters to do so. In the process, for the first time it made legal marriage possible for those freed informally, and created legally recognized family relationships, including those of freeborn children. Junian Latinity is not to be seen, as it was sometimes in later antiquity, as a punishment or demotion from full citizen status.[15] The penalty, if anywhere, was imposed on their freeborn children by expressly depriving them of their rights of inheritance to their free parents' estates. This was

[14] On the *lex Fufia Caninia*, which impinges on the *lex Iunia* in purpose, timing, and content, see Gardner (1991).

[15] e.g. a freedman could be reduced to Latin status for ingratitude: *C.Th.* 2. 22. 1 (326).

blatantly and uncharacteristically discriminatory, and the discrimination lasted for more than five centuries. Despite some mitigating concessions, concern for family values had little to do with it. Many scores of thousands, even hundreds of thousands, of children were involved. Rome was, after all, a slave society.

Children of Junian Latin parents (i.e. of those who were still *Latini*) can be either slave-born or freeborn, depending on their mother's status at the time of their birth. By contrast with formally manumitted slaves, where age at manumission is determined by the 30-year minimum prescribed by the *lex Aelia Sentia*, Junian Latin status is quite unpredictable on grounds of age. The inscriptional evidence from tombstones shows that female slaves were freed informally at any age from 1 year upwards. Their children, if slave-born, could either have remained slaves or have been freed, again at any age and independently of either parent. They would simply follow the same paths as their parents, whether as slaves or informally freed Junian Latins themselves. They could even have been formally manumitted and become Roman citizens while their parents remained Junian Latins.

More problematic, and more interesting for our purpose, are the *freeborn* children of Junian Latins, i.e. those born after their parents, or at least their mother, had acquired Junian Latin status. How many came into this category? We can only guess. The sources, legal, epigraphic, or literary, say virtually nothing at all about them. That does not mean that they did not exist in large numbers (Weaver 1990: 281–304). The legal sources in particular have little or nothing to say about freeborn Latins of any sort, to the point where it has been argued that individual *ciues Latini* did not exist anywhere in the *municipia* throughout the empire, even in communities with the *ius Latii* (Millar 1977: 406, 483–7, 630–5).[16] But the point needs to be made that a much higher proportion of children of Junian Latin parents, perhaps a large majority of them, would have been freeborn (because their mothers could be informally manumitted at any age) than was likely, or indeed possible, for children of formally manumitted parents (who would normally have to wait till they were 30 for manumission). If the conversion of Latin status to Roman citizenship status was as restrictive as seems to me likely, the provisions in the *lex Aelia Sentia* for early formal manumission of Junian Latin parents would not have altered this situation significantly. Even parents formally manumitted by iteration at the regular age of

---

[16] Cf. N. Mackie, *Local Administration in Roman Spain AD 14–212* (1983), 201–6. But see González (1986: 148, 206); and further below.

30 or over may not, initially at least, have won citizen status for
their children also (Ulpian, *Reg.* 3. 4).[17] Freeborn children of Junian
Latins, under these conditions, are likely to have substantially out-
numbered freeborn children by the first marriage of formally manumitted slaves, when both partners (*contubernales*) would normally
have 'married' as slaves.[18]

Where can we expect to find them? Anywhere where there were
Roman citizens owning slaves and wanting to set them free for
whatever reason; especially in Rome, Ostia, and throughout Italy,
from Herculaneum and Pompeii to Pliny's third wife's grandfather
in Ticinum (Pliny 7. 16), as well as in the provinces from Spain to
Asia and Egypt.[19] The *leges Iunia*, *Aelia Sentia*, and *Fufia Caninia*
together, as carrot and stick, were designed to mitigate the institution of Roman slavery in practice by making freedom easier to
achieve, while at the same time reducing the flow of Roman *citizen*
freedmen by restricting formal manumission, especially by testamentary manumission, where the 30-year age bar most strictly applied.
It follows that under the civil law only Roman citizens could create
freed Junian Latins just as they alone could also create freedmen who
were Roman citizens. But at all times the interests of the patrons
come first. The reasons given by Gaius (3. 56)[20] for the discriminatory provisions of the *lex Iunia* are essentially that, if a freedman
became a Latin in the usual 'coloniary' sense, his Roman patron
would otherwise have had no claim on his freedman's property by
right of manumission, because it was not a formal civil law manumission, whereas he would have such a claim with a freedman who was
a Roman citizen. So, to prevent the benefit which was being conferred on the Latin freedman rebounding to the disadvantage of his
already generous patron, in order to protect his right of succession
to his portion of the freedman's property, by a legal fiction it was

[17] See Gardner, ch. 2, n. 7 above. On *iteratio*, see further below.

[18] As to second marriages of *ciues Romani liberti* after manumission with freeborn women,
including *ciues Romanae*, no account is taken here. These undoubtedly occurred quite often,
especially with younger women. I know of no basis for making even a guestimate of numbers, despite the fact that the children of such unions clearly played a very significant role
in the penetration of the freedman class into the municipal élites throughout Italy. On this
subject, see Garnscy (1975: 167–80; 1981: 359–71).

[19] For Junian Latins in Egypt, cf. *Gnomon Idiologi* (*FIRA* 1. 470–8, no. 99) 19, 21, 22,
26.

[20] 'Legis itaque Iuniae lator cum intellegeret futurum, ut ea fictione res Latinorum defunc-
torum ad patronos pertinere desinerent, quia scilicet neque ut serui decederent, ut possent
iure peculii res eorum ad patronos pertinere, neque liberti Latini hominis bona possent
manumissionis iure ad patronos pertinere, necessarium existimauit, ne beneficium istis datum
in iniuriam patronorum conuerteretur, cauere uoluit, ut bona eorum proinde ad manumissores
pertinerent, ac si lex lata non esset; itaque iure quodammodo peculii bona Latinorum ad
manumissores ea lege pertinent.' Cf. *Fragmentum Dositheanum* 5.

deemed after his death that no such manumission had taken place. This solution had the drastic consequence that it then became a question of ownership of a slave's *peculium*, not succession to a freedman's inheritance. A slave not only has no rights to property, but has no family or kin either. This did not mean that the situation of her/his children reverted to that obtaining before the *lex Iunia*, where slaves who were informally free and under the protection of the praetor in civil law strictly speaking still had no rights at all. That would have meant that *iure peculii* the *children* as well as their parents were the property of the master, being still slaves. Under the *lex Iunia*, however, this was not the case. Gaius does not draw a precise parallel with the time before that law, but qualifies the situation of Junian Latins with the phrase '*as it were* by right of *peculium*' (*iure quodammodo peculii*). It is only for the purposes of succession that their children are deemed not to exist. And that thoroughly so. Even if the patron's right was for any reason defective, the children still did not benefit—the whole estate fell to the state (3. 62).[21] But at least they were born and remained free.

On this paradoxical situation Gaius comments that the rights over the property of Junian Latins are very different ('accidit ut longe differant') from those obtaining over the inheritance of freedmen who were Roman citizens (3. 57).[22] He then proceeds in the following *twenty-three* chapters to demonstrate, at inordinate length for a student textbook, just how different these legal rights were in practice— in relation to heirs outside the family (*heredes extranei*), to joint owners or patrons, the division of property between the patron's children, etc. etc., detailing modifications made in two *senatusconsulta* of AD 42 and 75 respectively, and the opinions of jurisconsults Caelius Sabinus and Cassius (3. 63–71). In all this there is not a mention of the children of the Junian Latin freedmen themselves! They are, of course, irrelevant to these strictly legal issues.

What, then, was the status of the freeborn children of Junian Latins?[23] Did they also come under the provisions of the *lex Iunia* or were they Latins in the sense of the now defunct coloniary Latins, or come under what one supposes was the definition of Latins and the law of citizens of towns with the *ius Latii*?[24] There are problems

[21] 'Bona autem Latini pro parte deficientis patroni caduca fiunt et ad populum pertinent.'
[22] 'Unde accidit, ut longe differant ea iura quae in bonis Latinorum ex lege Iunia constituta sunt, ab his quae in hereditate ciuium Romanorum libertorum obseruantur.'
[23] See esp. Sirks (1983: 262–5), where the views of the few previous writers on this question are recorded.
[24] The first two tablets of the *lex Irnitana*, which must have contained such a definition, are unfortunately missing. Cf. González (1986: 200).

with each of these alternatives. The children, being freeborn, have no legal patron and thus cannot be subject to the testamentary constraints or other patronal obligations which their parents had. In this respect they cannot be classed as Junian Latins as the key provision of the *lex Iunia* could not apply to them. If it did, the silence of the sources, especially Gaius, is inexplicable, even allowing for the gaps in his text. On the other hand, if Junian Latins did not have the right to conclude a marriage recognized by the civil law (*ius conubii*) (Ulpian, *Reg.* 5. 9; cf. 5. 4; Gaius 1. 80), these children should have derived their status from their mother under the law of nations (*ius gentium*),[25] and if she were a *Latina Iuniana*, and perhaps even if she were a *ciuis Romana* in the period before Hadrian, they should have been *Latini Iuniani* themselves.

More likely they reverted to the full status of coloniary Latins but without being subject to the fiction of the *lex Iunia* 'ac si lex lata non esset'.[26] As *Latini* they would have possessed the full *ius commercii*, which included the right to make a will, to receive inheritances and be appointed *tutor*. But as *Latini coloniarii* they ought to have been citizens of a Latin colony, which of course they weren't. In practice did they follow their Junian Latin parents who derived their *origo* from the home town of their manumitter?[27] The latter would have been a Roman citizen. It is clear, and has become even clearer since the discovery of the *lex Irnitana*, that *Latini* were closely assimilated to Roman citizens for practical legal purposes, the most significant exception being eligibility for municipal office in Italy or Roman colonies and *municipia ciuium Romanorum* in the provinces. It is less clear, but nevertheless probable, although seemingly anomalous, that a Junian Latin mother conferred on her freeborn children a status that was *better* than her own (cf. Sirks 1983: 263–4).

A similar but more intriguing line of thinking emerges from considering the freedmen of Junian Latins. What status did they have? There is no reason to think that Junian Latins could not have acquired slaves by virtue of their right to conduct business on equal terms with Roman citizens (*ius commercii*) and then manumitted them. But in what form? Formally or informally? Surely that did not matter, as their patrons were in any case not *ciues Romani* and so not subject to the *lex Iunia* or the *lex Aelia Sentia*. But, if we

---

[25] Cf. Gaius 1. 81: 'ut . . . <qui> ex peregrino et Latina nascitur, is matris condicionem sequatur'.

[26] For the phrase 'Latina ingenua' in Paulus, *Sententiae* 4. 9. 8; cf. 2. 21a. 1, see Millar (1977: 634).

[27] Cf. C. 10. 40. 7; *Fragmenta Vaticana* 193, 221. These sources, however, are not conclusive; see Sirks (1983: 260–1).

equate the 'Latini' (i.e. 'Latini Iuniani') of the legal sources with 'coloniary' Latins for all purposes other than in relation to those restrictions to their *ius commercii* placed on them by the *lex Iunia* which we have been considering above, the manumission by municipal 'Latini' in the provinces is relevant, on the assumption that, if they existed at all, their legal status was identical with that of *Latini coloniarii*. Chapter 28 of the *lex municipii Salpensani* under Domitian (AD 82–4), and now the same chapter of the *lex municipii Irnitani* (AD 91), deal with the manumission of slaves by a citizen of either town who is of Latin status ('municeps municipi . . . qui Latinus erit') before a duumvir in charge of the administration of justice, the equivalent of the praetor at Rome in their respective *municipia*. The procedure is formal, being equivalent to manumission *uindicta*, and confers 'Latin freedman' status with 'full rights' ('uti qui optimo iure Latini libertini liberi sunt erunt'). It takes cognizance of the *lex Aelia Sentia* only to the extent that it provides for the municipal equivalent of the *apud consilium* procedure for manumitters under 20 years.[28] No mention is made at this appropriate point of a similar procedure for slave manumittees under 30 years, nor indeed is informal manumission or Junian Latin status suggested as a possibility. The only hint is the reference to 'full rights' ('optimo iure') which might be taken to imply that lesser rights could sometimes be conferred.[29] If the phrase is taken to suggest Junian Latins, it is not applicable to Latin manumitters, but only to Roman citizen manumitters in the *municipium*, who came directly under the provisions of the *lex Iunia*, and the *lex Aelia Sentia*. As for the meaning of 'full rights', the *lex Irnitana*, ch. 72, concerning the manumission of public slaves, is helpful—in becoming free, the *serui publici* also become 'Latini' and 'municipes municipi Flaui Irnitani', both men and women; that is, the citizens of Irni are *Latini*. Furthermore, as their estates revert to their patrons not *iure peculii* but as *hereditas*, in the same way as public slaves freed by a *municipium* of Italy,[30] they cannot be Junian Latins. They must be *ciues Latini*.[31] Also of interest is another legal fiction which provided that Latin patrons, whose freedmen or

---

[28] Ibid. 28: 'dum is qui minor XX annorum erit ita manumittat, si causam manumittendi iustam esse is numerus decurionum, per quem decreta h(ac) l(ege) facta rata sunt, censuerit.'

[29] Cf. ibid. ch. 30, where the phrase 'optimo iure optimaque lege' is also used in an absolute sense. See González (1986: 207).

[30] Ch. 72: 'idem ius municipi Flaui Irnitani esto, quod esset, si municipi Italiae libertus liberta esset'.

[31] *Pace* Millar (1977: 630–5) and Fear (1990). See González (1986: 223; cf. 148–9, 206). For the term 'ciues Latini', distinguished from 'ciues Romani', see *lex municipii Malacitani* ch. 53 (*FIRA* 1. 210): 'incolae, qui ciues R(omani) Latiniue ciues erunt'; and, by implication, ch. 54.

freedwomen obtained Roman citizenship through the *ius Latii* as a
result of their sons or husbands holding magisterial office, should
have the same rights over them and their goods as they would have
had if they had not been made Roman citizens.[32] That is, the freedmen of Latin patrons could have a higher status than their patrons.

We may reasonably conclude that freedmen of Junian Latins too,
under certain conditions, could acquire a higher status than their
patrons. If they were formally freed *uindicta* before an appropriate
municipal magistrate, in the same way as the freedmen of municipal *Latini*, they would become *Latini coloniarii*, not *Latini Iuniani*.
Manumission *testamento* was obviously not available for slaves of
Junian Latins as the latter had no testamentary right to make a will.
For the same reason, it seems unlikely that informally freed slaves
of Junian Latins could have themselves become Junian Latins. Such
manumissions may well have been invalid.

Returning to the status of the children of Junian Latins, what were
their prospects of advancing to become full Roman citizens? These,
it seems, apart from a special grant from the emperor (*beneficium
principale*), depended entirely on their parents. Two main avenues
lay open to them: the *anniculi probatio* procedure and iteration
(*iteratio*) by repeating the manumission, this time formally and without the defect that had made the original procedure informal.[33] A
successful completion of either procedure by the parents carried with
it citizen status for their freeborn children as well.[34] Both presented
rewards and difficulties. The rewards consisted not just of citizenship, but citizenship at an early age—as soon as they were 1 year
old under *anniculi probatio*, as the name implies, and under *iteratio*
as soon as their mother was 30 years old; that is when they themselves were about 10–15 years old, as they would be born free at
any time after their mother's early manumission. The difficulties were
inherent in the formalities of the procedures themselves. Iteration
was by no means automatic when their parents came of age, so to
speak, at 30. Apart from the difficulties of manumission *uindicta*
itself outside Rome, which required the presence of a senior magistrate, there was the formal requirement that the person repeating

---

[32] *Lex Irnitana* ch. 97: 'idem ius esto quod fuisset si ei eae ciues Romani Romanae facti
factae non essent'.

[33] In numerical terms, the other avenues to citizenship for Junian Latins, listed in Gaius
1. 32*b*–4 and Ulpian *Reg.* 3, were minor, mostly centred on Rome and involving those who
had considerable wealth at their disposal.

[34] It seems to me likely that the same applied to all the other methods of obtaining full
citizenship available to Junian Latins; but see Gardner, ch. 2 n. 7 above.

the manumission (the iterant) must, by a complexity of the Roman forms of legal ownership, be the former quiritary (*de iure*) owner, not the bonitary (*de facto*) owner or possessor who might have originally manumitted the slave informally and become his patron.[35] The Junian Latin could thus acquire two different patrons possibly from different towns or, more seriously, the quiritary owner years later might not agree to manumit or may have died without expressing any intention to do so, or the original manumission under age might have been by testament and thus unrepeatable, and so on.[36] Neither method was at all guaranteed or predictable. As for the emperor's *beneficium*, that may not have been granted as routinely as is suggested by Millar (1977: 486–7) and, whether initiated by the Junian Latin himself or not, certainly required the knowledge and consent of the patron whose financial interests were involved (cf. Pliny 10. 5, 11; Gaius 3. 72).[37]

If their parents died under the age of 30 or otherwise did not succeed in obtaining citizenship, what remedies lay open to the children? As far as I can see, very few or none at all, apart from the *beneficium* of the emperor. Could they become Roman citizens by holding office or becoming decurions in *municipia* with the *ius Latii*? As they were freeborn *Latini*, there would seem to be no legal impediment, provided they were among the eligible local citizens. This would require their *origo* to be the same, which in turn would imply that their parents' manumitter, who would have to be a Roman citizen, had the same *origo* also.[38] In the Italian *municipia*, where the largest numbers of Junian Latins must have lived in the period before the *constitutio Antoniniana*, the *ius Latii* did not apply. In the Spanish provinces, in places such as Malaca, Irni, and no doubt elsewhere, where it did apply, they would be in the same position as other freeborn *Latini*, but without the inherited wealth of their parents which was available to Latins of non-servile descent. It is difficult to see how they could compete on reasonably equal terms

---

[35] The two capacities could (and might usually) coincide, but by no means always did; it depended on the mode of acquisition, as when a slave was acquired *in bonis*, not by formal *mancipatio*.

[36] For the remarkable complexities possible under the iteration procedure, see especially Sirks (1983: 244–71).

[37] The consequences of not having the patron's consent, by a constitution of Trajan, were that he kept his citizenship during his lifetime and his children also were citizens ('iusti liberi'), but at death he was treated as a Junian Latin, so that his children could not be his heirs. This situation was modified but not fundamentally changed by Hadrian (Gaius 3. 73).

[38] In the *lex Malacitana*, ch. 53, residents of non-local citizen status (*incolae*), whether *ciues Latini* or even *ciues Romani*, were only allowed to vote in the local elections in a single *curia*, selected by lot by the presiding magistrate.

or succeed in obtaining municipal office there in anything like significant numbers.

THE HERCULANEUM INHERITANCE

L. *Venidius Ennychus*

It is a curious accident that, but for the discovery of the Herculaneum Tablets over fifty years ago, we would have had no single example of *anniculi causae probatio*, a procedure that has been reckoned to be so common as to be routine for many, many thousands of couples in the Junian Latin class. In order to obtain citizenship for himself, wife, and children, a Junian Latin marrying a *Latina* or *ciuis Romana* was required to do so before seven citizen witnesses, declaring that it was expressly for the purpose of begetting children, then to present himself later before the praetor in Rome or provincial governor with a child at least 1 year old, and prove his case (Gaius 1. 29; Ulpian, *Reg.* 3. 3). The name of L. Venidius Ennychus appears several times in a dossier of documents[39] the earliest of which, in July 60, records his attestation of the birth of a daughter.[40] Another, a year later in 61, probably records his successful application for Roman citizenship by *anniculi probatio*.[41] Two further tablets, some years later, probably in 72 or soon thereafter, record his deposition for a case in which someone had challenged his claim to the 'ius honoris';[42] this must mean his eligibility to be elected to the order of *Augustales* in Herculaneum, in whose *album Augustalium* his name subsequently appears.[43] Ennychus is the earliest identifiable Junian Latin, predating Antonia Harmeris, L. Satrius Abascantus, P. Caesius Phosphorus, Pancharia Soteris, and the trio C. Valerius Astraeus, C. Valerius Dionysius and C. Valerius Aper,

---

[39] *HT* 5, 83, 84, 89; cf. 62, 82, 88; reconstructed and explicated in a masterly article by V. Arangio-Ruiz in *Mélanges H. Lévy-Bruhl* (1959), 9–24 = V. Arangio-Ruiz, *Studi epigrafici e papirologici*, ed. L. Bove (1974), 535–51.

[40] *HT* 5: 'L. Venidius Ennychus testatus est | sibi filiam natam esse ex Liuia | Acte uxore sua.'

[41] *HT* 89: '[. . . . . .] | eorum el[. . . . qui lege Aelia Sentia] | causam prob[auissent . . L. Venidii] | Ennychi e[t Liuiae Actes uxoris eius] | quod filiam [a se procreatam anniculam] | habere pr[o]fe[ssi sunt . . . qua de re agitur] | eorum s[ibi causam probam esse Romano]ls[que c[iues] esse' (using the reconstruction of Arangio-Ruiz (n. 39) 22). It is to be noted that the name of the daughter is nowhere mentioned or considered to be relevant.

[42] *HT* 83: 'L. V[e]nidius En[ny]chus testand[i ca]usa dixs[i]t | [L.] An[n]io Rufo se honoris ius emerere [ut] | si uellet ex numero decurionum aut au[gus]ltalium nominatis a se decem de petition[ibus] | nostris discep[t]atorem dicas [. . . . .]'; cf. 84: 'si minus necessario c[oa]ctus a te spo[n]lsionem tecum faciam'.

[43] Guadagno (1977: 114 ff.) = *AE* 1978, 119 + *CIL* 10. 1403, at B.a.12.

Junian Latins rescued from the correspondence of Pliny with Trajan (10. 5, 11, 104) and who qualified for citizenship by the emperor's *beneficium*. Ennychus used his unnamed daughter—her name seems not to have mattered—to obtain citizenship for his family as well as a place in Herculanean society which he coveted for himself, despite his servile origins and conjectured modest economic standing in the community.[44] And yet this did not come unchallenged as a matter of course, much less as a right. His qualification to be elected *Augustalis* by the local decurions was his Roman citizenship, not his enjoyment of *ius commercii* as a Junian Latin. But, in the not un-litigious atmosphere of Herculaneum in the 70s, even these credentials he had to defend with vigour and at some cost. How typical this case is of Junian Latins and their motives for converting to Roman citizenship, we have no means of knowing. But even in the context of Italian municipal society in the first century AD, as compared with that of the provinces where Roman citizens were much less concentrated, citizenship was by no means to be taken for granted by those released from slavery.[45]

Petronia Justa Again

This leads us back again to the case of 'the woman who calls herself Petronia Justa'.[46] The story so far: in AD 74 and 75 at Herculaneum, 'Petronia Sp. f. Iusta', the child of Petronia Vitalis, a freedwoman of Petronius Stephanus and Calatoria Themis, was claiming that she was freeborn (i.e. that she was born after the manumission of her mother) but that she was illegitimate ('Spurii filia', i.e. that her father did not have *conubium* with Vitalis her mother, or was unknown). Calatoria Themis, on the other hand, was claiming that Justa was her freedwoman (i.e. that she had been born *before* the manumission of her mother and was thus slave-born). There are no incontrovertible documents to prove either claim, and the situation is made more difficult as in the meantime both Themis' husband Stephanus and Justa's mother Vitalis have died. As the suit was not inexpensive, there must have been property and/or inheritance at stake. From the age data it is likely that, if Justa was not freeborn, she would have been freed at well under 30 years and be a Junian

---

[44] Arangio-Ruiz (n. 39) 9.
[45] The Venidius Ennychus dossier raises several interesting matters in relation to a Junian Latin's exercise of *commercium iure Quiritium* in the field of ownership, contracts, etc. which it is not possible to discuss here. See Arangio-Ruiz (n. 39).
[46] *HT* 14–30: see G. Pugliese Carratelli, *Parola del Passato* 3 (1948), 165–84; V. Arangio-Ruiz, *Bullettino dell' Istituto di Diritto Romano*, 1 (1959), 223–45. For convenience only, see the refs., bibliography, and discussion in Weaver (1991: 166–72).

Latin. The result of the suit is unknown, but the odds, as also the dossier of tablets, lay with the wealthy but grasping Calatoria Themis. For our purposes it is a specific example that raises interesting questions about children and status.

But how does Vitalis, the mother of Justa, fit into the scenario? At what age was *she* manumitted? The fact of her manumission is not in question, but what sort of manumission was it—formal or informal? Was she over 30, formally freed *uindicta* by a magistrate, presumably the praetor in Rome, in the presence of witnesses? Or by Petronius Stephanus in his will (*testamento*), she being over 30 years of age? In either case, she should be a Roman citizen—that is, if we can reasonably assume that Stephanus himself was a Roman citizen. A tribal indication certainly, or at least filiation probably, would put *that* beyond doubt, but these are missing, not as with a good number of other persons named in the tablets. In either case the documentary evidence should have put the date of Vitalis' manumission out of contention. If it was shown that Justa was born after that date, her free birth would have been settled, but would she have also been born a *ciuis Romana*, though illegitimate? Not necessarily, if her (unidentified) father was a Junian Latin. Before Hadrian settled the matter with a *senatusconsultum*, there was doubt whether the child of a (Junian) Latin father and a *ciuis Romana* followed the status of the mother. This would have been the case in AD 75.

Oddly, amid all this preoccupation with status, no one in the Herculaneum Tablets, either Justa herself or any of the witnesses, either in their promissory documents (*uadimonia*) or in their *testimonia*, makes any reference to the *citizenship* of Justa: the most anyone claims for her is that she is freeborn (*ingenua*). How significant is this? At least it opens the possibility that Justa was claiming only freeborn *Latin* status. The reason for this would not be hard to seek, if her mother was herself a *Latina Iuniana*, having been freed informally by Petronius Stephanus when she was under the age of 30. In that case, unless Vitalis was a foster-child (*alumna*) of Stephanus and Calatoria Themis, it is hard to see her qualifying for formal manumission under any of the *causae iustae* of the *lex Aelia Sentia*, such as *matrimonium* with her manumitter or, given the anonymity of her father, under the *anniculi probatio* procedure. Even if Justa was not Vitalis' only child, it would be quite likely that she was born before her mother's thirtieth birthday. Thus Vitalis herself could easily have been a *Latina Iuniana*, informally freed at any age, or at least well before she turned 30.

Perhaps Justa was relying on just this fact. It would certainly have made her case for freeborn status easier to establish, the earlier the age at which her mother had been manumitted. It would also explain the otherwise awkward absence of documentation which Junian Latinity did not require. All that was needed for that was evidence of intention (*uoluntas domini*) on the part of the intending manumitter, which need not be in written form. It would also have made it more difficult for Calatoria Themis to refute Justa's claim to free birth.

Under these circumstances, what consequences would follow for Justa herself? Two areas are relevant: first, inheritance; second, status. In regard to inheritance, as a Junian Latin her mother would not have possessed any right to make or take under a will. All her property would have passed *iure quodammodo peculii* to her patron Stephanus (and to Themis as well, if she was a joint-patron), thereby totally excluding Justa. On the other hand, if Stephanus had predeceased Vitalis, the latter would not have been able to accept any legacy or bequest, except by way of *fideicommissa* through his heir; and if his widow Themis was joint-patron of Vitalis, the *ius patronatus* would then have been hers, either alone or in conjunction with any agnate heir(s) of Stephanus.

As for status, if Justa's mother was freed informally before Justa was born, the latter would inherit her Latin status. But as she was in that case freeborn, she would not be subject as regards her own property to the restrictive clauses of the *lex Iunia* which denied her the inheritance rights to her slave-born Junian Latin mother. Whether we call Justa a 'Latina Iuniana' or a 'Latina coloniaria' would not strictly matter, except in so far as the latter makes clear her full right to acquire and dispose of property, subject if appropriate to the permission of her tutor. In particular, she would not be subject to any patronal rights (*ius patronatus*). In this case, Justa would be independent of any rights that Calatoria Themis as joint-patron of Vitalis or as heir of Stephanus could claim over her. Worse still from Themis' point of view, Justa could keep without restriction gifts given her by Stephanus during his lifetime and could inherit freely by way of legacies from Stephanus after his death. Otherwise, where did the resources and resolve to take on Calatoria Themis in the praetor's court in Rome come from? Perhaps the balance in the case of 'the woman who calls herself Petronia Justa' now begins to tilt back decisively in her favour.

The Album Augustalium

Finally from Herculaneum, an item of nomenclature. The *album Augustalium* referred to above (n. 43) contains the names of some

110 *Augustales* all with *tria nomina*, arranged in eight columns, of which the first three have names uniformly with filiation and tribal indication, the names in columns four and five have no status indication at all, while those in the last three columns all have the freed indication. The first group has the heading '(centuria) Cla(udia) ingen(uorum)' which points to a significantly high proportion of freeborn *Augustales* at Herculaneum, matched almost exactly by those that are specifically shown as freedmen. Particularly interesting, however, is the status of those uniformly recorded without status indication on the columns in between. They would otherwise be classed as *incerti*. Why, if they are *ciues Romani liberti*, do they not have status indication like those following, and why do they appear to take precedence over those that do? Intriguingly, among them occur several names that correspond with those in the tablets we have been discussing, including L. Venidius Ennychus and C. Petronius Stephanus.[47] On the assumption that all *Augustales* must be *ciues Romani*, it is possible that, like Venidius Ennychus, they are all former Junian Latins who have been granted full citizenship status. They would have the right freedman credentials. It also seems likely that relatives of Petronius Stephanus are among them. But these ought to be freeborn and, if *ciues Romani*, why are they not on the preceding columns? Freeborn children of Junian Latins, as *Latini coloniarii*, are no doubt excluded by their status. It would perhaps be outrageous to suggest otherwise.[48]

[47] See Guadagno (1977: 120–3).
[48] On the Herculaneum material, see now Wallace-Hadrill (1994: 175–86).

4

Rome and the Outside World: Senatorial Families and the World They Lived In

Minicius Fundanus, one of Pliny's closest friends (1. 9; 4. 15; 5. 16; 6. 6; 7. 12), is a person we know better still because he was also one of Plutarch's friends and appears as a participant in several of Plutarch's Essays.[1] For a long time it was debated how the acquaintance with Plutarch arose. It seemed plausible to suppose that Fundanus had held office in the province of Achaia at some stage in his preconsular career, either as quaestor or as legate to the governor, or indeed as proconsul.[2] He could have got to know the sage of Chaeronea at this time, as was the case, so it is assumed, with Sosius Senecio, the *consul ordinarius* of AD 99. The latter may indeed have been quaestor in Greece (Jones 1970: 98 ff.). However, an inscription, long overlooked, which supplies the *cursus honorum* of Minicius Fundanus up to the point just before his consulship in 107, has made it plain that Fundanus never visited Greece in an official capacity.[3] Where then did these two philosophically inclined persons meet? Ronald Syme, in one of his last papers (1991: 603–19, at 619), argued persuasively, from the fact that Fundanus spent the entire period between quaestorship and praetorship in Rome, that it was at Rome itself that this first contact took place. 'Plutarch had visited Rome several times, for certain in 88 and 92. Rome was the intellectual centre of the Greek world, the goal of ambition, the resort of talkers and thinkers.'

Rome was the magnet for many, not just for literary types and

For help in the preparation of this article I must thank Annemarie Andermahr and Alexandru Diaconescu, as well as Hannah M. Cotton for discussing the ideas in it with me, and Tony Birley for translating the text from the original German. References to inscriptions are to *CIL* unless stated otherwise.

[1] Cf. *PIR*[2] M 612.

[2] See e.g. Groag, *RE* 15. 2, 1820–6 (no. 13), 1820–6; Groag (1939: 44–5).

[3] Sergejevski, *Glasnik* 38 (1926) 156 = A. & J. Šašel (1986: 100, no. 1627) = Syme (1991: 609 ff.).

philosophers. The whole known world looked on the imperial capital as its goal—not always to the approval of those who lived there.
Still, everyone was free to decide whether to come to Rome or to
go away again. No one was tied to Rome by legal obligations—with
one exception: the members of the Roman senate. The very fact of
belonging to this, the highest order in the empire, carried with it the
requirement to be present in Rome. Up to a certain age the senators
were obliged to take part in senatorial meetings: so, at any rate, it
was laid down in the regulations of the early principate (Talbert
1984: 152–4). Furthermore, in the early period Rome was the legal
origo of all senators. They were thereby detached from any legal
tie with their previous home town and ceased to be subject to the
duties and obligations of their communities of origin.[4]

These circumstances could lead to the inference—and have indeed
done so—that Rome was in reality the principal centre of activity
for the members of the senatorial order in the early and middle
principate. The world outside the metropolis may, to be sure, have
supplied the senators with the economic basis for their existence, in
that the surplus production from their estates was delivered to Rome
and consumed there (Whittaker 1985: 49–75). All the same, Rome
was in other respects the central point, to which ties of emotion also
bound them. It was in Rome and in its immediate surroundings, in
towns such as Tibur and Praeneste, that the life of members of the
ordo senatorius was spent, from birth till death, so to speak. The
countless tombs of senatorial families along the roads leading to
Rome appear to bear witness to this view.

Considerations of this kind reflect the concrete facts; but they
illustrate only part of the real situation. Many senators by no means
exclusively focused their attention on Rome. The outside world, specifically the realities of daily life in other towns in Italy and in the
provinces, played an important role, in many cases, indeed, a decisive
role, in their thoughts and in their mentalities.[5] Trajan's comment
that many candidates for senatorial magistracies looked on Rome
and Italy 'non pro patria, sed pro hospitio aut stabulo', is enough to
give the game away (Pliny 6. 19. 4). It is true that most of the sources
which supply information on the connections of senators with other
places and other communities are not always easy to interpret. None
the less, it is worth making the attempt.

The remarks that follow will not offer a comprehensive investigation of the senatorial lifestyle. The main focus will be, rather, on
those aspects of their lives that have left traces in the epigraphic

---

[4] Chastagnol (1977: 43 ff.; 1992: 196 ff.); Eck (1977: 372 ff.); Talbert (1984: 40).
[5] On specific aspects, cf. Talbert (1984: 40–1) and esp. Eck (1980: 283 ff.).

record, especially in funerary inscriptions, both in Rome and else-where. It should then be possible to compare the realities of sen-ators' lives at Rome with those of their lives in other places.

In one form or another all senators, and the immediate members of their families as well, had to conform to the conventions which senatorial membership imposed on them. That applied in princ-iple to everyone who took up a place in the senate. But the con-sequences were of course necessarily far more marked for those who came from the remoter parts of Italy or, as was increasingly the case from the Augustan period onwards, from the provinces. It was not merely the fact that for them the distance from Rome was greater, involving journeys to the home town which were correspondingly longer and more burdensome. The differences in lifestyle, in cultural norms, in the whole ethos of another place,[6] would become ever more pronounced—in spite of the existence of a 'common Graeco-Roman culture'. There was a corresponding pressure to conform to the behaviour patterns standard at Rome, especially in the senatorial order. Hardly anyone could hold out against these social pressures. It began with the necessity to be present at Rome. A senatorial career could last for more than forty years. Thus Cn. Calpurnius Piso, in the letter of farewell that he addressed to Tiberius in the night of 8/9 December in the year 20, wrote that he had served the late emperor Augustus and thereafter Tiberius for forty-five years (Tacitus, *Annales* 3. 16. 4). During this long period functions in Rome and in the provinces could alternate. But above all in the first years of the senatorial career, in the standard five-year intervals between quaestorship and praetorship, almost all the young mem-bers of the senate would stay in Rome. There were practically no posts which could be held outside the capital at this stage in their career. For this reason a session of the senate was never just an assembly of grey-haired old gentlemen. Rather, even with an attend-ance figure of 300, which was probably not achieved all that often,[7] a considerable proportion would be made up of those in the younger age group.[8] The juniors would all be stamped, in these years, with the mentality peculiar to the *ordo senatorius* and its members. As

---

[6] Cf. the overall presentation by Millar (1993), e.g. for the provinces from Syria in the north to Arabia and Judaea in the south.

[7] Cf. Talbert (1984: 137–52). Even in the final vote in the trial of Calpurnius Piso on 10 Dec. AD 20 only 301 senators took part.

[8] One can recognize this by the following consideration. The *cursus* between quaestorship and praetorship lasted on average five years. Of the 100 young senators that belonged to these year-groups, only 10 each year as a rule went to the provinces as quaestor; proconsular legates were only occasionally drawn from men of this rank. Thus at least 80 young senators, including those serving as quaestors and praetors at any given time, must always have been present in the senate.

for the older senators, especially the consulars, they were far more frequently, at least relative to their total number, away on official duties. Still, they too always returned to Rome and it was at Rome, at least as long as they were active (McAlindon 1957: 108), that they generally lived their lives.

So every senator was, for a start, more or less compelled to acquire a house for himself at Rome, or at least quarters appropriate to his rank. Apart from occasional mentions in authors such as Tacitus, Pliny, Statius, or Martial, it is above all the lead water-pipes, the *fistulae aquariae*, that supply information about the residences of senators at Rome. Well over half of the names of persons known from surviving water-pipes are those of members from the *ordo senatorius*, male and female. By contrast there are relatively few names known of knights who, like senators, acquired a house at Rome and applied to the emperor for the right to piped water. Against a total of more than 180 members of the senatorial order whose names are on these pipes we can set a mere seventeen members of the *ordo equester*. Even imperial slaves and freedmen crop up in greater numbers on the lead water-pipes (Eck 1982: 197–225). This ratio reflects the marked difference in the strength of the ties that bound the two *ordines* to Rome.[9] It is true that the development of the administration and the growing assignment of new tasks to knights increased the importance of the equestrians. In absolute terms, as well, there were ever more high equestrian functionaries who were active over long spells in Rome. Yet this does not mean that more than a limited number of these people transferred their family residence as a result.[10] Rather, when their appointment in Rome came to an end, many of these equestrian office-holders went back home— 'back to the old plantation'—or to another town of their own choosing.[11] This meant that it was not really necessary to acquire a house in Rome and bother about a proper water-supply with a private connection to the mains.[12] This also applied to the intervals between

[9] The *fistulae aquariae* are the more reliable indicator for the place of residence of the individual higher-status groups than are the literary sources. In the latter, the highest status group, i.e. the consular senators, is the most strongly represented. The *fistulae* provide a more objective source from this point of view.

[10] Occasionally, however, one of them acquired property, as the case of Septimius Severus in Statius, *Siluae* 4. 5, shows.

[11] Cf. the case of the praetorian prefect Gauius Maximus at Firmum Picenum (Eck 1993: 368–77).

[12] In this connection one must, to be sure, consider the difference in the financial means of the knights, which in principle could have played some part in the case of house-purchase. Still, this difference may not have been all that decisive, since at least the knights who served as procurators also enjoyed a good salary.

posts in the provinces, in cases where there was a gap between appointments: the place of *origo*, not Rome, would be the point of reference for an *eques*. This is demonstrated particularly clearly by funerary inscriptions for knights at Rome. In spite of the fact that there were immeasurably more knights than senators, there are markedly fewer tombs of equestrians than of senators at Rome. The great majority were buried elsewhere, in the towns of Italy and of the provinces. Senators and their families were tied to Rome, at any rate to a far greater extent than were the knights. Hence they made the effort to ensure a higher standard of civilized living for themselves by acquiring their own connection to the city water-supply.

The topographical distribution of senatorial *domus* can be worked out by study of the *fistulae aquariae* in particular, although there is of course other evidence as well. It is clear that from the first half of the first century AD the districts favoured for senatorial residence were the Quirinal and the Esquiline. This is easy to explain, since it was there above all that spacious gardens could be laid out, an essential feature of the lifestyle deemed appropriate for senatorial families. It is true that many of these great *horti* of the early principate were transferred to imperial hands, for example the *horti Epagathiani*, the *horti* of Statilius Taurus or the *horti Maecenatiani*. On the other hand, such parks were often granted to loyal followers of the ruler. We know, for example, that Cornelius Fronto, Marcus Aurelius' tutor in rhetoric and suffect consul in 142, was the possessor of the gardens of Maecenas, which he was later to bequeath to his daughter and his son-in-law Aufidius Victorinus. They had probably been presented to the successful teacher as a gift by Antoninus Pius or Marcus Aurelius.[13] In the course of the second century, however, and subsequently above all from the third century onwards, it was the Aventine, once the plebeian hill, that became more and more attractive to senators: in late antiquity the Aventine out of all *colles* of Rome became the really aristocratic one. The fact that Licinius Sura, Trajan's closest confidant, and later Fabius Cilo, City Prefect under Septimius Severus, had residences there, may have contributed to this development. All the same, it may not be a complete coincidence that the first senatorial *domus* which we can probably assign to the Aventine belonged to one Larcius Macedo, whose father Larcius Lydus, in the time of Nero, had been only a slave, then a freedman.[14]

---

[13] Champlin (1980: 21–2); on the consulship in 142 (not 143, as hitherto assumed), cf. Roxan and Eck in *Festschrift H. Lieb* (Basle 1995).
[14] Pietrangeli (1951: 21); Eck (1981a: 245–6; 1982: 201–2, 217); *Lexicon topographicum urbis Romae* 2, s.v. 'domus Larcii'.

These senatorial houses and parks, together with the villas in the *suburbium*, played an important part in the lives of their owners and their families, probably to a greater extent than had been the case under the Republic. There was an important change in the significance which the public sphere had for senatorial self-representation or for honours shown to senators by others in the transition from Republic to Empire. During the last decades of the Republic, above all, it had been the public places or the great public buildings at Rome that were evidently the sole arena for such display. The Forum, in particular, and likewise the open space on the Capitol, were the preferred locations in which, in competition with other members of the ruling élite, senators could play out the struggle to influence public opinion. This changed with Augustus and with the dominant position exercised by the ruler in Rome. The public sphere was no longer available for anyone, that is for anyone in the great senatorial families. Control over its use was now held by the ruler, or better perhaps, exercised in his interest by the senate (Eck 1984a: 129–67; Lahusen 1983: 97–107). As a result a partial withdrawal of the senators from the public sphere in Rome took place: the substitutes for the public places and public buildings, the *opera et loca publica*, were the senatorial mansions and parks (Eck 1992: 359–76). These continued to offer unrestricted space in which an individual senator's family itself, his friends and clients, and further, cities in Italy and in the provinces could honour him. There it was possible to put on display the importance of his family as well as of the individual senator himself. It is in this private sphere—which admittedly Elder Pliny describes precisely as the continuation of the public into the private (*NH* 34. 12)—that all forms of showing honour were to be found, exactly as they could be in public places and buildings in Rome. In the latter, however, they were under the supervision of the senate and, increasingly, under the control of the *curatores aedium sacrarum et operum locorumque publicorum* (cf. Kolb 1993: 114–21). Let me give some examples. P. Numicius Pica Caesianus, a senator who probably belongs to the time of Augustus, was honoured in his mansion on the Esquiline by two *trapezophora*, dedicated by the province of Asia, which had commissioned eight men to go to Rome for this purpose.[15] L. Cornelius Pusio, a legionary legate in Germania Inferior at the end of the Claudian period, was honoured by one of his subordinates, a centurion of the Sixteenth Legion, who dedicated a bronze bust to Pusio with a bronze

---

[15] 6. 31742–3; cf. *PIR*[2] N 203; Eck, *Lexicon topographicum urbis Romae* 2, s.v. 'domus P. Numicii Picae Caesiani'.

inscription, set up inside the senator's house on the Quirinal.[16] A similar honour was shown to Marius Maximus, *cos. II* in the year 223, on the Caelian, although in his case four separate persons were involved (6. 1450–3). The monuments that honoured Cornelius Pusio and Marius Maximus consisted respectively of a portrait bust and the usual *statuae pedestres*. As for M. Didius Seuerus Iulianus, who was later to become emperor for a few weeks in the year 193, he had a great monument erected in his honour in his private residence by the *municipium* Biscia Lucana in the province of Africa (6. 1401 = *ILS* 412),[17] evidently after his proconsulship of that province. It consisted probably of a *biga* or even of a *quadriga*, a type of monument which is by no means uncommon even for senators and knights outside Rome, but for which there seems to be no precedent as a public form of honour in the capital other than for the ruler.[18] It was evidently quite in order even in imperial Rome for any form of honour, whether offered by individuals or by communities, to be displayed on private land. Public places, by contrast, were subject to imperial control and this prevented unwanted large-scale display by individuals. In private and at the same time for a restricted, selected part of the public, the individual senator and his family could none the less make use of all forms of self-representation or of honouring by third parties and direct this to serve their own interests. This was possible even in Rome itself. To find a larger public for such forms of honour, of course, one had generally to go outside Rome. Not a few senators did in fact do just this.

All these statues and monuments also served the purpose of keeping fresh the memory of the person honoured, not only in their lifetime but even more so after their death. It is precisely over this point, however, that one comes up against particular problems of interpretation. There were various quite different places where someone's *memoria* could be preserved after their death—especially, of course, by means of a funerary monument or at least in connection with

[16] 6. 31706 = 37056; Lahusen and Formigli (1990: 65–77).

[17] See the reconstruction in Pflaum (1966: 60, 94–5). It is noteworthy that the majority of dedications set up for senators at Rome by communities (see the list in Eck (1984*b*: 212–17)) were not carved on solid bases but on slabs. This may indicate that in most cases we are dealing with quite large monuments, the bases of which were built of substantial blocks or had a walled core. That could point to *statuae equestres* of *bigae/quadrigae*. Direct archaeological evidence for monuments of this kind is, however, as far as I am aware, not known for Rome.

[18] All the same, Martial 10. 2. 10 talks of the broken *equi* of Crispus, which from the context can most plausibly be explained in a funerary context; in that case a *biga* or a *quadriga* could be involved here. On equestrian statues in funerary contexts, Bergemann (1990: 49); E 13 on pp. 123–4 could also have been set up on a tomb.

FIG. 4.1. Tomb of members of senatorial Plautii family beside Anio R. near Tibur (Tivoli). Cylindrical structure (1st century AD) with several inscriptions. Circumference 23m., diameter 18m., height 13.2m.

one. But this could just as well be in the town house of a senatorial family or in a villa outside the city walls. These alternatives mean that neither the concrete expression of the memorial nor the intention behind it was the same in each case. They tell us something different about the survival or continuance of a family.[19] If there were no further descendants, the *memoria* was generally confined to the tomb; the private house was in such an event no longer the appropriate place. From the epigraphic texts that we possess it is, to be sure, usually easy enough to determine straightaway that they were first set up after the death of the person named in them. But whether an inscription was merely posthumous or was the actual text belonging to a funerary monument, what the precise function of the inscription was and where it was originally set up are questions that cannot be so readily answered. Very few inscriptions have been found *in situ*. But with funerary inscriptions of senators there is a particular problem: the otherwise completely normal formulas, such as *dis manibus*, *hic situs est*, which thereby make the purpose of the stone totally unambiguous, or the details of the person's age, very seldom get a mention—particularly in the case of adult male members of the senatorial order. To give the age was in their case unnecessary, since the offices which were generally named, whether the complete set or at least a selection of the highest posts held, supplied a far more important message (Eck 1981*b*: 127–34).

The situation is perfectly clear and straightforward if precise information is available about the context to which the inscriptions belong. In the case of some of the Plautii, for example, the inscriptions can still be seen on the funerary monument by the Anio River near Tivoli. One of them is set on the tomb itself, the others are placed on monumental slabs in front of the Mausoleum (Fig. 4.1).[20] In three of the texts the funerary context can also be directly inferred from the wording. In each case husband and wife are named in the nominative, the one above the other, and furthermore in two cases a child is also mentioned, whose age is given (cf. Eck 1981*b*: 127–9). This is usually—although not always—an indication that the inscription is funerary (Eck 1995). It is also a common feature of these texts that no one is named as responsible for the burial (14. 3605–7). This also applies to the long inscription of Ti. Plautius

---

[19] If it can be proved that a deceased senator was honoured by a statue in a private house, this may, very frequently at least, have occurred in the house belonging to his own family. Such a statue can thereby be taken as evidence for the survival of a family.

[20] 14. 3605–8 = *I.It.* 4. 1. 122–5 = *ILS* 921. On the mausoleum itself, Eisner (1986: 105–8).

Siluanus Aelianus, although in this case the name and offices of the
dead man are in the dative (14. 3608 = *ILS* 986 = *I.It.* 4. 1. 125).

Of course, if we did not know the context of this inscription and
only had the text, say in a manuscript reading (which is often the
case), it would by no means be so certain that it should be assigned
to a tomb. After all, texts which are in their structure totally comparable to this one have been found in the villa of the Volusii at
Lucus Feroniae, for the consul of 3 BC, L. Volusius Saturninus,
and for Q. Volusius Saturninus, *consul ordinarius* in AD 56. These
texts name the two senators in the dative with their most important offices and there is no name of a dedicator at the end, exactly as
with the inscription of Ti. Plautius Siluanus Aelianus. But at Lucus
Feroniae the archaeological context demonstrates that the inscriptions were set up in the *lararium* and were connected to statues or
at least to portrait busts.[21] Here too, then, the context helps with the
interpretation: an exact definition of the type of inscription would
otherwise hardly have been possible. Experience tells us that this
information is mostly not available. The following example may
indicate what problems in defining the function of an inscription
can arise as a result.

An inscription from Cures Sabini of L. Iulius Marinus Caecilius
Simplex, suffect consul in AD 101, has long been known (9. 4965
= *ILS* 1026). From the way the text is printed in *CIL*,[22] it appears
to have been carved on a slab of which the width was greater than
the height. Since Iulius Marinus is, furthermore, named in the dative
and no dedicator is mentioned, the various elements here appear to
point to an inscription slab which was attached to a funerary monument. Yet in 1945 a further text, also from Cures Sabini and referring
to this senator, was published in *Notizie degli Scavi* which was quite
definitely a marble slab measuring 4.5m. wide, 1m. high, and 6cm.
thick.[23] The senator's name is given in the dative in this inscription
as well and once again no dedicator is named. The text is in both
cases the same; even the abbreviations, broadly speaking, match. Only
the way the text is set out on individual lines is different, and the
total number of lines varies: in the first case the text takes up thirteen
lines, in the second only seven. With both inscriptions, then, we have
the criteria which point to a funerary context—yet it is impossible
that both of them were the actual funerary inscription. There are

---

[21] Eck (1972: 461–84; 1973: 128); *AE* 1972, 174; M. Moretti and A. M. Sgubini Moretti,
La Villa dei Volusii à Lucus Feroniae (Rome 1977), with texts, 33 ff.
[22] No description of the inscription is given, although Bormann had seen the original at
Pisaurum.   [23] M. Marella Vianello, *NS* 1944/5, 23 ff. = *AE* 1947, 156 = 1980, 357.

other conceivable explanations. The first inscription might, for example, be the base of a statue, which, since there is no dedicator, obviously belongs to private surroundings, in other words it had not been set up in a public place in the town of Cures. Hence one could imagine that it belonged in a *domus* of the senator in or near Cures Sabini, in which the statue with inscription had been erected to him after his death. But it is equally possible to conceive of the statue base being in front of a mausoleum, just as in the case of the funerary monument of the Plautii at Tivoli, where the inscriptions stood in front of the structure.[24]

The second text, the one published in 1945, can likewise be given a different interpretation. Marble slabs of this type and size are often found on the front of large honorific monuments. Given the dimensions in this case (1m. high and 4.5m. wide), it ought to have been at least for a *quadriga*. Approximately this scale of inscription occurs, for example, on a monument excavated during the 1970s in the Forum at Volsinii: some 77cm. high and at least 4.2m. wide. In this case the inscription unquestionably belongs to a large monument, erected for Pompeius Vopiscus C. Arrun[tius Cate]llius Celer Allius Sabinus, after his proconsulship in Africa. The difference between this inscription and the large inscription of Iulius Marinus from Cures Sabini consists only in the fact that at Volsinii it was a publicly erected monument, dedicated by the *colonia Iulia Carthago* (*AE* 1980, 426). But in Iulius Marinus' case there is no dedicator. Still, can one imagine that there would have been such a massive monument for a presumably deceased senator at Cures Sabini, in other words a long way from Rome, on a private estate? Or should such a monument belong to a funerary context? This too should not be totally ruled out: after all, Martial speaks of the *equi* of one Crispus, which have fallen apart and hence can no longer preserve his memory. The context suggests that these horses (at least a pair) would have stood on a tomb.[25] That would give the funerary monument all the more distinction.

The information so far at our disposal does not allow a definite decision about the function which the inscriptions of Iulius Marinus

---

[24] Iulius Marinus, who was a second-generation senator, probably derived from the east (cf. Bowersock (1982: 667); Halfmann (1979: 110, 118)). Yet not only was he evidently buried at Cures Sabini but his father probably was as well. This may be inferred from the formulation which is found only in the two inscriptions from this town: 'leg. pro pr. prouinciae Ponti et Bithyniae proconsulatu patris sui'; by contrast, this detail is not mentioned in a text with *cursus honorum* from Xanthos (Balland (1981: 133)). In the area of Cures Sabini the father too may thus have been a well-known person; one may suppose that the tombs of father and son were set up in the same spot. [25] Cf. above, n. 18.

at Cures Sabini originally had. But the same problems crop up with many other epigraphic documents of this kind. A single example may be sufficient to illustrate this. At Hispellum the left-hand side of an inscription of Cn. Pinarius Cornelius Clemens, consular governor of Germania Superior about the year 74, is still preserved, walled into a modern building. The text is composed in the nominative case and hence, from the point of view of the text alone, could have belonged to a building inscription (11. 5271). In fact, however, the slab can be seen to have a slight curve[26] and can thus clearly be defined as a funerary inscription which belonged to a circular tomb.[27] That means that this senator was buried at Hispellum, a few kilometres south of Assisi.

In quite a few cases it is impossible, in the light of our present information, to decide between a funerary context or merely a posthumous honouring of the dead.[28] That applies above all to inscriptions, often with a very brief text, in which the person to whom the stone, mostly a statue base, refers, is given in the dative without mention of a dedicator. Often enough with such epigraphic evidence the inscriptions are indeed funerary; the same applies with many texts in which the person is named in the nominative but with no verb added, particularly texts from the early imperial period. None the less, both sorts of a base could derive from a context quite different from the funerary. They could belong to a larger monument on which several persons were honoured. Let me give an example, which may be enough to demonstrate what problems can arise from

[26] Autopsy, Sept. 1981; other examples (involving equestrian families) in Devijver (1989: 416–49); Devijver and Wonterghem (1992: 180–4).

[27] Of course, the difficulty in specific instances of defining the exact function of an epigraphic monument and the exact position of the tomb can be seen from the honorific decree for M. Nonius Balbus (*AE* 1976, 144). An altar was to be erected on the spot where the body was cremated with the simple text 'M. Nonio Men. Balbo'. If the full text of the decree of the town council had not been preserved, we would probably always attribute an altar with a text like this to the burial-place of a dead man, rather than to the place of cremation.

[28] One may here simply refer to the special problem of cenotaphs. One of these was postulated for Nouellius Atticus, for example, who came from Mediolanum and died during his proconsulship in Narbonensis, and whose 'funerary inscription' was found at Tibur (14. 3602 = *ILS* 950). This inscription, which was set up 'memoriae Torquati Nouelli Attici', is regarded as coming from a cenotaph (*PIR*[2] N 175), whether correctly or not cannot be determined. Nor is a definite decision possible in the case of P. Paquius Scaeua. 9. 2845–6 = *ILS* 915, a text that belongs to the inside (!) of a sarcophagus at Histonium, appears to be a clear indicator of burial at that place, especially as the text speaks in the case of Scaeua and his wife of 'simul condere'. On the other hand, 6. 1483 (Rome) has 'dis manibus P. Paqui Scaeuae', which points to a grave at Rome. If both texts refer to the same man, one would have to postulate that one of them was a cenotaph. Yet in fact 6. 1483 should be regarded as a funerary altar which, however, served only the cult of the deceased Paquius Scaeua, but did not refer to his burial. The *ara* was found in the place where there was a *columbarium* of the *liberti* and *familia* of P. Paquius Scaeua (information from A. Diaconescu).

larger-scale monuments of this kind, which involve more than one person. The so-called Arch of the Sergii at Pola is still preserved. The attic is divided by three bases on which there once stood statues of the non-senatorial persons whose names are inscribed on them. In each case the name, in the nominative, and the offices are given.[29] Because the monument is preserved complete, the function of the individual inscriptions is perfectly clear. But it is obvious that the majority of the monuments of this kind which once existed have subsequently been destroyed. If individual inscriptions from such monuments have been preserved, cut off from their context, they could perfectly well appear to be funerary, even though their original function was quite different. Our problem is simply that the original can no longer be recognized.

The problems in interpretation that I have illustrated apply to epigraphic material everywhere, both in Rome and its immediate vicinity as well as in Italy and in the provinces. This means, more or less inevitably, that we still cannot make clear statements about the relative distribution of senatorial tombs in Rome itself and the rest of the empire—not yet, at any rate. With progressively more exact publication of inscriptions, or when they are restudied, it will be possible to assess them on a more secure basis.[30]

All the same, it is worth attempting at least to detect what tendencies can be inferred from the material so far collected, in so far as it appears to be relevant. As was to be expected, the largest group of all the senatorial funerary inscriptions, in which the find-spot is given more specifically than just 'Rome', has been found in the immediate surroundings of the city, mainly along the roads leading out of Rome but also, of course, inside the later Walls of Aurelian.[31] The tombs are as varied in their type as are the individual places of

---

[29] 5. 50 = *ILS* 2229 = *I.It.* 10. 1. 72.

[30] This will be very clear, e.g. in the case of the city of Rome as a result of the revision of all senatorial and equestrian inscriptions by G. Alföldy. He has kindly made available to me the already completed parts of the *Supplement* to 6. Cf. further Boschung (1987: no. 110 = 6. 1463; no. 319 = 6. 1485; no. 432 = 6. 1486)—the type of monument in question can be correctly recognized here for the first time. A further important criterion by which funerary or at least posthumous inscriptions can be identified is the expression *designatus* attached to the final office in a *cursus*. This is of course not an absolutely decisive yardstick, especially when an inscription is set up to a governor in a province by a subordinate (this is particularly clear in the case of the legates of the *legio III Augusta* at Lambaesis). But when inscriptions of this kind are set up by relatives or friends at Rome or in another place which has no connection with the office in question, the death of the man honoured is in most cases the occasion for the inscription and the mention of the designation (cf. *ILS* 1064). In some cases this has implications for the identification of the individuals.

[31] No study dealing with tomb-complexes of this socio-political group has yet been written. It would have to cover the archaeological as well as the epigraphic material.

burial in which members of the senatorial order found their last resting-place. On the one hand there are gigantic tumulus graves such as that of Caecilia Metella on the Via Appia, the circular tomb of C. Asinius Turcianus with a diameter of *c*.25m. on the Vatican Hill,[32] or the extravagant Pyramid of Cestius on the Ostia road (Nash 1962: ii. 321–3). Against these one may set relatively small and modest structures such as the so-called Mausoleum of Sulpicius Platorinus on the right bank of the Tiber, measuring 4.46m. by 3.12m. along the sides,[33] or the Mausoleum of C. Minicius Fundanus on Monte Mario, of which the internal measurements are 3.9m. by 4.95m.[34] Whereas in the first two examples no individual burial-places are known, we do have some details from the tombs of Sulpicius Platorinus and Minicius Fundanus. In that of Sulpicius Platorinus, in which a marble slab above the entrance gives the names in the nominative of two of the persons buried, there were several marble or alabaster urns, each bearing the name of the dead without any details of their social status.[35] Had these inscriptions been divorced from the context of a senatorial tomb, it would have been impossible to determine their status. There were also, it is true, on the outer side of the tomb, facing the Tiber bank, funerary inscriptions of at least five persons, which by registering their offices or grades of family relationship made the social connections clear (6. 31765–7). The tomb of Minicius Fundanus no longer preserves the actual dedicatory inscription. It might have supplied details which would show whether this senator, a man with active philosophical interests, had followed the widespread practice of his peers in giving his entire official career, or whether he had conceived his funerary inscription in some other form.[36] However this may be, inside the tomb itself were found two funerary *cippi* in which the ashes of Fundanus' wife, Statoria Marcella, and of his daughter, only 13 years old, Minicia Marcella, had been placed (6. 16631–2). Here the name alone was enough, with, in the case of the daughter, her age.

In other tombs, however, reference was made, with all possible emphasis, to rank and public office. Often this is evident only in

[32] Eck (1986: 281–2) = *AE* 1987, 134; Alföldy (1992: 129 ff.).

[33] For a new reconstruction of the funerary complex with two separate entrances and an attribution to M. Artorius Geminus, cf. Silvestrini (1987).

[34] Lanciani, *NS* 1881, 60; *Bull. Comm.* 9 (1881), 22–3; Dressel, *Bullettino dell' Instituto* 53 (1881), 13 ff.   [35] 6. 31762–4; cf. Sinn (1987: 20, 25).

[36] It now appears that the funerary inscription of Minicius Fundanus' contemporary, the historian Tacitus, is known, if the attribution to Tacitus of 6. 1574, with restorations, by Alföldy (1995) is correct. The inscription presents the normal type of a senatorial career, as in many other funerary texts.

part. On the one hand we have monumental tomb inscriptions, which had generally been placed above the entrance to the monument and gave either the complete career of a senator or at any rate its most important phase. In other cases senatorial prestige was illustrated in concrete form by the depiction of *fasces* and *sellae curules* or in the portrayal of the dead man by a statue in front of the tomb, often standing on a base—and on this, again, a visitor could read an inscription with details of the career. However, in the immediate area of Rome virtually none of the senatorial burial-places or mausoleums are preserved intact. For the most part only fragments of inscriptions or reliefs survive to show how the members of the imperial ruling élite had conceived the appearance of their last resting-place.[37] There is the tomb of the Plautii near Tivoli, which achieves an effect by its sheer monumental scale (see Fig. 4.1 above). But otherwise, to gain an idea of the overall impression such a structure could give, we have from the vicinity of Rome only the funerary monument of P. Cluuius Maximus Paullinus, suffect consul at the beginning of Antoninus Pius' reign. This was found in 1931 at Monteporzio Catone and is now re-erected in the Museo delle Terme. It was built in Luna marble, on a substructure with two steps, measuring 11m. by 10m. Over the entrance doorway was part of the funerary inscription, giving the names of the dead man, his consulship, and his priestly office of *VIIuir epulonum*. The greater part of the *cursus* was set out on the side wall. There twelve *fasces* also were carved in relief, indicating the dead man's consular rank. A tripod on the other side was to represent the priestly office of a *quindecimuir sacris faciundis*.[38] The wording of the inscription shows none of the features which are otherwise normal in funerary texts. It could just as well have come from a statue base, as is the case, for example, with Ser. Calpurnius Dexter, whose daughter set up a statue to him 'secundum uoluntatem eius' on the base of which the complete *cursus honorum* is set out. It probably came from directly in front of Calpurnius Dexter's tomb.[39] All the elements are preserved in the tomb of Cluuius Maximus Paullinus and thus offer the total impression that such a tomb was intended to give. If one compares this with the other examples from Rome and its vicinity—of reliefs with *fasces*, *sellae curules*, and other symbols of office[40]—only a handful, to

---

[37] Cf. esp. Schäfer (1989: 363 ff.).
[38] The inscription is *AE* 1940, 99; interpretation of the entire monument, Schäfer (1989: 364–5).   [39] 6. 1368 = *ILS* 1175 = Camodeca (1979: 225–8).
[40] Fragmentary reliefs depicting scenes which could well belong in a funerary context create a particular problem. As yet there is no collection of this evidence.

be sure, and mostly fragments—it is still clear that such decoration was also used on many other funerary monuments of senators, right into the third century AD (Schäfer 1989: 363 ff.; Ronke 1987).

As already mentioned, a significant proportion of all known senatorial tombs comes from Rome itself or the immediate vicinity. At least 200 inscriptions are to be interpreted in this way, even if in not a few cases it remains slightly uncertain whether they come from the immediate funerary context, or, rather, belong to posthumous memorials in town houses or large suburban villas.[41] Nor do these 200 inscriptions necessarily represent exactly the same number of tombs, since often enough individual funerary texts derive from a single tomb-complex.[42] It is frequently possible to infer from a single funerary inscription the existence of a large family tomb.[43] The dead who are documented by these 200 inscriptions belonged to families which came from every part of Italy as well as from the provinces.[44] Against this group from Rome and vicinity one may set a not inconsiderable number in the various regions of Italy and in the provinces.[45] In Latium and Campania there are some thirty examples, from Picenum down to Lucania at least twenty-five, the region Etruria-Umbria-Aemilia offers fifteen, and the same number is found north of the Po. Outside Italy all the provinces that supplied Rome with many senators are represented in this category of record. Narbonensis leads with at least thirteen examples, Baetica has six, Tarraconensis seven, and Greece the same number. Even provinces from which so far only a few senators are known[46] can show clearly specimens of senatorial tombs, for example Lusitania

[41] Uncertainty of this kind applies e.g. to 6. 1341, 1345, 1351 (funerary altar?), 1359, 1360, 1368, 1371, 1378, 1389, 1397 and 1398 (statue bases?), 1413, 1447, 1448, etc.

[42] Thus e.g. 6. 1348, 1349.

[43] *AE* 1990, 129, from Grottaferrata, names 'Mesia Titiana, c(larissima) p(uella)' simply as 'pronept(is) Aspri iunioris'. In my view, this description ought merely to mean that because of this relationship it was permissible to bury the girl in the tomb of the Iulii Aspri, who had property at Grottaferrata. If the point at issue was the social rank, one would have had to mention a good many other people as well. Cf. also Dondin-Payre (1994: 127–63, esp. 155–6).

[44] A few examples should suffice: 6. 1359, L. Baebius Auitus, who probably came from Tarraconensis; 1373, Cassius Paulinus, perhaps from northern Italy; 1387–8, all the Cornelii and Corneliae here named came from Baetica; 1402, C. Dillius Vocula, from Baetica; 1403, Domitius Decidius, from Narbonensis; 1449, Macrinius Auitus, from Gaul or Germany; 1528, D. Valerius Asiaticus, from Narbonensis. On their origin, cf. *Epigrafia e ordine senatorio* 2, with the articles on the different regions of Italy and the provinces.

[45] I was assisted in my checking of the evidence outside Rome by Frau A. Andermahr, to whom I express my thanks.

[46] That does not of course mean that only very few senators came from there; rather, it can be conditioned by the specific nature of the epigraphic tradition, e.g. in the Gallic provinces; cf. Eck (1991*b*).

with four and Aquitania—it is a surprise—with two, likewise Macedonia.[47] The province of Asia seems rather poorly represented with only three senatorial tombs,[48] in spite of the fact that an extraordinarily high number of families from Asia gained entry to the senate (cf. Halfmann 1982: 603–50). However, the types of inscription found here and, in particular, the unsatisfactory state of excavation in cemeteries outside the cities in this province do not permit reliable conclusions to be drawn. In fact, the impression gained from the inscriptions inside the cities in the province of Asia is rather that senatorial families here maintained continuous links with their places of origin.[49] Hence one would assume that members of the senatorial order were regularly buried in the province. Two spectacular examples can make this point clear.

At Ephesus a library was founded by Ti. Iulius Celsus Polemaeanus, suffect consul in AD 92, and he was later interred in a sarcophagus in its crypt.[50] This burial must have been decided upon before building work started, otherwise the sarcophagus could not have been fitted into the very confined space. The expensive and lavishly adorned library building, which was at the same time the tomb of this senator, who came from Sardes, was erected in a central position at Ephesus, where two main streets meet and where the massive gateway leads into the lower market. In order to use the building as a tomb, a decision by the *boule* of Ephesus was required, for in this Asian city, too, burials normally occurred only outside the city centre.[51] If a decision by the council at Ephesus permitted this place of burial for Celsus, one may assume that he had previously expressed the wish for it. What motive the consular senator had for choosing Ephesus as his last resting-place is, one must add, not explicit in the texts.

In all there are six inscriptions dedicated to Celsus that are connected to the library. Five of them stand on bases and belonged to statues (*I.Eph.* 7. 2. 5102–6). The inscriptions give no indication that they have a funerary function and could all perfectly well have been set up in some other connection. If the library had been completely destroyed, as were so many other buildings, but the inscriptions had

---

[47] Lusitania: 2. 111, Canidia Albina; 112, Q. Iulius Maximus and his two sons; Aquitania: 13. 395, C. Valerius Valerianus Sanctus; 1129, Claudia Varenilla; Macedonia. L. Saluius Secundinus, text in Schäfer (1989: 261, no. 15) (in my view his *origo* was Philippi).

[48] See below, C. Iulius Quadratus Bassus and Ti. Iulius Celsus Polemaeanus; further, [Ul]pius Flauius Claudianus Ponticus (Drew-Bear and Eck 1976: 304–5).

[49] Halfmann (1979: 52 ff., and esp. his list, 100 ff.).

[50] Cf. the texts in Keil, *Forschungen in Ephesos* 5. 1; *I.Eph.* 7. 2. 5101–14.

[51] See e.g. *I.Eph.* 3. 614b–c, with permission for the burial of Laeuia Paula and M. Antonius Albus.

survived, nothing would show that they had served to adorn this 'tomb' of Polemaeanus.

The second remarkable specimen of a senatorial burial, this time at Pergamum, also allows one to distinguish certain fundamental characteristics. In AD 117 C. Iulius Quadratus Bassus, suffect consul in 105 and one of Trajan's most important army commanders in the ·Parthian war, died in the province of Dacia. Hadrian ordered his remains to be transported to Asia, presumably to Pergamum. The cortège was escorted by soldiers under the command of the *primuspilus* Quintilius Capito and the tomb was constructed at the expense of the *fiscus* (*Pergamon* 8. 3. 21). Thus, although Quadratus Bassus had been a member of the senate for more than twenty-five years—perhaps indeed thirty years—it was apparently completely natural to bury him in Asia, his home province. He had probably given specific instructions to this effect himself. For Hadrian, too, it must have been no problem to have the tomb erected in Asia; the monument, which was unquestionably expensive, was anyway paid for from imperial funds. Bassus must therefore have been more closely tied to his home town than to Rome, which was legally his domicile. Here one must observe that he spent perhaps the greater part of his senatorial career not in Rome but in the provinces, above all as governor or as army commander. Hence he had probably less opportunity than many other senators to build up strong links with Rome. Besides this, he did not die in Rome itself but in the recently conquered province of Dacia. The actual tomb has not yet been found.[52]

By contrast the tomb of C. Iulius Antiochus Philopappus is still preserved to this day on the Hill of the Muses at Athens. This descendant of the last king of Commagene had taken up residence in Athens and was first made senator, with praetorian rank, under Trajan. He reached a suffect consulship in 109.[53] In his case it is scarcely surprising that he had his tomb built at Athens and not at Rome—he had spent most of his life there, so at least it is generally assumed. How then could links with Rome have arisen? It is perfectly logical that the inscriptions below the statues of his ancestors were composed in Greek.[54] Yet even in his case the powerful effect of being a member of the *ordo senatorius* comes through. The *titulus* beneath the statue of Philopappus in philosopher's dress is in Latin: only his

---

[52] See *PIR²* J 508; Habicht, commentary on *Pergamon* 8. 3. 21.

[53] *PIR²* J 151; 3. 552 = *ILS* 845. 2; Schäfer (1989: 380); but there is no reason to suppose, as Schäfer does, that he was not in Rome during his suffect consulship.

[54] 3. 552 = *ILS* 845. 3-5 = *IG* 2². 3451.

senatorial posts are named, but not the archonship which he had held at Athens as early as the 80s (*PIR*² J. 151). Further, the frieze relief which dominates the monuments depicts his festive processions on the occasion of his consulship at Rome: twelve *togati* with the *fasces* show in pictorial form where at least one, if not the main, point of reference for his public prestige was to be found for this descendant of a Hellenistic king (Kleiner 1983). Nevertheless this tomb was erected in Athens.

A similar mixture of the link with the home town and of the Roman forms can be recognized on a funerary monument which stands in a dominant position above the cliffs by the sea at Attaleia, now Antalya, on the south coast of Turkey.[55] Above the rectangular substructure, measuring 17m. by 18m., rises a drum-shaped construction, which perhaps originally supported a tumulus. The decisive point, however, is that near the entrance to the grave twelve *fasces* are carved, which define the occupant as senator of consular rank. Who this senator was we do not know—the inscription is lost. At all events, at the present stage of our knowledge there can be no doubt that the senatorial occupant of this grave was not, for example, a governor of the province of Lycia-Pamphylia, even though there are, obviously, examples of senatorial office-holders who were buried in the provinces in which they served.[56] For the imperial legate of Lycia-Pamphylia was always of praetorian rank. Hence this unknown senator must derive from Lycia-Pamphylia itself, probably from Attaleia. The monument can be dated to the second half of the first century AD.[57]

In all the cases of senatorial funerary monuments in the provinces that have been examined in some detail so far, except for that of Antiochus Philopappus, the persons had had no break with their political past. Hence it cannot have been disappointment that was the reason for a return home. It must have been some especially close link, which we cannot now identify. Disappointment, or a sense of resignation, however, can very well be assumed for a senator who played an important role in a year of crisis, AD 97:

---

[55] Schäfer (1989: 373–4); Stupperich (1991: 417–22).

[56] Thus e.g. T. Aninius Sextius Florentinus at Petra (3. 87); M. Heluius Geminus and M. Calpurnius Rufus at Ephesus (3. 6074 = *ILS* 975 = *I.Eph.* 3. 683; 3. 6072 = *I.Eph.* 3. 631, on which see Eck (1991*a*: 102)); Q. Gargilius Aufidianus, M. Maecius Probus, L. Tadius Simplex, Q. Umbricius Proculus (*RIT* 138, 142, 147, 148; here, however, it is also possible that posthumous commemorative statues are at issue, since only the statue-bases survive, while the context to which they belonged is unknown). In principle, one could of course suppose that only a cenotaph was set up in the province, while the ashes would have been brought back to Rome (or elsewhere), as happened e.g. with L. Antistius Rusticus (Martial 9. 30).   [57] For a proposed identification, cf. Birley and Eck (1993: 45 ff.).

M. Cornelius Nigrinus Curiatius Maternus.[58] At that time governor of
Syria, Nigrinus lost the struggle for the succession to Nerva—to M.
Ulpius Traianus. It is thoroughly understandable that there was thereafter no place for this man at Rome. The result was a return to his
Spanish home, to Liria Edetanorum in Tarraconensis. There too he
had his tomb built, of which Géza Alföldy and Helmut Halfmann
have reconstructed the *titulus*.[59] But great as his disappointment may
have been, however embittered, perhaps, he was about political
developments at Rome, none of this can be detected in his funerary inscription. He uses the normal standard formula, which had
become the usual sign of senatorial rank at this time, the full *cursus
honorum*.

Still, as far as we can tell from the sources at our disposal, it was
not, in most of the cases we can get to grips with, reasons such as
disappointment, embitterment, exclusion from the political process
—in other words, reasons that could deter people from remaining
permanently in Rome—that were decisive for the return back home
and the provision of a grave there. Rather the motives will have
been the emotional ties with the home town, the connection with its
citizens and with the senator's own family, perhaps too the recognition that a single senator of the Roman People would occupy a
far more prominent position at home, among those who were not
his equals, than he could at Rome, where competition was strong
and an individual senator could at best fill second place, but never
the first. By no means the only one to appreciate this was Ti. Claudius
Herodes Atticus, *consul ordinarius* in 143 and teacher of rhetoric to
Marcus Aurelius. He saw his native Greece as his proper sphere of
activity, especially Athens and Attica, above all Cephisia, where his
favourite villa stood. There he buried all those of his children who
predeceased him, likewise his wife Annia Regilla. The province, which
was above all the focus of his benefactions, was also the place where
his entire family, and finally Herodes himself, were laid to rest.[60]

This combination of benefaction towards the home town and the
erection of a tomb there is found with other senatorial families too.
Casinum in southern Latium was the place of origin of C. Ummidius

---

[58] Cf. Syme (1988: 274–7); Schwarte (1979: 139 ff.).

[59] Alföldy and Halfmann (1973: 331–73). There, however, the great inscription is not
described as funerary; on p. 345 there is only reference to 'honorary inscriptions'. It seems
to me doubtful whether this expression can be at all meaningfully applied in this case. In
none of the five texts which can be identified as referring to Nigrinus is there any reference
to a public setting up of an inscription. In my view, all the inscriptions (apart from the funerary inscription) belong to bases which were, rather, set up in the private domain. Cf. now
also 2²/14. 124; and, further, 125–7 (for Nigrinus); 128 and perhaps 129 (for his son).

[60] For the complete dossier, Ameling (1983: i. 95 ff.; ii. 138 ff., 211 ff.).

Durmius Quadratus, governor of Syria in the last years of Claudius, and also his burial-place (10. 5182 = *ILS* 972). As much as half a century later his daughter, who likewise belonged to the *ordo senatorius*, was also active as a benefactress towards her home town: she not only built an amphitheatre and a temple, but enlarged the theatre too.[61] Yet up to a very advanced age she had her actual residence at Rome (Pliny 7. 24). The Picentine town of Urbs Saluia evidently enjoyed its greatest prosperity in the Flavian period, above all thanks to the involvement of two senatorial families that were related to one another. The family of Saluius Liberalis Nonius Bassus, suffect consul probably in 85 or 86, took an emphatic part in his activity, among other things by the erection of a *porticus*, by the adornment (of buildings?) with marble columns and statues as well as by supplying money, probably for the upkeep (*tutela*) of buildings.[62] Liberalis himself became *quinquennalis* in the town four times, his son Vitellianus three times. If a fragmentary inscription can be referred to a further son, he too is attested as *quinquennalis*.[63] Liberalis' wife served as *flaminica Salutis Augustae* (9. 5534 = *ILS* 1012). In spite of all the involvement of its menfolk with Rome and the provinces, the family was extraordinarily closely connected with its home town and the place was seen by it as an important point of reference. In all probability it enjoyed very special esteem there too. Hence it is in no way surprising to find the funerary inscription for Saluius Liberalis, his wife Vitellia Rufilla and for at least one son, Vitellianus, in this town. Probably these inscriptions were all originally attached to a single large funerary monument. The connection with its Picentine *origo* that had proved to be so significant in the family's lifetime was continued after death by the erection of a large family tomb. The *memoria* of the family was in a real way tied to this place.

This is even clearer in the case of M. Nonius Balbus, who evidently came from Nuceria, but who found a 'spiritual home' at Herculaneum.[64] There are numerous statues set up there to him and to members of his family by the Herculanenses themselves, by the Nucerini, but also by the *koinon* of the island of Crete and by the cities of Gortyn and Cnossos.[65] These communities thus registered their gratitude and esteem towards Balbus not at Rome but in this Campanian town. This can only mean that Nonius Balbus wished

---

[61] 10. 5183 = *ILS* 5628; *AE* 1946, 174 = Fora (1992: 269–73).
[62] Bormann (1896: 120–3); cf. Delplace (1990: 101).
[63] Cf. on the family, with the relevant evidence, Eck (1992/3).
[64] See on this man most recently *PIR²* N. 129.
[65] 10. 1426 = *ILS* 896; 1427, 1429 = *ILS* 896a, 1430–4.

it to be so, because there was more to tie him to Herculaneum: he had, after all, made a significant contribution to the renewal of the town's buildings by financing the erection of a basilica, the enclosure wall and doors belonging to the basilica (10. 1425 = *ILS* 5527). Here in this town he was better able than he would have been in Rome to enjoy the sense of satisfaction that resulted from his bene-factions, as well as the honours that they brought in return. Maybe this is all connected with the fact that at Rome itself honours of this kind were mostly possible only in the private sphere, but no longer in public places (Eck 1984*a*: 129–67). A town such as Herculaneum offered many a senator a far more 'grateful' public than did Rome. Balbus was not subject to competition with people of the same social standing at Herculaneum. This is probably very largely the reason why, as in this case, numerous communities and also private indi-viduals set up statues or other monuments to senators, above all in their home towns but less often at Rome.[66] How strong the link between Nonius Balbus and Herculaneum was is especially clear from the fact that after his death, which evidently occurred at Herculaneum, the decurions had the place where he was cremated marked by a special altar. From here an annual procession in Balbus' honour, at the Parentalia, was to set out, evidently to the deceased senator's tomb. All this is clearly reminiscent of the honours which were de-creed at Rome for the members of the *domus Augusta*. The appro-priate place for such ceremonies for this senator was not Rome, but Herculaneum, where he lived, 'quo hac uixerit'.[67]

Such an unusual amount of documentation, with evidence of benefactions, honours during a man's lifetime, and his burial, in one and the same place, does not survive for anyone other than Nonius Balbus. Herculaneum in any case is a special place. All the same, even the less copiously preserved sources for other senatorial fam-ilies allow us to recognize similarly strong connections with a par-ticular town, usually the original home.

Brixia may serve as an example, even though not all the attested senators from there can be taken into account. Especially striking is the great number of statues, which were erected to several members of the senatorial family of the Nonii between the Hadrianic period and the end of the second century AD by various people.[68] On the one hand the *cultores Larum* were involved, on the other the local

---

[66] Eck (1984*b*: 212–17), with the documents deriving from the community. There is as yet no collection and analysis of those deriving from private individuals.

[67] *AE* 1947, 53 = 1976, 144 = Schumacher (1976: 165–84).

[68] Cf. Garzetti (1977: 175–85); id., *I.It.* 10. 5. 1, pp. 80 ff.; see further *PIR*[2] N. 114, 115, 116, 140, 145. For the remarks that follow, the individual attributions are of no relevance.

collegium dendrophorum.[69] Further there were people from outside
Brixia, for example a *tribunus cohortis* or a *commilito*, who had
had some military position under a member of the Nonii family
in a province (*I.It.* 10. 5. 1. 129, 130; cf. 127). But within the family, as well, many participated in multiplying the number of statues
for their own relatives (ibid. 128, 131, 136), as well as honouring
people outside the family, to some extent *ex testamento* (ibid. 112,
124, 150).[70] In addition there are dedications to the gods made by
the same people at Brixia (ibid. 56; 2. 812). This can be established
for Postumia Paulla, wife of the suffect consul Iuuenius Secundus.
She was honoured by the erection of a statue at Brixia by six separate people, most of them senatorial family members (ibid. 139–
42). But a senator's wife of another family was also involved, that
of the Nummii, which is likewise attested at Brixia in various ways
(ibid. 143, 144, 137).

But what does this allow us to conclude? Such a concentration of
honours in the form of statues for various people from the same
family over a long period of time in one and the same place is only
conceivable if the town itself had some emotional worth for the
people honoured. The connection cannot have been merely mar-
ginal, such as that the Nonii had extensive landholdings around
Brixia, which can in fact be documented. No: Brixia must have
been, at least from time to time, the actual place of residence for the
family or at least parts of it, just as the decree of the decurions of
Herculaneum expressed it for Nonius Balbus.[71] How that worked
out in practice cannot be demonstrated on the basis of the epigraphic material. But it is at any rate indisputable that the town of
Brixia was a living point of reference for the Nonii, which affected
their lives. Where they were buried is yet unknown. Rome, at all
events, took up only part of their life.

One can very well make a similar assertion about C. Antius A.
Iulius Quadratus, an older kinsman of the previously mentioned C.
Iulius Quadratus Bassus of Pergamum. This senator of the Flavio-
Trajanic period, suffect consul in AD 94, governor of Syria *c.*100–
103/4 and *consul ordinarius* II in 105, is represented by a mass of
inscriptions at Pergamum, the like of which, apart from Herodes
Atticus in Attica, we know for no other senator.[72] In all, well
over twenty-five more or less completely preserved inscriptions of

---

[69] *I.It.* 10. 5. 1. 134 (probably set up in the private house), 135.
[70] These statues were possibly set up on the testator's tomb, so that he could in this way
assemble his friends around it after his death (the suggestion comes from A. Diaconescu).
[71] See above, n. 67.
[72] The evidence is in *PIR*² J 507 and in Halfmann (1979: 112 ff., no. 17).

honorific character are known for this man at Pergamum. To some extent the city itself had initiated the erecting of a statue, otherwise it was the *iuuenes* or private individuals, also other cities, outside the province of Asia. As well as holding various offices at Pergamum, Quadratus had also shouldered the expenses for a competition that was named after Trajan. Naturally Pergamum was the senator's place of origin and an honour from Pergamum itself alone in the form of one or more statues would have been quite within the bounds of the normal and predictable. But here markedly more than this occurred and, in particular, not just on the initiative of Pergamum itself but through that of other cities. These honours imply, if not definitely attest to the fact, that Iulius Quadratus wanted to see statues erected in his honour in this city in Asia, and not in Rome. There, in the imperial capital, at least as yet, not a single relevant monument in his honour has been found. Should one suppose that Quadratus, as soon as his duties at Rome allowed, returned back home, to spend the last years of his life in the place where recognition for his public activity was everywhere tangible in the form of statues and inscriptions? His tomb has not yet been found, any more than has that of his kinsman Quadratus Bassus, who, as is well attested, was buried in Asia, presumably at Pergamum. At all events, one can hardly seriously dispute that a significant part of Iulius Quadratus' existence, over and above his ownership of property, was bound up with Pergamum, even though he had to spend many years far away, as a senator *populi Romani*. Christian Habicht has inferred from an inscription of Pergamum, which cannot be dated earlier than AD 120, that Iulius Quadratus did in fact return to Pergamum at an advanced age,[73] and that, among other things, he there assumed the office of the provincial priesthood. No senatorial offices are mentioned in the honorific inscription which was set up to him by Pergamum in this connection:[74] they were evidently in this context no longer of significance. If we may assume that he held his first consulship at the usual age of a little over 40, he must have been some 70 years old about the year 120.[75]

The Nonii, Postumii, and Nummii at Brixia, like C. Iulius Quadratus at Pergamum, cannot be regarded as exceptional cases in

---

[73] Other senators, even in old age, did not return to their original home, e.g. Vestricius Spurinna; as shown by Pliny 3. 1, he must have been living near Rome at the age of 78; on his origin, perhaps in northern Italy, see most recently Syme (1991: 541–50).

[74] Habicht, commentary on *Pergamon* 8. 3. 20.

[75] For a comparable, if numerically less pronounced, concentration of evidence for a senatorial family in its place of origin or perhaps in some other place too, e.g. Halfmann (1979: nos. 71 and 106, pp. 84, 89, 101). In Italy, one could refer, amongst others, to the Neratii whose centre remained for hundreds of years at Saepinum.

their relationship to their original home and in their intimate ties with places outside Rome. All that is out of the ordinary in their cases is the great volume of the epigraphic material. Numerous other examples display the same basic phenomenon, merely by slightly different means and above all with far fewer texts.

At Cirta P. Iulius Geminius Marcianus, suffect consul in the time of Marcus Aurelius, was honoured by one of his former subordinates in the province of Arabia, likewise by the Arabian city of Petra. But far more is implied by the fact that the senator himself laid down in his testament the instruction that a statue which the Adraheni from the province of Arabia had set up to him in his *domus* at Rome should be brought to Cirta after his death and set up there (8. 7050–2 = *ILS* 1102–3a). Whether he had senatorial descendants is unknown. At all events he must have reckoned that there would be a greater chance of his memory being kept alive by the statue being at Cirta, in the place where other statues of him and of members of his family already stood.[76]

At Centuripae in Sicily a large complex of buildings was excavated outside the city in 1926, in which, among other things, numerous statues of men and women were found, set up on stone bases clad with marble slabs. Only part of this large collection was published and only in an unsatisfactory fashion at that.[77] However, a careful analysis of the surviving fragments has made it possible to recognize that Q. Pompeius Sosius Priscus, *cos. ord.* in AD 149, around the middle of the second century honoured the memory of his long deceased ancestors in Sicily, in a purely private context, by means of statues and inscriptions, which give only the names and the relationship (Eck 1994). We can identify the paternal grandparents as well as his father or uncle. By comparing inscriptions in neighbouring towns it is possible to establish that both the families of Q. Pompeius Falco, suffect consul in 108, and of Q. Sosius Senecio, *cos. ord.* in 99 and again in 107, had evidently long had connections with this area. If more than half a century later one of their descendants, who was by now a third-generation member of the Roman senate, revived the memory of his ancestors in a private context far from Rome, the place must have had for him too a special meaning. His family identity must have been, at least in part, determined by this place.

One may postulate this in a slightly different way for C. Herennius Caecilianus, a *nouus homo* under Hadrian. The decurions of Verona

---

[76] One may also postulate posthumous setting up of a memorial in 11. 3364–5 = *ILS* 1047, 1081. Both statues of the Tullii were erected by a freedman of the family in the baths at Tarquinii.   [77] Libertini 1926: 45–6; cf. Manganaro (1989: 161–209).

erected a statue to him (Albertini 1971: 439 ff.; Alföldy 1984: 141), probably an equestrian one (Eck 1992: 368–9), at Sirmione on Lake Garda, probably on one of his estates. That cannot have occurred without his consent, indeed one may well assume that it was at his express wish. The city centre of Verona itself or the senator's own private residence at Rome would have been the more obvious place to erect the statue. But to Herennius Caecilianus the private area on his estate in the Transpadana apparently had greater significance. At the time when he received the honour he had in any case belonged to the senate for only a relatively short time, at most five years.[78]

For another Transpadane, Younger Pliny, the link with Comum, his home town, and the interests of its citizens, remained active during his entire life. His letters allow us detailed insight into this. Journeys that he made back to Comum from time to time are also known to us from his letters, just as we know that other senators visited their home towns.[79] It is true that if we were restricted in Pliny's case to epigraphic records from Comum, as happens with almost all other senators, his involvement with the town would not be so apparent, at least as far as the quantity is concerned. Only three texts from Comum refer directly to Pliny. Two attest statues that were set up to him in his lifetime, both in the dative and neither very informative (5. 5263; AE 1972, 212). It is another matter with the third one, which was engraved only after his death. After presenting his entire *cursus*, it relates the *beneficia* of Pliny towards the town and its citizens, and towards his freedmen. To this extent the inscription might not be so out of the ordinary (5. 5262 = ILS 2927). But as far as I can see, no one has yet pointed out the fact that the inscription, although it was set up after Pliny's death, does not directly name anyone as responsible for carrying this out. It must

---

[78] One could of course speculate that the senator, who was still young, did not yet possess at Rome or in its close vicinity a suitable *domus* in which the monument donated by Verona could have found an appropriate place.

[79] Thus Herodes Atticus must have stayed initially for very long periods and then permanently in Attica (cf. Ameling 1983: 84 ff.), whereas by contrast Cornelius Fronto clearly never returned to his home in North Africa (cf. Champlin 1980: 5). On the other side, Domitius Apollinaris journeyed after his suffect consulship in 97 to his home town Vercellae (Martial 10. 12). Above all, older senators could have withdrawn from Rome frequently. The relatively low numbers of senators registered as present for the vote on *senatusconsulta* allow one to suppose that not a few senators were absent from Rome, even without any official duties. But if, in that case, only 300 or less were present at sessions of the senate, one must seek an explanation why so many were absent. The possibilities are numerous; individual senators were, for example, at least during the first century AD, serving as judges or, like Pliny, in individual instances summoned to the imperial *consilium*, and thus unable to attend senate meetings. All this is of course insufficient to explain the relatively low figures. Absence from Rome for private reasons may not in fact have been all that uncommon: a temporary stay in the home town can belong in this category.

in fact have been Pliny himself, since he is named in the nominative. What then was the function of the inscription? From the dimensions of the stone it is unlikely that it was set up inside a house.[80] The listing of *beneficia* for *pueri et puellae* and for the *plebs* of Comum would also have little point inside a house. The text with this mixture of offices and *beneficia*, that means the *res gestae Plinii Secundi*, was therefore intended for a public place. But that can only mean that it was either attached to a posthumous monument—which, if Pliny himself was responsible for it, is difficult to conceive—or it was on Pliny's tomb. In either case Pliny would have given the instructions for the text, as is shown by the use of the nominative case. He did not want to rely on other people, whether private persons or indeed the magistrates of the community.[81] The text shows, above all, that for Pliny too, who had spent long years away, principally at Rome, it was not the world metropolis which was the sole or lasting point of reference for his life, but Comum, his old *patria*. This unites Pliny with many of his peers. The legal tie with Rome and the practical constraints of duties in the individual posts and in the senate shaped the life of senators in many different respects. But the world outside Rome was also able to assert its rights.[82]

---

[80] As A. Sartori and G. Manella inform me, the size of the still surviving fragment is 87 × 85cm. From this one may calculate the minimum width of the inscription as about 3.2m. I hope to discuss the text more fully elsewhere.

[81] Cf. Pliny 6. 10. 5–6: one ought to give thought to the erection of a tomb before one's death.

[82] The subject of this paper needs further detailed investigation, which it has not yet been possible to undertake. For one thing, the entire epigraphic material must be examined again with attention to its chronological development—for with the change in political circumstances the behaviour of senators in respect of the world they lived in could have been influenced too. One should further inquire whether there is a detectable difference in the way they behaved *vis-à-vis* Rome or the wider world between *noui homines* and senators of several generations' standing—which would not surprise. For *noui homines* very probably had spent at least their youth in the old *patria*. In this case the ties would naturally have been stronger. Further, in their case their parents may well have remained at home. On the other hand, however, there are not a few cases in which senators' children were buried in the old home. This makes it at least plausible that the children were brought up there (see e.g. the list in Eck (1981*b*: 129–31); cf. further 10. 1689, 3855; 11. 3882, 5208; 13. 1129). In this connection one needs to examine all inscriptions of *nutritores* and *nutrices* of senatorial families: they may readily be supposed to have lived—and with them their senatorial charges—at the place where they set up an inscription (cf. e.g. 11. 1740). [See also Bradley (1991: 13–36) on *nutrices* in Italy and the provinces; cf. ibid. 37–75, *nutritores* in Rome. Edd.] If a knight at Thibilis was *tutor* of a senatorial child (8. 5528–9), then the *puer* too must have grown up in this town. It is known that Hadrian as a youth returned for some time to Italica (SHA, *Hadrian* 2. 1). One could pose further questions. In particular, however, for more precise answers there should first, in many cases, be a much more exact examination of individual inscriptions on the original stone (cf. above). This would take time to carry out.

5
Sons, Slaves—and Christians

PETER GARNSEY

INTRODUCTION

If we can believe Ambrose, bishop of Milan in the late fourth century, his friend Simplicianus appreciated his sermons on St Paul. This, and Paul's status as a profound but difficult thinker, was Ambrose's excuse for writing Simplicianus a long letter on 1 Corinthians 7: 23, in which Paul 'calls us from slavery to liberty, with the words: "You have been bought with a price; do not become the slaves of men."' Paul was asserting, according to Ambrose, 'that our freedom is in Christ, and that our freedom is in the knowledge of wisdom' (*CSEL* 82, no. 7, para. 4). The language of wisdom, *sapientia*, is not employed in this place by Paul, and the discussion of Ambrose appears to owe less to the apostle than to Paul's older contemporary Philo of Alexandria. The letter is a Christianizing version of Philo's treatise on the first part of the Stoic adage that 'every wise man is free, every fool is a slave'.[1] It is noticeable that when Ambrose returns to the Corinthians passage at the end of his Letter, he renders the second clause as 'do not become the slaves of men *and of the passions*'. This emendation brings it close to orthodox Stoic doctrine according to which true slavery is of the mind or soul.

It may certainly be doubted whether, after reading the letter of Ambrose, Simplicianus was anything the wiser about 1 Corinthians 7: 23. Ambrose provides no discussion of redemption, nor any analysis of the advice not to become 'the slaves of men'. Such instruction would have been problematic, indeed provocative, if it were taken as advice to avoid or escape from physical slavery. Interpreted thus, it would have contradicted the whole tenor of the passage, and the general message of Paul, according to which we should be content with our present status, be it slave or free.

I have profited from the comments of Margaret Atkins and Caroline Humfress on an earlier draft, and from the discussion at the conference, especially the comments of the respondent, Judith Evans-Grubbs. This chapter should be regarded as merely a preliminary exploration of a large and difficult theme.

[1] For Philo as slave theorist, see Garnsey (1994).

But the more fundamental problem for us, in approaching the sentence in question and the passage as a whole, lies in Paul's indiscriminate use of status terms. We are free in Christ, we are slaves of Christ, we are freedmen of Christ. 'Iuris consultus abesto!' Paul appears to be thumbing his nose at contemporary social and cultural hierarchies, as upheld by Roman and other legal systems. His point is the irrelevance of human divisions of any sort in the divine scheme of things. As he writes in Galatians 3: 28 (and in a slightly different form in Colossians 3: 11—if indeed this letter is his—and 1 Corinthians 12: 13): 'There can be neither Jew nor Greek. There can be neither slave nor free. There can be no male and female. For you are one in Christ Jesus.'

What difference did this doctrine make in real life? The historian of slavery in particular will want to know whether a new spirit of egalitarianism transformed master–slave relationships within the Christian community, if not in Graeco-Roman society as a whole; or whether, on the other hand, existing social hierarchies were confirmed. For the pronouncement 'there can be neither bond nor free' might in principle lead in either direction. It might imply that slaves and free men (if the distinction between them were to be preserved at all) should be treated in the same manner—a radical doctrine. Or the implication might be that existing social relations and distinctions should stay in place, as being irrelevant to the level of existence that matters, which is the spiritual—a conservative doctrine.

There is a separate though related question: whether Paul viewed his teaching as reformist, whether he wanted or expected it to have social consequences. This is a question about social attitudes; it is more accessible than the first question, and can be pursued by a study of whatever relevant prescriptive passages exist in the writings of Paul.

The first question has to do with social change and is more difficult to address. Not surprisingly, scholars have divided over the issue. Improvement in the position of slaves has commonly been postulated, and credited to Christianity, or to Stoicism. In the former case, the argument has focused on the period of late antiquity (in the latter, the period of the Principate), and this is appropriate, for the Christian Church was then in a position of power and beginning to dominate society. Attention has been drawn, for example, to the content and tenor of specific late-imperial laws, and to the promotion of manumission in church (a practice which, it is claimed, increased the frequency of manumissions). Others disagree. De Ste Croix, for example, has charged that Christianity actually tightened the grip of slavery on Graeco-Roman society. And the case that Christianity had in general a retrograde effect on society has recently been put (with some attention to slavery) by MacMullen in a swashbuckling article entitled 'What Difference did Christianity Make?' (de Ste Croix 1981; MacMullen 1990).[2]

It is not my intention to enter or survey this controversy now. I confine myself to five remarks:

1. I am with MacMullen (though he does not argue the case) in believing that Christianity did make a difference. Whether that difference was predominantly positive or negative (or even whether it is sensible to pose the question in these terms) need not concern us now. One corollary of this is that I distance myself from the approach of Eyben in his recent discussion of father–son relationships (though he too fails to argue *his* case) (Eyben 1991). Eyben assumes that there was an essential stability and continuity of attitude and behaviour over the period covered. I infer this from his free juxtaposition of texts pagan and Christian, early and late. It is risky enough to move from one Christian source to another over time. One can find common ground between, for example, Paul and Augustine writing on slavery, but it does not follow that Augustine's general attitude to slaves and slavery marked no change—let alone that the attitudes of Christians and others had remained static over the centuries.

The attitudes of pagan and Christian authors may well be found to coincide to a degree (and this is no surprise) when they talk of father-and-son, as with master–slave relationships. But an argument which documents similarities without countenancing the possibility that there might be dissimilarities will be seriously flawed.

2. If I were to explore the impact of Christianity on Graeco-Roman society, I would be less inclined than scholars in general have been to take the 'top-down' approach, that is to say, to attack the question by focusing on imperial laws or the public behaviour of officials, soldiers, and the clergy.[3] Rather, I would try to penetrate to Christian attitudes and practice 'on the ground'. This approach can be countenanced because of an important new development, one which marked Christianity off from the pagan philosophies. Philosophical ideas in antiquity tended to circulate only among the educated élite or, more realistically, within pockets of the élite. In contrast, Christian doctrines, at any rate after Christianity became a *religio licita*, were

---

[2] Other, generally more optimistic, discussions, include Roberti (1935); Biondi (1954); Gaudemet (1959; 1962); Crifo (1988); Herrmann (1980). Evans-Grubbs (1993*a*) argues for a conservative approach by Constantine and succeeding emperors.

[3] Evans-Grubbs (1993*b*) does not explicitly address the question of the impact of Christianity, but the force of her argument is that the legislation of emperors did not affect domestic behaviour (specifically in the area of male slave–mistress relations).

preached to the multitudes, from every pulpit in the *orbis terrarum*. We can therefore approach the Christian preacher and his message with higher than usual expectations. My own expectation is that the message had some influence upon those who came to listen.

3. The question of audience-response is not a straightforward one, especially if the message turns out to be ambiguous. This is bound to be the situation where the preacher is operating at different levels, on the one hand, the spiritual, theological, metaphorical, and on the other, the material, physical, actual. Slavery is a case in point.

4. It remains the case that the first step in any inquiry into the impact of Christianity on society must be the clarification of the content of Christian thinking—in the case under consideration, on the relation between slave and son. There is anyway no reason why an inquiry of this sort should be geared to the short-term goal of studying the effect of Christianity on contemporary society. As any student of intellectual history knows, ideas can have a history and make an impact beyond the society in which they evolved and circulated. In any case, I would suggest that in the matter before us the task of the historian of ideas has priority over that of the social historian.

5. The social historian, when his turn comes, should set himself objectives appropriate to the quality of his data, that is, strictly limited objectives. For example, he may be able to discover something of the nature of North African society through the pages of Augustine, following the example of Brent Shaw (1987*a*) in a classic article (though I have reservations). But can he show how that particular society evolved from the pagan to the Christian era? And supposing that he can pin down relevant trends, can he isolate those causes of such developments which can be said convincingly to have emanated from Christianity?[4] For the 'MacMullen question', is, I suspect, insoluble, certainly in the present state of the evidence, and probably absolutely.

The business of this chapter is to investigate one side of the role of slavery in Christian theology, that is, the relation of slave and son. I must be selective. I confine myself to remarks on Paul, Lactantius, and Augustine. Paul provides a starting-point: he makes some use of the metaphor of the household, and also has some advice for both masters and (especially) for slaves. Lactantius discusses relationships within the household, albeit in the service of his theological explorations, and in the process raises status-tension between sons and

---

[4] It is a theme of Brown (1988: e.g. 205–7, 250), that changes in moral attitudes were neither the creation of Christianity nor restricted to Christian circles.

slaves. But we see him as theologian, not preacher, interested more
in doctrinal exploration than in changing the lives of men. His contact with the world outside is insubstantial. He does, however, make
some interestingly unconventional statements about social divisions.
The volume of Augustine's work and his contribution in this area
are far greater than those of his two predecessors. Like Paul, he oper-
ates on several levels. He takes the theology of Paul and Lactantius
a step further, but also reveals his own social attitudes, while enabling
some deductions or plausible speculations to be made concerning the
attitudes and behaviour of members of his audience.[5]

SLAVES AND SONS IN ST PAUL

The son–slave distinction is not one of those listed as meaningless
in the sight of God. In fact, Paul in the Galatians passage moves on,
leaning on Roman law,[6] to confront slaves and sons, to the (even-
tual) disadvantage of the former:

3: 28   'There is neither Jew nor Greek, there is neither bond nor
free, there is neither male and female; for you are all one
in Christ Jesus.'

3: 29   'And if you are Christ's, then you are Abraham's offspring,
heirs according to promise.'

4: 1   'I mean that the heir, so long as he is a child, is no better
than a slave, though he is owner of all the estate;'

4: 2   'but is under guardians and trustees until the date set by
the father.'

4: 3   'So with us; when we were children, we were slaves to the
elemental spirits of the universe.'

Slave and son begin as near status-equals—for as long as the son
is an infant (νήπιος) he is a quasi-slave. But Paul goes on to explain
how the situation of the son improves as he matures and gains his
inheritance:

4: 4–7 'But when the time had come fully, God sent forth his
Son, born of a woman, born under the law, to redeem

---

[5] My choice of Paul and Augustine needs no special justification. Lactantius is an unjustly
neglected thinker. His discussion of the relevant themes, while owing something to Tertullian
(see e.g. *Aduersus Marcionem* 3. 2. 13–16) and Cyprian (e.g. *De bono patientiae* 3)—both
African, as it happens—is much more detailed and elaborate. Of eastern Church Fathers,
Origen and Anastasius in particular have much to contribute. See Widdicombe (1994).
[6] C. Humfress has persuaded me that Paul has in mind here Roman law rather than any
other legal system. For *tutela impuberis* (guardianship of an underage person), see e.g. Buckland
(1963: 142–3); de Zulueta (1953: ii. 49–50).

> those who were under the law, so that we might receive
> adoption as sons. . . . So through God you are no longer
> a slave, but a son; and if a son then an heir.'

Slave and son begin close together, but their paths separate, the great divider being the capacity of the son to inherit.

It is interesting that Paul chooses the context of guardianship, and specifically guardianship of minors (*tutela impuberis*), by which to advance his argument. This is a deliberate choice, to suit a complex exposition which exploits technicalities of Roman law.[7] An alternative would have been to present slaves and sons as equally subject to *patria potestas*. This might have achieved a similar side-effect, that of blurring the status distinction between them. But the implications would have been unfortunate: a son (that is, follower of Christ) claiming his inheritance by escaping from the *potestas* of his father (that is, God).

It is striking that Paul has used Roman law as a tool to develop his theology, and has used it accurately. He has captured at once the ambiguity of the position of the son *qua* infant, and the clarity of the son's position once he has received his inheritance, in both cases by comparing his condition with that of a slave. Later we will find Lactantius actually claiming for a theological argument on a similar subject that it is validated by Roman law.

For a different perspective on the son–slave distinction we turn to the Epistle to the Romans. Here sons and slaves are virtually substitutable.

In Romans 8: 14 we read: 'For all who are led by the Spirit of God are sons of God (υἱοί)' and again (vv. 16–17): 'It is the Spirit himself bearing witness with our spirit that we are children (τέκνα) of God; and if children, then heirs, heirs of God and fellow-heirs with Christ.'

Two chapters earlier, followers of Christ have been 'set free from sin and have become slaves to God' (6: 15–23, at 22); and at the very beginning of the work the author styles himself 'Paul, a slave of Christ'.

We saw that in 1 Corinthians Christians enjoyed in the sight of their God the status of slaves, of free men, of freedmen. We can now add—of sons.

What lies behind the positive connotation given to slavery in some contexts by Paul, involving the apparent elision of the slave–free and

---

[7] On slavery in Paul, see Martin (1990); for legal metaphors in Paul, see Lyall (1984); for sons in Paul, see Byrne (1979). For the influence of Roman law on the Church Fathers, see Gaudemet (1975).

slave–son distinctions, his proud self-styling as 'the slave of Christ', and his encouragement of Christians to be slaves to one another? Is this 'pure theology', or was he moved by ideological considerations (always supposing that this is a valid distinction)? Briefly, I do not believe that where Paul presented slavery in a metaphorically favourable light he was influenced by the social/historical context, specifically, the phenomenon of upwardly mobile slaves in contemporary Graeco-Roman society.[8] Still less do I think that Paul saw himself as advancing the cause of social reform.

Paul as a Jew, Saul, knew that Old Testament writers had claimed for the ancient Israelites as a race the uniquely privileged status of slaves of God, having been rescued by Him from slavery in Egypt. Paul as a Christian was moved by the humiliation, the self-enslavement of Christ, as shown in his birth as a man, his life of service, and his death in the manner of a slave. As Paul wrote in Philippians,

Who, though he was in the form of God, did not count equality with God a thing to be grasped. But emptied himself, taking the form of a slave, being born in the likeness of men. And being found in human form, he humbled himself, and became obedient unto death, even death on a cross. (2: 6–8)

So slavery became a key metaphor, with highly favourable overtones, for describing the demands, and the rewards, of Christian discipleship.

An implication of accepting that the source for Paul's views does not lie in the social/historical context is that any benefits that Christianity brought for real, physical slaves were to be enjoyed on the spiritual rather than the material level. No knock-on effects for the legal status of slaves were entailed.

One can arrive at the same conclusion by a more direct route, by studying what Paul and other authors of Pastoral Epistles say of a prescriptive nature on master–slave relations. In particular, they firmly instruct slaves to stay in their present station and loyally serve their masters, good or bad, as if they were serving Christ.[9] This last clause might be taken as particularly significant, in so far as it carries the implication that slavery was acceptable in the sight of God. This is the kind of consideration that provoked de Ste Croix into the charge that Christianity underpinned the institution of slavery.

We can only speculate as to how Christian slaves reacted to the Pauline instructions, and whether Christian masters adjusted their behaviour in response to the doctrine of the fundamental equality of

[8] In this matter my view differs from that of Martin (1990).
[9] 1 Corinthians 7: 20–4; Ephesians 6: 5–8; Colossians 3: 22–4. 1; Titus 2: 9–10; 1 Timothy 6: 1; 1 Peter 2: 18–21; Philemon 10–19.

men in the sight of God. It is in principle possible that early Christianity, while not at all abolitionist, did foster the better treatment of slaves, at least among Christians—a possibility, incidentally, not considered by de Ste Croix. At any rate, the means to settle the issue are not available.

SONS AND SLAVES IN LACTANTIUS

Discussion of sons and slaves occurs in Lactantius in two main contexts, arguments against polytheism in the *Divine Institutes* (*Diuinae institutiones*) and the argument for a God who is angry as well as merciful in the treatise *On Anger* (*De ira*). It will emerge, first, that there are two clear tendencies: one is to elide the distinction between son and slave, the other (which is related) is to give heavy emphasis to the disciplinary and coercive role of the head of the household (and, by analogy, God). Both points are interesting in view of the finding of Richard Saller (1991), building on earlier scholarship, that in Roman law sons and slaves were clearly distinguished, and that the distinction was particularly visible in the field of corporal punishment. Slaves were beaten, sons were not.

The explicit appeal to Roman law (referred to earlier) comes in a passage of the *Divine Institutes* (4. 3. 14–15) where Lactantius is developing a metaphor from the household:

Therefore one God is to be worshipped, who can truly be called 'father'. The same must also be 'master', because just as he can show mercy, so too can he coerce. He deserves the name 'father' because he showers on us many and great gifts; but he is equally master, because he has the supreme power of chastisement and punishment. That master and father are one is established by civil law doctrine (*iuris ciuilis ratio*).

In the next sentence but one, *pater* becomes *paterfamilias,* underscoring the Roman law context. What Lactantius says at that point (4. 3. 15–17) is striking:

Who can bring up sons unless he has the power of a master over them? The father is deservedly called the 'father of the family' (*paterfamilias*) though he might have children only: it is easy to see that the name 'father' embraces slaves too, because of the 'family' (*familias*) that follows, and the name 'family' embraces also sons, because father comes before it. It is clear, then, that the same man is both father of slaves and master of sons. Then again, the son is manumitted as if he were a slave, and the slave who is freed receives the name of his patron as if he were a son. But if he is called 'father of the family', to indicate that he is endowed with a twofold authority, so that he should show mercy because he is the father, and coerce because he is the master, it follows that the one who is a slave is a son also, and the master and father are likewise one and the same.

This is curious, and perhaps unexpected. The discussion might have gone in another direction. Lactantius might have proven the unity of the Godhead (his main purpose) while preserving a clear distinction between sons and slaves. The *paterfamilias*, he might have said, displays the indulgence of a father towards his children and the coercive authority of a master towards his slaves; by analogy, God combines both these qualities, performs both these roles. Instead, Lactantius breaks down the differences and confuses the categories of dependent relationship. He goes on to couple bad slaves and bad sons in the following sentence (and elsewhere), in which he compares 'philosophers and those who worship false gods' with 'children who have been disowned, or fugitive slaves' (4. 4. 5).

Lactantius was aware that the relations of the *paterfamilias qua pater* with the son and *qua dominus* with the slave were different, but he does not allow himself more than a gesture towards this difference, as in the sentence (4. 4. 1) that begins: 'From these things it is clear how wisdom and religion are connected one with the other. Wisdom looks toward children; it exacts love. Religion looks toward slaves; it exacts fear. For just as the former ought to love and honour their father, so the latter should serve and fear their master.' But he soon reverts to the earlier position, asserting that, just as God combines two attributes (father, master), so also do we, in so far as we are his followers (children, slaves): 'Since however God, who is one, embraces the character both of a father and a master, we ought to love Him because we are His children, and we ought to fear Him because we are His slaves.'

In *De ira*, Lactantius returns to these themes: God's relationship to humanity is actually the subject of the treatise. We find that the God–man relationship is expressed in terms of the same, elaborate metaphor from the household. God is the *paterfamilias* in whom are united the qualities of father and of master, *pater* and *dominus*. It is noticeable that, in this treatise too, Lactantius does not set up a polarity between *pater/filius/gratia*, on the one hand, and *dominus/seruus/ira*, on the other. On the contrary, there is a clear tendency to collapse the father–son distinction. This is no more marked than in the classic sentence: 'Mundus tamquam dei domus est, et homines tamquam serui (The world is like the household of God, and men are like slaves)' (17. 11).

It is striking that of all the vertical relationships within the household, it is the 'despotic' that Lactantius has singled out here as the appropriate metaphor for the relationship between God and man. Moreover, it is noticeable that when he does produce a comprehensive list of those subject to *patria potestas*—*serui, liberi, coniuges,* and *discipuli*—it is to remind the *paterfamilias* of his duty to coerce.

It is perhaps understandable in a treatise which is entirely devoted to proving that God does, should, must show anger, that the coercive role of the *paterfamilias* is centre-stage. Can we, however, go further and make an inference about Lactantius' social as distinct from theological attitudes? It is hard not to believe that this writer was a disciplinarian by conviction, and that for him the disciplining of children was, and should be, as routine as the disciplining of slaves; and that, in general, in his view coercion of dependants was in accordance with the will of God. For that is the effect of the analogy of the household: as with God, so with men. Formally, the argument is presented the other way around, because Lactantius is trying to prove the reality and necessity of divine anger: as we ought (sc. to coerce), so God ought. Lactantius is in fact little interested in issuing advice for heads of households, let alone in describing existing patterns of behaviour within the household. This, I imagine, is why we hear little about the nature of the punishment with which sons as well as slaves are threatened.

Although little or nothing is said about the manner of punishment inflicted by the *paterfamilias*, Lactantius does say something about motives. It is an attribute of the anger of God that it is just, and aimed at correction not vengeance. And so it should be among men. Lactantius does not go so far as to claim that punishment is a mark of affection, that *gratia* is displayed through *ira*. Augustine would drum home that message—and in general provide a more detailed account, with some novelties, of the status of sons and slaves in relation to both divine and human authority.

Lactantius does confront the complaint of the faithful that while they, the slaves of God, are marked down for punishment and suffer correction, sinners appear to be free and prosperous. The exemplary sinners happen to be *fugitiui* and *abdicati*, runaway slaves and disowned sons. Lactantius' answer is chilling. There is no hurry. God is patient. The eternal fires are being stoked for them.

We saw that in a classic statement in *De ira* men are compared to slaves within the household of God, that is the world. But Lactantius is equally capable of saying, as in *Diuinae institutiones* 5. 14. 17, that 'we are all his sons, enjoying equal rights', and he goes on to use the related concept of brotherhood. The context seems to make a difference: slavery is perhaps seen as more appropriate where punishment or correction is at issue, sonship where God's blessings are under discussion. In Paul, slavery goes with redemption and liberation, sonship with the promise of inheritance. The nuance in each case is significant, betraying the fact that the writer is in touch with the 'real world', even when speaking in metaphor. In fact, Lactantius' contact with reality is not here confined to a delicate hint, for the sentence in question is part of a longer passage in the course of which he moves freely, and confusingly, between the spiritual world and the material world, and in the process flirts with a radical vision of society. He is discussing equity, an aspect of justice. This he equates with Cicero's concept of *aequabilitas*, which means that men are on the same level: 'The other aspect of justice is equity: I do not refer to the equity of judging well, laudable though it is in a just man, but that which involves putting oneself on the same level as others— what Cicero calls equability'. *Aequabilitas* was not a central plank of Cicero's political philosophy. It was, nevertheless, according to Lactantius, part of God's vision for men when he created them:

God, who creates and breathes life into men, wanted all to be on the same level, that is equal; he set before them all the same conditions of life, he endowed them all with a capacity for wisdom, he promised them all immortality: no one is cut off from his heavenly blessings. For just as He gives all an equal share of his one Light, and showers his rain upon all, supplies them with food, and accords them the sweet rest of sleep, so he bestows on all equity and virtue.

God appears, however, to have settled for spiritual equality. Lactantius now reverts to language familiar from earlier theologians:

In his eyes no one is a slave, no one a master; and if we all have the same father, so we are all his sons, enjoying equal rights. No one is poor in his sight unless he lacks justice, no one is rich unless he is laden with the virtues, no one has reached the heights of perfection unless he has achieved all the grades of virtue.

There follows, however, a remarkable critique of Graeco-Roman society for being inegalitarian, for failing to realize God's utopian vision:

That is why neither Romans nor Greeks have been capable of possessing justice, because they have kept men unequal, divided into many different grades, from poor to rich, from lowly to powerful, from private citizen to the highest regal power. Where all are not equal, there is no equality, and that very inequality excludes justice, for the whole force of justice lies in making equal those who when they come into this life have been established in the same condition.

This is not fortuitous. When slavery makes a reappearance, which it does immediately, the social critique is finished, and Lactantius has taken refuge in the safe haven of Pauline metaphor. He can now acknowledge institutional slavery as an aspect of his own world and dismiss it as of no consequence in the sight of God. The passage ends with the juxtaposition and virtual identification of brotherhood (and by implication sonship) and slavery:

> Someone will say: 'Are there not among you some poor, some rich, some slaves, some masters?' ... Since we measure all human things not by the body, but by the spirit, and, though the condition of the bodies may be diversified, there are not slaves among us, but we regard them and we speak of them as brothers in spirit and as fellow-slaves in religion ...
>
> (*Diuinae institutiones* 5. 14. 15–15. 6)

SONS AND SLAVES IN AUGUSTINE

Augustine's voluminous works yield a rich harvest of texts relating to sons and slaves (Klein 1988; Corcoran 1985; Poque 1984; Shaw 1987a). My three main texts are taken from sermons recently discovered by Dolbeau at Mainz, and I choose them because they are both unfamiliar and inherently interesting (even if not entirely novel in all their details).[10]

Mainz 62, *De calendis ianuariis: contra paganos, de uero mediatore Christo et de falso mediatore diabolo*, is a sermon of 1545 lines.[11] Its message is that Christians should not undermine the attack on pagan idol-worship by themselves indulging in the veneration of columns, statues, churches, angels, or martyrs and their shrines. God alone should be worshipped. In the course of the discussion of martyrs, Augustine conjures up the image of the household in the following way (lines 264–81):

> Why have we said this? So that, when we attack the pagans, we do not give them an excuse for attacking us. You come to the places of the martyrs so as to take away a pious memory in your hearts, and so that, from the honour won by the martyrs, there may arise a devotion for the God who did not desert the martyrs in their suffering, but aided them as they did battle, and crowned them in their victory. Thus you make yourselves worthy objects of the prayers of martyrs. As a rule a good slave is deeply indignant if he is honoured while his master is despised, a good slave who has actually been transformed from a slave into a son. In one respect he is still a slave, who is destined to be made a son out of a slave, and in another respect he is already a son. To be a slave in fear is one thing, and

---

[10] As announced in *Revue des Études Augustiniennes* 36/2 (1990), 355–9.

[11] *Recherches Augustiniennes* 26 (1992), 90–141.

a son in love another. A great house has everything: hired workers, slaves and sons. Hired workers are those who look for worldly gains within the church; they are those of whom the apostle says that they do not proclaim the good news in purity. And yet he permits them, saying: 'Let Christ be proclaimed, whether for opportunistic reasons or in truth.' Slaves are those who do what a master bids them in fear. They are actually of the house, in fact they are nearer the centre of a great house than hired workers are; of these slaves sons are made, when they begin to serve out of love. So, as I said at the beginning, a great house has everything.

What do we think the martyrs are, my brothers? God forbid that we classify them among the hired workers, nor among those who are not yet sons. For they loved Christ, and out of love for him despised not only all the pleasures of the world but also all torments...

Much later Augustine returns to the earlier theme, according to which only God is to be worshipped, referring this time to the angels (lines 1164–72):

They are servants, doing what they have been bidden to do, referring our prayers to God, not themselves exacting them from God. No angel says to man: 'I have offered your prayer in the sight of the glory of God.' Yet *he* did not ask the angel, and *he* did not ask God: as a servant, he offered his prayer. Surely he did not say, as do perverse and corrupt ministers of certain powers: 'Give me something, if you want me to take a message, if you want me to admit you.' Our Lord does not have a great house of that kind. His slaves love him, his sons love him.

The main points for our purposes are two:

1. At the heart of the text is a distinction between sons and slaves. Slaves obey their master out of fear, whereas the hallmark of the father–son relationship is love: 'aliud seruus timore, aliud filius caritate' (lines 272–3). The *timor/caritas* distinction, though conventional and somewhat prescriptive, is grounded in the status distinction between slaves and sons recognized in law and custom; it also presumably draws to some extent from experience in the household. However, it would be quite another thing to claim that it tallied with actual attitudes and behaviour in contemporary North African society.[12]

2. Next, Augustine has slave evolving into son—not any slave, but a *bonus seruus*. All that is required is that the slave begin to serve with love. The martyr is like neither the hired worker nor the

[12] The *timor/caritas* distinction may be broken down or qualified. See e.g. *Sermones* 297. 2 (PL 39. 2314): both slave and son fear, but the slave fears torture, the son love (i.e. the love that issues in punishment); *Enarrationes in Psalmos* (hereafter *En. Ps.*) 70. 1. 1 (CCL 39. 941): 'multum enim mouet Dei amor et timor: timor Dei quia iustus est, amor, quia misericors est'; *En. Ps.* 118. 31. 3 (CCL 40. 1771): fathers are feared and loved by pious sons.

'not yet son', but is rather a model *bonus seruus* who is now called *filius*. Slave and son in this usage would seem to be synonymous, and we note that Christ is introduced several times as the archetypical *bonus seruus*. But Augustine can also write: 'his slaves love him, his sons love him', preserving the shell of the distinction, at least. But in general, there can be no dispute that with this stage in the argument Augustine is operating within another realm, that of the spirit. Nor am I tempted to suggest that his argument reflects and is influenced by behaviour patterns in his society; for example, the status confusion that apparently arose from mixed marriages, in particular between slave men and free women.[13]

In Mainz 54, *Super uerbis apostoli: O altitudo diuitiarum et scientia Dei*,[14] Augustine blurs the son–slave distinction in a different way: instead of envisaging the promotion of the slave, that is, the good slave, into a son, he appears to depress the son to the level of the slave, making them equally subject to coercion from the *paterfamilias* and from God. The theme is already familiar from Lactantius. Augustine shares his predecessor's concern with explaining and justifying the anger of God. The key passage runs as follows (lines 91–125):

But first see this working out in actual daily life—you can learn from this how God's mercy has not abandoned mortal men—there being certain comparisons that can be drawn from human existence which show us that punishment can be inflicted in mercy. What am I to say? You administer discipline to your slave, and in the act of disciplining you show pity precisely at the moment when you appear to be inflicting punishment; however, I do not say this to the slave. Perhaps you are angry with the slave to the point of hating him. You should not be, if you are a Christian. You should not be, if you keep before you that while 'slave' and 'master' are different words, 'man' and 'man' are not. You should not pursue a sinning slave with hatred. But, insofar as slaves are men, let us discard this comparison, and replace slave with son. No one is capable of not loving his sons, and there is no praise to be earned by a man for loving his son. The master says: 'For what profit will you gain if you love them who love you? Surely tax-collectors do as much?' How much more are sons loved, whom

---

[13] For this phenomenon, see Evans-Grubbs (1993*b*), drawing almost entirely on legal sources. My impression is that this world is not reflected in the sermons and theological works of Augustine, and this despite the fact, revealed in a letter, that the status of the children born of just such unions was sometimes at issue before Augustine's own episcopal court. It is interesting that Augustine has to seek advice on the subject from his fellow-bishop and trained jurisconsult Alypius. See *Epistulae* 24* in *CSEL* 88. The idea of the promotion of slaves into (adopted) sons is found already in Origen and Anastasius: see Widdicombe (1994). See also Augustine, *En. Ps.* 32. 2. 7 (*CCL* 38. 253).

[14] *Revue des Études Augustiniennes* 27/2 (1991), 271–88.

men beget to succeed them. No one, to be sure, can by the very law of nature hate him whom he has brought into the world. There is nothing to praise a man in this, which is found also in the animal kingdom. No one praises a man who loves his sons. You don't just find this among tame animals. Fierce lions soften over their cubs, tigers love their progeny, snakes tend their eggs and nurture their young. So, if those things which are apparently created savage and cruel do not maintain their savagery and cruelty towards their offspring, what is so special about a man loving his son? But, my brethren, I have said these things besides so that you may see that a punishment can be inflicted in mercy, taking children as an example, taking a case where hatred is impossible. A man sees his son descending to pride, lifting himself up against his father, taking for himself more than he should, wanting to dissolve himself in empty pleasures, wanting to squander what he does not yet possess. And when he does all this he is cheerful, laughing, rejoicing, gloating. His father, however, stops all this with reproof, punishment, beatings. He wipes the grin off his son's face, and substitutes tears. It looks as if he has taken away something good and brought evil in its place (Look what he has banished: mirth; and look what he has introduced: groans). Yet, if he had let that mirth go unpunished, he would have been cruel; it is in the forcing of tears that mercy is located. Thus, if a father who induces tears is found to be merciful, why do we not understand that our creator could have done what we proclaimed in song: 'God, you rejected us and put us down'? But why did he do this? Surely not for destruction, surely not for perdition? Hear what comes next: 'You were angered and you showed us pity.' Why is he angry with you, and justly so? Read the following words in conjunction: 'Before I was humiliated, I sinned.' What benefit did it bring you that you were rejected and put down? 'It is good for me that you have humiliated me, so that I may learn your judgments.'

Augustine takes the argument a stage further with an elaborate comparison between two tripartite vertical structures. The first is the order of existence, with God above men, and men above other created things. The second is the hierarchy of the household, with a master of free status at the top, below him a slave who, however, doubles up as master because he too has a slave, and at the third and lowest level, the slave of a slave, a *seruus uicarius*.

Augustine has the slave/master punished for raising himself against his master. The agent of punishment is the slave of the slave, who is instructed by the overall master to beat his own master; or, in another formulation, it is our body, which also plays a second role as the cause of our sin, our attempting to rise above our station. As Augustine puts it (lines 245–9):

Thus our God, because we offended him, gave orders that we be tortured in relation to our body; our body was made mortal, and that is why we both suffer punishments and have dared to puff ourselves up against the master. Therefore we are now being beaten by our slave. We are being tortured in the torments of our flesh; the master humiliated us by having us beaten by a slave.

The argument about the motivation of God's punishment is clinched with a reference to the crucifixion: the father handed over his own son for punishment in mercy, the son handed himself over in mercy (lines 300–1).

I confine myself to two observations arising from this sermon which fit our present purposes:

1. Augustine does recognize a distinction between son and slave, not so much in the way they are treated, as in the way they are viewed. In both cases punishment can, and should, be imposed in mercy; in neither case should the miscreant be hated. With slaves, this is because they are men. But there the similarity between sons and slaves ends. Augustine switches from slaves to sons in order to advance the argument to its next stage, where he wants to claim that punishment is inflicted not just out of pity but out of love. It can be said only of sons that they are loved in accordance with the law of nature, a law respected as much by beasts as by men, as much by wild beasts as by tame beasts.

2. Slave and son have a lot in common, and that includes liability to physical punishment. It does not seem to matter to Augustine who is being beaten, son or slave, in the service of the theological point that he is making. In the first part of the argument it is mainly the son, in the second part it is the slave. Both stand equally for us humans, who are subject to punishment, and deservedly so, because we sinned first (lines 250–1).

If there is some surface inconsistency in Augustine's handling of sons and slaves, the reason is that Augustine has a foot in two worlds, the material and the spiritual. But there is a complication, because the two worlds appear to come together in the matter of punishment. Augustine is talking theologically of the consequences of the Fall, for man and for God, the necessity and inevitability of suffering; and his theology of punishment is based on biblical texts. At the same time, his doctrine may well—and is commonly thought to—reflect behavioural patterns in contemporary North African society. For Suzanne Poque, who has most usefully compiled an assemblage of Augustinian texts relating to domestic discipline, the image of the chastising father 'qui semblait à première vue tout devoir à l'Écriture, apparaît profondément enracinée dans le vécu quotidien de l'Antiquité romaine tardive' (Poque 1984: 203). In other words, the physical punishment of sons was ubiquitous in contemporary society; and the *flagellum* (whip), the weapon which is most commonly mentioned in such contexts, was routinely used against sons (ibid. 193–224). It would follow, incidentally, that the *flagellum* could not have served as the dividing line between free and slave in late antiquity—as it did, according to Saller, in the world governed by Roman law in the classical period of Roman history (Saller 1991: 151–65).

I would advise caution, even in this case where the issue might seem clear-cut,[15] for two main reasons. First, Augustine's teaching on punishment is, as I have indicated already, deeply rooted in the Scriptures. His discussion frequently leans on well-known biblical texts such as Proverbs 3: 11–12 and Hebrews 12: 5–8, which support the physical punishment of sons by fathers. Moreover, as with the symbolism of slavery, so with that of flagellation, Augustine has the suffering of the sinless Christ before him as the supreme example. In consequence, no one can say he is unjustly disciplined, not even a 'slave of God', because all have sinned (Poque 1984: 215–16).

Second, Augustine's utterances, even when he is apparently operating in descriptive mode, need to be weighed with care. What price this generalization? 'It is a general characteristic of mankind that the son is set against his father.'[16] How trustworthy is this comment?: 'Parents are accustomed to disown bad sons, lest they suffer embarrassment because of them.'[17] Again, when Augustine writes: 'We see fathers whip their rebellious sons, but sometimes in despair they dismiss them to live where they might,'[18] we can legitimately ask of how many such cases he had first-hand experience.

It would be wrong to dismiss out of hand Augustine the preacher and theologian as a source for social history.[19] One may nevertheless wonder whether his view of North African society, in so far as it is revealed in his homilies and doctrinal treatises, was not darkened by his own deeply pessimistic view of humanity, and whether in his work description is not to some extent contaminated by prescription.

Be that as it may, the safer course undoubtedly is to stay with Augustine's own attitudes. His enthusiasm for discipline, both inside and outside the household, is notorious, and needs no special emphasis.[20] What of his attitude to slavery and to slaves? We should

---

[15] My approach differs from that of Shaw (1987*a*), who harbours few doubts.

[16] e.g. *Annotationes in Iob* 38 (CSEL 28. 2. 600–1).

[17] *En. Ps.* 44. 11 (CCL 38. 501–2).   [18] *Epistula ad Galatas* 39 (PL 35. 2132).

[19] *En. Ps.* 93. 17 (CCL 39. 1318).

[20] Poque (1984: 194, 222–3), referring e.g. to *En. Ps.* 37. 18 (CCL 38. 397); *Sermones* 56. 17 (PL 38. 385).

be no readier to ascribe to him than to Paul progressive, let alone egalitarian, views. Augustine was as keen as Paul in keeping slaves in their servile state. In the following passage, for example, the content of the message is thoroughly Pauline, even if it is stated with a lack of inhibition more characteristic of Augustine than of Paul:

Look, he has not made free men out of slaves, but good slaves out of bad slaves. How much the rich owe to Christ, who is keeping their house at peace for them! If there was an unfaithful slave somewhere, Christ would turn him round; he would not say to him: 'Get rid of your master. Now you know who the true master is; your earthly master may be impious and hostile, while you are faithful and just; it is unworthy for so just and faithful a slave to serve an impious and unfaithful master.' But he has not said *that* to the slave, but rather: 'Serve.' And to encourage the slave, he has said: 'Serve as I have done; I served bad masters before you.' If the Lord of Heaven and earth through whom all things were made was a slave to unworthy people . . . how much more should a man not disdain to serve even a bad master with all his heart and with complete goodwill?

(*Enarrationes in Psalmos* 124. 7)[21]

But we are given a more interesting insight into the mind of Augustine from another of the new sermons, Mainz 5, *De oboedientia*.[22] Here Augustine is chiding the congregation at Carthage for creating a rumpus in the church the previous day and forcing him to abandon his sermon. After chastising himself for not consulting his host, the primate Aurelius, before he gave up, he rebukes the congregation for their display of disobedience to their bishops. In so doing, he gives the New Testament message to Christians to serve one another an inegalitarian twist (lines 223–43):

But someone might say, 'My bishop should follow my Lord's example and serve me.' My dear people, I say to this—and let those who are capable understand this—if your bishop were not a servant, he would not be giving orders. For he is a servant who gives beneficial orders, he serves with vigilance, he serves with consideration, he serves with concern, he serves, in a word, with love. For he who came here to minister certainly gave orders to his disciples. [Augustine's first example is of the preparation of the Paschal feast, which Jesus delegated to others. He then turns to the entry into Jerusalem.] . . . He said, 'Go into the village opposite and you will find there the colt of an ass tied up, on which no one has sat; bring it to me . . .' They listened to him, went off, and did his bidding. Did anyone hold back, did anyone say: 'Why does he want the colt brought to him? It can't be the case that someone who has brought the dead back

---

[21] Cf. *En. Ps.* 32. 2. 6 (CCL 38. 252): it is better to be a slave to a man than to a vice.
[22] *Revue des Études Augustiniennes* 28/1 (1992), 63–79.

to life has worn himself out with walking.' Listen, slave: do what you are bidden by him who looks after your welfare, who attends to your safety.

Augustine turns to allegory—the village stands for this world and its values, which include disobedience; the colt stands for the Gentiles, bound up by the devil and not yet having carried a prophet. Augustine still has to find a *dramatis persona* for his audience, and indeed for himself and bishop Aurelius (lines 263–76):

What then do you want to be, my brethren: those who released the colt, or the colt itself? You would not dare claim for yourselves the role of those by whom the colt was released; it was the apostles who filled that role. That is the role of people under orders: we sustain that role, with our utmost solicitude, by means of the powers that the lord thinks fit to assign to us. No, we are talking of you. You are the colt, you obey those who lead you off so that you can carry the lord. So, my dear people, consider how the disciples released the colt and led it to the master. They led it, and it followed them; they did not drag it along, and it did not resist them. Yet—and we are speaking now of the service that we perform—when the disciples led the colt to the lord, they were doing a service for the colt; so too we do a service for you when we lead you to the lord, when we teach and advise obedience; if service were not being given you in your weakness, you would not be listening to us today.[23]

CONCLUSION

Nietzsche criticized the 'slave morality', the ethic of humiliation, which Christianity supposedly fostered, building on the Jewish heritage. Why did Christian theologians from Paul to Augustine (and beyond) make such free use of the image of slavery, applying it even to themselves and their Christian brethren, 'fellow-slaves in religion' (Lactantius), so that to be called a slave was a compliment and a privilege? Self-abasement, suffering, service, slavery are at the heart of Christian doctrine.

The other side of the coin, however, is that slavery is the key to salvation, and as such the badge of a rather exclusive club. This theme, already adumbrated by Paul (and drawn ultimately from Old Testament sources), is developed and elaborated by Augustine. We are all slaves, but there are slaves and slaves.

First, within the Christian community of slaves, there is a hierarchy of authority, of which the living proof and exemplum is the

---

[23] Cf. *En. Ps.* 31. 2. 23 (*CCL* 38. 241): a different version of the colt image, emphasizing discipline, and involving promotion from pack-animal to son!

vertically structured institutional church. There are slaves who serve by giving orders, and there are slaves who serve by carrying out those orders without question. Did Paul have that vision? He could only have had it in embryo. The best part of four centuries of the historical development of an ecclesiastical establishment separated the two theologians.

Secondly, if we think in terms of the totality of humanity, there is a division between bad slaves, that is, Jews, pagans, heretics, and Christians still enslaved to sin (Klein 1988), and good slaves, who are faithful servants of the Christian God.

Slavery, then, both divides mankind from God, and divides men from men, the damned from the called (or better, the chosen). It is within the latter group, of the called, that conventional status-divisions fade away, as slave and son become substitutable (as in Paul or Lactantius), or as slave evolves into son (as in Augustine). True, in the darker vision of Lactantius and Augustine, slave and son merge as joint objects of divine chastisement, although we are constantly reminded that without such punishment (better, correction) we cannot qualify for the inheritance.

All this is metaphor. We have to ask whether, for the Church Fathers, slavery and sonship had two more or less independent existences, one metaphorical, in the land of theology, the other physical, in Graeco-Roman society. As I read the evidence, the two worlds intersected surprisingly little.

Thus, despite the blurring of the son–slave distinction that occurs in Christian writers from Paul to Augustine, they regarded the legal distinction between sons and slaves as still holding good in all essentials: Augustine certainly writes as if the distinction still operated in the fields of punishment and reward, so that slaves were still subjected to severer punishments, and sons were still looked to as heirs.[24] In general, Augustine clearly had no more interest in eliding the son–slave distinction in actuality than he had in breaking down the divisions between master and slave, father and son, and husband and wife.[25]

But because the metaphor in question is a 'homely' one, drawn from daily life, we must certainly consider the possibility that it can be treated as evidence not just for the existence of particular social

---

[24] Augustine oftens talks of the son as the potential heir who must be groomed for this role by stern discipline. See Poque (1984: 210–11); Shaw (1987a: 20–6). On brutal punishments (much worse than the *flagellum*) to which slaves were liable, see Poque (1984: 284–96).

[25] *Tractatus in Iohannis Euangelium* 30. 8 (CCL 36. 293 = PL 35. 1636): inequality of father and son. For husband and wife, see now Mainz 41 (*De bono nuptiarum*) and 42 (*De honorandis uel contemnendis parentibus*), *Revue Bénédictine* 102 (1992), 275–82, 288–97.

and legal institutions, but also for the way they operated in contemporary society. The most plausible case for this is the theory of
divine punishment, which has been thought to reflect the relationship of African sons to their fathers. But how could this be shown?
How can we be led to agree with Shaw (1987a: 28) that the relationship was 'servile'? Weighing the patristic texts carefully (separat-
ing descriptive from prescriptive elements) is an essential first step.
But ideally one wants to have evidence of a different kind to draw
on. Finally, there is the problem of measuring the putative impact of
'real' father–son relations on Augustine's (or for that matter Lactantius')
theology as against other possible influences. As to the promotion of
slaves into sons, it would in my view be a mistake to see the development of this theological doctrine as a reflection of social phenomena,
for example, the status confusion between free and slave that apparently existed within certain households.[26]

As for the possibility that influence flowed in the other direction,
from the preacher to his audience: this is plausible enough as a
hypothesis, but is safest left at that level. Did the Christian heads
of households who listened to Augustine's sermons think twice before
disciplining their sons and slaves, temper their punishments, make
generous use of the facility of *manumissio in ecclesia* (freedom granted
in a church in the presence of the congregation), and so on? We
cannot know if they did, and in any case, the modest 'programme'
of humane treatment of dependants sketched above does not coincide with the prescriptions of the bishop of Hippo Regius, as we
have them.

[26] Evans-Grubbs (1993b) describes the phenomenon but does not raise the issue of its
possible impact on patristic writing.

6

Out of Sight, Out of Mind: Elderly Members of the Roman Family

TIM PARKIN

While the nuclear family has been the focus of most recent work on the Roman family, scholarly attention is beginning to turn again towards less central figures. But one group which has received very little attention has been the elderly. Full treatment would require, among other things, consideration of general social attitudes towards the elderly. Here I wish to consider only a few aspects of one sector of this age group within the family: the status of elderly parents and their means of livelihood, and their degree of dependence in differing circumstances.[1] What ties of affection and duty existed between adult offspring and their aged parents? How different was the life of the aged male head of a wealthy family, for example, from that of an impoverished, elderly widow with no surviving descendants? I will first consider the expectations and rights people had with regard to forms of support or welfare in their old age, and then the effect old age itself might have had on such rights.

WELFARE FOR THE ELDERLY: IDEALS AND REALITIES

In any society welfare aid towards the elderly, as towards other sectors in society, may be of various types, and may be given on a formal, institutionalized, and regular basis, or at an informal, individual level, as a single act. Again, it may take different forms, through the provision of food and goods, of money or housing, of medicine and nursing, or less directly as exemption from certain financial burdens or the granting of certain privileges. It may even take the form of 'moral support' or the enhancement of status. In the

I wish to acknowledge a special debt of gratitude to Fergus Millar, who guided and encouraged me in the early stages of writing this paper.

[1] Brief general treatment in Dixon (1992: 149–57). There are particularly good insights into lower-class families needing children as a form of old-age security in Bradley (1991: 117–18). In a different context, note also Shaw (1991: 66–90).

modern Western world, there are institutionalized pension schemes and the like, and an increased awareness both of the problems faced by old people and of the contributions they can make to society—not to mention their voting power. As a consequence most elderly people today can expect some form of old-age welfare independent of their own or their families' resources, though some may still live within the family group. In the ancient world the situation was very different. Furthermore, the situation in ancient Greece—or, more specifically, in classical Athens—contrasts sharply with that in Roman society, and so it will be useful to consider the differences between the two classical societies.

The precept of honouring one's parents is an ancient one, common to most civilizations and to most periods of history.[2] Among the Romans *pietas* (duty towards gods, country, and parents) expressed this virtue very well. It was epitomized in the character of Aeneas, himself a father, and his 'dutifulness' towards his aged father Anchises. *Pietas*, it must be remembered, was a reciprocal arrangement: parents had the duty of bringing up their children, and the children in return were expected to repay this 'debt', of both life and nurture, by providing support for their parents when they in their turn were in need—in their old age.[3] This expected reciprocity, in short, may be seen as a form of old-age security, operated privately but promoted at a public level, sometimes by legislation. But did it operate effectively?

In ancient Greece the notion of a debt owed to one's parents for having been reared, which must be repaid in their old age (by providing food and shelter, and burial when they died) is at least as old as Homer and continues throughout the classical period and beyond.[4] The same idea may be found among the Romans too, particularly under the influence of the Stoic creed.[5] The idea was commonly

---

[2] In general, cf. A. Lumpe and H. Karpp, 'Eltern', *RAC* 4 (1959), 1198–1203; and for more recent history e.g. Thomson (1991: 194–221).

[3] This expectation, frequently expressed in Greek literature also and reinforced throughout the education of the young Greek or Roman, may sound coldly calculating, bereft as it is of any notion of familial love: cf. e.g. Xenophon, *Memorabilia* 2. 2. 3; Seneca, *De beneficiis, passim*, esp. 3. 31–2. On the reciprocal nature of *patria potestas*, see esp. Saller (1988; 1991).

[4] To take only one, trivial example, as synonyms for παῖδες: Pollux (*Onomasticon* 3. 12) includes among his list νοσοκόμοι, γηροτρόφοι, and ταφεῖς (those who nurse the sick, care for the elderly, and bury the dead). In view of recent new trends in expectations regarding the welfare state in the Western world, the phenomenon of childbearing as a form of old-age security in various modern societies has increasingly become a renewed object of investigation, with especial interest in the fact that fertility levels are recorded as increasing over time in such societies, apparently in order to ensure old-age security; see e.g. D. C. Clay and J. E. Vander Haar, 'Patterns of Intergenerational Support and Childbearing in the Third World', *Population Studies* 47 (1993), 67–83.

[5] e.g. Cicero, *De officiis* 1. 17. 58 (influenced by Panaetius, the 2nd-cent. BC Stoic philosopher) and Seneca, *De beneficiis, passim*; cf. Musonius Rufus 15, 17. Lucretius 4. 1256 states that a man and woman have children 'ut possent gnatis munire senectam'; cf. Cornelius

expressed, indeed, that one motivation for a couple to have children was just so that they might have someone to tend them in their old age. Certainly a common lament at the death of one's offspring was for the loss of support in one's old age, and the prospect of being childless was regarded as most unfortunate, especially because a potential source of solace and welfare in one's old age had been lost.[6] This could be criticized in antiquity as a rather selfish sentiment on the part of parents,[7] and there was some philosophical debate as to whether a child's devotion towards his or her parents was due to natural feelings or to a sense of obligation.[8] At any rate, people who lived to see several generations of descendants born were regarded as particularly fortunate,[9] both because they were sure to have someone to tend their old age and because they could die in the secure knowledge that their name would live on. What is of particular interest at this stage is to discover whether such a 'duty' was merely hoped for or expected, or whether it was in fact directly imposed on children by the state.

It was commonly regarded as a law of nature and of the gods that children should treat their parents well.[10] Nature, indeed, provided a model for this in the way that some animals were believed to nurse

Nepos, frag. 59, the alleged letter of Cornelia to her son Gaius Gracchus, upbraiding him for causing trouble when it is his duty to see to it 'ut quam minimum sollicitudinis in senecta haberem'. For the same idea in St Augustine, cf. Shaw (1987*a*: 19–20, 43).

[6] e.g. Hesiod, *Theogony* 604–5; Aeschylus, *Persae* 576–84; Euripides, frag. 952 [Nauck], *Medea* 1033; *Anthologia Palatina* 7. 466, 7. 647, 16. 131; Cicero, *Pro Caelio* 80; *Pro Rege Deiotaro* 2; [Cicero], *Ad Herennium* 4. 39. 51; Vergil, *Aeneid* 9. 481, 11. 160–3, 12. 43–57; [Vergil], *Ciris* 314; [Quintilian], *Declamationes maiores* 10. 1; Apuleius, *Metamorphoses* 8. 19–20; Quintus Smyrnaeus 3. 446–51, 477–8; Ausonius, *Parentalia* 11 (his grief at the death of his grandson, his *spes certa*). Cf. Wiedemann (1989: 40–1) for relevant inscriptional material, and *CIL* 6. 18086. Compare the popular story of Pythes, who pleaded (to no avail) with Xerxes to let him keep at home one son to tend his old age (Herodotus 7. 27, 38; Seneca, *De ira* 3. 16. 3–4; Elder Pliny, *NH* 33. 47. 137; Plutarch, *Moralia* 263a–b).

[7] [Plutarch], *Moralia* 111e, asserts that parents who mourn for those who die young mourn selfishly if their grief is due to the fact that 'they have been cut off from some gratification or profit or comfort in old age (γηροβοσκία)'. Seneca, *De matrimonio* (frag. 13. 58, *ap.* Jerome, *Aduersus Iouinianum* 1. 47), states that it is sheer stupidity to marry and have children in order to ensure the immortality of one's name, to secure heirs, and to have help in old age: it matters little when you are dead, and in any case a son may die before you or else be unwilling to help.   [8] Diogenes Laertius 2. 93, 96; Plutarch, *Moralia* 497a–b.

[9] Cf. Elder Pliny, *NH* 7. 13. 60: one of the many exceptional circumstances connected with Augustus was that he lived to see his granddaughter's grandson (*neptis suae nepotem*, M. Iunius Silanus) who was born in the year of his death. Q. Metellus Macedonicus died leaving 6 children and 11 grandchildren (cf. Valerius Maximus 7. 1. 1 (*De felicitate*); Velleius Paterculus 1. 11. 5–7; *Anthologia Palatina* 7. 260; Elder Pliny, *NH* 7. 43. 139–40). In 4 BC a freeborn plebeian ('ex ingenua plebe') of Fiesole, C. Crispinius Hilarus, had in his procession 27 grandchildren and 18 great-grandchildren (Elder Pliny, *NH* 7. 3. 60). Cf. Pliny's letter to his wife's grandfather (8.10) on Calpurnia's miscarriage.

[10] e.g. Xenophon, *Memorabilia* 4. 4. 19–20; Demosthenes 10. 40–1; [Demosthenes] 25. 65–6; Plutarch, *Moralia* 479f; Theophrastus, frag. 152 [Wimmer] (= Stobaeus, *Eclogues* 3. 3. 42); Diogenes Laertius 7. 108; Valerius Maximus 1. 1. 13; 5. 4. 7.

their old parents,[11] in particular the stork, a bird which came to symbolize filial piety by—so it was believed—voluntarily caring for its old parents by providing them with food and shelter.[12] It was felt that humans too often failed to live up to the model that nature provided. For even if one's children lived long enough themselves, there was always the possibility that they would be financially unable or unwilling to support their aged parents.[13] One way round this problem might be to force offspring to see to the welfare of their elderly parents. In classical Athens legislation existed to ensure just that: children had a *legal* as well as a moral obligation to maintain their parents in their old age.[14]

This Athenian statute, attributed to Solon, stated that he who did not τρέφειν his parents was to be ἄτιμος, deprived of citizen rights. Children accused of maltreatment of parents were liable under a charge of γονέων κάκωσις, a charge which—uniquely in the case of a *graphe* (public prosecution)—any third party could bring without the risk of penalty if they withdrew the case or failed to secure at least one-fifth of the votes.[15] Furthermore, it appears that this legal duty extended as far as grandparents and even great-grandparents, though special pleading rather than legal reality may account for this suggestion. Our evidence for such an extension of the obligation comes from legal cases where a party argues that, as they would have been bound to maintain grandparents if they were alive, they should be legally able to inherit from them now that they are dead (Isaeus 1. 39, 8. 32). However, the primary stress was on the maintenance of

[11] Aelian, *De natura animalium* 9. 1 (the old lion is cared for by its young—no legislation is necessary, since nature teaches them; cf. 6. 61 and 7. 2 for old elephants); Oppian, *Cynegetica* 2. 343 ff. (with an explicit contrast with humans); Elder Pliny, *NH* 8. 82. 224: shrew-mice, *sorices*, 'genitores suos fessos senecta alunt insigni pietate'.

[12] Among many examples, cf. e.g. Elder Pliny, *NH* 10. 32. 63, and Petronius, *Satyricon* 55: 'ciconia . . . grata peregrina hospita pietaticultrix'. That the symbolism of the stork was widespread may be seen also in the verb ἀντιπελαργεῖν, 'to repay care' (cf. *Suda* s.v.; Hesychius 5453; *Etymologicum magnum* 114. 11; Zenobius, *Epitome* 1. 94; Origen, *Contra Celsum* 4. 98). For the stork in Roman art and on coins, cf. J. M. C. Toynbee, *Animals in Roman Life and Art* (London, 1973), 244–5. For birds as symbols of *pietas*, cf. Thompson (1936: 99, 176, 203, 223, 330).

[13] Herondas, *Mimiambi* 3: the complaints of a mother concerning her useless son who offers no prospect of support in his parents' old age.

[14] This need not imply that a legal obligation had more force than a moral one or an unwritten law (contrast Lacey (1968: 116): 'the city laid it on children as a legal obligation, not merely a moral duty'). The opposite could in fact be true, especially if a law is imposed to mend a breakdown in social sanctions. One thinks of Tacitus on the Germans (*Germania* 19. 5): 'plusque ibi boni mores ualent quam alibi bonae leges'; cf. Horace, *Odes* 3. 24. 35–6.

[15] Diogenes Laertius 1. 55, describing it as one of Solon's finest laws; [Aristotle], *Athenaion Politeia* 56. 6; cf. Lysias 13. 91. Harrison (1968: 77–8) believes that this was a *graphe*, not a *dike* (private action); though this is probable (cf. e.g. Demosthenes 58. 32), it is not certain (Harpocration, s.v. κάκωσις, calls it a *dike*).

one's parents. Indeed, 'Do you treat your parents well?' was one of the questions asked of a candidate for the archonship and for other public offices.[16] Athenians seem to have taken their duty seriously.

Of course it was not just a case of refraining from maltreating one's parents: positive services were also expected, such as the provision of food and shelter, and the observation of the due rites after death.[17] Such a duty, we are told, was laid on all offspring, with very few exceptions. Hence, keeping an eye on the future, there was every motivation to have children or, failing that possibility, to adopt them.[18] But there were potential negative aspects to such a system as well as beneficial ones: the elderly could be seen to be totally dependent on the younger generation and lose their power when they no longer held the purse-strings. Such, for example, is the situation described in Aristophanes' *Wasps*, where the son Bdelykleon is depicted as the master of the house and his aged father Philokleon is reduced to childlike dependency. Bdelykleon promises support for his father, but there is a marked lack of any filial respect here (736–40, trans. A. H. Sommerstein):[19] 'I'll support him, providing everything that's suitable for an old man, gruel to lick up, a soft thick cloak, a goatskin mantle, a whore to massage his prick and his loins.' As Philokleon later complains, he is being treated like a child by his own son—a complete reversal of roles: 'At the moment I'm not in control of my own property, because I'm young; and I'm closely watched—my little son keeps his eye on me and he's mean-tempered, and a cress-paring-cumin-splitter into the bargain' (1354–7). This is of course a scene from comedy, not a depiction

---

[16] Dinarchus 2. 17–18; [Aristotle], *Athenaion Politeia* 55. 3; Demosthenes 57. 70; Aeschines 1. 28; Andocides 1. 74; Xenophon, *Memorabilia* 2. 2. 13; Pollux, *Onomasticon* 8. 85.

[17] Xenophon, *Memorabilia* 2. 2; Demosthenes 24. 107; Lysias 13. 45; Theophrastus, *Characters* 6. 6. The moral duty persisted, as the 2nd-cent. AD Stoic philosopher Hierocles (*ap.* Stobaeus, *Florilegium* 25. 53 (Hense 4. 642)) makes clear in discussing proper conduct towards parents: 'For our parents, therefore, we should provide food freely, and such as is fitting for the weakness of old age; besides this, a bed, sleep, oil, a bath, and clothing—in short, general physical necessities, so that they should never lack any of these things; thus we imitate the care they took in rearing ourselves when we were infants.' Cf. id. *ap.* Stobaeus, *Florilegium* 22. 1. 24 (4. 503H), on marriage being beneficial, since it produces children who help us now while we are strong 'and when we are worn out, burdened with old age, they will be fine allies'.

[18] Cf. notes 4, 5 above. In Isaeus 2. 10 it is stated that Menecles adopted a son in order to have someone to tend his old age (γηροτροφεῖν). For the Romans also adoption was an effective means of ensuring that there was someone there to tend one's old age; on *adrogatio* being possible only for those in old age, see *D.* 1. 7. 15. 2, Ulpian, with Cicero, *De domo sua* 13. 34–14. 38, and Aulus Gellius 5. 19. 4–6. For adoption as an inheritance strategy, cf. e.g. M. Corbier (1991).

[19] Cf. Aristophanes, *Wasps*, 67–70 (Philokleon is a prisoner in his own home), 340–1, 441–7, 1003–7, 1380–1 (Bdelykleon to Philokleon: 'you're worn out and not able to do anything'). Cf. also *Birds* 757–9, 1347–71.

128   *Elderly Members of the Roman Family*

of real life, but its humour surely lies at least in part in its underlying reality, that an aged father could be treated in this way by his own son. Philokleon's complaint of being treated like a child is reminiscent of a common proverb, to be found not only in Attic comedy but in classical literature in general, that old age is a second childhood.[20] The logic behind such a metaphor, if indeed any underlying logic is to be expected, may be partly explained by the observation of the physical and mental decline experienced by many of the elderly and the dependence on others brought about by this. In Athens, in economic terms at any rate, old people may have been seen as children for the very reason that they had lost their independence and, like Philokleon, felt themselves to be prisoners in their own (or rather their children's) homes.[21]

While actual legislation did exist in Athens of the fourth century and apparently earlier which aimed to enforce the moral precept of treating one's parents well, particularly in their old age, the legislation may not have been conceived of or implemented *purely* in the interests of the elderly, but also to secure the welfare of the *oikos* as a whole. Athenian legislation in effect made the son (and in some cases, perhaps, the daughter—or rather her husband) the head of the household; at times, no doubt, this happened against the wishes of the father. We shall return to this point below in dealing with the effects of senility in old age, where it will be seen that just such a situation as that of which Philokleon complained was a potential legal reality.

According to Vitruvius (6, pr. 3), the comic poet Alexis stated that the Athenians deserved praise:[22] 'quod omnium Graecorum leges cogunt parentes <ali> a liberis, Atheniensium non omnes nisi eos qui liberos artibus erudissent' ('because the laws of all the other Greeks compel children to maintain their parents, but those of Athens only applied to parents who had their children taught a trade'). If the first part of this statement is true we lack good evidence for it, but perhaps that is not so surprising since our sources are primarily concerned with Athens. There does survive, however, an inscription of the late fourth or early third century BC from Delphi which

---

[20] Δὶς παῖδες οἱ γέροντες, *bis pueri senes*. Among several dozen extant examples from as early as the 6th cent. BC, cf. e.g. Plautus, *Mercator* 295–6, 976; Varro, *Menippean Satires*, frag. 91 Bücheler (= Aulus Gellius 7. 5. 10) cf. Cèbe 3. 406–7; Seneca, *Historiae, ap.* Lactantius, *Institutiones diuinae* 2. 4. 14; Clement of Alexandria, *Stromata* 6. 2. 19. 5–8; *Suda* s.v. δὶς παῖδες and καταγηράσαις.

[21] As Schaps (1979: 84) points out, the protection bestowed on the elderly parent by the archon also extended to orphans, *epikleroi*, and pregnant widows remaining in their husbands' homes—'to all those, in short, who were easily abused by the members of their *oikoi*'.

[22] It appears from Plutarch, *Moralia* 420d, that Alexis lived to be 106 years old (c.375–270 BC), so presumably he had some interest in the treatment of the elderly!

records the law that 'if anyone does not support (τρέφειν) his father and mother, this is to be reported to the *boule* who will bind the "non-provider" and send him off to prison'.[23]

From an earlier period, Herodotus (2. 35) reports that in Egypt, 'sons need not support their parents unless they choose, but daughters must, whether they choose to or not'. The main point here is clearly to contrast the situation with that in Athens, where it would naturally have been conceived of as the son's duty—how true it was in Egypt at the time is impossible to know. From Roman Egypt, however, we have more substantial evidence for the care expected from children by their elderly parents (Taubenschlag 1932; 1956), though no legislation seems to have enforced such welfare. Often it appears to have been the case of parents negotiating with their children. The papyri preserve cases where the elderly father, and sometimes mother, promise to leave their property to their children after their death on the condition that they care for them in their old age and provide proper burial for them when they die.[24] Normally the changeover in legal ownership is explicitly stated to take place only after the death of the donor, but sometimes, in practice if not also in theory, during his own lifetime the father hands over ownership entirely to his children and becomes dependent on them.[25] Such may be seen to have been a regular function under Roman law of the *donatio mortis causa*, a gift in contemplation or anticipation of

[23] L. Lerat, 'Une loi de Delphes sur les devoirs des enfants envers leurs parents', *Revue de Philologie* 17 (1943), 62–86. It is noteworthy that in this case imprisonment is the punishment, rather than *atimia*, the penalty in Athens. But note Demosthenes 24. 103, 105, where it is stated that Solon enacted that if a person who had been found guilty of maltreating his parents had the temerity to enter the *agora* he would be put into prison. See also *Ephemeris Archaiologike* (1892), 67 (= *IG* 4. 493) for an inscription which suggests that a law protecting parents existed at Mycenae.

[24] For a list of the relevant papyri, see O. Montevecchi in *Aegyptus* 15 (1935), 73, supplemented by the list in *P. Vindob. Tandem* (1976), 204, to which add *P. Upss. Frid.* 1. On the Roman law in relation to Egypt, cf. Taubenschlag (1955: 204–7), and Husselmann (1957: 135–54), citing earlier literature.

[25] Thus, e.g. in *P. Mich.* 321 (AD 42), at the age of 65 the father, Orseus, divides his property among his four children (three sons and one daughter); it is stated that the division is to take place after Orseus' death but in effect it takes place immediately. One son (probably the oldest), Nestnephis, is to receive most of the property. In return, for the rest of Orseus' life Nestnephis is to provide his father with 12 artabas of wheat and 12 silver drachmas annually for food, clothes, and other expenses, and is to pay the tax due on the land and Orseus' trade taxes as a flute-player. For his part Orseus promises to keep the property intact until his death and not to give it to anyone else. In *P. Mich.* 322a (AD 46), on the other hand, there is no mention of the legal changeover of ownership taking place after the death of the father: here 69-year-old Psuphis and his 60-year-old wife Tetosiris divide their property (individually) among their sons, daughters, and a grandson (the son of a deceased third son). Possession is immediate, and in return the offspring are to provide food and money, pay any debts, and furnish burial for the elderly couple when they die.

death.[26] Strictly speaking, a *donatio mortis causa* was made where the donor felt himself to be in imminent danger of death, including being 'aetate fessus' ('worn out by old age': D. 39. 6. 5, Ulpian).[27] The *donatio* facilitated the exchange of property without recourse to a *testamentum*,[28] but it could also be used to strike a bargain with the donee. *Donationes* from the *paterfamilias* to those in his *potestas*, as to his wife, were generally forbidden, since those in *potestas* were *alieni iuris* and therefore were incapable of owning property apart from their *peculium* while their *paterfamilias* remained alive (A. Watson 1968: 51–3, 232). But a *donatio* to a person under the donor's power was valid if confirmed in the will; in the meantime, the donor had the right to revoke the gift—hence perhaps it acted as a guarantee of good and dutiful behaviour on the part of the donee.

But there is no evidence from Egypt, at least in the first centuries of Roman rule, to suggest that the duty of caring for one's aged parents was compulsory. Some elderly fathers saw the need to make an official complaint or take personal revenge when they felt that their children were not performing their (moral) duty.[29] One first-century papyrus (*P.Oxy.* 275, AD 66) provides a neat example of a father both seeing to his own old age and making sure his son learns a

[26] In general, cf. D. 39. 6; C. 8. 56; and—especially relevant to my arguments here—*Fragmenta Vaticana* 294–6. Note also P. Simonius, *Die donatio mortis causa im klassischen römischen Recht* (Basle 1958); Kaser (1971: i. 763–5, ii. 564–7). For the institution under Jewish law in relation to Roman law, cf. Yaron (1960).

[27] It is specifically stated in a rescript of Diocletian and Maximian (C. 8. 53. 16, AD 293) that old age alone does not prevent making a gift ('senectus ad donationem faciendam sola non est impedimento'); nor does being mute and deaf (D. 39. 5. 33. 2, Hermogenianus). Other reasons given for making a *donatio mortis causa* include weak health, attack by enemies or robbers, 'the hatred of a powerful man', and an imminent sea voyage or journey through 'dangerous places' (D. 39. 6. 3–6). Originally it would appear that the mere general awareness of one's mortality was not sufficient cause, but by the time of Ulpian 'sola cogitatio mortalitatis' sufficed (cf. D. 39. 6. 2; also 39. 6. 31. 2, Gaius; 39. 6. 35. 4, Paulus).

[28] It is worth noting that, in a rescript of Diocletian and Maximian (C. 6. 22. 3, AD 294), it is stated that 'senium quidem aetatis uel aegritudinem corporis sinceritatem mentis tenentibus testamenti factionem certum est non auferre' ('it is established that feebleness of age or bodily infirmity does not take away the capacity to make a will from those who are still of sound mind'); on *senium*, see below. On the *querela inofficiosi testamenti* and the legal fiction that the testator is insane (when in reality he is just not acting according to *pietas*), cf. D. 5. 2. 2, Marcianus; and Gardner (1993: 64, 172).

[29] Cf. e.g. *P. Mil. Vogl.* 84 (= *P. Kronion* 50), Tebtunis, AD 138, where a father in his 70s, while distributing his property, all but disinherits his eldest son because of the son's allegedly undutiful behaviour; instead he leaves most of his estate to his other two sons and his granddaughter. In *BGU* 5. 1578 (3rd cent. AD) a veteran complains to the acting-prefect of Egypt about his daughter, charging her with ingratitude for not caring for him in his old age. In a much later case (*P. Lond.* 5. 1708, Antinoopolis, AD 567–68), the eldest son defends his right to take most of his deceased father's estate on the grounds that he spent a small fortune on his father's debts and maintenance when he was alive (his father, we are told, had gone blind and needed taking care of), and after his father's death paid for his burial and maintained the rest of the family at his own expense.

trade (just as the law of Athens would have required): he sends his son off to serve as an apprentice to a weaver for a year and receives from the weaver a set amount for food and clothing for himself.

Roman Egypt provides us with one more intriguing piece of information in this context. In a poll-tax register dating to the first half of the first century AD (*P.Oxy.* 1210, lines 4–5), mention is made of those men from the Oxyrhynchite and Cynopolite nomes 'chosen by their parents from their sons to support them in old age (γηροβοσκία)'. The implication is that such sons, by performing this service, received partial if not full exemption from the poll-tax: if this was the case it is our sole piece of evidence for such compensation, and possibly it may be an institution inherited from the Ptolemaic period which did not last long under Roman rule (Wallace 1938: 120).[30] This does not necessarily mean, however, that sons were *compelled* to render such a service to their parents,[31] only that those who did so apparently enjoyed some privilege from the state.

What, then, of Roman society? The contrast is striking. To put it quite bluntly, the Roman legislators do not seem to have given much thought as to how parents in their old age might look after themselves or be looked after. The reasoning behind this is probably not too difficult to find. Under Roman law, as opposed to the situation in Athens, the oldest male relative—be he father or grandfather or even great-grandfather—in theory retained power (*patria potestas*) until death, and as such retained control over the purse-strings.[32] One potential threat to the security of the *paterfamilias* will be discussed presently. First I offer a more general overview of some evidence from Rome for *pietas* towards aged parents working in practice.

Evidence for the intervention of the state in the treatment of parents by their offspring (short of parricide) is negligible before the second century AD. Dionysius of Halicarnassus (20. 13. 3) mentions that the Roman censors, as one of their invasions into the privacy of citizens, made sure that children were not disobedient to their aged

---

[30] In *P. Flor.* 382 (c.AD 193), lines 38–40, an old man seems to be saying that his son should be exempt from a liturgy because he has to take care of his father (γηροτροφίαν): this is the father's wish—whether it was complied with is quite another matter.

[31] *Pace* Taubenschlag (1932: 509–10; 1956: 175, 177).

[32] See further below. As for the elderly female, her situation must have varied depending upon her status: husband alive or dead; married with or without *manus*; children surviving (and co-operative) or not, etc.; cf. Dixon (1988: 47–51, 188–94). Widowed women without children, or for that matter unmarried women—presumably few in number—must have had the most difficult circumstances if they did not have control over inherited property and their own means of support. Note Seneca, *Consolatio ad Marciam* 19. 2 (even with wealth old-age security is a concern).

parents. Perhaps such scrutiny did come under the aegis of the *cura morum* (supervision of public morals), though no concrete evidence for such intervention survives. Extant declamatory speeches, however, show that the maintenance of parents by their children was an issue of some interest. The relationship such *declamationes* have to legal reality, however, is less clear. A 'law' requiring that children maintain their parents or be imprisoned is frequently debated in such exercises;[33] there is even a case where it is recognized that such maintenance for the elderly brought with its immediate benefits a loss of independence and power for one old man who is made to say to his son (Elder Seneca, *Controuersiae* 1. 7. 10): 'ad te legem meam transfero: licet alliges, et alas' ('I transfer my rights to you: go ahead and bind me, but please also feed me'). Were the rhetoricians simply arguing about theoretical niceties, quite divorced from the reality of Roman life but influenced by what was known to have been the case in Athens at any rate,[34] or did such a law actually exist in the time of Elder Seneca and later?

It is only in the second century AD that we begin to find in the legal corpus (itself, it must be remembered, not compiled until several centuries later) discussion of the duty of parents toward children and vice versa in terms of maintenance (*alimenta*) (Sachers 1951: 347–56). An undated rescript of Antoninus Pius (C. 5. 25. 1) states that 'parentum necessitatibus liberos succurrere iustum est' ('it is right for children to look after the needs of parents'); that is, it is just and befits *pietas*, but is not necessarily compulsory. The moral obligation is reciprocal.[35] A few years later Marcus Aurelius and Lucius Verus (C. 5. 25. 2, AD 161) inform a certain Celer that 'competens iudex a filio te ali iubebit, si in ea facultate est, ut tibi alimenta praestare possit' ('the competent judge will order that you

---

[33] 'Liberi parentes alant aut uinciantur'; cf. Elder Seneca *Controuersiae* 1. 1, 1. 7, 7. 4 (the mother is to be maintained, not just the father: 7. 4. 3–4; cf. 7. 4. 1 and 10: 'if you won't feed your mother, at least bury her'); Quintilian 5. 10. 97, 7. 6. 5 (raising the difficulty that an infant or a soldier away on service cannot be expected to maintain his parents; cf. C. Chirius Fortunatianus (4th cent. AD?), *Ars rhetorica* 2. 10: '"qui parentes non aluerit, uinciatur"; neque enim infantes aut debilis alere possunt'); Quintilian 7. 1. 55 (some parents may not deserve to be maintained at their children's expense if they have not treated them well in their turn); [Quintilian], *Declamationes minores* 368 ('patrem ali non solum oportet, uerum etiam necesse est'); Ennodius (AD 473/4–521), *Dictio* 21. In one case the 'law' states that only 'needy' parents must be maintained: [Quintilian], *Declamationes maiores* 5 pr.: 'liberi parentes in egestate aut alant aut uinciantur'. Cf. F. Lanfranchi, *Il diritto nei retori romani: Contributo alla storia dello sviluppo del diritto romano* (Milan 1938), 274–82; Bonner (1969: 95–6).

[34] It will be noted that the declamatory 'law' specifies imprisonment as the penalty for conviction, not loss of citizen rights (in Roman terms *capitis deminutio*). Cf. n. 23 above.

[35] The heading in the *Codex* is 'De alendis liberis ac parentibus'; cf. e.g. C. 5. 25. 4 (AD 197). Note also D. 3. 5. 33 (34), Paulus (where a grandmother is said to maintain her grandson 'iure pietatis').

be maintained by your son, if he has the means to be able to provide support for you').[36] In other words, the son is expected to maintain his father if he has the means to do so. But the obligation is not automatic—a judge must order the son to perform this duty if he feels the situation calls for it.

Ulpian in the *Digest* makes the position clearer. In a lengthy extract from his *Duties of a Consul*, a work written in the reign of Caracalla and therefore practically contemporaneous with the passages from the *Codex* cited above, the obligations of parents towards their children and vice versa are discussed. It is first stated (*D.* 25. 3. 5. pr.) that 'si quis a liberis ali desideret uel si liberi, ut a parente exhibeantur, iudex de ea re cognoscet' ('if anyone asks his children to support him or children ask to be maintained by their parent, a judge will look into the matter');[37] the duty of maintenance, not an automatic one (though some families may have treated it as such), is seen as reciprocal and treated in the same context. Subsequently Ulpian discusses specific circumstances: for example, a son may have a natural obligation towards his *paterfamilias*, but what if the son had been emancipated while still an *impubes*? He is no longer in *potestas* and therefore, technically, under no obligation to his father. Ulpian states that in such a case a son can be compelled (sc. by the *iudex*) to support his father if the former is financially able and the latter is in need ('patrem inopem alere cogetur'). The duty is seen as a moral or natural one, rather than one strictly required by the letter of the law.[38] Similarly, a son serving in the army, if he is in funds, has a duty due to *pietas* to support his parents.[39] Another rescript which Ulpian cites states that, while a son might support his father out of a sense of *pietas*, if the son dies his heirs should not be compelled to provide maintenance for the father if they are unwilling to do so, 'nisi in summam egestatem pater deductus est' ('unless the father is reduced to extreme poverty').[40]

---

[36] Cf. similarly C. 5. 25. 3 (AD 162).

[37] 'Exhibeantur' here means to 'provide support or maintenance': cf. *TLL* 5. 2. 1432–3; *Vocabularium Iurisprudentiae Romanae* 2. 689–90.

[38] *D.* 25. 3. 5. 13: 'iniquissimum enim quis merito dixerit patrem egere, cum filius sit in facultatibus.' At ibid. 16 Ulpian notes that it is stated in a rescript that the duty of a *filius* to support his parents is 'ratione naturali', and does not extend so far as the payment of a father's debts. For the poverty of parents being a factor in this context, cf. ibid. 17 (cited below, n. 40), and [Quintilian], *Declamationes maiores* 5 pr. (cited above, n. 33).

[39] *D.* 25. 3. 5. 15: 'ratio pietatis' (cf. ibid. 37. 15. 1. pr., Ulpian).

[40] *D.* 25. 3. 5. 17. Presumably this son had been emancipated, or perhaps the reference is to the inheritance of his *peculium castrense*. Since one was not legally under the *potestas* of one's ascendants on the maternal side (such as the maternal grandfather but also one's mother), it was asked whether *pietas* should extend to the maintenance of such elderly people: cf. *D.* 25. 3. 5. 2, Ulpian, where it is stated that the *iudex* should give consideration to these relatives' physical and financial position, 'cum ex aequitate haec res descendat caritateque

In short, therefore, the care of the elderly within the Roman family was felt to lie naturally with their children, but direct legislation to impose this obligation, such as has been seen to have existed in Athens (and as was set down, for example, in the Elizabethan Poor Law Act of 1601, and apparently in Singapore in 1994), was never introduced at Rome. The institution of *patria potestas* in theory meant that the *paterfamilias* could expect total and immediate support from his dependants for as long as he lived and continued to control the purse-strings. The position of elderly relatives, such as the mother and the maternal grandparents, who did not carry such sway in legal terms, is less straightforward, and the expectation that they would receive support seems to have rested on general feelings of *pietas*, at times enforced by the decision of a *iudex*. Exactly what sort of care should be provided was not made explicit, but it seems to have been limited to financial aid, expected if the son was financially capable and the elderly parent was in need.

Incidentally, while the traditional image of the extended family in antiquity has been effectively quashed by recent historians of the family, it must still be realized that it would have been inevitable that some more distant relatives (including grandparents, paternal and maternal, and grandchildren) remained within the family home, especially among the lower classes and away from the city.[41] Multigenerational families, though the exception and very rarely mentioned in the literary sources or recorded on inscriptions, would not have been totally unheard of.[42] The moral duty of caring for one's aged parents, therefore, may have extended to sharing one's roof with them—possibly the elderly relations could perform functions such as child-minding. Due to demographics, however, such an arrangement would usually have been of a short-term nature (cf. Saller 1986a).

The Romans, perhaps influenced by Greek ideas and practices, may have debated the duties owed by children to their parents, particularly in the rhetorical schools, but in reality the laws did not secure the welfare of the elderly. The contrast here with the situation in

sanguinis'; cf. also *D.* 27. 3. 1. 4, Labeo *ap.* Ulpian. Similarly it is asked whether ascendants on the female side have a duty to support descendants: *D.* 25. 3. 5. 5 (Pius said a maternal grandfather must support his grandchildren); 25. 3. 8 (a daughter's child is not the liability of a maternal grandfather but of the father, unless the latter is destitute himself). Elder Seneca, *Controuersiae* 9. 5, asserts that the ties felt between a maternal grandfather and his grandchildren are due to nature rather than to law.

[41] Cf. Dixon (1992: 6–7, 22, etc.); Bradley (1991: esp. chs. 6–7); Treggiari (1991: 410–12). For comparison, see Laslett (1977: ch. 5; 1983: 92 ff.; 1989: 107–21); Mitterauer and Sieder (1982: ch. 7).

[42] Standard citations include Plutarch, *Crassus* 1, *Aemilius Paullus* 5; Valerius Maximus 4. 4. 8; *D.* 7. 8. 4–6, Ulpian, Paulus.

classical Athens is striking, and one may wonder about the general validity of the well-known passage from Dionysius of Halicarnassus (2. 26), himself a Greek,[43] where he describes the Roman institution of *patria potestas* as being far superior, in terms of ensuring the obedience and dutifulness of children towards their parents, to that which had obtained among the Greeks. Certainly the *paterfamilias* may have been happy, but what of others? *Patria potestas* revolved around the male head of the family, perhaps to the detriment of other elderly members. Whether the *paterfamilias* himself was concerned with the welfare of such other elderly relatives probably depended upon the individual and his circumstances. What is clear is that the Roman legislator, unlike Solon and his successors, saw no need to intervene for their benefit.

In this context it is worth considering briefly what other sources of welfare might have been available to elderly members of Roman society. While there was no secular, institutionalized system of old-age welfare, recourse might be had to friends and neighbours. If one's wealth permitted, *captatores* (legacy-hunters) might be attracted, and there was always the hope that slaves and freedmen would be there as support.[44] Poorer classes might have achieved some security, at least after death, through *collegia*. But there can be no doubt that the care of such individuals as survived into old age was a matter of private rather than public concern. The duty of caring for elderly parents lay primarily with the children, whether naturally, morally, or in strict legal terms, and such support must have been particularly needed by the poorer classes of the elderly population; for the wealthy members of society for whom we have the most evidence the need would have been far less urgent, though not insignificant. When such a source of welfare failed, whether through never having had children, having lost children, or having undutiful children, a Roman had only two possible choices in seeking someone to help—a spouse, or oneself.

[43] Writing at Rome at the end of the 1st cent. BC, he was, to quote D. Daube (*Roman Law: Linguistic, Social and Philosophical Aspects* (Edinburgh 1969), 86), 'more Roman than most Romans' (cf. E. Gabba, *Dionysius and the History of Archaic Rome* (Berkeley 1991), esp., in this context, 148–51).

[44] Cf. D. 1. 12. 1. 2, Ulpian, 25. 3. 5. 18–25, Ulpian, 25. 3. 6, Modestinus, for the freedman's obligations of maintenance towards his needy patron (and even towards his patron's parents, 25. 3. 5. 26, Ulpian). The Delphic manumission records of the last two centuries BC make this obligation (παραμονή), whether in money or in personal services, very explicit: cf. W. L. Westermann, 'Slave Maintenance and Slave Revolts', *Classical Philology* 40 (1945), 1–10; Hopkins (1978: ch. 3). Schaps (1979: 147 n. 95) cites a Delphic inscription which records that a girl is manumitted on the condition that she care for *her own* (slave) parents in their old age, an interesting twist. For *paramone* in the Egyptian papyri, cf. Adams (1964: esp. 152 ff.).

The probable demographic regime of the ancient world meant that a typical marriage, if it did not end in divorce,[45] was terminated after less than twenty years by the death of one of the couple. However, remarriage appears to have been the norm, and was deliberately encouraged under the terms of Augustus' marriage legislation.[46] It would therefore probably have been quite common still to have a husband or wife in one's old age, even if one's children were no longer living. The idea that a spouse could provide comfort, if not also material support, in one's old age is regularly expressed. Indeed, one of the encouragements to marriage that Dio (56. 3. 3) has Augustus express to the assembled equestrians in AD 9 is that a wife will 'temper the untimely harshness' of old age.[47] Pliny expresses his contentment at the fact that his young third wife, Calpurnia, will love him, even though he will grow old in body.[48]

Nature again provides a model in the way that the male kingfisher, when it becomes too old to fly and support itself, is carried by the female and fed by her (Plutarch, *Moralia* 983a–b).[49] Aelian, in citing this example, states that human beings fail to live up to the ideal: women, he says, despise their old husbands and chase after young men, while elderly husbands ogle girls and ignore their elderly, lawfully wedded wives (*De natura animalium* 7. 17).[50] Ulpian discusses the case of a wife who suffers from *saeuissimus furor* (raging insanity) but who receives no form of support from her husband; in such a case, he says, the woman's guardian (*curator*, i.e. she should be

---

[45] And indeed under later Roman law it is said that the infirmities of old age offer grounds for divorce; cf. *D.* 24. 1. 61, Gaius: 'propter . . . uel senectutem aut ualetudinem aut militiam satis commode retineri matrimonium non possit'. Plutarch for one expresses indignation at such grounds for divorce (*Moralia* 789b; cf. *Cicero* 41. 6), which might suggest that in his day it was not too uncommon.

[46] Up until the age of 60 years for males and 50 for females. Incidentally, Plato, *Laws* 11. 930, states that a man with no children whose wife dies must remarry so as to have children. On the possible advantages of concubinage over remarriage for elderly Roman males, see Saller (1987: 74–6).

[47] It is a commonly expressed wish in Latin poetry that a couple may grow old together: e.g. Tibullus 2. 2. 19–20, 3. 3. 8; Propertius 1. 8. 46 (and also Martial 4. 13). And an elderly couple, even of slender means, may be regarded as happy and fortunate: Tibullus 1. 10. 39–44; Ovid, *Metamorphoses* 8. 631–4; *Fasti* 3. 541–2; cf. *Anthologia Palatina* 7. 260, and Simonides, frag. 7 West, 83–93, for the bee-woman who 'grows old with a husband whom she loves and who loves her'. For inscriptional evidence of exceptionally long married lives, cf. e.g. *CIL* 6. 8684, 12388, 18137, 18758, 19008, 20241, 21303a, 21319, 25697, 25905, 33087, 34407, 34706, as well as, of course, the *Laudatio 'Turiae'* (*ILS* 8393 = *CIL* 6. 1527, 31670, 37053).

[48] 4. 19. 5: 'non enim aetatem meam aut corpus, quae paulatim occidunt ac senescunt, sed gloriam diligit'. Pliny was probably only about 40 years old at the time.

[49] Cf. Antigonus, *Historiarum mirabilium collectio* 23, quoting lines from Alcman (frag. 26 Page). See Thompson (1936: 139–40).

[50] Cf. Seneca, *De remediis fortuitorum* 16. 5, for old wives deserting their husbands; Treggiari (1991: 476–7).

under *cura furiosi*) or relatives (*cognati*) should either force the husband to care for her or else take back her dowry and let the woman provide for herself (*D*. 24. 3. 22. 8). Normally a husband would have been on average some ten years older than his wife, and they might—if they survived—have grown old together and provided comfort and perhaps support for one another.[51] No legislation, however, forced a man or woman to provide for an elderly spouse; again, it was felt that a natural sense of obligation should ensure that this happened. If death, divorce, or desertion meant that in old age a person was on his or her own, only one other source of maintenance was available: oneself.

The dread of a combination of old age and poverty is one strongly expressed in the extant literature, even though for our writers no such combination would have been a realistic prospect. Even Cicero, in his consolation for old age, has Cato admit, when asked by Laelius whether it is not true that old age is more tolerable for him only because he possesses 'opes et copias et dignitatem' ('wealth and resources and rank') which many others lack, that 'nec enim in summa inopia leuis esse senectus potest, ne sapienti quidem, nec insipienti etiam in summa copia non grauis' ('an old age of extreme poverty cannot be tolerable even for a wise man, nor can it fail to be burdensome, even amidst the greatest wealth, for a fool') (*De senectute* 3. 8).[52] In the same dialogue Cicero states that the two greatest burdens of life are thought to be poverty (*paupertas*) and old age (*senectus*), a sentiment shared by many; both factors in combination must have proved highly unfortunate.[53] But the literary sources, on which we are dependent for testimony, fail to furnish us with reliable and realistic depictions of the life of the elderly poor, despite the fact that we may assume that some 5 to 10 per cent of the overall population of the Roman world at any one time would have been over the age of 60 years. The concern of the literature remains

---

[51] There appears to have been a fairly common (literary) tradition that a young wife was not suited to an old man: e.g. Athenaeus, *Deipnosophistae* 13. 559f–560a. Cf. Pliny 8. 18 for Domitius Tullus' wife caring for him in his very decrepit old age.

[52] J. G. F. Powell (ed.), *Cicero: Cato Maior de senectute* (Cambridge 1988), 119–20.

[53] *De senectute* 5. 14, describing Ennius at the age of 70 years; cf. Ennius, *Hecuba*, frag. 92. 183–4 [Jocelyn]: 'senex sum: utinam mortem obpetam priusquam euenat quod in pauperie mea senex grauiter gemam' (cf. Euripides, *Hecuba* 492–8); not that Ennius was exactly poverty-stricken—see E. Gruen, *Studies in Greek Culture and Roman Policy* (Leiden 1990), 119. Cf. Aeschines 1. 88 ('old age and poverty, the greatest evils among men'); Plato, *Phaedrus* 267c; Diogenes the Cynic *ap.* Diogenes Laertius 6. 51 ('on being asked what is the most miserable thing in life, Diogenes replied: "an old man who is destitute"'); Menander, *Monosticha* 656 Jaekel; Menander, *Sicyonius* 375–6; Philemon, frags. 125K (= Stobaeus, *Florilegium* 50. 2. 51), 127K ('old age can be a fine thing only if one condition is met, namely if you're wealthy when you're old'), 128K ('if you chance to meet a poor, lonely old man, don't bother asking how he is: for everything's bad with him').

within the circle of the writer and his contemporary audience who, like Cicero's Cato, were assumed to have the power and resources— if not also the mental fortitude—to find consolation and support in old age. Nor does the legal corpus concern itself too much with the impoverished elderly members of society.[54]

Only in a passage from the second-century AD philosopher Iuncus[55] do we find the admission, without it being developed for satirical or humorous purposes, that for some members of society old age presented an impossible burden. In dealing with the hardships of old age, Iuncus notes the additional miseries that true poverty would bring (Stobaeus, *Florilegium* 50. 2. 85 (Hense, p. 1051, lines 17–22)):

And if as well poverty should happen to befall an aged man, he himself would pray to be completely freed from life on the grounds of his complete impoverishment, since he has no one to guide him, no source of support, cannot clothe himself adequately, does not have enough money for shelter or for food, and sometimes has no one to even draw water for him.

This is held to be the most horrible reality of old age, 'an oppressive, painful, grievous and decrepit spectacle', to use Iuncus' own words. There is some realization here that true poverty does not mean merely the inability to be comfortable in old age, to enjoy *otium cum dignitate*; it is the grim reality of complete destitution without the basic necessities of life such as shelter and sustenance, not to mention self-respect. And it is a condition for which there can be no relief (except in death)—neither the state nor the wealthier members of society provided any tangible aid. In this passage, whatever Iuncus' motives in writing it, we have a depiction which begins to go beyond the philosophizing platitudes of a Cicero, beyond the derogatory and wry remarks of a Martial, and there emerges, however distant, a picture of the real misery, degradation, and helplessness that old age might bring to the less privileged members of an ancient society.

---

[54] The poor could of course turn to begging in old age—note the fears of Naevolus in Juvenal 9. 125–40. One late legal 'concession' made to aged beggars may be seen in *C. Th.* 14. 18. 1 (cf. *C.* 11. 26), AD 382, where it is stated that all beggars are to be tested concerning their 'integritas corporum et robur annorum' and that if they have not been reduced to *mendicitas* through any *debilitas*, they are to become the slaves of those who report them and are to be taken off the streets—in other words, the only 'legal' sort of beggar was one who was old and/or physically handicapped.

[55] Iuncus writes, despite his very Roman name, in good, undatable Attic Greek, and he mentions nothing specifically Roman; the influence of Plato and Cicero is detectable. The 2nd-cent. date seems to be based primarily on the hypothesis that he belongs to the Second Sophistic movement. J. H. Oliver, *Hesperia* 16 (1967), 42–56, argues that he was Aemilius Iuncus, suffect consul in AD 127 and mentioned by Juvenal (15. 27); this is possible but unprovable. One thing we may presume, however, is that it is unlikely that Iuncus wrote about an impoverished old age from personal experience.

I have been dealing here with means of support for the elderly and have contrasted in particular the situations in Athens and Rome at different periods (a contrast which is not made in any extant Roman text). In Roman society it would appear that the duty lay primarily with a man or woman's immediate descendants, as part of a sense of *pietas*, but it was only in the second century AD that such a duty found expression in law. While no form of direct public aid or welfare was ever available, help might be expected from other family members or from powerful friends—always supposing that such people were alive and willing. Eventually the old person must look to his or her own resources, and the pervading mentality that one's lot was what one deserved (a sentiment with a modern ring to it, in fact) left little room for genuine interest or sympathy. This negative conclusion is of course a subjective generalization—to be gleaned as much from inference as from the inadequate ancient sources—but is, I believe, a necessary antidote to a longstanding myth that in past cultures, both in antiquity and in more recent history,[56] the elderly enjoyed a life of prestige, comfort, and respect (with an implied contrast to the present day). That some did is certain. That most did not must be recognized.

OLD PEOPLE IN THE FAMILY: THE THREAT OF SENILITY

Hesiod depicts the fifth age of humankind, the Iron Age, as a time of misery, marked with disputes within the family, where men dishonour their aged parents and are so degenerate that even infants are born with grey hairs on their heads (*Works and Days* 174–89).[57] The notion that a child should be dutiful to his or her aged parents has already been seen above, where some indication was also given that it was felt that some offspring failed to perform their duty. This is one aspect of generational conflict and it is a theme which frequently appears in classical literature.[58] It is not, however, a question that I wish to become embroiled in here, for the simple reason that an exhaustive collection of literary references to the

[56] Cf. Laslett (1977: 174 ff.; 1989: ch. 8); C. Freer, 'Old Myths: Frequent Misconceptions about the Elderly', in N. Wells and C. Freer (edd.), *The Ageing Population: Burden or Challenge?* (London 1988), 3–15.
[57] Cf. T. M. Falkner, 'Slouching towards Boeotia: Age and Age-Grading in the Hesiodic Myth of the Five Races', *Classical Antiquity* 8 (1989), 42–60.
[58] M. Reinhold, 'The Generation Gap in Antiquity', *Proceedings of the American Philosophical Society* 114 (1970), 347–65, is a comprehensive if rather unimaginative survey of the depiction of generational conflict in Greek literature from Hesiod to Menander, together with some mention of Egyptian, Jewish, Indian, and (only briefly, 362–5) Roman sources. The collection of essays of varying quality in S. Bertman (ed.), *The Conflict of Generations*

conflict between the young and old would achieve little more than making us aware of something that is quite obvious anyway.[59] Most of the depictions in classical literature of this conflict fall into one of two categories: (1) moralizing by the elderly on how the young should (but apparently do not) behave, and (2) comic descriptions (not necessarily written by the young) of the struggle of a rebellious son against a conservative (or in some cases even more rebellious!) old father. Of more interest in the context of this chapter are the reasons why this conflict of generations arose, if in fact the conflict is more than just a literary motif or a sign of the paranoia of the elderly, and the repercussions such a conflict might have had on the family. Two types of generational conflict need to be differentiated (something most of the literature on the subject fails to do). The conflict within a family, between father and son (or mother and daughter, etc.), may be common to any family at any time;[60] the potentially more serious conflict of the younger generation of a society with the elder members is a public one which breaks out in particular during times of crisis. The former may in its extreme state result in family disintegration, the latter in civil strife. What will most concern us in what follows is one particular product of intra-familial generational conflict, namely the threatened usurpation by a son of the control held by a father, and again the contrast between Athens and Rome will be important. First, however, it is necessary to discuss an aspect of old age that is rarely mentioned in the ancient sources. In practically all negative depictions of old age and of the elderly in ancient literature, the emphasis is on *physical* debilities. For what follows, on the legal and social effects of senility[61] on the elderly person, it will be necessary first to consider to what extent

---

in Ancient Greece and Rome (Amsterdam 1976), including a reprint of Reinhold's essay, is also of some interest. For more perceptive studies, cf. J. de Romilly, *Time in Greek Tragedy* (New York 1968), 143–71, and J. F. Gardner, 'Aristophanes and Male Anxiety: The Defence of the *Oikos*', *Greece & Rome* 36 (1989), 51–62, at 59–61.

[59] The tradition of the conflict can be seen e.g. in the mythologies of many cultures—such as in Greece, with Ouranos being overpowered by Kronos who was in turn overthrown by Zeus. In Maori creation mythology the two original gods, Rangi (the sky) and Papa (the earth), are in close embrace until their six male children—Tawhirimatea (the wind), Tane (the forests), Tu (war), Tangaroa (the sea), Rongo (the *kumara*, sweet potato), and Haumia (the fern root)—plot to separate them; Tane accomplishes this by growing (as a tree) between them, pushing between them with his hands (the roots) and his legs and feet (the branches).

[60] Most cases of family generational conflict in classical literature, especially in tragedy and comedy, focus not on everyday, mundane disagreement, but on crucial moments, such as the marriage of the young son or daughter. For one particularly vivid portrayal of father–son conflict at a time of real crisis, cf. the *agon* at Euripides, *Alcestis* 614–746, together with E. M. Thury, 'Euripides' *Alcestis* and the Athenian Generation Gap', *Arethusa* 21 (1988), 197–214.

[61] By the term 'senility' I mean primarily the potential mental repercussions of old age (i.e. senile dementia), as opposed to the strictly physical ones, though the English word may carry both senses (and indeed the two may be interrelated).

the mental disabilities that might accompany old age were recognized in Roman society.[62]

Moses Finley noted in his brief survey of the status of the elderly in the ancient world (Finley 1981: 170) that 'I can find hardly any reference [sc. in classical literature] specific to mental illness in old age, and then only of the most casual kind.' This is true enough, since the emphasis in the literature is on the easily visible, physical drawbacks suffered in old age. But the awareness of the mental short-comings is still there, and it will be of use to survey the evidence briefly. The term *senium* is commonly differentiated from *senectus* or *senecta*, general terms for old age, by reference to particular neg-ative aspects.[63] This tradition is made very clear in the following comment by Isidorus, in describing the last of the (six) ages of man (*Origines* 11. 2. 8, 30):[64]

senium autem pars est ultima senectutis, dicta quod sit terminus sextae aetatis ... senectus autem multa secum et bona adfert et mala. bona, quia nos ab inpotentissimis dominis liberat, uoluptatibus inponit modum, libidinis frangit impetus, auget sapientiam, dat maturiora consilia. mala autem, quia senium miserrimum est debilitate et odio.

('Senium' is the final stage of 'senectus', so called because it is the end of the sixth age ... Now 'senectus' brings with it many things, some good, some bad. Good, since it frees us from the most violent masters: it imposes a limit on pleasures, it smashes the force of lust, it increases wisdom, it grants wiser counsels. Bad, however, because 'senium' is most wretched in terms of both the disabilities it inflicts and the loathing it incurs.)

---

[62] This precludes a detailed analysis of the medical literature. Our primary concern here is with the awareness at a more general social level, as evidenced in literary and legal sources.

[63] Cf. D. Slusanski, 'Le vocabulaire latin des *gradus aetatum*', *Revue roumaine de Linguistique* 19 (1974), 113, 352–4, 566–7. The *Oxford Latin Dictionary* defines *senium* as: (i) the con-dition of old age, usually implying decay or debility; (ii) the period of old age, senility, dot-age, long life; (iii) melancholy, gloom, hypochondria. The negative element is omnipresent. In the Latin legal corpus, *senium* is similarly used, without any special legal significance; it can refer to general ill-health through age, without necessarily implying mental illness, to the decrepitude of the ancient laws before the recodification under Justinian, to the disrepair of old buildings, or to the alleged decline in eloquence of a speaker in his old age.

[64] Cf. Jerome, *PL* 25. 1021, clearly Isidorus' source here. On *senium*, cf. Charisius, *Ars grammatica* 1. 11 (Barwick 39. 17–18): 'senium, μέριμνα φύσεως, senilis morbus'; Festus 454L: 'senium a senili acerbitate et uitiis dictum'; Donatus *ad* Terence, *Eunuchus* 2. 3. 11: 'senex ad aetatem refertur, senium ad conuitium [sic]'; Serenus *ap.* Nonius Marcellus 393. 3L: 'callet senium arte bibendi' (cf. below on λήρησις); Nonius Marcellus 1. 1 (3–5L): 'senium est taedium et odium: dictum a senectute, quod senes omnibus odio sint et taedio'; Laevius, *Alcestis* frag. 8 [Baehrens] (*ap.* Aulus Gellius 19. 7. 3): 'Corpore pectoreque undique obeso ac mente exsensa tardigenuclo ("slow of pace") senio obpressum'; Valerius Maximus 9. 3. 8, of Sulla: 'nec senio iam prolapsus, utpote sexagesimum ingrediens annum'. Cf. *delira senecta* (TLL 5. 1. 466. 77–82). Less common words were applied specifically to women: *anilitas* (cf. TLL 2. 69. 72–6; Isidorus, *Origines* 11. 2. 28: 'sicut autem a sene senectus, ita ab anu anilitas nominata est'; Catullus 61. 155) and *anas* (Paulus *ex* Festus 26L: 'anatem dicebant morbum anuum, id est uetularum, sicut senium morbum senum'; cf. Flavius Caper in Keil, *Grammatici Latini* 7. 107. 15).

Loss of mental prowess was one negative feature of old age that was recognized. As Juvenal puts it (10. 232–3), after describing all the physical horrors of old age as he saw them, 'greater than the loss of every limb is madness' ('sed omni membrorum damno maior dementia').[65] Assorted references, most of them casual, may be collected to show this general awareness of the fact that in old age the mind may fail.[66] One particularly interesting reference—and far from casual—is to be found in a passage by the second-century AD medical writer, Aretaeus (3. 6. 2),[67] where, in discussing *mania*, he differentiates between *mania* and λήρησις, the latter being 'the misfortune of old age', which is 'a numbness or deadness of the senses' and 'a benumbing of the *gnome*[68] and of the *nous* through cooling', unlike *mania*. *Leresis*, he goes on to say, begins in old age and, again unlike *mania*, does not go away, but dies with the person. We have already seen earlier in this chapter one image of the mental disabilities associated with *senectus*: the proverb that old age is a second childhood, which relates to both physical and mental debilities among the elderly. The loss of memory in old age, also remarked upon, is another feature of relevance here.[69] An old man suffering from such disabilities might be felt by the younger members of his family,

[65] Juvenal lists such features as forgetting the names of one's slaves, and not recognizing the faces of old friends and one's own children—the second recognized today as one symptom of Alzheimer's disease. For such signs of madness, cf. Lucretius 3. 467–9; Cicero, *In Pisonem* 20. 47 (with Nisbet's comments ad loc.); Elder Seneca, *Controuersiae* 2. 4. 2.

[66] e.g. Herodotus 3. 143. 3; Sophocles, *Oedipus at Colonus* 930–1, *Antigone* 281; Euripides, *Bacchae* 251–2, *Aeolus* frag. 25 [Nauck] (= Stobaeus, *Florilegium* 50. 38); Aristotle, *De anima* 1. 4. 408b; Xenophon, *Apologia* 6–8; Plautus, *Bacchides* 820–1 (a slave talking about his aged master: 'terrai <iam> odium ambulat, iam nil sapit nec sentit, tantist quantist fungus putidus'); Lucretius 3. 453–4: 'claudicat ingenium, delirat lingua, labat mens, omnia deficiunt atque uno tempore desunt'; cf. 3. 168–9 (with Lactantius, *Institutiones diuinae* 7. 12. 1); Sallust, *Bellum Iugurthinum* 11. 5; Vergil, *Aeneid* 7. 440; Elder Pliny, *NH* 7. 50. 169; Tacitus, *Annales* 6. 38 (for the *delator* Fulcinius Trio in his will accusing Tiberius of suffering from 'fluxa senio mens'; cf. Dio 58. 25. 2; also Tacitus, *Annales* 4. 52, for the failing powers of the aged Domitius Afer: 'aetas extrema . . . fessa mente'); Seneca, *Letters* 58. 36 (cf. *De beneficiis* 7. 26. 4: 'torporem mentis ac senium'); Marcus Aurelius, *Meditations* 3. 1; Censorinus, *De die natali* 14. 6; Arnobius, *Aduersus nationes* 2. 7.

[67] Iude (ed.), *Corpus Medicorum Graecorum* 2 (1958), 41. 18–23. Note also Galen, *De symptomatum causis* (7. 201K).

[68] Hippocrates, *Aphorisms* 5. 16 has the same phrase, used of the effect of heat! For the term λήρησις, elsewhere used by Stoics of foolish talk associated with drunkenness, cf. Plutarch, *Moralia* 504b, 716f; Diogenes Laertius 7. 118; and Chrysippus, *Fragmenta Moralia* 643 (von Arnim, *Stoicorum Veterum Fragmenta*, iii. 163 = Stobaeus, *Eclogues* 2. 7, p. 109 Hense). Note the nouns παράληρος and λῆρος, used of delirium, and see also Galen 4. 786K.

[69] Cf. Cicero, *De senectute* 7. 21; Lucretius 3. 1039–42; Elder Seneca, *Controuersiae* 1. pr. 2–3 (though this is probably false modesty, since Seneca was known to have a prodigious memory!); Suetonius, *De grammaticis* 9; Maximianus, *Elegies* 1. 123–6, 195 ff. Messalla Corvinus is a particularly noteworthy case: Elder Pliny (*NH*. 7. 24. 90) states that he forgot his own name, and Jerome (*Chronicon* 2027, AD 11, *PL* 27. 563–4) provides further details: 'Messala Coruinus orator ante biennium quam moreretur, ita memoriam ac sensum amisit,

whether through genuine concern or for more selfish reasons (control of property meaning power), to be incapable of retaining control of the home. It is just such a situation that we must now consider, not as a literary motif but as a legal reality.[70]

What happened in ancient society when an old man who, as oldest male member of the family controlled the social and economic life of his household, became incapable through senility of performing effectively this function and furthermore acted recklessly in dealing with the family property? In Athens an action (*graphe*) for παράνοια (insanity) existed which a son could bring against his father in such circumstances, aimed primarily at preventing the old man from squandering and thereby dissipating the estate of the *oikos*.[71] Though no concrete evidence for such a charge ever having been brought by a son against his father exists, the existence of the law is clear enough and is frequently referred to in the literature.[72] Indeed one very famous account, doubtless fictitious, of a son prosecuting a father on just such a charge had long currency in antiquity.[73] The

ut uix pauca uerba coniungeret, et ad extremum ulcere sibi circa sacram spinam nato, inedia se confecit, anno aetatis LXXII' (see R. Syme, *The Augustan Aristocracy* (Oxford 1986), 219–20). On the other hand, special note was made of those who survived into old age with their memory intact: cf. e.g. Simonides, frag. 14 West (of himself at the age of 80 years; cf. S. Goldhill, *Phoenix* 42 (1988), 189–97); Elder Pliny, *NH* 25. 5. 9 (of Castor the botanist); Philostratus, *Lives of the Sophists* 1. 11. 495–6 (of Hippias of Elis who had extraordinary powers of memory, even in old age—as, apparently, did most of the sophists; cf. id. 2. 21. 604, etc.); cf. Elder Seneca, *Controuersiae* 2. 6. 13 (reportedly a common assertion): 'the *νοῦς* blossoms (συνανθεῖ) in old age'; Seneca, *Letters* 26. 2; Jerome, *Letters* 10. 2.

[70] For other legal restrictions affecting the elderly within the family, cf. *D.* 26. 1. 13. pr., Pomponius (a curator may be appointed for someone who has a tutor on account of the tutor's ill-health or *senium aetatis*); and *C.* 6. 22. 3, cited above, n. 28.

[71] [Aristotle], *Athenaion Politeia* 56. 6: the duties of the archon include the *anakrisis* of public and private lawsuits, among which is included the charge of 'παράνοια, when a man is accused of squandering his property through insanity'. Cf. Isaeus 6. 18, where Euktemon, whose senility is stressed throughout the speech, is said to have fallen in love and to have thereby ruined his *oikia* by spending too much money on the woman.

[72] e.g. Aristophanes, *Clouds* 844–6 (Pheidippides wonders if he should take his insane father to court and get him judged insane, or if he should just alert the coffin-makers!); Xenophon, *Memorabilia* 1. 2. 49 (Socrates was accused of teaching children to show contempt for their parents, persuading his followers that he rendered them wiser than their fathers, and observing that a son was allowed by the law to confine his father on convicting him of insanity); so too 1. 2. 51; cf. Plato, *Apology* 20; Aristophanes, *Clouds* 1407. See also Plato, *Laws* 11. 928–9; Aeschines 3. 251–2. Plato, *Epistles* 7. 331c states that 'a father or mother I think it not right (ὅσιος) to constrain, unless they are suffering from mental derangement (παραφρονία)'.

[73] Sophocles accused by his son Iophon: Cicero, *De senectute* 7. 22 (he implies a Roman parallel: 'quemadmodum nostro more male rem gerentibus patribus bonis interdici solet'; see n. 90 below); Anonymous, *Vita Sophoclis* 13 (quoting Satyrus, 3rd cent. BC); Plutarch, *Moralia* 785a; [Lucian], *Makrobioi* 24; Apuleius, *Apologia* 37; Jerome, *Letters* 52. 3. 6 (copying Cicero); cf. Valerius Maximus 8. 7. ext. 12; M. R. Lefkowitz, *The Lives of the Greek Poets* (London 1981) 84–5.

action existed as a possibility and as a potential threat to old age; the fact that we know of no genuine case from the period may be due either to our own inadequate knowledge or to the fact that the existence of the law meant that sons in many cases almost automatically took over control of the *oikos* in their father's old age, whatever the latter's mental condition.[74] When an Athenian son married, at around the age of 30 years, this may have been seen as the appropriate time for control of the household to pass to him, it being his duty to care for his aged parents if they were still alive.[75]

What then of the Roman situation? The contrast again is apparent. It was a well-known feature of Roman law that the *paterfamilias* retained control of the household until his death,[76] and of this unique feature the Roman legal system was insistently proud. Daube (1969: 75–6) has presented a well-known caricature of the repercussions of this legal situation:[77]

Suppose the head of a family was ninety, his two sons seventy-five and seventy, their sons between sixty and fifty-five, the sons of these in their forties and thirties, and the great-greatgrandsons in their twenties, none of them except the ninety-year-old Head owned a penny. If the seventy-five-year-old senator or the forty-year-old General or the twenty-year-old student wanted to buy a bar of chocolate, he had to ask the *senex* for the money. This is really quite extraordinary.

It certainly is. Demographic realities meant that many, in fact most, Roman males of about the age of 30 years did not have a father— let alone a grandfather or great-grandfather—still alive and so were no longer *in potestate*.[78] But the fact remains that *some* did remain under the complete control of the elderly male members of their family well into their adult life. That such a situation might lead to very real interfamilial conflict is obvious enough, and indeed the spectre

[74] As Lacey (1968: 106–7, 117–18, 130), asserts; see also M. Golden's comments in *Phoenix* 35 (1981), 322 n. 21. Cf. Plato, *Lysis* 209c, for the young Lysis' assumption that his father will hand over everything to him when he considers his son to 'know better than himself'. Lysis' father may have had something different to say on the subject.

[75] Aristotle (*Politics* 7. 16. 9–10. 1335a) approves of just such a scheme in theory. Note too that in Aristophanes' *Wasps* it is Bdelykleon, not Philokleon, who runs the house.

[76] Unless (thus Gaius 1. 127–36) the *paterfamilias* or his dependants suffered *capitis deminutio* (*maxima* or *media*), or if a *filiusfamilias* became a *flamen Dialis* or a *filiafamilias* a Vestal, or if they became enrolled in a Latin colony (thereby losing Roman citizenship) or were emancipated by the *paterfamilias* (if adopted by someone else they would then fall under his *potestas*). Taking all this into account, it appears that most Romans remained *in potestate* until their father died.

[77] The age differences, given that a Roman male on average married in his late twenties (cf. Saller 1987a: 20–35), are probably not quite right, but the point remains just as valid.

[78] Saller (1986a: 7–22). Some doubts have recently been expressed about these figures. Those who need convincing would do well to read Laslett (1988), which incorporates the imperial Roman figures.

of parricide finds room for an appearance here, particularly when a *filiusfamilias* was in debt to a moneylender and had no means of repaying the debt while his father remained alive.[79]

For Roman society, as opposed to that of Athens, there is no testimony that it was the norm nor indeed that it was even considered appropriate for an elderly father to hand over practical control of the family property to his sons, though this would have been one way in which the potential conflict engendered by the system of *patria potestas* might have been eased. The fact that a *filiusfamilias* could hold a *peculium* (savings)—and, from the time of Augustus, a *peculium castrense* (property acquired during military service) independent of his father's property[80]—may have made the situation slightly more tolerable, as would the possibility of division of the father's property in anticipation of his death.[81] But such a dramatic move as allowing the children total independence from, say, the age of 25 years (when they reached full adulthood as *maiores*) would have done a lot more.[82] But that is beside the point—it did not happen, no doubt because it would have been such a revolutionary step; indeed, the suggestion probably never arose, except perhaps in the minds of some particularly rebellious young sons.[83] In wealthier circles a young male may commonly have left the family home to set up his own residence and family,[84] but ordinarily it must often have been the case that a son stayed at home, ready and waiting to take over the family estate on the death of the father.

[79] Cf. Cicero, *Pro Roscio Amerino*, and the *senatusconsultum Macedonianum* (1st cent. AD), on which see Daube (1947). Note also id. (1969: 88–90); Hopkins (1983: 244–5); see now Gardner (1993: 63–6). Cf. Ovid, *Metamorphoses* I. 148–9, and Statius, *Siluae* 3. 3. 14–16: 'procul hinc, procul ite nocentes, si cui corde nefas tacitum fessique senectus longa patris'.

[80] Cf. Juvenal 16. 51–6 for the case of a 'tremulus pater' who courts ('captat') his son who earns a soldier's pay—a neat inversion of roles. Cf. Daube (1950: 435–74). See also Gardner (1993: 57–62) on sons as their fathers' *institores*.

[81] Discussed above; note also *D.* 10. 2. 20. 3, Ulpian; 10. 2. 39. 5, Scaevola; 41. 10. 4. 1, Pomponius; cf. Saller (1991: 40). *D.* 28. 2. 11, Paulus, even makes it sound as if in reality the distinction between father and son as property owners was minimal.

[82] Cf. Daube (1947: 303). While a young Athenian male became independent (i.e. no longer under the control of a *kurios*) on being entered on the deme's register at the age of 18 years, a Roman remained *in potestate* even after reaching the age of 25 years. *Emancipatio* of a son *in patria potestate*, though often discussed in the legal texts, seems not to have been a common reality; cf. Saller (1986a: 16), and see now Gardner (1993: 66–72).

[83] The only suggestion of such a practice from Roman times that I know of is in the declamatory school—see Elder Seneca, *Controuersiae* 3. 3: 'cum tricenario filio pater patrimonium diuidat'; i.e. when a son reaches the age of 30, his father must divide his property with him. The old man, having given his estate to his sons, is described as 'solus, senex, inops'. In this case there seems to be no relationship to Roman reality; cf. Bonner (1969: 106); Garnsey and Saller (1987: 141). Cf. above on *donationes*, and also Shaw (1987b: 21–6). For a valuable comparative study, see D. Gaunt, 'The Property and Kin Relationships of Retired Farmers in Northern and Central Europe', in Wall *et al.* (1983: 249–79); also C. B. Brettell, 'Property, Kinship, and Gender: A Mediterranean Perspective', in Kertzer and Saller (1991: 340–53).

[84] Saller and Shaw (1984a: 137); Saller (1986a: 17).

Such, then, very briefly, is the generalized Roman situation. But what if the father was regarded as mentally incapable of effectively running the household and there was a perceived danger of the family estate being lost? The old man would retain his legal status as *paterfamilias*[85] but did he in practice retain all his rights? The Roman institution of the *cura furiosi et prodigi* (supervision of one who is mad and a spendthrift) is relevant here. From the time of the XII Tables[86] it was admitted that a *furiosus* or a 'prodigal' should not be considered capable of looking after his own property and that therefore a *curator* should be appointed for him (as with the supervision of minors and of women *sui iuris*) until his madness or prodigality abated. This duty was traditionally assigned to the agnatic relatives; failing this a suitable *curator* might be appointed by the praetor or *praeses* (D. 27. 10. 1. pr., Ulpian; 27. 10. 13, Gaius). It is expressly stated under later law that a son who is upright (*probus*) may be the *curator* of his own father (or mother).[87] In such cases the son effectively gained control over the family property, while still remaining *in potestate*. Such cases are not, of course, restricted to elderly parents, and in fact the old age of the parents is not specifically mentioned as a factor in the legal texts. But it may be assumed, in the light of what has already been said above about the observed mental incapacity associated with old age, that a father suffering from senile dementia may indeed have been assigned to the *cura* of his son on the latter's application. There is a problem of terminology here—the man suffering from *furor* may be assigned a *curator*, while the mental disability experienced by the elderly is generally termed *insania* or *dementia*. However, not too much should be made of this.[88] The main difference appears to have been that while a *furiosus* of younger years may have lucid intervals and may be expected to

[85] D. 1. 6. 8, Ulpian. On the whole subject of insanity in Roman law see Nardi (1983: esp. 100–7), and Gardner (1993: 167–78), esp. on the disadvantageous legal position of the son of a *furiosus pater*.

[86] XII Tables 5. 7; cf. Cicero, *De inuentione* 2. 50. 148, [Cicero], *Ad Herennium* 1. 13. 23; D. 27. 10; Paulus, *Sententiae* 3. 4a. 7: 'moribus per praetorem bonis interdicitur hoc modo: quando tibi bona paterna auitaque nequitia tua disperdis liberosque tuos ad egestatem perducis, ob eam rem tibi [ea re] <aere> commercioque interdico' (for the reading *aere*, see Watson 1967: 157).

[87] D. 26. 5. 12. 1, Ulpian (citing a rescript of Antoninus Pius, that a son, 'si sobrie uiuat', may be the *curator* of his father; this apparently went against the view of Celsus *et al.* that it was *indecorum* for a father to be ruled by his son); 27. 10. 1. 1, Ulpian; 27. 10. 2, Paulus; 27. 10. 4, Ulpian (referring to *pietas*). For the position of daughters in a similar context, cf. D. 3. 3. 41, Paulus.

[88] For the distinction between *furor* and *insania*, see A. Watson (1967: 155–6), with Cicero, *Tusculan Disputations* 3. 5. 11, and L. Bonfante, *Corso di diritto romano*, i. *Diritto di famiglia* (Milan 1963), 642 ff. What about *dementia*? Note that Ulpian in discussing the *cura* of the *furiosus* (D. 27. 10. 6) uses both *furor* and *dementia* (though not necessarily as

recover eventually, the *insania* of old age generally persists continuously and until death.[89] In both cases the same action lay open to the *sani* relatives.[90]

This leads us again to the declamatory school. A specific action for *dementia* is mentioned several times, usually in bizarre circumstances, where a son prosecutes a father.[91] Again it is difficult to judge the degree of legal reality underlying these exercises.[92] It seems most probable that in these exercises the declaimers have in mind both the Greek action for παράνοια and the Roman institution of *cura* for the *furiosus*.[93] But it must be pointed out that the praetor or *praeses* would presumably only have placed a father in *cura* for *furor* or prodigality in extreme cases,[94] whereas the situations the declamatory exercises portray are in most cases bizarre but trivial.[95] In 'real life' accusing one's father of insanity is an extreme step, and not one that the legal system regarded lightly.[96] Whatever the degree

synonyms). Julian (*D.* 27. 10. 7) speaks of both *curatio furiosi* and *curatio dementis*, apparently interchangeably. But note C. 5. 4. 25. 2, AD 530, for a clear distinction. On terminology, see also E. Renier, 'Observations sur la terminologie de l'aliénation mentale', *Revue Internationale des Droits de l'Antiquité* 3 (*Mélanges F. de Visscher* IV, 1950), 429–55; Nardi (1983: 18–23); Gardner (1993: 168, 175).

[89] Cf. the passage from Aretaeus cited above (n. 67), and [Quintilian], *Declamationes minores* 349: 'dementiam non posse curari'.

[90] It may be to this action, rather than just interdiction of a prodigal by a magistrate, that Cicero is referring when he says (*De senectute* 7. 22; see n. 73 above) that the action taken by Iophon against his father has a parallel in Roman society.

[91] Cf. Elder Seneca, *Controuersiae* 2. 3 (a rapist wins over the father of a girl he has raped, but not his own father, so he accuses him of *dementia*); 2. 4 (a man disinherits his son, the latter has a child by a prostitute, whom he acknowledges (*sustulit*); the son falls ill, calls his father, and entrusts the *nepos* to the grandfather; the son dies, the grandfather adopts the child, and is accused of *dementia* by his other son; cf. Calpurnius Flaccus (2nd cent. AD), *Declamationes* 30); 2. 6 (a man began to lead a life of debauchery (*luxurians*), his son already doing so; the son accuses his father of *dementia*, on the grounds that debauchery belongs to youth, not old age); 6. 7; 7. 6; 9. 5. 7; 10. 3; [Quintilian], *Declamationes minores* 295 ('datum est hoc ius contra patrem. legum lator prospexit senectuti: ideo medicinam filiis imperauit'), 316, 328, 349, 367 (including a brief list of alleged symptoms of such *dementia*).

[92] Quintilian (11. 1. 82) describes similar cases as 'scholastica materia, sed non <quae in foro non> possit accidere'.

[93] Note ibid. 7. 4. 11 (cf. 7. 4. 29); Elder Seneca, *Controuersiae* 2. 3. 12–13: 'ego [the speaker, Asinius Pollio, or Seneca himself?] scio nulli a praetore curatorem dari, quia iniquus pater sit aut impius, sed semper quia furiosus; hoc autem in foro esse curatorem petere, quod in scholastica dementiae agere'.

[94] Cf. Paulus, *Sententiae* 3. 4a. 7, quoted above, n. 86.

[95] Only in the case of Elder Seneca, *Controuersiae* 2. 6, has the father been accused of leading 'liberos tuos ad egestatem'; in the other cases, the son accuses his father of *dementia* for some decision or action he has made which adversely affects the rest of the family (or, more typically, just the son). As Bonner (1969: 94) says, the cases Seneca describes 'seem to be as far-fetched as possible and in most of them a praetor would almost certainly have rejected the application'. Cf. Gardner (1993: 172).

[96] Cf. Paulus, *Sententiae* 1. 1b. 1 (= *D.* 2. 4. 6): 'parentes naturales in ius uocare nemo potest: una est enim omnibus parentibus seruanda reuerentia'; [Quintilian], *Declamationes*

of reality underlying this *scholastica materia*, however, it seems most probable that the theoretical possibility of an action for insanity being brought by a son against his aged father might be enough—in both Athens and Rome—for a compromise to be reached out of court and within the home (at Rome, no doubt, in a family *consilium*), but without such an agreement being legally binding. That the Roman system of *patria potestas* was in cold legal terms much harsher than the situation in Athens is clear enough. But in reality it might be expected that the Roman *filiusfamilias* was not totally subject to the whims of a despotic old father. Senile dementia was at least recognized, if not dwelt on, in antiquity, and the son's capability to act as *curator* for a *furiosus* or *prodigus* father opened up one legal loophole whereby a son might in practice succeed to his father's position while the latter was still alive.

On the other side of the coin, however, one must remember the position of the elderly parent in this relationship. From what has been said in this chapter, the implication appears to have been that the elderly in the family could be in many respects in a position of almost childlike dependency. But the absence of wage-earning as a fundamental element in the structure of Roman society, and with it the absence of a notion of institutionalized retirement, meant in effect that an elderly person, so long as he or she possessed some means of financial independence—be it a patch of garden[97] or a slave—would not be totally helpless. The words Cicero has Cato speak at *De senectute* 11. 38 (trans. M. Grant) must have rung true with many elderly Romans:[98] 'ita enim senectus honesta est, si se ipsa defendit, si ius suum retinet, si nemini emancipata est, si usque ad ultimum spiritum dominatur in suos' ('Age will only be respected if it fights for itself, maintains its own rights, avoids dependence, and asserts control over its own sphere as long as life lasts.'). When a person's failing state of physical and mental health led to total inability to be self-supporting, then, in the absence of effective medication, dependence on others may have been short-lived anyway.

---

minores 346: 'aduersus patrem ne qua sit actio nisi dementiae' (likewise C. Chirius Fortunatianus, *Ars rhetorica* 1. 22). Menander, frag. 601 [Koerte = Stobaeus, *Eclogues* 4. 25. 32] refers to the madness of prosecuting (δίκας γραφόμενος) one's parents.

[97] As with the aged Philetas in Longus, *Daphnis and Chloe* 2. 3.

[98] Powell (as at n. 52), 177–8, detects some legal overtones here, particularly in *emancipata*.

7
Conflict in the Roman Family

SUZANNE DIXON

In this chapter, I consider how conflict in the Roman family was viewed in the Roman moral system and how it might be analysed from modern theoretical perspectives. Debates and programmes emanating from the International Year of the Family have highlighted some changing perceptions of family life. In some senses, the family as an institution has been increasingly exposed in recent years as the site of violence and abuse, rather than the idyllic haven constructed in the nineteenth century and propagated in modern representations such as situation comedies and advertisements for processed food. Yet families are still perceived as the vital building blocks of any society and social workers are now more reluctant than their fore-runners to destroy families by removing children or gaoling errant parents, because they acknowledge the symbolic and emotional significance of the family unit to all its members, including victims, oppressors, and accomplices. This emotional emphasis coexists with the persistent state perspective of the family as a core social unit for producing and rearing citizens, workers, and soldiers.

It is not a recent discovery that individuals have been oppressed and maltreated within families. Moral and ideological perspectives on conflict and power struggles have traditionally split on political and academic lines. Politically, the family has since the nineteenth century been appropriated by the right, which has tended to up-hold the authority of the 'head of the household', usually the father-husband, against most challenges.[1] In many states, nineteenth- and

This work formed part of my project on 'Freedom and the Family' carried out during a two-month fellowship at the Humanities Research Centre, Australian National University, in 1994, and combined its annual theme of 'Freedom' with that of the International Year of the Family. I am grateful to the HRC for the award of the fellowship and for its sponsorship of the third international Roman Family Seminar. I particularly appreciated the support of the Director, Professor Graeme Clarke, and of the administrative staff and other fellows, including Professor Paul Weaver. At the conference in Canberra in August 1994, I had the benefit of a response from Dr Kathryn Welch, of the University of Sydney, an expert in the politics of the 50s BC. I have not modified my central thesis, but I have incorporated in this published version of the paper responses to some of her perceptive critical comments.

[1] See the review in Dixon (1992: 19–20). Cf. Donzelot (1979) and Mount (1982).

early twentieth-century legislation modified the 'right' of husbands/ fathers to assault family members for 'reasonable' correction. In practice, however, enforcement of the new legal view of individual rights was (and continues to be) erratic for a number of reasons connected with official and community approaches to the inviolability of the family, which generally translates to endorsing all but the most extreme behaviours by its most powerful members. In Roman society, the legal restrictions were few and excessive violence within the family was more likely to be moderated by social constraints. The dowry system and ease of divorce might have acted as a deterrent to some husbands, for example, but the institution of *patria potestas* and the persistence of school- and folk-tales bolstering its extreme applications formed a culture which in the last analysis validated its abuse.[2] Casual references in the Roman sources (which always take the perspective of the *paterfamilias*) take for granted a degree of violence towards wives and children,[3] but yield more material on penalties and ideologies than circumstantial information about violent incidents. Nor is violence in all contexts to be equated with conflict, which is the focus of this paper.

The latest generation of historians and sociologists of the family has often drawn on radical philosophies—notably Marxism and feminism—which emphasize the conflicting interests of different family members and characterize the family as a tainted institution serving the powers that be, especially capitalism and patriarchy, and institutionalizing the oppression of women and children.[4] In some

[2] See Dixon (1992: 45–8) for the gradual and generally reluctant incorporation in the legal system of socially acknowledged limits of the legitimate exercise of paternal authority, especially paternal rights to kill children or to end their marriages against their will, and ibid. (145–7) on paternal paranoia. Eyben (1993: 47–9) analyses traditional stories endorsing paternal severity, usually fathers executing sons for the public good. See also ibid. (65–7).

[3] The elder Cato's alleged comment that men who beat their wives and children harm their most precious possession (Plutarch, *Cato maior* 20) implies that such behaviour is standard. The comments of Valerius Maximus 2. 1. 6 on the worship of Juno Viriplaca (husband-placator?) imply that women at Rome felt the need to avert marital violence in their daily lives. Tales like that of the wife beaten to death for drinking wine for non-medicinal purposes (Elder Pliny, *NH* 14. 89; Aulus Gellius 10. 23. 4) and the many stories of fathers putting recalcitrant sons to death (e.g. Livy 8. 7; Valerius Maximus 5. 8) are certainly not typical and not necessarily factual, but they represent public approval of violent enforcement by the *paterfamilias* of moral and civic values; cf. Dionysius of Halicarnassus 2. 26. 27. This is in marked contrast to the tone of sources reporting rumours that wives might have poisoned husbands (e.g. Livy, *Epitome* 59; Orosius 5. 10. 10; see Münzer, *RE* 2A. 1445 = Sempronius no. 99, on Sempronia; Tacitus, *Annales* 1. 5 on Livia, 3. 23 on Aemilia Lepida, 4. 60 on Julia Livilla) or stepmothers their stepchildren (Cicero, *Pro Cluentio* 26–7; Juvenal 6. 626–33; Tacitus, *Annales* 1. 3, again on Livia).

[4] See Engels's classic 1884 work on the evolution and function of the family. Cf. Lund (1971), Reed (1975). Rapp, Ross, and Bridenthal (1979); Yanagisako (1979; 1991) represent

studies of the family, there has been a scholarly reaction against the mid-twentieth-century vision of the family as a solid, harmonious unit, with consistently common interests, socializing a new generation for its proper economic and political destination. Functional approaches to the family as performing certain roles—social reproduction, reciprocal lifelong care, emotional support, economic co-operation—dominated the social sciences in the 1950s and 1960s and tended to perpetuate a static and rather benign image of families.[5] Since the 1960s, however, conflict—once treated as symptomatic of 'deviant' families—has increasingly been perceived by scholars to be a normal and perhaps necessary part of family life.[6]

I agree that conflict of various kinds is a normal, continuing part of family dynamics. I would even argue that the common ideological stress on public shows of family solidarity and specific cultural elaborations (such as *pietas* and *concordia*) on harmony, love, and duty stem from a general awareness that siblings, in-laws, and spouses have conflicting interests which continually threaten the economic and other needs for the family to operate as a unit. With some reservations, I endorse a Marxist–feminist perception of families as serving to reproduce the means of sustaining the economic and social values desired by the ruling class to maintain its dominance. I accept, therefore, that the family *is* regularly a locus of conflict and a means of oppression, particularly of women and of the younger generation. I wish, however, to refine and modify this stance with the propositions that much of the conflict is an almost ritual renegotiation of family roles over a fairly predictable life-course pattern and does not threaten the family or its individual members, but that some of it is more dangerous and involves grave losses for some. Most domestic violence falls into this category. I would add the argument that,

feminist views of inbuilt family conflict. In general, psychoanalytic approaches have had less impact on social-historical studies, but it is worth noting the strong psychoanalytic attack by Laing (e.g. 1971) on the family, as an oppressor of the individual psyche, feeding collectively off the pain of the individual. The psycho-history school tends rather to take a power-relations approach to the family, drawing on classic Freudian psychoanalytic assumptions.

[5] Cf. Skolnick (1975: 704): 'Sociology, anthropology and psychology have defined the family as an agency of integration and adjustment for both the individual and the society as a whole.' She relates this (pp. 704–7 of her excellent review article) to US economic and intellectual trends of the period c.1940–60.

[6] Skolnick points out (ibid. 715) that in some respects this concept marks a return to the assumptions of Freud and Simmel that individuals in close contact are bound to be in competition with each other for various goods. Cf. Goode (1971: 624): 'Like all other social units or systems, the family is a power system. All rest to some degree on force or its threat, whatever else may be their foundations.' Sprey (1988: 137) on the socio-biological approach 'in which conflicts of interest are seen as endemic to the structures of both human marriages and families'.

however oppressive the family is as an institution, it is also typically an important economic and emotional support for people at all
levels of society.[7] The most familiar example of this paradox is that
of the severely abused child who desperately wishes to remain in a
family situation and aligns with negligent or abusive parents against
authorities.

It is patently more difficult to test these propositions against Roman
evidence than with modern intensive studies of specific communities, where observation and questionnaires can be structured to that
purpose and the basis of choice and controls is better defined,[8] but
it is not hopeless. Richard Saller has led the way in many respects,
in his 1991 analysis of the evidence for parental whipping of free
Roman children and now in his more recent 1993 study of paternal–
child conflict over choice of marriage partner and related questions.[9]
Like him, I have tried to use the available sources critically to gain
a more nuanced and therefore more accurate view of Roman family
relations, particularly in my comments on the socially defined authority of the older, widowed Roman mother and a more pragmatic view
of the actual workings of *patria potestas*.[10] Too many discussions in
the past accepted the legal provisions and literary stereotypes of the
tyrannical *paterfamilias* with lifelong powers over his children as a
realistic reflection of practice. The stereotypes do, however, have some
value in reconstructing moral positions and ideologies.

The Roman material reveals that certain kinds of conflict were to
be expected and social and legal institutions offered partial remedies. In most sources (literary, epigraphic, or juristic), the hero is the
paterfamilias and the popular villains the wayward young son and
the wicked stepmother (with the stepfather creeping in as a poor
second). Rules limiting the husband's access to his wife's dowry, or
protecting the interests of children not only against the depredations
of a scheming stepmother or stepfather but against the whimsical

---

[7] Radical historical scholarship—particularly on the Black family in the USA—has tended
towards this modification, which is reflected in other radical approaches to working class his
tory. But consider Lund's scathing denunciation (esp. 1971: 12–13) of US communist party
arguments that the Black and working-class family does not oppress women. Goode's (1963;
1964) emphasis on revolutionary aspects of the family should perhaps be distinguished
from Mount's (1982) characterization of the family as the bastion of liberty against an all-
encroaching state. See also Bush (1990: 90–4) on the Black slave family in the Caribbean.

[8] Cf. the opening statements of method by Herzfeld (1980: 92–3) in his discussion of fraternal competition for patrimonial shares in three modern Greek regions and of Otterbein and
Otterbein (1965: 1470–2) in their cross-cultural study of blood-feuds.

[9] Contrast Saller's (1991) observations (esp. 157–64) on the beating and whipping of
ingenui with the uncritical remarks of J. K. Evans (1991: 170–2) (although Evans is elsewhere more judicious, e.g. pp. 177–80).

[10] Dixon (1992: 46–8) on *patria potestas*; id. (1988: 61–7, 177–9) on the mother's authority.

disinheritance of dutiful children reflect the same ideologies (and often feature the same characters) as the literary stereotypes of conflict in family life which we see in comedy and satire.[11]

Since I have introduced a sliding scale of gravity for family conflict, I should offer examples of different types of conflict. In-law tension can be a minor matter of oblique remarks or overt criticism. Permanent or inbuilt conflict is likely to occur between spouses over expenditure and sexual jealousy and need not be serious, although it always has that potential. Siblings or cousins are likely to be in constant, mild competition for parental approval. All of these forms of conflict are likely to be shown in a stronger light at particular times, such as the organization of family parties at annual festivals. They typically flare up for life-cycle occasions such as births, engagements, weddings, and deaths and funerals, which involve reassignments of family roles and, where property is in question, reassignments of material dispositions. Death can lead, among other things, to inheritance disputes and divorce can lead to similar squabbles about property which might be the real cause of conflict or an excuse for airing existing grievances.

I argued in *The Roman Family* that, for all the artistic stress on generation conflict between the adolescent and the middle-aged parent, the power struggle between the middle-aged and the elderly is more serious. The younger generation in Roman society was most likely to rebel over decisions affecting their own lives, such as marriage choice, but although such conflicts are often very painful to the participants, I regard them as (in most cases) minor, cyclical disagreements. Like other conflicts centring on life-cycle events, they simply reflect the fact that families do not always acknowledge the changing roles of members, who have to renegotiate them personally by confrontation or manipulation (sulking, nagging, non-cooperation). If there are efficient social or family procedures for the changes, they are likely to be less traumatic. In principle, 50- and 60-year-old parents and in-laws should be able to foresee that the next generation will want to replace them. They could plan a form of retirement or

---

[11] e.g. *D*. 5. 2, *C.Th*. 2. 19 (*De inofficioso testamento*), *Inst*. 2. 13 (*De exheredatione liberorum*). On the remarrying mother and the rights of her children against the new husband/stepfather to the dowry, see *C.Th*. 2. 21; 3. 8; on property which she inherited from the children's father, see *C*. 5. 9. The profligate or extravagant *adulescens* and his mean old father feature in Plautus' *Mercator* and *Trinummus*, to name only two, and in Horace, *Ars poetica* (*Epistles* 2. 3), 160–74. For comic purposes, the *paterfamilias* is satirized for his strictness and frugality, but in more serious media (in which I include the otherwise hilarious Valerius Maximus and the *declamationes* and *suasoriae* in Elder Seneca) the stern and provident *paterfamilias* is the upholder of traditional values and power structures. Cf. the examples of Evans (1991: 177–8); Dixon (1992: 145–6).

semi-retirement to accommodate the transfer of responsibilities, but it does not always happen in that painless way.[12]

In this chapter, I analyse Roman examples of each grade of conflict: the normal, the moderately serious and the positively dangerous. Cicero's letters provide us with the most intimate glimpses of Roman family life, particularly in his correspondence with his friend Atticus, who became a connection *c.*67 BC when Atticus' sister Pomponia married Cicero's younger brother, Quintus.[13] Intermittent (or possibly continuous) difficulties between the brothers-in-law Quintus and Atticus and between husband and wife eventually give way to the more serious step of divorce in 44 BC (a step which had been mooted since 50 BC). Young Quintus Cicero, product of the union, provides an interesting example of generation conflict —with his uncles and mother and, above all, with his father from early 59 BC (he was then 17). There is a striking contrast between the actual strategies employed by Quintus senior and the notorious legal and economic powers available to the Roman *paterfamilias*. The Quintus *v.* Quintus (and the Young Quintus *v.* Pomponia) skirmish is a classic example of ritual conflict focusing on marriage choice, politics, and manners. The most dangerous conflict is the one which emerges between Marcus Cicero and his brother Quintus (with the two sons aligned with their fathers) during the civil war in October 48 BC (after Pompey's defeat at Pharsalus, where all four had fought on the losing side). At that stage the conflict became public and involved literally warring sides. The basic principle of maintaining the appearance of family solidarity was therefore breached even more violently than it would have been in a court case.[14]

[12] Detail and references on these issues is provided in Dixon (1992: 138–57).
[13] It is interesting that Shackleton Bailey felt bound to comment (1965: i. 278) on Cicero's use of the word *adfinis* (*Att.* 1. 5. 1 = SB 1) to describe Atticus' relationship with Cicero's recently deceased cousin Lucius: 'Technically neither Lucius nor Marcus Cicero was Atticus' *adfinis* (cf. *D.* 38. 10. 4. 3–4, Modestinus)'. Cf. Cicero's use of 'fraterne amari' (*Att.* 1. 5. 8).
[14] See Cox (1988) and Hunter (1994) for the tension between notional fraternal solidarity and the reality of Athenian inheritance disputes. In fact, this tension is routinely expressed in Roman sources, as it is in modern media reports of very public family conflicts. Much of the appeal of US day-time talk shows and the irresistible *Sylvania Waters* (a controversial BBC documentary which exposed the intimate life of an Australian family) lies in the horrified disapproval of the spectator at the very notion of airing to millions the routine clashes which take place in every home. Australians, generally unlitigious, continue to marvel at ruinous family inheritance cases, e.g. *Time Australia* 7/9 (2 March 1992), 56–62, cover story, 'Families that Fight Together' by R. Callick. Husband–wife disputes, though equally riveting, are not generally perceived in the same way as sibling and—most shocking and sensational of all—parent–child clashes conducted through the courts. Analogous ancient attitudes underlie the characterization of Euthyphro in Plato's dialogue and Valerius Maximus' praise of the daughter unjustly disinherited by her mother, who was too filial to dispute the maternal testament before the praetor (Valerius Maximus 7. 8. 2). It is also interesting to see how Cicero, who admits that public opinion at Larinum is against Cluentius (*Pro Cluentio* 11–12), tries to argue away his client's unfilial and unsavoury reputation (ibid. 7).

As Keith Bradley (1987) has reminded us, successive remarriage was even more popular with élite Romans than it is in our societies and created a range of step- and half-relations. In practice, these relationships generally seem to have extended Roman kinship categories amicably enough. Our sources have little reference to conflict between step- and half-siblings, but a strong ideological emphasis on the step-parent as a threat to the material interests—and even the physical safety—of the children of earlier marriages. The wicked stepmother is a familiar demon in Latin literature and idiom,[15] while the wicked stepfather becomes a greater concern to Roman jurists.[16] Pliny (6. 33) records his appearance in the centumviral court (some time early in the 2nd cent. AD) on behalf of an adult daughter against her stepmother. I shall also consider Apuleius' *Apologia*, delivered at Oea in North Africa AD 155–8, in which the speaker claims he was not a fortune-hunting wicked stepfather.

In the court cases (*Apologia* and Pliny 6. 33), the ideological presumption of intrinsic conflict allows—indeed, positively encourages —the manipulation in court of received stereotypes of the grasping intruder (stepmother or stepfather) into the family and fuels or even creates conflict between the generations. I shall argue that this represents a structural inducement to push conflict of the ritual, life-cycle type into the more serious category. The stepmother of Pliny's friend faced public ignominy and loss of fortune, while Apuleius (charged by his stepson with magic) was at threat of loss of freedom and civic status and punishment as a criminal.

For a detailed examination of family conflict, it is difficult to avoid Cicero's letters, which provide a uniquely intimate, longitudinal view of a family's life. When we come to the surviving *corpus* of the letters to Atticus, we find Cicero in 68 BC assuring his friend—perhaps too insistently—that his brother Quintus feels toward Atticus' sister Pomponia as they both wish and by May 67 Pomponia is expecting young Quintus.[17] This introduces the family characters on whom I shall concentrate in this chapter.

---

[15] On the stereotype of the scheming stepmother, see Dixon (1988: 155–9); Gray-Fow (1988); Noy (1991). For factual examples of predominantly good stepmothers, cf. Phillips (1978: 76–7); Hallett (1984: 257–8) and Dixon (1988). Livy 39. 9. 2–4 is a rarer literary example of the wicked stepfather. Cf. Dixon (1992: 143–5) for both stepmothers and stepfathers. See now also P. Watson (1995).

[16] On legal safeguards against the designs of second (and later) wives and husbands, see C. 5. 9; 5. 10, *C.Th.* 2. 21, 3. 8, and the discussions by Dixon (1988: 49–51) and Humbert (1972: 387–446).

[17] *Att.* 1. 5. 2 (Nov. 68), where Cicero rather ominously reports that in correspondence with Quintus 'et placarem ut fratrem et monerem ut minorem et obiurgarem ut errantem' to produce the desired frame of mind. See also 1. 6. 2; 1. 8. 1 and, for news of the pregnancy, 1. 10. 5.

Difficulties between the brothers-in-law Atticus and Quintus were
apparent in 61, when Atticus, who had apparently ignored Cicero's
strong hints that he should accompany Quintus to his proconsular
province of Asia, complained to Cicero that Quintus had written him
abusive letters (which he enclosed). He also had it on good authority
that Quintus regularly ran him down to common acquaintance in
Rome and on his journey to the province. Cicero responded with
the information that he knew Quintus had some grievance against
Atticus, and implies that it would all have blown over if Atticus had
met up with him in Greece. Without Atticus' presence, poor Quintus
—a good-hearted chap quick to take offence but equally quick to
calm down[18]—was at the mercy of the opinions of others. There is
a strongly implied criticism of Pomponia and of Quintus' freedman
Statius in Cicero's response, as well as more than a hint that Quintus
might have grounds for offence.[19] This is pretty much the pattern of
such correspondence, in which Cicero makes some concessions, but
tends to defend his brother to Atticus until the serious rift between
the brothers. In this case, Atticus was eventually persuaded to make
overtures to Quintus, and the tension seems to have dissipated.
Atticus, his sister Pomponia and their mother spent the Compitalia
together at Arpinum in December 60 (Quintus was still in Asia).[20]
So this particular in-law conflict—potentially serious enough to lead
to divorce—had been smoothed over.

Quintus' period as governor was prolonged, and he did not meet
Cicero again before his exile (March 58–August 57). In the meantime, Cicero had written strong words of admonition and reproach
for his harsh, quick-tempered approach to personal relations and
judicial decision-making in the province.[21] Oddly enough, Quintus

[18] But contrast the comments on Quintus' temper and behaviour in *Q.fr.* 1. 1 and 1. 2.
[19] *Att.* 1. 17. 3: 'atque huius incommodi culpa ubi resideat facilius possum existimare
quam scribere; uereor enim ne, dum defendam meos, non parcam tuis. nam sic intellego, ut
nihil a domesticis uulneris factum sit, illum quidem quod erat eos certe sanare potuisse.' And
cf. 4: 'ecquid tantum causae sit ignoro'.
[20] *Att.* 1. 19. 11; 1. 20. 1; 2. 3. 4. In 2. 6. 2 (April 59), Cicero casually assumes that Atticus
is aligned with the family interests and can be expected to chase up Quintus' stipend.
[21] *Q.fr.* 1. 1 (late 60/early 59) is a long essay on good government from an older brother
who has never governed a province to a younger one who has been doing so for two years
now. Sections 37 ff. deal in a fairly polite way with the problems posed by Quintus' reported
failure to control his temper. In *Q.fr.* 1. 2, written in late 59, towards the end of Quintus'
term, Cicero is much more pointed and upbraids his brother for ill-judged and partial behaviour, actually instructs him to reverse some of his decisions and quotes in understandable
dismay certain violently expressed passages from Quintus' official letters, now circulating in
Rome. Perhaps most intriguing of all is Cicero's apology (12) for his own intemperance in
writing 'an unbrotherly letter' ('littteras ad te parum fraterne') under a misapprehension, and
confidently asks Quintus' brotherly forgiveness for them ('huic tu epistulae non fraterne scriptae
fraterne debes ignoscere'). Given the hair-raising tone of the letter that has survived, one can
but imagine what the unbrotherly one contained!

does not seem to have resented this, or not sufficiently to affect his performance during Cicero's time of trial. The whole family—including the in-laws Pomponia and Atticus, and Tullia's husband C. Calpurnius Piso Frugi (quaestor in 58)—pulled together to secure Cicero's return. Quintus, himself in debt, not only allowed Cicero free use of his funds but offered more and it was his personal guarantee to Pompey of Cicero's good political behaviour which persuaded Caesar to agree to Cicero's return.[22] This is a classic example of families uniting against external threats and providing every kind of material and emotional support.

The correspondence during the years 57–51 gives evidence of routine family dissatisfactions and grumbles, but in general the brothers are affectionate towards each other, while the in-laws sustained relations at least.[23] In 51 both brothers and their adolescent sons went to Cilicia, where Marcus Cicero was proconsul. During this period, there were clearly more serious in-law problems. In a much-quoted letter written from Minturnae in May 51, Cicero responds to complaints by Atticus about Quintus' behaviour towards Pomponia. He reports that he had a long talk to Quintus at Arpinum about Atticus and about his concerns and Cicero felt Quintus was placatory towards Pomponia, not showing signs of any resentment. Cicero then gives an example of Quintus' excellent behaviour and Pomponia's rudeness in her last days with her husband before his departure (*Att.* 5. 1. 3–4):

We dined at Arcanum (you know the farm). When I arrived, Quintus very nicely said, 'Pomponia, you ask the women in and I'll fetch the boys.' As far as I could see, nothing could have been more pleasant, his words, his manner, his expression. But in my hearing, she said, 'I am a guest here myself.' I suppose the point of that was that Statius had gone ahead of us to arrange our meal. Then Quintus said to me, 'See? This is what I have to endure every day.' 'What of it?' you may say. It *is* important, and upset me at any rate, that she had answered so stupidly, her language and tone so nasty. I was upset but hid it. Everyone but Pomponia sat down to the meal and Quintus sent her share from the table, but she rejected it. What more do you want? I thought nobody could have been nicer than my brother, nobody more unpleasant than your sister.

And so it goes on. We have all heard such accounts. Doubtless Atticus could counter with similar one-sided anecdotes—indeed, he

[22] Shackleton Bailey (1971: 64–72); Dixon (1984: 80–7).
[23] Cf. Shackleton Bailey (1971: 92) on the correspondence between the Cicero brothers in 54: 'Difficulties and misunderstandings—Quintus' disregard of fraternal advice in certain dealings with their home town, further trouble with Pomponia, touchiness over Marcus Cicero's omission to press for his company on a trip to the country—seem to have been few and fleeting. The tone of the correspondence is relaxed, sometimes jovial, always friendly.'

had probably done so. Cicero pettishly points the moral, that Atticus should recognize the need for instruction and admonition on his side of the family as well as Cicero's. He then proceeds with a series of practical and political instructions in the firm belief that relations are as before.

But things seem not to have improved and in the correspondence between the province and Italy, including some that has not survived, divorce was under discussion. Writing from Laodicea in April 50, Cicero denies a suggestion from Atticus that he had been encouraging Quintus to divorce Pomponia. He blames Quintus' freedman Statius for the report (*Att.* 6. 2. 1–2). In May or June, young Quintus (then 16) came to his uncle in tears. He had been encouraged to open his father's mail in his temporary absence and had come upon a reference to the possibility of divorce. Cicero was moved by his distress and encouraged him to do his best to reconcile his parents (*Att.* 6. 3. 8; 6. 7). The subject does not recur in correspondence after this period.[24]

In the meantime, more cosmic events were also affecting the family. All four Cicero men fought with Pompey and after his defeat in August 48 parted company at Patrae, where there must have been some kind of disagreement, although Cicero does not seem to have realized how serious it was. There had been ill-feeling in Greece from other Republicans at Cicero's refusal to take a command (*Att.* 11. 7; Plutarch, *Cicero* 39). It is not clear whether this was related to the quarrel between the brothers. Cicero returned to Italy in October, but had a long wait in Brundisium for Caesar's pardon. At first, he speculated innocently about the movements of the Quinti and *their* prospects for pardon,[25] but by December 48 he had heard that young Quintus had been maligning him before Caesar and others (*Att.* 11. 8. 2) and in January 47 he learned that his brother Quintus had been writing to friends in Italy denouncing him (*Att.* 11. 9). From now until the return to Italy of the Quinti in mid-45 this is a serious concern of Cicero's, linked with his anxiety about his own pardon, for he hears that Quintus has prepared a speech attacking him, to deliver before Caesar (*Att.* 11. 10. 1). Roles have changed since 50 BC. Now it is Atticus who mediates between the brothers, while Cicero assumes that Pomponia will help *him* by resealing Quintus' letters which Cicero had opened before sending on to their proper recipients (*Att.* 11. 9. 2).

---

[24] The divorce had definitely taken place by mid-44: *Att.* 14. 10. 4; 14. 17. 3.
[25] *Att.* 11. 6. 7; 11. 7. 7. In March 47, he quotes to Atticus from a letter he had written to Caesar exonerating Quintus from any part in Cicero's decision to join Pompey: *Att.* 11. 12.

We never find out the precise reasons for this savage behaviour by the Quinti, although it is likely that Caesar blamed Quintus for Cicero's enlistment in Pompey's cause and Quintus might well have believed this was based on something Cicero had said.[26] In March 47, Cicero received from Quintus *frater* an explanatory letter which Atticus seemed to think of as an overture, but Cicero described as written 'in most disgraceful terms' (*spurcissime*). The only thing Cicero mentions specifically from this letter is the charge that he had been mean and given Quintus no material help—which seems reasonable in view of Quintus' past generosity. Cicero's response is weak. Quintus now apologizes to Atticus for displeasing *him* by his conduct (*Att.* 11. 13. 2–4; 11. 15. 2)! Even so, it is interesting that Quintus later complains to Atticus that Cicero does not write to him and Cicero answers the charge (*Att.* 11. 16. 4). Relations were not, then, assumed to have ended. The two brothers finally met and resumed relations. Shackleton Bailey (1971: 184–5) strongly argues that they were never fully restored, but it is difficult to be sure of this in the absence of correspondence between them. From mid-45, the focus of Cicero's fear and disapproval was his nephew, who moved in influential Caesarian circles and violently criticized both his uncle and his father at dinner parties—according to those helpful friends who continually rushed to inform Cicero of such attacks, which were potentially very dangerous. Young Quintus was alleged to be spreading it about that both Cicerones were hostile to Caesar and Marcus Cicero particularly suspect.[27] These grave imputations mingled with more homely criticism of Marcus Cicero's paternal tyranny towards his cousin, young Cicero.

Quintus in fact had at the age of 20 (or 21) entered a stage in which he was at loggerheads with the older generation. The two brothers might still be cool towards each other, Pomponia and Quintus were certainly arranging a divorce and the associated settlements, which also meant that Atticus and Quintus senior were likely to be out of sympathy with each other, but young Quintus managed in the end to unite them all. His important political connections were no proof against parental and avuncular criticism on

---

[26] In *Att.* 11. 12. 1–3, Cicero makes it clear to Atticus that he had written the opposite to Caesar—doubtless so that Atticus could pass it on to Quintus. Caesar would have played his own game. Cicero had left Italy for Pompey against Caesar's express instructions and Caesar deliberately let him sweat it out at Brundisium until September 47, when they had a showy reconciliation—Plutarch, *Cicero* 39. Moreover, Caesar had virtually published the letters Quintus had written about Cicero to all and sundry—*Att.* 11. 22.

[27] *Att.* 13. 37 (August 45), e.g. 2: 'nihil autem ab eo tam ἀξιοπίστως dici quam alienissimos nos esse a Caesare, fidem nobis habendam non esse, me uero etiam cauendum (φοβερὸν ἄν ἦν) nisi uiderem scire regem me animi nihil habere.'

the perennial grounds of his indebtedness, his politics, and the question of his marriage. It is a New Comedy topos. Perhaps the divorce provided him with some opportunity to play his parents off against each other, as Cicero seemed to think, but then Cicero made trouble as well, by revealing to his brother that young Quintus' version of relations with his mother were not as bad as he told his father and by representing his comments about his mother in the worst possible light to Atticus.[28] There is trouble not only over the question of young Quintus' own marriage but his vigorously expressed distaste for potential stepmothers.[29]

Beaten down by the united forces of the older generation and by a (possibly related) lack of funds, young Quintus finally agreed to the idea of his own marriage in December 45. Cicero has left his version of the dialogue between himself and his nephew on this subject. In this creation, the orator is all cool dignity and wears down the ungraciousness of his young pup of a nephew, sternly reminding him of his duty to his father and mother (*Att.* 13. 42). It makes for vivid reading, but one imagines young Quintus' version of the incident might have been different. Politics continued to be a good way of annoying the older generation even after Caesar's assassination in March 44, so the elder Quintus was delighted that his son chose in June to offend Antonius rather than himself over some matter and came to live with his father. Cicero was sceptical about young Quintus' explanation of the political change but encouraged him to make overtures to Brutus and Cassius (*Att.* 15. 21. 1; 15. 29. 2).[30] But in December, Cicero responded in the senate to an attack by Antonius on his nephew (*Att.* 16. 3. 3; 16. 4. 4) and all four Cicero men were proscribed by the triumvirs in November 43. According to Plutarch, the two brothers parted with a tearful embrace. The two Quinti died together, each expressing the final wish that he should

---

[28] Cf. *Att.* 13. 41. 1 (August 45), where the two uncles are considering the appropriately dignified way to readmit their nephew to their favour, with clear reservations, and Cicero proudly reports his exposure to Quintus *frater* of the fact that young Quintus had corresponded with his mother. In *Att* 13. 37, written at the same time, Cicero recaps the contents of an allegedly conciliatory letter from young Quintus in a way designed to alienate the other uncle.

[29] In *Att.* 14. 17. 3 (May 44), Cicero indignantly sympathizes with his brother, who has received a nasty letter (a hereditary trait) about the prospect of Aquilia as a stepmother and stating that young Quintus owes more to Caesar than to his father—a classic father–son red rag.

[30] In July, Cicero pretended to young Quintus that he believed in his change of heart (which seems to have had moral *and* political implications), but wrote a secret letter to Atticus telling him not to trust their nephew or to believe the letter Cicero had given him for Atticus (*Att.* 16. 5; 16. 16)! If they had all lived longer, this double-dealing could have been used to fan family quarrels most effectively in subsequent years.

not witness the other's death. The assassins therefore executed them simultaneously. In the end, family solidarity prevailed.

There is little need to belabour the distinction between denouncing a brother before a powerful autocrat and sniping at a nephew in a letter to a fellow-uncle. What is perhaps particularly interesting is that the lower level of very routine generation conflict can coexist with the other—but no more interesting than the reminder that people living through extraordinary upheavals, personal and national, are as preoccupied as ever with maintaining 'normal' family relations—including the maintenance of low-level and medium-level conflict. There were three divorces in the Cicero family in the period between the return of the men to Italy and Caesar's assassination. The political pressures could well have exacerbated difficulties, but not necessarily any more than separation imposed by provincial service in less disruptive times. One could even speculate about the impact of correspondence, as distinct from the possibility that everyday opportunities for face-to-face bickering might be an important means of dissipating conflict before it reaches serious levels—serious enough, that is, to lead to divorce. Certainly the Roman practice of recycling correspondence inflamed many situations and it is extraordinary that in such a society people continued to be so indiscreet about what they committed to paper (or tablets). Publishing abroad family problems must usually be judged an extreme form of conflict which breaches the understood limits of keeping things within the family. After years of affectionate mutual help and of accepting fraternal advice about everything from his marriage to his provincial administration, Quintus must have been badly hurt to go to the lengths he did in vilifying his older brother, in the full knowledge that his words could have caused Cicero's death.

In the other two instances of conflict I examine below, it might seem less surprising that matters are made public, for they involve stepparents. Any relationships by marriage, even those of husband and wife, are in some sense viewed as less basic and permanent than 'blood' ties and their breach therefore less shocking. Yet the children involved in the cases concerned have almost necessarily fallen out with their parents and the accusation of undue influence by the stepparent implies the exposure of the parent. In the two cases I take, the parent is represented as a helpless pawn—the father of Attia Viriola was *amore captus* at the age of 80, a ridiculous figure (Pliny 6. 33. 2). Perhaps it was more pious of the son of Pudentilla of Oea to claim that she was induced by magic to marry Apuleius, but the prosecution argument—that only greed would have led him to marry an ugly old woman of 60—was hardly respectful (Apuleius, *Apologia* 89).

Pliny's letter accompanied a polished version of the speech he delivered on behalf of Attia Viriola, a woman of equestrian rank, married to a former praetor.[31] Many aspects of the case are obscure. Pliny's covering letter is intended to lay out the main features for his friend so that he can concentrate on the beauties of the speech. This has been frustrating for those who have tried to use it to recreate the conditions of the centumviral court or the state of the *querela de inofficioso testamento* in the early second century, but for our purposes his account is quite telling. It was, he says, a *cause célèbre*. A huge audience strained to hear from the upper gallery of the Basilica Iulia (6. 33. 4): 'magna exspectatio patrum, magna filiarum, magna etiam nouercarum' ('the anticipation of fathers, of daughters, of stepdaughters was intense'). The implication is that the judgment would be of interest to others in analogous situations. Pliny mentions that complex calculations were involved, but seems otherwise to have relied unashamedly on bombast (10): 'dedimus uela indignationi, dedimus irae, dedimus dolori, et in amplissima causa quasi magno mari pluribus uentis sumus uecti' ('I gave full rein to outrage, to fury, to grief: I went at a gallop, rhetorically speaking, in the interests of such a significant cause'). For all that, the result was not conclusive, although he crows (6) 'uicta est nouerca' ('the stepmother was beaten')—rather reminiscent of 'the wicked witch is dead'—for all the world as if he had never held up Fannia, stepmother of Helvidius Priscus, as a model of womanhood.[32] Even the way he summarizes the situation for his friend is imbued with stereotypes—the noble, dignified daughter who has been cut out by the scheming, seductive stepmother; the infatuated old fool who forgets his duty to his own children: 'For a woman of equestrian rank, married to a former praetor, was seeking the due award of her patrimony in a full centumviral court hearing, because she had been disinherited by her eighty-year-old father within eleven days of his infatuation with the stepmother.'[33]

This is precisely the image, with genders reversed, which is presented in an assize court in North Africa some fifty years later, initially with the embellishment that Apuleius had secured the death of his stepson and erstwhile friend Sicinius Pontianus (Apuleius, *Apologia* 1–2). He counters the charges with sober information about the low dowry and the nature of the dotal agreement (91–2) and

---

[31] Pliny 6. 33. 2. See Tellegen (1982: 112); Sherwin-White (1966: 398–9).

[32] Pliny 9. 13. 3; 3. 16; 7. 9.

[33] Pliny 6. 33. 2: 'nam femina splendide nata, nupta praetorio uiro, exheredata ab octogenario patre intra undecim dies quam illi nouercam amore captus induxerat, quadruplici iudicio bona paterna repetebat'.

Pudentilla's real age (89), but the stereotype of the scheming step-father is the core of the case which he must demolish. He admits that the elder son, Pontianus, feared the worst when his mother wrote to him in Rome that she had received strong medical advice (69) on the urgency of ending her fourteen years of chaste widowhood with a new union: 'As soon as Pontianus received his mother's letter, he hurried from Rome. He was afraid that she would take a greedy husband and bestow all her wealth on the husband and his kin, as often happens. That anxiety was all the more pressing because all his hopes—and his brother's—of enrichment lay in their mother's wealth.'[34] With a personal fortune worth four million sesterces Pudentilla was not in Pliny's class, but she was wealthy—probably wealthier than her husband's family, for the sons had by now in-herited their father's share of the estate. Apuleius' version is that Pontianus himself wished Apuleius to court her to *prevent* her fall-ing into the hands of an adventurer.

Apuleius represents the threat of the scheming stepfather as real ('ut saepe fit'). He is simply at pains to show that he is not that kind of boy. Not only did he settle for a modest dowry and a marriage contract which favoured the sons, but he claims that he interceded with the mother on their behalf, persuading her to settle valuable property on them (93) in her lifetime and to make proper provision for them in her will. He counters the image of the fortune-hunting stepfather with that of the scheming uncle (Sicinius Aemilianus) and the bankrupt pimp father (Herennius Rufinus, father-in-law of the now dead Pontianus), who brought the suit on behalf of Apuleius' younger stepson Sicinius Pudens. Pudens must have been at least 17 by this time, quite old enough to bring a case in his own right,[35] but it suited Apuleius to represent him as an impressionable child.

In this case, the stepfather seems to have conquered, for Apuleius' *Florida* dates from his residence in Carthage a few years later, but it could have been otherwise. A conviction would have been very serious—much more so than a defeat of the stepmother in Pliny's case. It also marks an extreme stage in family conflict, a public de-claration of the incompetence of the mother and the fact that her son and brother-in-law did not trust her to put her child's inter-ests first. One can only speculate about the impact the trial had on Pudentilla herself—perhaps she *did* disinherit her son as a result? But, as we have seen from the Ciceronian examples, families can

---

[34] Apuleius, Apologia 71: 'nam Pontianus acceptis litteris matris confestim Roma aduolauit, metuens ne, si quem auarum uirum nacta esset, omnia, ut saepe fit, in mariti domum conferret. ea sollicitudo non mediocriter animum angebat, omnes illi fratrique diuitiarum spes in facul-tatibus matris sitae erant'.   [35] Cf. Butler and Owen (1917: pp. xx–xxi n.).

recover even from the most public and extreme forms of exposure and conflict.

The examples of conflict analysed in this chapter are uneven in detail. The stepparent cases both reveal murky depths in family relations which are exaggerated by the intense light of the court and the need to articulate rival versions of events which exonerate the speakers and condemn their opponents. This adversarial style is apparent in squabbles within families but is probably heightened when competing judgements and versions of events are written in letters. Even vigorous confrontations at family gatherings can be modified by the presence of other family members and the distractions of practical arrangements and necessary interruptions. Up to a point, families are structured so that the numerous chronic irritations and clashes are accommodated in everyday exchanges or ritualistic complaints ('So-and-so is always mean'; 'Isn't that just like x?'). Alignments might take place over particular issues, but the conflict is not permitted to escalate beyond a certain level which would disrupt the peace of a particular gathering, let alone of the family as a unit. Once the lengthy routine grumbles are committed to paper, they have to become more focused, as if a case were being presented to the recipient, and this process can harden the grievances and make intercession a more cumbersome business than a few conciliatory words across the dinner table or private admonition of a sibling after the meal. The party approached who receives a written challenge from the mediator is in turn obliged to formulate a case in self-defence with a degree of counter-attack. The practicalities of ancient correspondence also lengthened the process considerably.

These factors apply even more to court cases, where the parties are obliged by the format to engage in the most extreme form of public mud-slinging. A reconciliation following a case like Apuleius' is certainly made very difficult. The cases themselves feed, as we have seen, on popular stereotypes about stepparents which are a structural recognition of the built-in competition for goods within families, and of the lack of confidence in the step-relationship as a moral brake. Sibling (especially fraternal) jealousy and rivalry and filial resentment —even homicidal resentment—were acknowledged in Roman culture and law, but they were cushioned more vigorously with notions of family solidarity and reciprocal duty and advantage. Even in-laws were assumed to have a strong stake in maintaining harmonious family relations, but the interests of stepparents were assumed to lie with themselves or their own children, in opposition to those of the children of an earlier marriage of the current spouse. By the same token, the rules for polite behaviour by a child towards a stepparent had none of the force of *pietas* expected towards parents, grandparents, or aunts and uncles. Any change in the attitude of the living parent would be readily put down to the influence of the new spouse and there would always be friends and other relatives (especially of the dead parent) to encourage suspicions. We have seen— particularly through the Ciceronian correspondence and the *Apologia* —the communal nature of feuding in Roman families, in which mediation and involvement of brothers, sisters, aunts, uncles was to an extent expected, but similar involvement from a stepparent had no such legitimacy. The possibilities were extended by a legal system which acknowledged the dangers of parental remarriage to the issue of earlier marriages. It is quite likely that any falling-out between Pudentilla and her sons would have happened anyway as a result of their changing ages and roles and particularly their marriages— but the existence of a stepfather provided a focus for resentment and blame. The law also provided escape clauses for any pangs of offended *pietas* in the possibility of asserting reduced responsibility on the part of the parent. In the cases I have cited, infatuation and magic are alleged to have clouded the parent's judgement. The *querela de inofficioso testamento* and Valerius Maximus' moralizing discussions of unjust parental wills which omitted or discriminated unduly between the testator's children both employ the language of madness (usually *furor*) to explain the unnatural phenomenon. A society which acknowledged a wide range of kin and quasi-kin ties and numerous, honourable non-kin claims on an estate still placed great emphasis on parental duty and the presumption that, all things being equal, a sane and normal parent would favour his or her children over all others in transmitting wealth.[36]

We return to the truism that families themselves contain individuals who are by definition competing with other family members for a host of goods, material, emotional, and symbolic. Conflict is not surprising. At the same time, society (and its many subcultures) needs family units. Individual family members need the family unit for a number of reasons—these are perhaps most obvious in families engaged in subsistence production, but they are fairly clear in the case of Roman senatorial families, too. There is therefore an inbuilt tension between the continuing competition and the intermittent reassignment of family roles on the one hand and the need for solidarity

---

[36] Champlin's recent study (1991: 107–20) makes it clear that this presumption of parental *pietas* was justified. For all the popular and literary preoccupation with the machinations of legacy-hunters (*captatores*) and stepparents, actual testamentary dispositions reveal an overwhelming preference for the children as heirs of the testator or testatrix.

on the other. This tension generates social mechanisms which are
reasonably successful in checking conflict before it reaches a serious
level. The view we have of the Cicero and the Sicinius families alerts
us to the trouble-making which went on in Roman families and could
be deliberately fostered by reporting to the parties what the others
had said or written about them.[37] They also demonstrate how the very
existence of outside mechanisms could exacerbate conflict, and even
transform it into a much more dangerous phenomenon. An aggrieved
brother who is to appear before Caesar or a suspicious son encouraged by his uncle to air his grievances against his mother through a
court case directed against his foreign stepfather becomes an incen-
diary with a torch to hand. Both the discourses and the mechanisms
available themselves shape an existing situation and therefore its
possible consequences.

I deliberately chose examples from quite different eras and medi-
ated through different genres, to illustrate my argument, that certain
kinds of conflict are virtually endemic. It is not so much the conflict
itself as the setting which provides the possibility of transforming it
into something really dangerous. The setting includes civil war, palace
politics, strong social prejudices (e.g. against stepparents), and the
incitement of interested parties. The seasoned politicians and killers
who reported young Quintus' disloyalties to his uncle, the already
wealthy adult daughter challenging her father's will, the son and
brother-in-law of Pudentilla all had something to gain from exacer-
bating family conflict and were reckless of (perhaps excited by) its
possible cost to others. Civil wars and civil or criminal actions alike
become convenient means for achieving an end. The participants are
precipitated into public, shameful, and dangerous family ruptures.
But the initial causes are ones to be found in more mundane settings
and played out in distressing but tolerable ways. Perhaps one of the
most striking things about Roman examples is the failure to threaten
or use the formidable powers theoretically available to a *paterfamilias*
faced with generational family conflict.

Rigid identifications of cause and effect are probably as dubious
as predictions, but both are tempting. One can, for example, imagine Quintus *frater* enjoying the visits of a young Quintus, mellowed

[37] Dr Welch pointed out that the interference of such actors as Balbus and Hirtius at this
stage of Roman history is hardly to be likened to general trouble-making or gossip. I see their
intervention (e.g. *Att.* 13. 37. 2), however, as a characteristic phenomenon of Roman social
(including family) dynamics, which takes on special meanings in these particular circumstances. It is central to my thesis that civil war—like the existence of criminal charges for
magic—provides a context and medium for styles of conflict which would have existed otherwise but taken a less serious form.

by marriage and paternity, the painful, intense conflicts blotted out as surely as they were in their last moments.[38] It is difficult, too, for us to shake off entirely the oddities of twentieth-century thinking, in which we are trying to reconcile a peculiarly homogeneous version of family happiness and childhood needs with a growing consciousness that violence can be present in the best of homes. We are also very preoccupied with the unconscious and the notion that frustrations must eventually cause problems. At one stage, Cicero thought that Quintus must always have hated him, yet the two brothers had seemed close and affectionate through more than half a century of vicissitudes and were reconciled to an extent before their deaths. Perhaps most of all we need a reminder that many kinds of conflict are a normal part of family dynamics and that, while such mechanisms as *patria potestas* and rules for dowry return or inheritance provide a legal and social framework for containing conflict, other structures—including prejudices against stepmothers, or in-laws, or insubordinate children—can themselves cause and shape more serious forms of conflict.

[38] The Plutarch account of their deaths might well be fanciful, but represents the kind of resolution deemed appropriate and likely by ancient and modern readers. It seems a proper reflection of ideology and observed reality.

8

Interpreting Epithets
in Roman Epitaphs

HANNE SIGISMUND NIELSEN

diis manibus | C Volusio Sp f Seuero | filio optimo et piissimo
uix | ann xv mens iiii diebus xiiii | Volusia Herois mater fecit
et | sibi et Phoebo coniugi optim | et carissimo | et libertis
libertabus posterisq | nostris omnibus (29540)[1]

Recent research has placed much emphasis on the interpretation of epitaphs to clarify important problems concerning the structure of the Roman family.[2] But only isolated pieces of information from each inscription have been registered and used in these quantitative studies. Inscriptions, like the one quoted above, consist of many different elements, and our interpretation of each epitaph depends on how these are interrelated. I have been interested to see what happened if a sample of inscriptions was made taking into consideration all possible information—or as much as possible—from each epitaph, and thus combining the advantages of the quantitative approach to the epigraphic material with the interpretation made on the basis of a reading of each epitaph.

In this chapter, the main emphasis will be on the interpretation of the epithets proper used in the epitaphs by dedicators to characterize the commemorated persons, but other 'epithetic' aspects of the information provided by the epitaphs will naturally be included in the analysis.

In my examination, I assume that no information in any epitaph is given without reason. No term of relationship, age indication,

References to inscriptions are to *CIL* 6, unless stated otherwise.

[1] Volusia was free at the time she had her son C. Volusius Seuerus. He died aged 15 and was commemorated by his mother. On the same epitaph, Volusia commemorates herself and Phoebus, whom she designates *coniux*. The union must have been a *contubernium* for Phoebus was evidently of slave status. Volusia cannot have been without means: the epitaph includes in the commemoration her freedmen and their descendants. Probably it was originally placed over the entrance door of a family grave, the occasion of its dedication being the death of C. Volusius Seuerus and the natural dedicator his mother, whose social status was higher than her husband's. Volusia describes her son as *optimus* and *piissimus* and her husband as *optimus* and *carissimus*.

[2] Saller and Shaw (1984a); Shaw (1984; 1991); Rawson (1986a); Treggiari (1975; 1981).

and epithet was chosen haphazardly, and it was not a coincidence whether some information—such as status or occupation—figured in the epitaph. This assumption is, of course, not properly valid. As in our own Western culture, Roman dedicators sometimes chose rather mechanically what was included in the epitaph for the passer-by to read, but usually there seems to have been good reason why an epitaph had a particular form. This does not imply that the epitaphs inform us what real life had been for the dedicators and the commemorated persons mentioned in the epitaphs. The pattern of commemoration of the Romans has always been puzzling, for it evidently did not reflect real life, but not until this was accepted and fully realized was it possible to make fruitful use of the epigraphic material in the study of the Roman family.[3]

I will not here enter into the problem of the original physical context of the epitaphs, but treat them—as is customary—simply as text (Sigismund Nielsen 1995).

THE SAMPLE

This study is based on a sample of every fifth readable epitaph from *CIL* 6, excluding all *additamenta*.[4] Also fragmented inscriptions have been included provided they yielded enough information. On the other hand, some inscriptions—despite being perfectly legible—have been excluded if they were too ambiguous and unclear to be of any use.

The sample consists of a total of 3,797 epitaphs representing various types of graves. In 616 of these epitaphs it is uncertain whether the person or persons mentioned are dedicators or commemorated. Usually these inscriptions come from *columbaria*, only very infrequently from single graves or family tombs (Sigismund Nielsen 1995). The person or persons in this type of epitaph are mentioned in the genitive or nominative. There are no age indications, no epithets, terms of relation, or other signs to show whether they are commemorated, rather than owners or dedicators.[5] It is of course of major

---

[3] Saller and Shaw (1984a: 130): 'The skewing is not an effect upon our data but rather is produced by the very differences in cultural preferences for funerary commemoration that we are studying. Whatever skewing there is in these data, therefore, represents the phenomena that we are seeking to measure.'

[4] That is, the material examined comprises the inscriptions 1345 to 29680.

[5] In the *columbarium* near the Arch of Drusus in the area once known as Vigna Codini, excavated by Pietro Campana in 1840, 198 inscriptions (4881–5078) can still be seen *in situ*. There are several instances of identical inscriptions of the type described here, making it reasonable to believe that these inscriptions most frequently inform us of ownership of the *loculus* rather than commemoration.

importance to the interpretation of an epitaph to know whether a person mentioned is commemorated or a dedicator. In these 616 epitaphs, 874 persons are mentioned. Due to uncertainty about their role in the epitaph, I have preferred to exclude them from the overall examination. In respect of both distribution of sex and status, they behave rather differently from the rest of the epitaphs of *CIL* 6 and in my opinion would, if included, skew the results too much.[6] The following survey is therefore based on the 3,181 epitaphs with a total of 4,508 commemorated from the sample of *CIL* 6 where the persons mentioned can with certainty be identified as commemorated or as dedicators.[7]

What will be said here about terms of relation and age distribution is well known and should not be discussed at length. It is, however, necessary to establish the framework, however familiar, if only because there are slight differences between my approach to an interpretation of the epigraphic material and that of other recent studies.

TERMS OF RELATIONSHIP USED IN THE EPITAPHS

Table 8.1 shows the distribution of relationships among the commemorated in the sample. It is evident from these distributions that, when relationships are mentioned, there is a strong emphasis on parents' dedications to their children and on dedications to spouses. Likewise, it was evidently not considered part of the normal pattern of commemoration to put up epitaphs to siblings and other members of the family, including grandparents, uncles, etc.[8] This characteristic

[6] The 874 persons mentioned in the possible owner epitaphs of *CIL* 6 constitute 16% of the 5,382 commemorated in the sample as a whole or 23% of the 3,789 dedicators. The sex ratio is 200 (583/291) compared with the 128 (2,121/1,654) of the commemorated in *CIL* 6 and 158 (1,787/1,128) of the dedicators if they are excluded. Nine of the commemorated are of uncertain sex, due to fragmentation of the epitaph.

[7] When so many components from each epitaph are included in the examination, it has been necessary to make the sample analysed extensive. Otherwise, some of the groups singled out would become too small to yield any result. If only a few characteristic features were analysed, e.g. term of relation or age, a smaller sample would suffice.

[8] This is not the place to go into detail with the definitions of the terms of relation found in the epigraphic material. My interpretation of the relationships is—with a few exceptions—in accordance with the one found in Saller and Shaw's studies. I do not, however, include *alumni* in the group 'other family'. Here they constitute—together with *uernae* and *deliciae*—the group of foster-children (Sigismund Nielsen 1987; 1990; 1991). In the group of fosterers are included nurses (*nutrices*) as well as male fosterers (*nutritores*) under any relevant term of relationship. The small group of foster-brothers and -sisters consists of the persons commemorated with the term *conlactaneus*. The only group defined negatively is the group 'other relation'. Here relationships are found that do not fit into any other group. It includes heirs (*heredes*), colleagues (*collegae*), friends and comrades (*comes, sodalis, amicus*), but also

TABLE 8.1. *Distribution of relationships*

Term of relation	CIL 6	
	%	no.
no term of relation	25	1,136
spouse	21	932
sibi	16	724
son/daughter	15	679
parent	5	245
patron	4	170
sibling	3	147
foster-child	3	144
client	2	108
other relation	2	107
conseruus, conlibertus	1	53
other family	1	32
fosterer, foster-brother/-sister	1	31

feature of the Roman pattern of commemoration has been used in modern research as the most important evidence to show that the Roman family was nuclear. One point should, however, immediately raise suspicion, namely the surprisingly low percentage of children's dedications to their parents. This is not necessarily an argument against the existence of the Roman nuclear family, but may manifest a lack of stability (Saller and Shaw 1984a: 138). Still, in the light of the probable age distribution of the Roman population (Frier (1982; 1983); Parkin (1992: 67–90)), of the emphasis in the *Digest* on the filial duty of sons to bury their fathers (*D.* 11. 7, esp. 11. 7. 14. 8, Ulpian), and of the importance of *pietas* that seems to have been prevalent in all status groups of Roman society, I find the lack of commemorated parents in the epigraphic material from Rome

a freedman's spouse (*coniux liberti*), a pupil and a teacher (*discens, magister*). Unlike Saller and Shaw, I include self-commemorations (*sibi* or *se uiuo*) and commemorated without any term of relation in my count of commemorated. Commemorated persons without any term of relationship differ significantly from those commemorated with a term of relationship. Probably Saller and Shaw are right in believing that the commemorated without any term of relationship represent the same relationships found elsewhere in the material, but it should be noted that there are significant differences between commemorated generally and commemorated without any term of relationship. For example, the sex ratio for the latter group is 160 (699/437) and thus much higher than the epigraphic norm. Self-commemorations are likewise fundamentally different from commemorations of others. I have included them in the overall count of commemorated, but excluded them from the following distributions in this analysis.

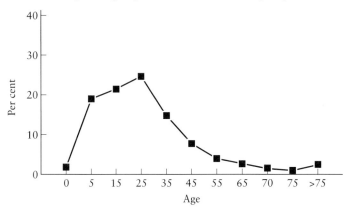

FIG. 8.1. Age distribution, *CIL* 6.

very strange, and would suggest that the missing dedications to parents and the high percentage of dedications to sons and daughters primarily reflect the expectations parents of all status groups had of their children and only secondarily the structure of the family.

Compared with the almost total lack of mention of all but the closest family, it is interesting to see that patronage relationships constitute 6 per cent of the commemorations and fosterage relationships 4 per cent. Relationships of patronage and fosterage were evidently frequently considered to be as important and as personal as close family ties[9] and the relatively high percentages of both alongside the close familial ones should be kept in mind.

THE AGE DISTRIBUTION OF COMMEMORATED IN *CIL* 6

Much effort has been squandered in a vain attempt to use the age indications of the epitaphs from the Roman empire to reconstruct the demographic structure of the population. These studies were definitely abandoned in the 1960s (Clauss 1973). Other approaches to the demographic problem have been made, and on the basis of stipulations, plausible results have been obtained (Frier 1982; 1983; Parkin 1992). The age distribution according to the inscriptions in *CIL* 6 is shown in Fig. 8.1. It is evident that the epigraphic age distribution does not reflect demographic reality. Of those commemorated

---

[9] Some patronage relationships were likewise familial. In these cases I have always registered the relationship as familial, just as patronage relationships, although they may have been familial as well, are registered as patronage relationships if the familial side of the relationship is not explicitly mentioned.

in *CIL* 6 as a whole, excluding self-commemorations, 34 per cent (1,298/3,784) are commemorated with an indication of age. The ratio between commemorated males and females in the material as a whole is 128 (2,121/1,654), while it is 148 (775/523) for commemorated with an indication of age at death.

Compared to what would have been demographically expected, the age groups between 5 and 25 years are overrepresented in the general age distribution of *CIL* 6, while hardly any infants are commemorated—demographically, infants ought to have constituted the largest part of the material. The question is, whether they were commemorated anonymously, or whether they were not commemorated at all. Unfortunately, it will probably never be possible to answer this question, but instead of concentrating on missing evidence, it is more productive to examine the material actually available. As far as I can see, this does in fact suggest why infants are absent from the epigraphic material, whether commemorated or not.

Table 8.2 shows the percentages and numbers of commemorated for whom age is indicated in the different relationship groups in *CIL* 6.

The only groups where those commemorated with an age indication outnumber those without one are the groups of foster-children and sons and daughters. The strong emphasis on youth makes it reasonable to conjecture that premature death was considered an

TABLE 8.2. *Distribution of age indications by relationship group*

Term of relationship	%	no.
son/daughter	68	461/679
foster-child	60	86/144
sibling	36	53/147
no term of relation	30	339/1,136
spouse	24	227/932
client	21	23/108
patron	17	29/170
parent	12	29/245

Note: The groups *conserui* and *conliberti*, other family, other relations, and fosterers and foster-brothers/-sisters, are passed over here and in the following. The number of inscriptions and epithets in these groups is too low. When information is given about these groups, it is normally only to complete the picture. For obvious reasons, self-commemorations are not included.

important motivation for commemoration. The epithets used to characterize the different relationships point in the same direction and make it possible to clarify more precisely why children and young adults were thought of in connection with premature death, while infants were not.

The epithets used to characterize the commemorated and his or her relationship to the dedicator in the epitaphs of *CIL* 6 have not been treated since Harrod wrote *Latin Terms of Endearment and Family Relationships* (Harrod 1909). This book is a remarkable study, written long before the age of computers made life both easier and at the same time much more complicated for social historians studying epitaphs. Harrod's main aim was to establish which epithets were most frequently used to characterize which relationships. Considering the magnitude of the compilation task, it is perfectly understandable that Harrod concentrated on the distribution of epithets applied to different relationships and been less occupied with their interpretation. Here I will first briefly present the epithets used in *CIL* 6, the general frequency of their occurrence, and their distribution of age indications, and discuss their interpretation on the basis of their use in the literary texts.

Of all commemorated, excluding self-commemorations, 49 per cent (1,840/3,784) are commemorated with at least one epithet. This means that it was considerably more common to be commemorated with an epithet than with an age indication.

A great variety of epithets is found in *CIL* 6. As many as 64 different adjectives and expressions are used in the sample examined in this study, although several of them are found only once or twice. A total of 2,220 epithets and expressions are used to characterize the commemorated. If the most infrequent epithets are deducted —that is epithets that constitute less than 1 per cent of all those found in the sample—we are left with a list of a mere 8 different epithets (see Table 8.3). *Bene merens, dulcissimus/a, carissimus/a,* and *pientissimus/a* or *piissimus/a* constitute 84 per cent (1,843/2,220) of all the epithets found. With the inclusion of *optimus/a, sanctissimus/ a, incomparabilis,* and 'expression or sentence', 93 per cent (2,070/ 2,220) of the epithets in *CIL* 6 are found among those mentioned above. This gives the impression of a very conventional choice of epithets that do not reveal much, either about the commemorated or the relationship between the commemorated and the dedicator.

TABLE 8.3. *Common epithets*

Epithet	%	No. of all epithets/2,220
bene merens	50	1,098
dulcissimus/a	12	262
carissimus/a	12	257
pientissimus/a or *piissimus/a*	10	226
optimus/a	5	113
sanctissimus/a	2	52
incomparabilis	1	31
expression/sentence	1	26

This is, of course, largely the case. The epithets of the Romans must have been as normative as the epitaphs in which they are mentioned: they express society's expectations, but therefore also the individual's expectations. The degree of reality behind the epithets is difficult to gauge. This is, however, of minor importance. The interesting thing is to observe the different expectations as they pertain to different types of relationships. In the following, I will discuss the use of the four most frequently found epithets in *CIL* 6.

EPITHETS USED TO CHARACTERIZE DIFFERENT RELATIONSHIPS

The number and type of epithets used to characterize the different relationships represented in *CIL* 6 vary significantly. Table 8.4 shows the number and percentage of commemorated of different types who are commemorated with at least one epithet.

Compared with Table 8.2 showing the percentage of persons commemorated with an indication of age, it is interesting to notice the shift in emphasis in the different terms of relation. The greatest emphasis as far as epithets are concerned lies on *patroni/ae*, parents and spouses, in contrast to the distribution of age indications, where the major emphasis was on sons and daughters and foster-children. The wording of each epitaph is dictated by the space available on the stone and the economic possibilities of the dedicator. In several instances—when the age at death of the commemorated was known —the dedicator must necessarily have chosen whether to indicate age or to use an epithet. On the basis of the distribution of epithets

TABLE 8.4. *Distribution of commemorated with at least one epithet*

Term of relationship	%	no.
spouse	74	693/932
to patron	71	120/170
parent	67	163/245
son/daughter	61	415/679
client	56	61/108
sibling	48	71/147
foster-child	40	57/144
no term of relation	11	129/1,136

proper in the epitaphs, it would not be unreasonable to conjecture that indication of age in an epitaph was looked upon much as an epithet, that is as something that primarily informed the reader of the epitaph of the nature of the relationship. In my opinion, this offers the best explanation of why epitaphs commemorating persons without an indication of age at death more frequently contain one or more epithets, compared with epitaphs commemorating persons with an indication of age. I will return to this point below in my discussion of the epithets proper in the inscriptions.

GENERAL INTERPRETATION OF THE EPITHETS

The question is, what type of information the reader is supposed to get from a certain epithet, and how the epithet characterizes the relationship mentioned. Despite the restricted number of epithets used in the inscriptions, they do not normally seem to have been used indiscriminately. Therefore it seems reasonable, on the basis of their pattern of distribution among the different relationships in the epigraphic material and in the literary sources, to attempt an interpretation of their character and the connotations they gave the ancient reader.

In Table 8.5 the percentage distribution of epithets in different types of relationships is presented.[10] This distribution includes all epithets applied in the sample, irrespective both of the epithet's position and number in the inscription. If the dedicator had the possibility of applying only a single epithet to the commemorated it might be expected

[10] The percentages are relative, i.e. the 33% sons and daughters characterized as *dulcissimi* represent the 156 of a total of 477 epithets applied to sons and daughters, not of the total number of 2,220 epithets.

TABLE 8.5. *Distribution of epithets by relationship group*

	total	foster-child	no term	other relative	parent	patron	client	sibling	son or daughter	spouse
no. of epitaphs	2,220	63	147	75	193	136	74	90	477	885
bene/										
%	30	24	29	25	28	55	46	21	14	34
no.	663	15	42	19	54	75	34	19	67	299
dulc/										
%	12	25	7	—	9	—	—	14	33	5
no.	262	15	10	—	17	1	—	13	156	47
caris/										
%	12	21	7	7	5	—	11	8	10	17
no.	257	13	10	5	10	2	8	7	49	152
pient/										
%	10	—	—	—	22	—	—	20	25	3
no.	226	2	3	2	43	2	3	18	121	29
optim/										
%	5	—	—	21	11	7	6	3	2	5
no.	113	1	2	16	21	10	4	3	8	46
sanc/										
%	2	—	—	—	—	—	—	—	1	5
no.	52	—	—	—	2	1	—	1	3	42
incom/										
%	1	—	—	—	—	—	—	3	—	3
no.	31	—	—	—	1	—	—	3	2	23
expr/										
%	1	—	5	—	—	—	—	—	1	1
no.	26	1	8	2	1	—	1	2	4	7

Note. **Here** only the instances where *bene merens* is written in full are included.

that this would be chosen with more care and precision than if several epithets were used.

Table 8.6 in part shows how many of the inscriptions mentioning an epithet in *CIL* 6 mention only a single epithet and the distribution of these epithets. This percentage is always very high, but it should be noted in particular that commemorated foster-children and sons and daughters are very frequently commemorated with only a single epithet. This is at first sight surprising. Together with spouses, sons and daughters represent the groups of commemorated accorded the greatest interest in *CIL* 6, and together with commemorated foster-children, sons and daughters represent the groups most frequently commemorated with an indication of age. Considering this heavy emphasis, it seems at first sight surprising that as many as 74 per cent (355/477) of the inscriptions containing epithets dedicated to sons and daughters contain only one epithet, while this is true of only 61 per cent (537/885) of the same type of inscriptions dedicated to spouses. The high percentage of 'single epithet' commemorations among sons and daughters should probably be seen in the light of their likewise high percentage of age indications. The dedicators of these epitaphs to sons and daughters have chosen to characterize the commemorated by one epithet and an age indication instead of by two or more epithets.

BENE MERENS

dis manib Veturiae | Daphne C Iulius Anthus | et Veturia Helena | parentes filiae suae | carissimae fecerunt | uixit anno i mensibus vii (5046)

dis manibus | Veturiae Daphne | uix an lxxii | Veturia | Helene patronae | benemerenti | fecit (5047)[11]

Bene merens[12] is by far the epithet most usually applied to commemorated persons in *CIL* 6 and therefore in many ways the most

---

[11] These two inscriptions are still found *in situ* thanks to the thorough excavation of the *columbarium* where they were found by P. Campana. Veturia Helena has dedicated these two epitaphs, one to her daughter together with her husband C. Iulius Anthus and the other to her *patrona*. According to his *nomen*, the husband was not the freedman of Veturia Daphne, as his wife was. Helena and Anthus had called their daughter after Helena's *patrona*. But the most interesting thing about these two epitaphs is that the elder Veturia Daphne is as a matter of course included in the biological family of Helena. None of these persons were probably very well off. They had chosen a *columbarium* for burial where the *loculi* were sold and resold—the cheap but decent way of being buried in Rome. The little girl is characterized as *carissima*, while the *patrona* is called *benemerens*.

[12] Or its equivalent *bene meritus/a*. *Bene merens* is by far the most common form of the epithet.

TABLE 8.6. *Distribution of single epitaph inscriptions*

	total	foster-child	no-term	other relative	parent	patron	client	sibling	son or daughter	spouse
all epitaphs										
%	69	83	79	79	70	79	68	61	74	61
no.	1,527/2,200	52/63	116/147	59/75	136/193	107/136	50/74	55/90	355/477	537/885
bene/										
%	34	25	33	25	29	61	54	27	13	42
no.	516	13	38	15	40	65	27	15	46	225
dulc/										
%	11	23	7	—	8	—	—	15	34	2
no.	172	12	8	—	11	—	—	8	121	12
caris/										
%	11	25	6	7	4	—	6	7	12	15
no.	161	13	7	4	6	1	3	4	42	81
pient/										
%	11	1	—	—	23	—	—	16	28	3
no.	160	1	2	2	31	1	1	9	98	14
optim/										
%	4	—	—	15	11	4	—	—	—	4
no.	55	—	2	9	15	4	1	—	4	19
sanc/										
%	1	—	—	—	—	—	—	—	—	4
no.	22	—	1	—	1	—	—	—	1	19
incom/										
%	1	—	—	—	—	—	—	—	—	—
no.	12	—	—	—	1	—	—	1	—	2
expr/										
%	1	—	5	—	—	—	—	—	—	2
no.	15	—	6	2	1	—	1	1	1	9

complicated expression to interpret. Harrod, in his study, did not even approach the problem of interpreting this epithet.[13] The fact that *bene merens* occurs very frequently suggests that it is mainly applied as a formula and not as a meaningful epithet carrying information about the relationship between the dedicator and the commemorated.[14] In contrast to the other epithets found in the inscriptions, *bene merens* is frequently used in an abbreviated formulaic form supporting the non-epithetical interpretation of the expression. In 30 per cent (663/2,220) of the instances, it is given in full, while in 11 per cent (242/2,220) it is abbreviated as the formulaic *b. m.* In another 7 per cent (158/2,220) this formulaic *b. m.* is placed at the end of the epitaph, while *d. m.* (*dis manibus*) is placed at the beginning. This use of the epithet *bene merens* must be considered the least epithetic. It should probably be regarded only as a graphic indicator of the beginning and end of the inscription proper, not as a proper epithet. In another 2 per cent (35/2,220), the formula *b. m.* is placed at the end of the epitaph without the *d. m.* formula at the beginning of the inscription. Perhaps this is likewise meant to be a graphic indication of where the inscription ends. It is less certain than with the *d. m./b. m.* formula, but may have been the case. If we concentrate on the instances in which *bene merens* is written as an epithet proper, the possibility of discerning the epithet behind the more automatic and formulaic use seems to become significantly better.

In Latin literature the expression *bene merens* or *bene meritus* is much less common than in the inscriptions. In contrast to the inscriptions in which the expression is applied to all types of relationship, both familial and non-familial—predominantly, however, to non-familial relations—in literature it is almost always used in a non-familial context to describe relationships denoting obligation and gratitude. Cicero provides us with some examples. See for example *De prouinciis consularibus* 24. 2: 'nemini ego possum esse bene merenti de re publica non amicus', and *De legibus* 1. 43. 3: 'ubi enim liberalitas, ubi patriae caritas, ubi pietas, ubi aut bene merendi de altero aut referendae gratiae uoluntas poterit existere?' Several times in the examples, *gratia* is naturally mentioned together with *bene merens*, thus in Cicero, *Philippics* 14. 13. 9: 'nonne satis est ab hominibus uirtutis ignaris gratiam bene merentibus non referri?'

---

[13] See Harrod (1909: 1): 'These two participles of *mereo* occur on the stones with such extreme frequency that it has not seemed advisable to collect the instances of their use and work out complete statistics as has been done in all other cases.'

[14] Thus also *TLL* s.v. *mereo* 812. 25: 'propter usum creberrimum haec formula significatione propria euanida etiam de iis adhibetur, in quibus aliquid meriti fuisse non potest, uelut de liberis breuissimae aetatis'.

In Cicero's letters, the only[15] example to my knowledge of a direct familial use of *bene merens* is *Att.* 14. 10. 4. 2: 'Quintus pater ad me grauia de filio, maxime quod matri nunc indulgeat cui antea bene merenti fuerit inimicus.' Cicero is of course referring to his sister-in-law Pomponia and her miserable relationship to his brother Quintus. In the *Digest*, a few instances refer to *amicos bene merentes*, but without going into detail about what they had done to deserve gratitude: for example, 39. 5. 5. pr., Ulpian: 'affectionis gratia neque honestae neque inhonestae donationes sunt prohibitae, honestae erga bene merentes amicos uel necessarios, inhonestae circa meretrices'. According to the *Digest, meretrices* were not in themselves *bene merentes*. This is the only example where *bene merens* seems to refer to sexual morals, but connotations in this direction do not seem to be part of the general meaning of the expression. According to the *meretrices* themselves—as they are presented by Plautus—nothing prevented them from being *bene merentes*. It all depended on whether they had done anything to deserve gratitude. The dialogue of the plays of Plautus makes the meaning of the expression *bene merens* very clear: only persons who had performed an actual service deserved gratitude and had the right to be called *bene merentes*. In *Captiui*, one of the young prisoners of war who has given the play its name warns the other young man's father that he will get his deserts: 313: 'est profecto deus, qui quae nos gerimus auditque et uidet: is, uti tu me hic habueris, proinde illum illic curauerit; bene merenti bene profuerit, male merenti par erit'. In *Menaechmi*—on another level—Erotium, the mistress of Menaechmus, maintains that she is *bene merens* on the basis of what she has done for her lover: 693: 'quando tu me bene merentem tibi habes despicatui, nisi feres argentum, frustra me ductare non potes'. He is reclaiming a cloak that she believes he has given to her. She feels that her anger is justified, for he actually owes her something substantial for her services. This very businesslike down-to-earth understanding of a relationship, in which one party is characterized as *bene merens*, because he or she had done something that deserved *gratia* from the other party,[16] is important to keep in mind when the epigraphic material is analysed.

As mentioned above, 30 per cent (663/2,220) of the epithets in the epigraphic material analysed are *bene merens* or its equivalent *bene meritus* written in full: see Table 8.5. Not surprisingly, *patroni/ae*

---

[15] See, however, also Hyginus, *Fabulae* 25. 2. 2 about Medea and Jason: 'Medea cum uidit se erga Iasonem bene merentem tanta contumelia esse affectam'.

[16] See also Plautus, *Pseudolus* 315–20: 'PS: face quod te rogamus, Ballio, mea fide, si isti formidas credere. ego in hoc triduo . . . euoluam id argentum tibi. BA: tibi ego credam? . . . CALL: sicine mihi aps te bene merenti male refertur gratia?'

are most frequently of all commemorated with the epithet *bene merens*. Of the epithets in this group, 55 per cent (75/136) are *bene merens*. The only other epithet employed in more than one or two inscriptions about *patroni/ae* is *optimus*. In all other groups of commemorated the range of epithets used is much wider. Just after commemorated *patroni*, *bene merens* is most frequently found in the group of persons commemorated by their patron, that is usually freedmen and servants commemorated by their master, but here a few instances of *carissimus*, *pientissimus*, and *optimus* are found as well, which makes the emphasis on *bene merens* seem less strong. Patronage relationships must invariably have been based on obligation and gratitude, probably often in a very concrete way. Foster-children are the only ones commemorated outside the biological family, with a slighter emphasis on *bene merens*. The emphasis here is almost equivalent to the one found among commemorated parents and siblings. Foster-children constitute a most interesting group among the commemorated in *CIL* 6: in many ways they are similar to commemorated sons and daughters and 'behave' much as one would expect close kin relations to do, but especially with respect to epithets there are important and interesting differences. Foster-children as a group in *CIL* 6 are slightly younger than commemorated sons and daughters, but this has not prevented their dedicators from characterizing them with a *bene merens* as frequently as they are called *dulcissimi* or *carissimi*. There may be several reasons for this. First, it should be noted that the percentage distribution of epithets used about foster-children is based on rather few epithets, but in all probability a sample containing a higher number of inscriptions would not show a different distribution. One of the reasons why the group of commemorated foster-children is quite frequently commemorated with this epithet may have been that the relationship to a foster-child was conceived of as something between kin and patronage. Unlike relationships within the family, a relationship to a foster-child was in one way or another a matter of choice.[17] This might naturally imply some sort of 'hidden contract' between fosterer and foster-child that made it natural to employ an epithet like *bene merens* about the foster-child, even if the child was actually fairly young. I will return to this point under my examination of the other epithets. To support this interpretation of the use of *bene merens*, it is relevant

---

[17] This is of course only to a certain extent true of *nutrices* who received wages for fostering a child, but nurses' relationships to their foster-children do not constitute the majority of relationships to foster-children in *CIL* 6. Most of them seem to belong to the type known from literature, where a child is chosen as a substitute for own children or simply because it was a sweet child. See Sigismund Nielsen (1987; 1990; 1991; 1996).

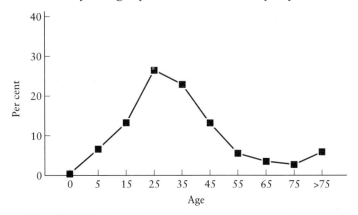

FIG. 8.2. Age distribution, *bene merens*.

to point to the commemoration of spouses and the number of times *bene merens* is found here. A priori it seems surprising that *bene merens* makes up 34 per cent (299/885) of the epithets applied to commemorated spouses—and as much as 42 per cent (225/537) of the cases where only one single epithet is used to characterize a commemorated spouse. Many of the persons called spouses in *CIL* 6 were not legally married to their partners,[18] but all types of marriage, including arrangements not legally sanctioned, would probably have required some contract or agreement between the partners that made it natural for the dedicating spouse to designate the commemorated as well-deserving, that is as having done what he or she was expected to do and thus deserving gratitude from his or her relatives.

It was mentioned above that 34 per cent (1,298/3,784) of the persons commemorated in *CIL* 6, excluding the self-commemorations, were commemorated with an indication of age. Equivalent to this, 34 per cent (223/663) of the commemorated characterized with *bene merens* are also commemorated with an indication of age. Fig. 8.2 shows the age distribution of persons commemorated both with an indication of age and with the epithet *bene merens*. This distribution shows that persons commemorated with *bene merens* were a little older than the epigraphic average, but apart from this, the *bene merens* age distribution corresponds pretty well to the epigraphic norm. A heavier percentual emphasis on age indications together with the use of *bene merens* would have been expected if the epithet carried some of the connotations of the age indication. But age

[18] For marriage-like unions see Rawson (1974), Treggiari (1981).

indication was obviously not used more frequently with *bene merens* compared with what could be expected in *CIL* 6.

Thus *bene merens*, when used as an epithet proper, seems primarily to have been used to characterize relationships based on obligation. The relatives of the commemorated persons express their gratitude towards the deceased, who has done what could be expected to make the relationship a harmonious one.

CARISSIMUS AND DULCISSIMUS

d m | Ducenio Agrippino infanti dulcissi\mo q u a iii m vi d xx | Ducenius Praesidius | et Varronia Nuceri | na alumno suo | fecerunt (17070)[19]

d m | Flauiae Aphrodite | coniugi | carissimae | bene merenti | Q Memmius | Daphnus | fecit (18280)[20]

After *bene merens* follow *dulcissimus*, *carissimus*, and *pientissimus* or *piissimus* as the epithets most frequently applied to commemorated in *CIL* 6. *Bene merens* is the epithet by far most frequently found. The latter epithets occur only as 12, 12, and 10 per cent of the epithets used. Normally, in accordance with the habits of daily language, the superlative of the epithet is used.

Carissimus makes up 12 per cent (257/2,220) of the epithets found in the sample of *CIL* 6 examined here. When I first began studying the epithets of *CIL* 6, I expected *carissimus* to be almost synonymous with *dulcissimus*, likewise representing 12 per cent (262/2,220) of the epithets found.[21] But many important differences between these seemingly very similar words appeared when their use in literature and epitaphs was examined more closely.

---

[19] Praesidius and Nucerina have dedicated this epitaph to their *alumnus* Agrippinus, who died when he was 3. Praesidius and Agrippinus have the same *nomen*: 'Ducenius'. Even very young children are found in the *CIL* 6 who had been manumitted. Therefore Agrippinus may have been the freedman of Praesidius, but we cannot tell. Agrippinus is characterized by the epithet *dulcissimus*. It is interesting to notice that there is no difference between the character of this dedication and one to a son, except in the term of relationship.

[20] Daphnus has dedicated an epitaph to his wife Aphrodite. He uses the term of relationship *coniux* about her. Nothing seems to have prevented the two from being lawfully married: they both have a *nomen* and could thus be citizens with a right to enter lawful marriage. There is no indication of age in the epitaph nor of any family outside the conjugal. Aphrodite is described as *carissima* and *bene merens*.

[21] Harrod (1909: 5–6) notes that *carissimus* is primarily applied to commemorated adults rather than children, and that it is favoured for spouses, while *dulcissimus* 'is the particular epithet not only of children but of younger children'. He does not, however, go into detail concerning the differences between them.

The distribution of epithets in the epigraphic material naturally depends on the distribution of terms of relation. Friends are only infrequently commemorated in the inscriptions and thus only infrequently characterized by an epithet. In literary texts, however, friendships—both personal close relationships and more political ones—play an important role. Friends are mentioned in all types of texts. In fact they constitute the largest single group of persons referred to as *dulces/dulcissimi* or *cari/carissimi* while they are hardly ever found in *CIL* 6 and therefore hardly ever characterized by these epithets.

It need hardly be mentioned that *dulcis* and *carus* have an underlying meaning also when used as a personal epithet, *dulcis* meaning 'sweet-tasting' and *carus* 'expensive' or 'dear'.[22] Both words have—as in English—kept some of this meaning when used as personal epithets. Occasionally, this meaning is referred to directly, when the word is used as a personal epithet. See, for example, Plautus, *Asinaria* 614: 'O melle dulci dulcior tu es', and Catullus 82: 'Quinti, si tibi uis oculos debere Catullum | aut aliud si quid carius est oculis | eripere ei noli, multo quod carius illi | est oculis seu quid carius est oculis.' This well-known fundamental difference between *carus* and *dulcis* is of importance for their use. In my analysis, I have included only examples in which *carus* and *dulcis* refer directly to a person, the other examples being of minor interest in this context. As mentioned above, *carus* is very frequently used in literature to characterize a personal friend. Especially in letters or poems addressed to friends, the epithet seems to have been particularly popular. See, for example, Cicero, *Fam.* 16. 14. 2, to Tiro: 'humanitatem . . . propter quam mihi es carissimus', Seneca, *Letters* 61. 4: 'uixi, Lucili carissime, quantum satis erat',[23] and Statius, *Siluae* 2. pr. 29: 'haec qualiacumque sunt, Melior carissime'. In the correspondence between Fronto and the imperial family, Fronto is almost invariably called *carissimus* in the letters addressed to him by Marcus Aurelius and Lucius: *Ad M. Caesarem* 3. 2. 2, from Marcus Aurelius to Fronto, ends with the words 'uale mi Fronto carissime et amicissime'. The character of the letters reveals a close bond of affection between Fronto and the imperial family, which seems to have been genuine. It is interesting that Fronto hardly ever uses the term *carissimus* when addressing Verus or Marcus Aurelius. As far as I can see, the epithet is applied only once to Marcus Aurelius in the *De nepote amisso* 4. 1. 7: 'grauiter male ualui, mi Marce carissime'. This may

---

[22] See the articles on *carus* and *dulcis*, TLL 507. 1 and 2188. 30.

[23] The expression is very frequent in the *Letters* of Seneca: 23. 6; 32. 3; 53. 7; 63. 16; 79. 13; 113. 1.

be purely accidental, but is interesting, both in the light of the use of the epithet *dulcissimus*—which is used freely in the letters—and in the light of the correspondence between Pliny and Trajan, book 10 of the letters of Pliny. The examples from this correspondence should certainly not be included in the group referring to personal friendships, but among the considerable number of instances where *carus* or *carissimus* is used in a political context. Trajan always addresses Pliny as *Secunde carissime* or *mi Secunde carissime*, while Pliny uses the term *domine* without any characterizing epithets. There can be no doubt that *carissimus* in the letters to Fronto designates the warm affection felt towards him by Verus and Marcus Aurelius, while Trajan on his part probably implies by the phrase that he considers Pliny a politically trustworthy and reliable magistrate. The interesting thing, of course, is that *carissimus* in both cases is used by a superior about his inferior. These few letters do not prove anything, and unfortunately the tendency cannot be traced with any certainty in the literary material.

It is not surprising that *carus* would be used to characterize the relation to a friend. More unexpected is the political use of the word. In frequency the number of political relationships characterized by *carus* is surpassed only by the number of personal friendships characterized in this way. In the material examined here, the political connotations of *carus* imply that the person thus characterized belongs to the same side or the same party. It is a favourite word of Cicero's, both in his speeches and letters. See, for example, Cicero, *Att.* 4. 15. 10: 'nos Caesari et carissimos et iucundissimos esse', *Fam.* 12. 12. 3 (from Cassius to Cicero): 'haec a te peto non solum reipublicae, quae tibi semper fuit carissima, sed etiam amicitiae nostrae nomine', *In Vatinium* 9. 1: 'nam ut tu me carum esse dixisti senatui populoque Romano non tam mea causa quam rei publicae', and finally *Philippics* 1. 33. 12: 'carum esse ciuem, bene de re publica mereri, laudari, coli, diligi gloriosum est; metui uero et in odio esse inuidiosum, detestabile, inbecillum, caducum'. I mention the political use of *carus* in connection with its use in characterizing friends, for some of these political relationships will at the same time have been personal relationships and vice versa.

In contrast to *carus*, *dulcis*—as could be expected—is never used in a political context, but frequently of close friends. Friends are the persons most frequently characterized by the epithet *dulcis* or *dulcissimus* in the texts. It should, however, be emphasized that most of the examples are from the letters of Fronto. The greetings in this correspondence are overwhelming and very intimate, for example, 2. 14. 1 from Marcus Aurelius: 'uale . . . amicissime, rarissime,

dulcissime magister', 4. 4. 2, likewise from Marcus Aurelius: 'uale
mihi homo amantissime . . . magister dulcissime', and finally 5. 55.
1, from Fronto to Marcus Aurelius: 'uale, domine dulcissime, desider-
antissime'. Notice the very emotionally loaded epithets used together
with *dulcissimus* in these instances. Also, in the letters of Cicero,
dulcissimus is used about very close relationships: *Fam.* 16. 21. 2,
to Tiro: 'gratos tibi optatosque esse, qui de me rumores afferentur
non dubito, mi dulcissime Tiro', and *Att.* 6. 2. 9: 'nimis, inquam,
in isto Brutum amasti, dulcissime Attice', perhaps ironically.

The political use of *carus* indicates that this word was considered
more formal than *dulcis*, but that this was not always the case, since
carus/carissimus also appears almost synonymously with *dulcis/dul-
cissimus*. It is difficult to tell whether the direction superior to inferior in the application of *carus* in the letters of Fronto and Pliny is
significant or purely accidental. The impression of the use of *dulcis/
dulcissimus* so far is that this epithet was considered more intimate
than *carus* and reserved for the characterization of very close relations.

This impression is supported by the frequent use of *dulcis/dulcis-
simus* by lovers to describe their loved ones. *Carus/carissimus* is also
found in these contexts, but less frequently—sometimes, however,
quite synonymously with *dulcis*. But as far as I can see, there is a
clear tendency for *dulcis* to have a heavy erotic undertone not so out-
spoken in connection with *carus/carissimus*. See, for example, Ovid,
Amores 2. 8. 21, to Cypassis: 'pro quibus officiis pretium mihi dulce
repende | concubitus hodie, fusca Cypassi, tuos', and Catullus 32.
1: 'amabo, mea dulcis Ipsitilla', and, less direct but no less explicit,
51.3: 'qui sedens aduersus identidem te | spectat et audit | dulce
ridentem'. See also Plautus, *Rudens* 364: 'ut amo te, mea Ampelisca,
ut dulcis es'. For *carus*, see Catullus 104. 1: 'credis me potuisse
meae maledicere uitae, | ambobus mihi quae carior est oculis', and
Propertius 1. 8b. 31, about Cynthia: 'illi carus ego et per me carissima
Roma dicitur', but see also Tibullus 1. 4. 53, a *priapeum* on how
to seduce boys—here there can be no doubt about the erotic con-
notations: 'tunc tibi mitis erit, rapias tum cara licebit | oscula'.

It is likewise interesting to see how *dulcis* and *carus* are used
about spouses in literary texts, for the same tendency is found here:
when *dulcis* is used, the emphasis is usually more on the erotic side
of married life than on anything else. This is not the case with *carus*.
See, for example, Apuleius, *Metamorphoses* 5. 6. 2 on Amor and
Psyche: 'centies moriar quam tuo isto dulcissimo connubio caream',
Statius, *Siluae* 1. 2. 211 on the wedding of Stella and Violentilla:
'dulcia cum dominae dexter conubia uultus | adnuit!', and Ovid,
Heroides 13. 122, from Laodameia to her dearly beloved Protesilaos:

'promptior est dulci lingua referre mora', about the kisses she is longing for.

The language of lovers often bears resemblance to the language used by adults about small children. According to the tendency so far emerging from the literary material, we would expect *dulcis* to be an epithet applied especially to small children. Harrod rightly points out that this is the case in the inscriptions,[24] and the literary examples confirm the truth of this assumption. In a number of instances, *dulcis* is used as the epithet proper about infants, so in the *Digest* 32. 1. 41. 14, Scaevola: 'reliquum omne reddas... Maeuiae infanti dulcissimae'. Pliny calls childhood 'illam aetatem dulcissimam' in one of his letters (2. 18. 1). Statius uses *dulcis* to characterize small crawling and prattling children in his *Siluae*, for example 4. 5. 34: 'quis non in omni uertice Romuli | reptasse dulcem Septimium putet?', and 2. 7. 37: 'primo murmure dulce uagientem'. There is also a tendency for sons and daughters characterized by *dulcis/dulcissimus* to be generally younger than sons and daughters characterized by *carus/carissimus*. See, for example, Juvenal 5. 138: 'nullus tibi paruulus aula | luserit Aeneas nec filia dulcior illo' and 6. 38: 'tollere dulcem cogitat heredem'; see also Lucretius 3. 895: 'uxor optima nec dulces occurrunt oscula nati'. There is no emphasis on early age in the examples where *carus/carissimus* is used about sons and daughters. The epithet is found six times in the *Digest* in direct speech, in examples illustrating obligations placed on sons and daughters through their parents' testament. These sons and daughters cannot have been minors, since they were expected to take upon them the responsibility of fulfilling their parents' wishes. See, for example: D. 36. 1. 79. pr., Scaevola: 'uosque, liberi carissimi, hoc fideicommisso'.[25] In other examples, it is usually difficult if not impossible to estimate the age of the son or daughter called *carus/carissimus*. Age seems to be of minor importance in these cases, but usually they seem to be older: Cicero, *De domo sua* 96: 'defleui coniugis miserae... liberorum carissimorum'; Plautus, *Captiui* 400, where Hegio talks about his missing son: 'meus mihi, suos cuique est carus'; Pliny 3. 16. 4: 'filius decessit eximia pulchritudine, pari uerecundia et parentibus non minus ob alia carus quam quod filius erat'.

It is dangerous to apply statistical methods to the quantitative distribution of epithets in literary material, but there seems to be

---

[24] Harrod (1909: 10): 'Everything points to the conclusion that *dulcissimus* is the particular epithet not only of children but of younger children.'

[25] The other examples are: 31. 1. 34. pr., 6, Modestinus; 32. 1. 34. 3, Scaevola; 40. 5. 41. 1, 15, Scaevola.

no doubt that *carus/carissimus* and *dulcis/dulcissimus* in many cases
are used to describe the same type of relationships, namely to friends,
sons and daughters, spouses, and other members of the close family
(siblings and parents). On the other hand, there can be no doubt
either that in some cases there were strong preferences for which
of the two epithets was chosen. *Dulcis* appears in no political contexts in which *carus* plays a predominant role, while *dulcis* is the
epithet chosen by an author if sexuality or small children are in
mind. Therefore it would not be unreasonable to expect these differences in colour between the two epithets also to exist in the epigraphic material: that *dulcissimus* should be considered the more
intimate epithet of the two, while *carissimus* may have had a more
formal ring to it.

If we turn to the epigraphic material, it is immediately evident
that the distribution of *dulcissimus* and *carissimus* is very different
among the various terms of relationship (see Table 8.5). *Dulcissimus*
refers predominantly to foster-children and sons and daughters. This
is in accordance with the connotations of an intimate relationship
and youth found in the literary material and is not surprising. *Carissimus* is used much more widely than *dulcissimus* in the inscriptions.
First of all, I find it very interesting to see that very many foster-
children compared with sons and daughters are called *carissimus*.
The numbers behind the percentages of the epithets applied to foster-
children are not high, but I see no reason why the tendency should
not be clear. In the preference for *carissimus* applied to foster-
children there may be seen a trace of the same preference that might
be traced in the correspondence between Trajan and Pliny and between Fronto and Marcus Aurelius and Lucius Verus. Many foster-
children were of lower status than their fosterers, though this was
not invariably the case (Rawson 1986a; Sigismund Nielsen 1987).
Carissimus is also found in 8 instances in patrons' dedications to
their freedmen. This amounts to 11 per cent of the epithets applied
to clients in the material. Still the numbers are too low to provide
any evidence, just as the tendency that seems to appear in the letters
mentioned suggests itself only dimly. But apart from this uncertainty, I find it interesting that some sense of direction from superior to inferior status is perhaps visible.

Carissimus, after *bene merens*, is the epithet most frequently applied to spouses, while *dulcissimus* is only infrequently seen. If we—
probably reasonably enough—assume that *dulcissimus* as well as
carissimus were used in the inscriptions to indicate friendly and warm
feelings towards the person characterized by one of these epithets,
but that *dulcissimus* was primarily chosen if the commemorated

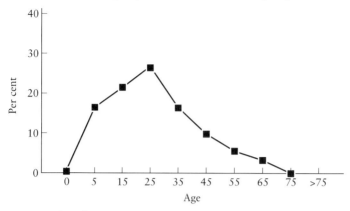

FIG. 8.3. Age distribution, *carissimus*.

was very young or if the relationship was very close, or both, the distribution of the two epithets in the epigraphic material still shows an interesting pattern. Notice that *dulcissimus* is more frequently used about parents and siblings than *carissimus*. This is interesting in the light of the frequency of *carissimus* in the dedications to spouses. Perhaps this may indicate more restricted expectations and less closeness in the relationship between spouses than between blood relations. The frequency of *pientissimus* among the different relationships does in fact point in this direction. I will return to this below, but first concentrate on the age distribution of those commemorated with the epithet *carissimus* and *dulcissimus* respectively.

  The wider use of *carissimus* in the epitaphs is supported by the age distribution of the persons commemorated with that epithet as well as an indication of age at death. It is closely in accordance with the overall distribution of age in *CIL* 6 (see Fig. 8.3 compared with Fig. 8.1). Of the commemorated persons characterized by *carissimus*, 40 per cent (103/257) have an indication of age at death. This is pretty well in accordance with the epigraphic norm for Rome of 34 per cent (1,298/3,784) of the commemorated with the exclusion of self-commemorations. This indicates, as was the case for the age distribution for commemorated with the epithet *bene merens*, that *carissimus* and its connotations were not specifically thought of in connection with indication of age. That is, a person with an age indication was not primarily thought of as *carus/carissimus*. That this is a point of some importance is stressed by the age distribution for commemorated with the epithet *dulcissimus* and the high percentage of these commemorated with an indication of age as well.

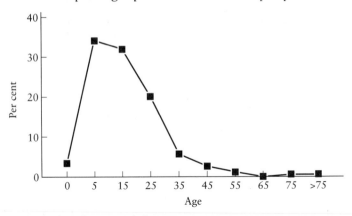

F IG. 8.4. Age distribution, *dulcissimus*.

As many as 65 per cent (171/262) of the commemorated characterized by the epithet *dulcis/dulcissimus* have an indication of age as
well. Fig. 8.4 shows that the age distribution of persons commemorated with the epithet *dulcissimus* is remarkably different, both from
the epigraphic norm of *CIL* 6 and the age distribution of persons
commemorated with the epithets *bene merens* and *carissimus*. This
is very interesting. In the first place it emphasizes that differences
of interpretation did exist between *carissimus* and *dulcissimus*. The
age distribution shows that persons described as *dulcissimi* were actually much younger than the epigraphic norm and generally also much
younger than persons called *carissimi*, and it seems evident that the
choice between *carissimus* and *dulcissimus* was certainly not an arbit-
rary one. In the second place, it ought to be possible at this point to
approach the problem of why some were commemorated with an
indication of age and some not, and what the indication of age in
an epitaph signified to the reader and dedicator of the epitaph.

It cannot be accidental that so many more of the commemorated
in *CIL* 6 characterized by the epithet *dulcissimus*, compared both
with the epigraphic norm and with those denoted *carissimi*, have an
indication of age. But at the same time as it seems possible to get
closer to an understanding of the age indication in Roman epitaphs
from *CIL* 6, new problems arise. The distribution of terms of relations for persons commemorated with an indication of age in *CIL*
6 shows, not surprisingly, a percentage increase in the groups representing commemorated children, notably sons and daughters, that
constitute the largest group compared with the overall distribution
shown in Table 8.1 (see Table 8.2).

Dulcissimus is found in 262 instances. In 156 (or 60 per cent) of these, the epithet characterizes a son or a daughter. It would not be wrong to conclude then that children who died young, with the exclusion of infants, were very frequently commemorated by their parents with an indication of age and that the epithet most frequently used about them was *dulcissimus*, and, as we shall see below, *pientissimus* or *piissimus*. This conclusion, however, is a poor one. It does not explain why parents chose exactly these epithets in combination with an age indication and why their choice was very different from fosterers' choice of epithets. As will be evident, foster-children are hardly ever called *pientissimi* or *piissimi*. I believe that the commemorative pattern of young sons and daughters should be taken as an expression of the broken expectations and hopes of parents to their now dead children. Unlike in modern Western society, relationships within the family were not on a purely emotional basis: grieving parents had lost more than their young children, they had lost their natural hope of support in old age and of a decent burial.[26] In other words, I imagine that the heavy emphasis on dedications to sons and daughters in *CIL* 6, the choice of epithets, and the frequent indication of age in these inscriptions, should be considered a strong indication of the important idea of *mors immatura*.

But before approaching the *mors immatura* or *acerba* motive, it will be appropriate to examine the use of the epithet *piissimus* or *pientissimus* very frequently applied precisely to sons and daughters.

PIENTISSIMUS AND *PIISSIMUS*

No difference in meaning can be discerned between *piissimus* and *pientissimus* in the epigraphic material of *CIL* 6.[27] The superlatives are hardly ever found in earlier literature. Cicero writes in *Philippics* 13. 43, in his invective against Mark Antony, that the superlative is very bad Latin: ' "nec Lepidi societatem uiolare, piissimi hominis" . . . tu porro ne pios quidem, sed "piissimos" quaeris et quod uerbum omnino nullum in lingua latina est, id propter tuam diuinam pietatem nouum inducis'. It appears frequently in later Latin literature and is the form preferred in the epigraphic material. *Pientissimus/piissimus*

---

[26] This thought is best expressed by Bradley in his review of Hopkins (1983) in *Classical Philology*, 82 (1986), 266–7.

[27] See Harrod (1909: 15): 'The meaning of *pientissimus* and of *piissimus* is treated here in one paragraph since their identity in meaning is apparent from these facts. In the first place, they are never used side by side as modifiers of a substantive . . . Finally and most convincing, the preferences shown in the application of the two words are in every case the same.'

occurs in 226 instances or 10 per cent (226/2,220) of all epitaphs in the sample of *CIL* 6 examined. As Table 8.5 shows, the distribution of the epithet in relation to the different terms of relationship is remarkable. It is restricted to close blood relations. Quasi-familial relationships and spouses are hardly ever denoted *pientissimi*. I will return to this below and first concentrate on how the epithet is used in Roman literature.

Unlike *carus* and *dulcis*, *pius* is a word loaded with connotations of fundamental importance to the Romans' understanding of themselves and to our understanding of the Roman mind.[28] In a very important paper, Richard Saller (1988: 410) has shown that *pietas* was a reciprocal feeling connoting not 'obedience' but 'affectionate devotion', 'due from all members of the family to all others'. In a later paper (1991: 150), he defines *pietas* as 'reciprocal, dutiful affection'. In dictionaries and handbooks, *pietas* is usually—when used of interpersonal relationships—defined as filial obligation and duty, that is the obedience owed by children to the head of the household, the *paterfamilias*. It is Saller's merit, on the basis of literature and legal sources, to have shown that this interpretation is much too narrow. Already in 1909, Harrod noted that there was a discrepancy between the interpretation of *pietas* found in dictionaries and what he saw in the inscriptions.[29]

Harrod primarily refers, as far as I can see, to the huge number of inscriptions where parents characterize their sons and daughters as *pientissimi* or *piissimi*. Thus his interpretation may seem less precise, but I believe that what he is expressing on the basis of his examination of the epigraphic material should be understood to be in line with Saller's interpretation of *pietas* in literature and legal texts.[30]

It is very difficult to measure affection. It is much easier to estimate the consequences of a possible feeling. *Pietas* seems always to have involved action or expectations of action. This is emphasized in almost all the examples presented by Saller. The two other epithets

---

[28] See Josef Liegle, '*Pietas*', *Zeitschrift für Numismatik* 42 (1932), 59–100, for a traditional approach to an interpretation of the political aspect of the word.

[29] Harrod (1909: 16): 'It is sufficiently evident that these two terms were applied most freely to the small circle of close blood kin. The articles on *pius* in the lexicons lay most stress on its meaning, dutiful to one's parents. For example, the statement in Forcellini, "pius proprie dicitur qui parentes, maiores, sanguine coniunctos, amicos, patriam amat colit, fouet iisque obsequitur et inseruit", would hardly give the reader the proper conception of its use as revealed by the sepulchral inscriptions, namely: that *piissimus* and *pientissimus* are used much more often to express the tender love of parent for child than the dutiful love of child for parent.'

[30] For the epigraphic material see also A. Betz: '*Pietas deorum erga homines* zu CIL III. 7954, aus Sarmizegetusa', in *Omagiu lui Constantin Daicoviciu cu prilejul împlinirii a 60 de ani* (1960), 33–7.

so far analysed here, *dulcis* and *carus*, do not contain this characteristic. The political sense sometimes given to *carus* or *carissimus* comes closest to giving connotations of action, but *pius* and the notion of *pietas* always as an important element incorporates action that shows the special qualities of this virtue. See, for example, Elder Seneca, *Controuersiae* 7. 4. 2: 'si matris exemplo pius esse uoluero, etiam oculos patri debeo', a rhetorical exercise with an exotic theme about a son who wants to save his father from pirates, while his mother, blinded by tears, wants him to stay with her and support her. See also Seneca, *Consolatio ad Heluiam* 19. 2. 9: 'illius manibus in urbem perlatus sum, illius pio maternoque nutricio per longum tempus aeger conualui', about a female relative, perhaps a sister or sister-in-law of Helvia; Ovid, *Tristia* 3. 3. 83–4: 'quamuis in cineres corpus mutauerit ignis, | sentiet officium maesta fauilla pium', about the poet's burial; Cicero, *Fam.* 6. 1. 3: 'officium iustum et pium et debitum rei publicae'. Livy frequently uses the epithet in connection with the expression 'pium et iustum bellum'.[31]

Saller rightly points out that *pietas* naturally often involved economic support of parents or children. This aspect is very important. Many parents, particularly from the lower economic classes of society, must have been totally dependent on help from their children in old age (Saller 1988: 406; Parkin, Ch. 6 above). There is another aspect of *pietas*, however, associated with this economic one, but at the same time part of the religious sphere, especially as far as death and mourning are concerned. It was possible to get a decent burial even if you had no family (Hopkins 1983: 211–17), but in many cases, especially in very small and accordingly often poor households, it must have been absolutely necessary to have relatives to make sure you had a decent burial and were commemorated properly.

In very many cases in literature, *pius* is used in connection with death and mourning. Ovid's sad description of his own funeral and the *officium pium* of his wife in this connection has already been mentioned above. See also D. 11. 7. 14. 7, Ulpian: 'potest tamen distingui et misericordiae modus, ut in hoc fuerit misericors uel pius qui funerauit, ut eum sepeliret, ne insepultus iaceret, non etiam ut suo sumptu fecerit: quod si iudici liqueat, non debet eum qui conuenitur absoluere: quis enim sine pietatis intentione alienum cadauer funerat?' In other examples[32] the person commemorating

---

[31] See e.g. 8. 6. 5; 9. 1. 10; 9. 8. 7; 37. 54. 19; 39. 36. 12; 42. 23. 6; 42. 47. 9.
[32] Ovid, *Heroides* 15. 113–16: 'postquam se dolor inuenit, nec pectora plangi | nec puduit scissis exululare comis, | non aliter, quam si nati pia mater adempti | portet ad exstructos

and grieving for a dead relative is naturally called *pius* and the duties in connection with funeral and commemoration are referred to as *officia* or *munera pia*, but notice that in Statius, *Siluae* 2. 1. 32: 'profusis | matribus atque piis cecini solacia natis' the deceased children are called *pii*.

When the dead are referred to as *pii* it is usually in a religious context, where their life in Elysium is imagined. See, for example, Lucan 6. 798: 'solum te . . . Brute, pias inter gaudentem uidimus umbras'; Martial 12. 52. 11: 'accipient olim cum te loca laeta piorum'; Ovid, *Amores* 3. 9. 66: 'auxisti numeros, culte Tibulle, pios'. Several other examples of this 'Elysiac' use of *pius* can be found. To my knowledge, in only two instances in literature, besides Statius, *Siluae* 2. 1. 32 mentioned above, is *pius* used of a recently deceased person not yet buried: Catullus 39. 4: 'ad pii rogum fili lugetur, orba cum flet unicum mater', and Martial 2. 41. 19–20: 'te maestae decet adsidere matri lugentiue uirum piumue fratrem'. In both these cases, the scene of a tragic burial is imagined, and in Catullus it is emphasized that the grieving mother has lost her only son. The question is, why these dead relatives are characterized as *pii*. There seems to me no doubt that the religious dimension of the word is not in question here. Being no longer alive, the dead were unable to demonstrate their *pietas* and thus to fulfil the expectations inherent in the notion. The dead son in Catullus would not be able to support his mother in old age and eventually bury her as he should have done. Instead the roles are reversed. She is now doing for him what he should have done for her. In a situation where the son receives *pietas* from his mother, he is still the one called *pius*. As the epigraphic evidence clearly shows, young sons and daughters dying before their parents and commemorated by them were actually very frequently characterized as *pientissimi* or *piissimi*, although their early death had made it impossible for them to act *pie* at the time their parents really needed it.

As mentioned above, *pientissimus/piissimus* is found 226 times in the epigraphic sample analysed here. In 121 of these cases or 54 per cent (121/226), the epithet is applied to commemorated sons and daughters. It is also frequently used about commemorated parents and siblings. It is very interesting, however, that it is only

corpus inane rogos', Pliny 8. 12. 4–5: 'scribit exitus inlustrium uirorum, in his quorundam mihi carissimorum. uideor ergo fungi pio munere, quorumque exsequias celebrare non licuit, horum quasi funeribus laudationibus seris quidem sed tanto magis ueris interesse'; Statius, *Siluae* 2. 1. 32: 'profusis | matribus atque piis cecini solacia natis', and 69: 'quid mirum tanto si te pius altor honorat | funere?'

infrequently used about spouses and foster-children: see Table 8.5.[33]
Saller (1988: 400 and n. 39) notes both the absence of conjugal
pietas in the legal texts and the emphasis on marital love and devotion found in the *exempla pietatis* in Elder Pliny, *NH* 7. 121–2.
There can be no doubt that *pietas* was expected between spouses.
There are several examples of this in literature.[34] *Contubernia*
(marital-type unions) between slaves are mentioned as equally important to blood relationships in *D.* 21. 1. 35, a paragraph stating
that *pietas* was quite fundamental and thus prior to law and social
status.[35] Slave families could (or should) not arbitrarily be split.
That this ideal was often in conflict with real life is evident from
the epigraphic material (Rawson 1966; Bradley 1987). Despite the
expectation of *pietas* in marriage, it is probably no coincidence
that *pietas* between spouses is so poorly attested in the *Digest* compared with *pietas* between parents and their children. The epithet
pientissimus/piissimus was not typically used to characterize spouses
in inscriptions. Just as was the case for persons characterized by the
epithet *dulcissimus*, a very high percentage—62 per cent (141/226)—
of commemorated persons characterized by *pientissimus/piissimus*
have at the same time an indication of age. The age distribution of
these persons is shown in Fig. 8.5. It shows much the same differences
compared with the epigraphic norm as the age distribution of persons
characterized by *dulcissimus*. The emphasis is clearly on young persons, but persons described as *pientissimi/piissimi* are not surprisingly
older than persons commemorated with the epithet *dulcissimus*.

Sons and daughters constitute the majority of commemorated characterized by *dulcissimus* and *pientissimus/piissimus* and they likewise
constitute the majority of those commemorated with an indication
of age. The sons and daughters commemorated as *pientissimi/piissimi*
had generally survived to an age where their parents expected to be
outlived by them. In ancient Rome the probability of dying after
having survived the first fifteen years of life was comparatively low,
though still high compared with our standards (Frier 1982, 1983;

[33] In 19% (43/226) of all cases *pientissimus* is applied to a parent, in 8% (18/226) to a
sibling, and in 13% (29/226) to a spouse, but see Table 8.5 for the relative distribution.
Spouses are very frequently commemorated with an epithet and only in 3% of cases (29/885)
is *pientissimus* chosen.

[34] See for example Ovid, *Ars amatoria* 3. 15: 'est pia Penelope lustris errante duobus';
Plautus, *Amphitruo* 1086: 'piam et pudicam esse tuam uxorem ut scias'; Propertius 3. 13. 18
and 3. 13. 24. Conjugal *pietas* frequently connotes sexual fidelity.

[35] *D.* 21. 1. 35, Ulpian: 'plerumque propter morbosa mancipia etiam non morbosa red-
hibentur, si separari non possint sine magno incommodo uel ad pietatis rationem offensam.
quid enim, si filio retento parentes redhibere maluerint uel contra? quod et in fratribus et in
personas contubernio sibi coniunctas obseruari oportet.'

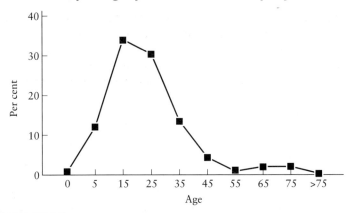

FIG. 8.5. Age distribution, *pientissimus/piissimus*.

Parkin 1992). Therefore it would not be unnatural if parents who lost sons and daughters at this age experienced their loss as much more painful than it would have been had the child died at an earlier age, when chances of survival were still small. Besides, parents who lost children about the age of 15 were themselves generally older than parents who lost small children, and their chances of having other children to replace the lost ones were accordingly diminished. This also implies that these parents, together with their children, had lost their possibilities of being supported and of being buried by the ones from whom they would naturally expect support and burial. The parents' expectation of *pietas* had been frustrated by their son or daughter's untimely death and this is what they express by mentioning both the age at death of their sons and daughters and by characterizing them as *pientissimi/piissimi* in a situation where they had themselves, contrary to nature, shown *pietas* towards their children.

PREMATURE DEATH

A priori, it seems strange that a culture in which early death was very common and in which it was most unusual for the surviving part of the population not to have lost several close relatives at an early age would emphasize a phenomenon like premature death. It occurs, however, with frequency in the literary material and the epitaphs of *CIL* 6. Evidently, premature death must have meant something different to the Roman mind than it does to a modern Western mind.

We consider any death at an early age premature, as we expect almost everyone to reach a considerable age before they die.

From calculations of the life expectancy of the Romans, death at an early age was more normal than the opposite. Loss of close relations by death at an early age must have been a common sad experience for most Romans. Infant mortality counted for most of the early deaths. It is calculated that about 50 per cent of a cohort would be dead before the age of 5. But also after these first years, life was very dangerous. Approximately 12 per cent of those who had survived till they were 5 would die before they were 25. Death at an early age in Roman society can therefore hardly be called unexpected. The Romans, however, did consider early death to be premature. It is therefore worth discussing what was meant by the expression *mors acerba* or *mors immatura*, as it is more than relevant to go into the discussion of the emotional and social implications of high infant mortality.

The question of whether parents in societies with high infant mortality grieved deeply when their children died has been discussed at length.[36] One of the great problems with the literary evidence from Rome is that it is possible to argue both that they did and that they did not. Not only was exposure of healthy infants practised, but authors such as Cicero and Seneca get away with saying that it was really not worth the trouble caring about the death of small children.[37] On the other hand, Seneca, in a very interesting passage, talks about all the expectations parents had of their infant children. He even states that nobody ever thought of death: *Consolatio ad Marciam* 9. 2: 'tot praeter domum nostram ducuntur exsequiae: de morte non cogitamus; tot acerba funera: nos togam nostrorum infantium, nos militiam et paternae hereditatis successionem agitamus animo'. Mark Golden (1988: 159) is probably right in saying that

---

[36] See Golden (1988) for references.

[37] Cicero, *Tusculan Disputations* 1. 39. 93: 'si puer paruus occidit, aequo animo ferendum putant, si uero in cunis, ne querendum quidem', and Seneca, *Letters* 99. 14, to a father who is actually grieving deeply for the loss of his little son: 'non est dolor iste, sed morsus; tu illum dolorem facis.' In 99. 2 Seneca mentions about the child: 'decessit filius incertae spei, paruulus; pusillum temporis periit.' The interesting thing of course is that Seneca can publish a letter like this and use as his argument that the boy was too small to be of any social importance and therefore not worth the grief his father felt by the loss. One of Seneca's points is that the nurse knew the child better than the father did (99. 14). That this point was probably of importance see also Quintilian 6. pr. 8 on the loss of his son: 'illud uero insidiantis quo me ualidius cruciaret fortunae fuit, ut ille mihi blandissimus me suis nutricibus, me auiae educanti, me omnibus qui sollicitare illas aetates solent anteferret.' The closeness of the relationship between father and son made the grief more unbearable. For a proverbial statement on the death of small children, see Publilius Syrus, *Sententiae*, under the letter M: 'Mors infanti felix, iuueni acerba, nimis sera est seni.'

expressions of emotion vary more widely than the emotions themselves, but this is an insoluble problem. Emotions existed in ancient Rome, as they do in our world, but they remain rather intractable and intangible. We can describe Cicero's immense grief at his loss of Tullia and his evident lack of interest in the death of his infant grandson.[38] We may conclude that Cicero was able to grieve for the loss of a dearly loved adult daughter, but that he did not automatically feel or express any considerable concern for her infant son except that he provided 'properly' for him.[39] This frustrating fact should not keep us from studying and discussing the feelings and emotions of the Romans. But it seems to be pointless to concentrate the discussion—as far as mourning is concerned—on the death of infants, since the Romans were not interested in giving any information on infant mortality. It will probably be a better idea to start discussion where the evidence is, that is with parents' response to the loss of older children.

Callistratus in *D.* 50. 16. 220. 3 mentions why it is important to raise children: 'natura nos quoque docet parentes pios, qui liberorum procreandorum animo et uoto uxores ducunt, filiorum appellatione omnes qui ex nobis descendunt continere: nec enim dulciore nomine possumus nepotes nostros quam filii appellare. etenim idcirco filios filiasue concipimus atque edimus, ut ex prole eorum earumue diuturnitatis nobis memoriam in aeuum relinquamus'. The text concentrates on the living memory established by the survival of direct descendants. But the wish to be buried and commemorated was an equally important part of what was expected from sons and daughters. These expectations were brought to nothing if children died before their parents. According to Seneca, death was always premature if a son or daughter predeceased his or her parents.[40]

Very infrequently in literature, infants are explicitly referred to as prematurely dead. In the *Aeneid*, Vergil places infants together with the innocently condemned in the first circle, emphasizing that they had died when they were still very young.[41] Usually young adults

---

[38] On Cicero's violent grief for Tullia, see *Att.* 12, *passim*; the little Lentulus is mentioned only a couple of times, see for example *Att.* 12. 28. 3: 'et uelim aliquando, cum erit tuum commodum, Lentulum puerum uisas eique de mancipiis quae tibi uidebitur attribuas.'

[39] The most detailed discussion of the question of grief and mourning is found in Hopkins (1983: 217–26).

[40] *Consolatio ad Marciam* 17. 7: 'nihil uetat illos tibi suprema praestare et laudari te a liberis tuis, sed sic te para tamquam in ignem impositurus uel puerum uel iuuenem uel senem; nihil enim ad rem pertinent anni, quoniam nullum non acerbum funus est, quod parens sequitur.'

[41] *Aeneid* 6. 426–9: 'continuo auditae uoces uagitus et ingens | infantumque animae flentes, in limine primo | quos dulcis uitae exsortis et ab ubere raptos | abstulit atra dies et funere mersit acerbo'. See also Fronto, *De nepote amisso* 2. 3: 'Victorinum pietate mansuetudine ueritate innocentia maxima, omnium denique optimarum artium praecipuum uirum acerbissima morte fili adflictum, hoccine ullo modo aequum aut iustum fuit?'

who had not yet accomplished what they had intended to do or ought to have done are meant, when premature death is mentioned in literary texts. Cicero and Pliny provide us with the best examples of this. In Cicero, *Fam.* 11. 28. 4, C. Matius, Caesar's close friend, in a letter to Cicero states that he wants everyone to regret Caesar's murder and consider his death premature: 'sed quid mihi suscensent si id opto ut paeniteat eos sui facti? cupio enim Caesaris mortem omnibus esse acerbam.' Violent death is frequently part of the concept of premature demise, but the idea of dying in the middle of his work is probably what is meant here. In his fourth oration against Catiline, Cicero states that death cannot come prematurely to a consular: 4.3: 'nam neque turpis mors forti uiro potest accidere neque immatura consulari nec misera sapienti'.[42] Pliny (5. 5) writes about C. Fannius, who was a lawyer and a writer of history: by his death, he left an unfinished work about the victims of Nero. Pliny found his death premature because: 'mihi autem uidetur acerba semper et immatura mors eorum, qui immortale aliquid parant'. Seneca's remarks on premature death and its implications for the family have already been mentioned above. In this context, it is natural to mention Pliny's well-known letter on the death of Minicia Marcella, who died when she was about 13 years old, just before her marriage: 5. 16. 6: 'O triste plane acerbumque funus! O morte ipsa mortis tempus indignius! iam destinata erat egregio iuueni, iam electus nuptiarum dies, iam nos uocati.' By her untimely death she crushed her father's hope of grandchildren and of continuing the family.[43] The loss of support in one's old age by a child's death is expressed in [Quintilian], *Declamationes maiores* 10. 1: 'eos, qui liberorum mortibus destituti cuncta uota et praeparatas spes in senectutem ante se egerunt' (cf. Parkin, Ch. 6 n. 6, above). This fundamental aspect of premature death is also naturally emphasized in the epigraphic material. See 26901, an altar inscribed on two sides: 'diis manibus | Successi fil | Caesia Gemella | mater piissimo | filio de suo | uix ann ix | m iiii dieb xv | fatis peractis mater | eode est condita quae | post obitum filii | uix ann iiii m xi d viii'. On the other side of the altar the following inscription is found: 'quod fas parenti | facere debuit filius | mors immatura fecit | ut faceret parens | pater Successus | supremum utrisque | praestitit officium'.[44]

---

[42] See likewise Cicero, *Philippics* 2. 119, where he refers to this statement made twenty years before: 'etenim si abhinc annos prope uiginti hoc ipso in templo negaui posse mortem immaturam esse consulari, quanto uerius nunc negabo seni?' See also Elder Seneca, *Suasoriae* 6. 12.

[43] This theme is treated by Lattimore (1962: 192–9); cf. Eck, Ch. 4 above.

[44] This inscription is very interesting. First Caesia Gemella, who was free, freeborn, or freedwoman, dedicated an epitaph to her son Successus. His status is unknown. He may have been freeborn, even if he has no *nomen*. The *nomina* of children are not always mentioned. The

Most of the inscriptions concerned with premature death are longer and more elaborately composed than epitaphs normally were in Rome. Most of the sons and daughters commemorated as prematurely dead were more than 5 years old when they died, but in a few instances infants are commemorated as well. The youngest was Speratus, who was under 1 year when he died. His parents express their grief as infinite: 26680: 'Speratus uix men v— | flet domus et cari lugunt sine fine parentes | abreptum fatis contegor hoc titulo | quis non exempli doleatur mortis acerbae | si me uidisses aut si mea funera nosses | fudisses lacrimas hospes in ossa mea | Speratus Attalus Politice'. Domitius Tiras expresses a more fatalistic attitude in his dedication to his daughter: 7574: 'mala in arbore pendunt | sic corpora nostra | aut matura cadunt aut | cito acerua ruunt | Domitius Tiras | filiae dulcissimae'. This fragmented epitaph is interesting in comparing human beings with fruit, and thus referring to the fundamental meaning of *immaturus*. In two inscriptions, the deceased tries to comfort the relatives by saying that premature death may befall everyone—even kings were not exempt from this grief: 7872: 'desine iam frustra mater mea desine fletu te | miseram totos exagitare dies | namque dolor talis non nunc tibi contigit uni | haec eadem et magnis regibus acciderunt'; in 23551, a fragmented epitaph commemorating a 6-year-old boy, the wording of the comforting verses accompanying the dedication is almost identical with 7872. That this was evidently a stock theme is shown by Seneca, *De ira* 3. 25: 'quomodo homini pusillo solacium in malis fuit etiam magnorum uirorum titubare fortunam et aequiore animo filium in angulo fleuit, qui uidit acerba funera etiam ex regia duci'.

OWN CHILDREN, FOSTER-CHILDREN

It might have been expected that the death of a child could be compensated for by adoption or quasi-adoption. This was probably also the case as far as the emotional side of the relationship was concerned (Sigismund Nielsen 1987), but I no longer believe that the same expectations were attached to relationships of fosterage

interesting thing is that he actually had a living father, who did not appear as dedicator of the epitaph. The reason may have been the father's inferior status compared with the mother's. He presents himself only with the *cognomen* 'Successus'. But there may be another reason. Women very frequently appear as dedicators of epitaphs to children. Not all of them were 'single' or heads of households. It may simply have been part of the convention that primarily women grieved for and commemorated children. See H. Sigismund Nielsen, 'Roman Family, the Evidence of the Epitaphs' (forthcoming). For further examples of epitaphs mentioning the theme of parents contrary to nature burying their children, see Lattimore (1962: 189–90).

and to blood kin relationships. Otherwise foster-children, like sons and daughters, ought to have been characterized with the epithet *pientissimus/piissimus*. As Table 8.5 shows, foster-children are hardly ever characterized by that epithet. I quoted *D*. 50. 16. 220 above, where the importance of direct descendants—blood relationships— is clearly expressed. In the epigraphic material, the wish to raise a family has been looked for in the inscriptions, especially through freedmen's emphasis on the freeborn status of their children.

STATUS

The question of why some of the persons mentioned in the epitaphs have an explicit status indication, while some have not, has been discussed at length for many years. There are, however, consider- able problems about using indication of status in the search for the Roman family. Only 28 per cent (1,060/3,784) of the commemor- ated, excluding self-commemorations, and 18 per cent (538/2,915) of the dedicators have an explicit status indication. Of the com- memorated persons with an indication of status, 62 per cent (661/ 1,060) are ex-slaves, 14 per cent (144/1,060) slaves, and 24 per cent (255/1,060) freeborn. Of the dedicators who mention their status, 67 per cent (362/538) are freedmen, 23 per cent (123/538) slaves, and 10 per cent (53/538) freeborn. This fact, combined with an estimate of actual status for the majority commemorated without any indication of status, has led to the conclusion that in *CIL* 6 as a whole freedmen or second-generation freeborn constitute the majority of the commemorated and the dedicators.[45] I will not go further into this, but merely remark that if freedmen were proud of their new status and wished to use it to establish a family they certainly did not show this in the epitaphs. On the contrary only 26 per cent (169/661) of the dedications to freedmen fall within the close family (parents, siblings, sons or daughters, and spouses), com- pared with 53 per cent (2,003/3,784) in *CIL* 6 as a whole, still with

---

[45] See Taylor (1961: 129) on the feeling of pride behind the announcement of citizenship, and ibid. 122 on the embarrassment that prevented freedmen from announcing their status; Treggiari (1969: 208) on the emotional background of announcing freedman status, a point taken up and developed by P. Zanker, 'Grabreliefs römischer Freigelassener', *Jahrbuch des Deutschen Archäologischen Instituts* 90 (1975), who (pp. 284–5) concludes, on the back- ground of an analysis of 125 reliefs with about 50 inscriptions about the whole class of freedmen in Rome: 'Die Dargestellten scheuen sich nicht, sich als *Libertini* vorzustellen. Für sie war es der entscheidende Erfolg ihres Lebens, dem Sklavendaseins entnommen zu sein. Ihre Grabrepräsentation wendet sich an ihres gleichen nicht an die Oberschicht . . . Ehe und Familie gehörten begreiflicherweise zu den erstrebtesten Zielen der Freigelassenen. Denn der soziale Tatbestand der Ehe machte das neue Bürgerrecht erst manifest.'

the exclusion of self-commemorations. The emphasis both among commemorated slaves and freedmen is on relationships in which their status was of importance to characterize the relationship. Among freedmen, 20 per cent (133/661) of the dedications fall within these relationships (other relations—which encompass relationships between colleagues—patronage relationships, and relationships between slaves or freedmen from the same household) compared with the 10 per cent (363/3,784) found in *CIL* 6 as a whole, with the exclusion of self-commemorations. It seems reasonable to contend that status was indicated if it was of importance to characterize the relationship described, otherwise not. Evidently, mentioning status did not play any significant role for freedmen who wished to establish a family.[46]

CHILDREN, MOST DUTIFUL AND SWEET

There cannot, however, be any doubt that family and close kin were of major importance to Romans of all social and economic classes, but the importance of the family and the wish to establish a family of one's own and raise children is not evident from the indications of status. Rather, I believe that the expectation or lack of expectation of *pietas* is of the greatest importance in estimating which relationships were considered the most important to the Romans, and here the relationship between parents and their children seems to have played the most important role. The closeness of that relationship is emphasized by the frequency of the epithet *dulcissimus* to characterize a son or daughter. In *CIL* 6, we usually meet parents who had not succeeded in raising a family. They had tried, but their hopes had been frustrated by the loss of their children. The extremely heavy emphasis on the commemoration of young sons and daughters, most of them characterized as *dulcissimi* and *pientissimi/piissimi*, shows the strong ambition in all status groups of creating a family and the profound loss felt when this hope was dashed.

---

[46] Only a handful of dedicating freedman parents are found in the *CIL* 6 who commemorate their freeborn sons or daughters: in this sample 14510, 15365, 15595, 26165. Many more would have been expected if citizenship played a very significant role in the minds of the new citizens.

9

The Iconography of Roman Childhood

BERYL RAWSON

INTRODUCTION

Philippe Ariès's 1960 book on childhood in pre-Revolutionary France[1] opened a new era in the historical study of children and childhood. His use of artistic representations of children was dramatically new, and his main thesis—that there had been no real concept of childhood before the seventeenth century—dominated the field for almost thirty years. Recently there have been reassessments of this thesis,[2] but although later scholars have modified the thesis the importance of iconographic evidence is fully accepted (and the difficulties recognized).

The French edition of Ariès was much helped by the positioning of plates through the text, reproducing two dozen of the works of art or monuments used as evidence in the argument. Most versions of the English-language edition and later versions of the French edition did readers a disservice in omitting the plates: readers could not properly assess the original argument nor can they now assess the re-evaluations. The plates[3] associated with this chapter are an integral part of the argument. The interpretation of some of the visual evidence is difficult, and sometimes more than one reading is

I owe warm thanks to Edyth Binkowski for assistance with this topic, especially with tracking down details and locations of monuments. I have also benefited from working with Janette McWilliam, whose Australian National University (ANU) theses (Honours 1990, MA 1994) have much to contribute on the legal and epigraphic evidence for children. I gratefully acknowledge support from the Australian Research Council.

[1] English trans. 1962, rev. edn. 1973.

[2] e.g. Burton (1989), Johansson (1987), Wilson (1980).

[3] A small proportion though they be of the large number of examples scattered in many repositories. The huge amount of material available poses an organizational problem but it does underline the basic argument of this chapter, that representations of children were highly visible in Roman society. Books and articles on ancient social life are still often unillustrated, and others draw their illustrations from commercial collections of reproductions which provide few contextual details. A catalogue of available material evidence, with basic details of provenance and context, would be a valuable contribution to this field of research and would enable others to refine interpretations and to advance the study of Roman children and childhood.

valid, but the cumulative impact of this evidence should leave no doubt about the appreciation of children and childhood in ancient Roman society.

Children are highly visible not only in the art of ancient Rome but also in its law and, to some extent, its literature. This reflects an active consciousness and high valuation of children and childhood in Roman society. An analysis of representations of children in all these media may illuminate further the role of children and attitudes to them in that society. This chapter focuses on artistic representations and on Italy.[4] The iconography, however, must be contextualized. The whole range of representations will eventually be considered together: art, epigraphy, coinage, law, literature (and a wide range of literature, not just selected examples from the literature where we expect children to be present).

The great majority of examples of children in Roman art can be dated to the imperial period, i.e. the period following Augustus' accession to virtual autocracy as *princeps* in 27 BC. They are particularly numerous in the second century AD. Does this reflect a real chronological development in sentiment and sensibility or merely the accidental distribution of what remains of Roman art? There is, after all, comparatively little Republican art extant. Nevertheless, of the remaining evidence very few Republican inscriptions and almost no art represent children. There are scenes in the literature of the late Republic which reveal a lively observation of children, but there is more in imperial literature, and the great developments in private law—which took much account of children—belong to the imperial period and especially the second century AD.

The suddenness of change under Augustus can be exaggerated. There must have been substantial continuity in *mentalité* from Republic to Principate, and Augustus' long reign (over forty years) allowed new attitudes to evolve gradually. Civil war had, however, intervened, entailing much loss of life for citizens and sharply increased scope for the victor to make his imprint on society. As Zanker writes (1988: p. v) in his extended and masterly study of images in the Augustan period, 'a fundamental change in the political system led to the creation of a new visual language that both

---

[4] For other areas of the Roman empire, pre-existing and continuing cultural traditions complicate the assessment of what is 'Roman'. Frenz (1985) argues that there are also significant differences between funerary reliefs made in Rome and those made in other parts of Italy. Kleiner, however, in her 1986 review, believes that city-Roman friezes must have been the models for those made in other parts of Italy, and Zanker (1988: 311–12) sees a uniform symbolism throughout Italy after Augustus.

reflects an altered mentality and contributed significantly to the process of change'.[5]

Zanker argues powerfully not only for fundamental change during the Augustan period but also for clearly identifiable phases in that process. There was a visual dimension to the political programme very early, certainly from 28 BC; but later there was a turning-point followed by new emphases. For our purposes 17 BC may be taken as a critical turning-point. The imagery of victory and self-justification gave way to that of prosperity, peace, stability, and optimism for the future. The Secular Games (*ludi saeculares*) of 17 BC had been preceded in the previous year by legislation to strengthen the basis of family life and to reward child-rearing. The Games themselves featured children prominently. Within the next decade the Altar of Peace (Ara Pacis) had been built, featuring children prominently and innovatively. The Anchises-Aeneas-Ascanius group was ubiquitous, a 'holy family'. The symbolism was reproduced endlessly until it became generalized into broad family virtues, especially *pietas*.[6]

There was probably subconscious acculturation to the new visual language at all levels of society, but ambitious ex-slaves and their families consciously adopted it—perhaps to show loyalty to the regime but certainly to mark their arrival in respectable, reasonably well-to-do free Roman society. Many had little to advertise except their status and family connections, and these appeared first in a large number of funerary friezes inspired by official art. After the Julio-Claudian period the fashion changed to altars, which continued to celebrate families well into the second century. The new taste for sarcophagi which developed in the second century provided greater scope for pictorial representation of life-cycles and family connections and some sarcophagi were sized, sculpted, and inscribed specifically for children. Early Christian society found the interest in children very congenial and continued to represent them on funerary memorials.

PRE-AUGUSTUS

There is some evidence of a native Italian interest in representations of infants and motherhood, e.g. the votive figures of women and

---

[5] Cf. p. 260: Augustan art was 'the result of a complete change in mentality'. There must have been 'some kind of identification between the artist and spirit of the new age'; the artist was 'contributing to the realization of a cultural program'. The text below, which deals with the Augustan period, draws heavily on Zanker, as will now be inevitable for anyone writing about this period. See also Kleiner (1978) and Kellum (1985; 1990).

[6] Kleiner (1977: 108) dates the increased frequency of children in non-imperial friezes from 13 BC, the year of the beginning of the Ara Pacis.

children from central and southern Italy from the fourth to the first centuries BC. The interpretation of these is difficult, but they appear to be Italian rather than Greek (Bonfante 1984; 1985). Moreover, although Hellenistic art in the East developed a greater interest in children than had been evinced in classical Athenian art, it is not clear that this was transferred directly to Rome. Other Hellenistic influences can be identified in the late Republic but there is little attention to children.

The subjects and style of Republican art reflected public life rather than private and focused on individual adult male Roman citizens— as generals, magistrates, priests.[7] There is the togate statue from Perusina of an orator, 'Arringatore',[8] there are the busts of such men as Cicero, Pompey, and Julius Caesar,[9] there is the prolific coinage of the late Republic advertising family history but increasingly glorifying individual contemporary men, and there is the occasional sculpted relief depicting magisterial duties—a forerunner to the later *curriculum uitae* reliefs on sarcophagi and other monuments—and perhaps a mythological genealogy.[10] There was also in the late Republic an increasing number of statues (including equestrian ones), in public places, of notable men.

This Republican art appears to be honorific rather than funerary. Where then, and how, did the upper classes bury and commemorate their family dead? Burials and cremations were legally prohibited within the walls of a town, so tombs lined the roads leading out of towns. For the imperial period these are a rich source of personal and family history but for the Republican period we know little of how private individuals were memorialized. Cicero's preoccupation with a memorial for his daughter Tullia when she died in 45 BC is well known and we have some description of the architectural plans he had in mind. (These include the first reference of which I am aware to *apotheosis* as the aim of the dedication: Cicero, *Att.* 12. 36.) Cicero knew that funerary inscriptions on such monuments had to be in a well-frequented place if they were to be read by many people—a prime objective of such memorials: he was thinking of a site on an estate outside of Rome but not too distant from the capital. Perhaps burial on or near rural family estates helps explain the

---

[7] Contrast the interest of imperial art in groups, females, the young, and ex-slaves.

[8] Florence, Museo Archeologico; Zanker (1988: fig. 4).

[9] Mansuelli (1981: i. 73–4); Zanker (1988: figs. 5–7).

[10] Probably the base of some monument: the so-called 'Ahenobarbus Base' in Munich (Glyptotek 239) and Paris (Louvre inv. Ma 975), illustrated and discussed by Zanker (1988: fig. 10, pp. 12–14), with a date of *c.*100 BC.

paucity of upper-class memorials in the vicinity of Rome.[11] There were some cases of burial in the Campus Martius, e.g. Julius Caesar's daughter Julia, perhaps C. Poplicius Bibulus (a plebeian aedile, probably of the first half-century BC), and the consuls A. Hirtius and C. Vibius Pansa who fell in battle in 43 BC, but these were conspicuous marks of honour.[12] Moreover, neither Tullia nor Julia nor any other example of Republican burial was a child in terms of age. We thus have no evidence of upper-class children's monuments from the Republican period—neither of their existence nor, if they did exist, what their form and style were.[13] Republican inscriptions which survive record magistracies and public honours. The portrayals of children in Republican literature, moving though some of these are, do not memorialize individual children in their own right but children are used as generalized symbols, e.g. in Lucretius, of the joys of family life which will be irrelevant after death.

The oldest surviving group of objects which might be called a family monument is that of the Scipiones (the monument, outside the Porta Capena, is still *in situ* but the contents are now in the Vatican): *CIL* 6. 1284–94 and *ILLRP (Imagines)* 132–8. This group includes a sarcophagus (of L. Cornelius Scipio Barbatus, consul 298 BC) and six inscriptions from the third and second centuries. Only one inscription is not for an adult male: that of Paulla Cornelia, wife of Hispallus, who died about 130 BC. There is no record of non-adult children. There is some sense of family in that reference is made to outstripping the best family tradition, 'gloria maiorum'.[14]

There is evidence of some late-Republican upper-class *sepulcra* in the environs of Rome, e.g. those on the Campus Martius and a few

---

[11] Munatius Plancus had a tomb at Gaeta, the Plautii at Tibur (cf. Eck, Ch. 4 and Fig. 4.1 above). There was uncertainty about where Scipio Africanus was buried. There were monuments to him both at Rome and at Liternum. Seneca (*Letters* 86.1) thought that an altar at Scipio's villa at Liternum might be his burial-place.

[12] Surviving monuments: Nash 2. 319, 341. Strabo (5. 3. 8) says that Romans erected 'the tombs of their most illustrious men and women' in the Campus Martius in the belief that this area was particularly sacred. This sounds like official commemoration rather than private. There was a Republican sumptuary law against excessive expenditure on *sepulcra* (Cicero, *Att.* 12. 36), but there is no record of its existence or implementation in imperial times. In 43 BC Cicero asked the senate to suspend such a law to allow allocation of a large area in the *campus Esquilinus* for the burial of Ser. Sulpicius Rufus, who had served the state well on an embassy to Mark Antony. This burial space was also to have official sanction as the burial-place for his children and descendants (Cicero, *Philippics* 9. 17).

[13] When Aemilius Paullus buried his two sons (aged 12 and 14) in 167 BC the burial site must have been close to Rome, as Paullus was in the middle of important public duties and he is reported as referring to Roman citizens having witnessed the funerals (Livy 45. 40–1; Plutarch, *Aemilius Paullus* 35–6).

[14] *CIL* 6. 1288. Cf. Cicero, *Tusculan Disputations* 1. 13.

others, but these are individual monuments, apparently not for family.[15] It would seem that other kinds of monument were preferred for the perpetuation of family memory (collective rather than individualized) at Rome, e.g. public works honouring the family name, such as the Basilica Aemilia. It is not clear that Augustus originally envisaged his mausoleum as a family tomb rather than an individual one, when he began it in 28 BC, but it became such (without, however, giving any prominence to children). A succession of family members, beginning with Marcellus in 23 BC, was buried and commemorated there. A mint official of Augustus' period (C. Sulpicius Platorinus, *triumuir monetalis* 13 BC) built a tomb which accommodated a number of people and had statues of his wife and himself at the door. The individual tombs of Caecilia Metella and of Cestius date to the last couple of decades of the first century BC, and Nash documents a few more for subsequent years, but even these are strikingly few when compared with the number of friezes, altars, urns, and sarcophagi of sub-élite families over the next couple of centuries.

Eck (1984*a*: 148) suggests that Augustus 'limited' monumental tombs for senators. They had to find other forms of memorial and often these were outside Rome, e.g. public benefactions in Italian towns (cf. Ch. 4 above). This political explanation has some force but there may be more to it than that. It may be that the upper classes lost interest in this kind of funerary monument as such monuments became widespread and were taken over by a new 'bourgeoisie'. A recent cross-cultural study of funerary monuments (Cannon 1989) has documented cyclical change in display ostentation. This highlights the role of status competition and aspiration in changing fashions. Growing affluence provides opportunity for expressive or competitive display. In these circumstances status uncertainty and social flux can lead to ambitious attempts to create material impressions of status. There is a need for symbols to express status and status aspirations. This seems to me to encapsulate the social environment of early imperial Rome and the circumstances in which funerary commemoration can provide the necessary symbols. However, as the use of such symbols becomes widely diffused in society the élite will move to practices which newly differentiate them: ostentation and restraint are effective in turn 'as an expression of social distinction'. It may not be restraint but another form of ostentation that the élite choose, as compensation. Cannon provides examples of this, e.g. in

---

[15] See Nash 2. 319, 327, 341, 357, 370. Of these, Sempronius' tomb on the slopes of the Quirinal includes his sister and his mother.

nineteenth-century England high-status funerals became simpler but church building and restoration flourished. This would fit well with the variety of funerary foundations in imperial Italy, e.g. *alimenta*, feasts, baths, and other public services.

The impetus for more widespread private funerary monuments is usually attributed to Augustan ideology and, in particular, the Ara Pacis. There are a few examples, however, which seem to belong to a slightly earlier period.[16] By the late Republic there were large numbers of slaves and ex-slaves (freedmen and freedwomen) in Italy who were assimilating to Roman society and seeking ways to advertise their improving status and wealth. In later periods, as we shall see, slaves and ex-slaves were prominent in funerary monuments and, having few of the trappings of official life to advertise, they memorialized particularly their family relationships, frequently including children.[17]

Inscriptions from tombs on the Via Statilia—one for two women, another for a group, mostly *liberti* but including two freeborn—date from the first half of the first century BC.[18] These seem to attest some *familia* links but no specific relationships. They do not include children. Probably the earliest example to include a child is the Seruilii relief of 30–20 BC,[19] representing the freed couple Q. Seruilius Hilarus (*pater*) and Sempronia Eune (*uxor*) and the freeborn child P. Seruilius Globulus (wearing a *bulla*) (Fig. 9.1). The portraits are individualized but rigidly frontal. This group is in the Augustan period but before the Ara Pacis. Similar is the Vibii relief, perhaps a decade later, representing a couple and (one may deduce) their son.[20] Cf. the relief of the child C. Vettius C. f. Secundus with three adults, all of freed status.[21] Thus by the late Republic and the Augustan period an interest in private portraiture, groups, and children was developing in Roman art. Augustus, once he was free of more pressing concerns, capitalized on this (rather than initiated it) to promote

---

[16] As with other areas of non-literary evidence for Roman society, there is a great need for surer criteria for dating. If we could be sure of the chronology of the monuments and inscriptions to be discussed below, we could identify real turning-points in *mentalité*. Kleiner's reviews of 1988 and 1989 provide useful criteria which might be used.

[17] The relationship between funerary inscriptions and the ex-slave community is particularly well delineated in Saller and Shaw (1984*a*). Cf. earlier studies in Taylor (1961) and Rawson (1966).

[18] Kleiner (1977: nos. 9, 40) gives 75–50 BC; Zanker (1988: fig. 12) gives a date of 100–80 BC, also favoured by Kockel (1993: 83–5 and pls. 1–3).

[19] *CIL* 6. 26410; Kockel (1993: 141–2 and pl. 51*a*); Kleiner (1977: no. 71) (with date of 13 BC to AD 5); Zanker (1975: fig. 19).

[20] *CIL* 6. 28774; Kockel (1993: 180–1 and pl. 94*a*); Kleiner (1977: no. 69); Zanker (1975: fig. 29). Zanker describes the child's bust as sculpted in the style of a prince of the imperial house.

[21] Kockel (1993: 145–6 and pl. 56*a*); Kleiner (1977: no. 84); Zanker (1975: fig. 25).

FIG. 9.1. Relief of Seruilii family, Rome, 30–20 BC. Freeborn son and freed couple ('father' and 'wife').

new policies and his own family and dynastic plans. This led to a great variety of representations and new forms in public art, to which in turn private art responded.

AUGUSTUS

In the revolutionary period which formed a transition from Republic to Principate, literature and art were preoccupied with the public crises and struggles for power which continued until 31 BC when Octavian (the later Augustus) won military victory over his opponents. The early years of Augustus' reign are marked by self-justification and his need to be seen as a successful military and political leader. In the long list of monuments begun in this period there was little scope for representing children or other aspects of private life: temples, libraries, the Saepta, a basilica, baths. There was, however, statuary in the Saepta precinct (dedicated by Agrippa in 26 BC) which represented pairs of mythological teachers and pupils (Elder Pliny, *NH* 36. 29).[22] Zanker (1988: 143) believes that the statuary was associated with a place where classes were held.

In 20 BC a grandson was born to Augustus—Gaius, the first son of his daughter Julia and her husband Agrippa. Another (Lucius) followed in 17 BC. Augustus' hopes of a dynasty promised stability and

[22] It was probably early in his reign that Augustus reinscribed the statue of Cornelia in the newly named *porticus Octauiae*, inserting 'daughter of Africanus' before 'mother of the Gracchi' ('Africani f. Gracchorum': *CIL* 6. 31610). There was, however, a strong political dimension to the representation of Cornelia as a symbol of Roman family life, to do both with Cornelia and the Gracchi and with the role of Octavia in Augustus' policies. See Coarelli (1978).

continuity of the new regime. In 17 BC the Secular Games were held, to celebrate Rome's long past history and optimism for the future. This festival, held approximately once a century to inaugurate a new age, was well overdue: the last celebration had been in 146 BC. The civil war period of the 40s and the 30s BC had not been appropriate for another celebration but Augustus could now choose his time carefully. There were not only two grandsons of Augustus' own blood: in 17 BC they were formally adopted by Augustus into the Julian house as his sons, C. (Iulius) Caesar and L. (Iulius) Caesar. In the previous year Augustus had personally introduced new legislation to strengthen family life: rewards for marriage and child-rearing, penalties for celibacy and adultery.[23] The Secular Games of 17 BC, held as late spring passed into early summer (May 30–June 3), celebrated fertility and gave a prominent role to mothers and children.[24] In particular, three choruses, each of seven boys and seven girls, sang the hymn (the *carmen saeculare*) written specially for the occasion by the poet Horace. As Zanker (1988: 172) comments, 'the state's real hope for the future, its children, was vividly embodied in the moving image of the young singers'.[25]

Children and family life remained an important focus for the rest of Augustus' reign. The virtue of *pietas* (loyalty to gods, country, and family) had already (before 19 BC) been made the centrepiece of Vergil's epic poem, the *Aeneid*. The image of Aeneas rescuing father Anchises and son Ascanius from burning Troy, a symbol of family devotion (in spite of the absence of wife Creusa), became ubiquitous. It was also closely associated with the Julian house, which traced its origins back to Aeneas and his mother Venus. Julius Caesar had capitalized on these associations[26] (Fig. 9.2) and Augustus featured the image on his coinage from before 31 BC.

Real, contemporary children as well as idealized symbols were given a prominent place on the friezes of the Ara Pacis which the senate, to honour Augustus, initiated in 13 BC and dedicated in 9

---

[23] Legislation commonly known as the *lex Iulia de maritandis ordinibus* and the *lex Iulia de adulteriis*, 18 BC.

[24] For details, see Zanker (1988: 167–72), drawing on the inscription *CIL* 6. 32323.

[25] Children had already been used in religious rites: a boy acolyte (*camillus*) had to have two parents living. There are *camilli* on the Ara Pacis.

[26] See e.g. Crawford (1974: 458/1 and pl. LIV. 10), a *denarius* of 47/46 BC whose reverse shows Aeneas fleeing from Troy holding Anchises on his shoulder. Augustus experimented with representations of this but it was probably quite early in his reign that the child Ascanius was added, being held by Aeneas' right hand: this became the definitive version. See the entry on coin 74.06 in the catalogue of the ANU Classics Department Museum, *Antiquities* (Green and Rawson 1981), 143–4. The comparison is made there with Sex. Pompeius' coin from Sicily of 42–40 BC, associating his own duty to his father Pompey with that of the Sicilian brothers Anapias and Amphinomos (Crawford 1974: 511/3a and plate LXII. 2).

FIG. 9.2. Reverse of Roman coin (denarius) of Julius Caesar, 47/46 BC. Aeneas fleeing from Troy, carrying father Anchises on left shoulder.

BC. On the southern long side Augustus' family is in procession. Realistically represented children—tugging at a parent's clothes, exchanging knowing glances—spill out of the foreground over the frame of the frieze. A similar child is part of the senatorial procession on the northern long side.[27] On one of the ends there is the fecund female figure variously interpreted, e.g. as Italia, or Pax (Peace), or Tellus (Earth). She nurses infants ready to suckle, surrounded by other symbols of fertility.

The children C. and L. Caesar continued to be prominent in public.[28] There were many portraits of them in public places. Livia and Augustus cherished statues of a great-grandson who had died early (Suetonius, *Gaius* 7). It may be from about this time that private busts and statues of boys and girls began to appear.[29] In 13 BC Augustus' coinage (*denarii*) showed Gaius and Lucius with their mother Julia on a reverse which clearly signified the dynasty and the

---

[27] Identifications of some figures are still controversial. Most recently, C. B. Rose (1990) has argued that the two boys usually identified as C. and L. Caesar are barbarian children representing the pacification of the Roman world in East and West. On the symbolism of children on the Altar, see now Currie (1995).

[28] See Suetonius, *Augustus* 64. 2 for Augustus' close interest in them.

[29] e.g. those listed in Gercke (1968: FM 2 and 3). The lack of illustrations in this book limits its usefulness. Provenance of examples is often unknown. When Gercke uses reliefs her dates are sometimes earlier than those of other scholars, e.g. Kleiner, Kockel. The great-grandson of Augustus and Livia who merited an *effigies* as a Cupid was older (*puerascens*) than the two who died as infants. This is consistent with the age of other children whose busts and statues seem to date from this period.

FIG. 9.3. (*left*) Reverse of Roman coin (denarius) of Augustus, 13 BC. Julia with sons Gaius and Lucius.

FIG. 9.4. (*right*) Reverse of Roman coin (denarius) of Augustus, 2 BC. Gaius and Lucius as *principes iuuentutis*, 'leaders of youth'.

intended imperial succession (Fig. 9.3).[30] In the same year Gaius, aged 7, took a leading role in the public presentation of the Trojan Games. Boys and adolescents were given an institutionalized role as cadres of youth, with Gaius being named *princeps iuuentutis* ('leader of youth') in 5 BC and both Gaius and Lucius represented with this title on coinage from 2 BC (Fig. 9.4).[31] In 2 BC Augustus was celebrated not only as the *paterfamilias* of the nation's first family but also as *pater patriae*, the father of the whole nation.

The new forum dedicated by Augustus in 2 BC embodied family and national virtues, often fusing the two. The central temple in this forum, dedicated to Mars Ultor (Mars as the avenger not only of Augustus' adoptive father Julius Caesar in Octavian's victory over Caesar's assassins at Philippi in 42 BC, but also of Rome's honour in the reclamation from the Parthians in 20 BC of the military standards captured from Crassus in 53 BC), was in future to be the place where Roman youths formally celebrated their recognition as adult citizens in the *toga uirilis* ceremony.

[30] *RIC* I². 72 nos. 404, 405. Julia and, before her, Augustus' sister Octavia were the first Roman women to be represented on coins in their own lifetime, and in each case it was in association with their roles as wife or mother.
[31] *RIC* I². 55–6 nos. 205, 212. All such coinage is silver or gold, which clearly emanated from Augustus himself.

In the new forum the Aeneas myth took its central place in Augustus' representation of national and family history. The statuary here no doubt set the myth in its received, official form. It was endlessly reproduced, on jewellery, lamps, and other artefacts. It apparently reached such a point of saturation that it was the subject of caricature.[32] But it became so internalized as a dominant ideal of the age that it was diffused from the political to the private sphere as a generalized representation of *pietas*, family devotion and duty.

Within a few years of the dedication of the Ara Pacis, private memorials recording families were becoming frequent. The memorials were overwhelmingly funerary and commemorated freedmen's families. For most freedmen, family was the primary thing they had to record, apart from their newly acquired citizen status, and the occasion for recording the family was usually the death of one of its members. The great families—the wealthy upper classes and especially parts of the imperial family—owned large numbers of slaves and were the patrons of many freedmen whom they had emancipated. Such families often made burial space available to these dependants, sometimes in a communal tomb shared by the donor family itself. Such dependants were members of the *familia* and might be the only ones left to maintain the tomb and its associated ritual. Freedmen continued the family name (the *nomen*). Huge examples of communal tombs (*columbaria*), with individual niches for urns and inscriptions and sometimes portraits, were set up by great houses, e.g. those of the Arruntii, of Marcella, of Statilius Taurus, in the Augustan and Julio-Claudian periods (approximately the first half of the first century AD). Children are amongst those memorialized in these tombs, but in comparatively small numbers.[33]

It was the individual family memorials which gave a special place to children. The Augustan family legislation offered incentives to freedmen as well as to freeborn to rear children and it is obvious that many responded. The funerary inscriptions from Rome of the early Principate belong largely to slaves and freed or to those who had recently emerged from that milieu. On the memorials embellished with sculpture the influence of the Ara Pacis and other examples of Augustan symbolism is clear.[34] The serious togate figures

---

[32] Not, perhaps, in Rome. Zanker's specific example is from Stabiae: Zanker (1988: fig. 162). But the poet Ovid's misjudgement, which brought about his exile from Rome, might have included facetious references to the myth in the very public circles of high Roman society (Zanker 1988: 209).

[33] See McWilliam (1994) for detailed analysis of *columbaria*.

[34] Zanker (1988: 8–11) comments on the fact that even the physical attributes of private individuals were copied from members of the imperial family. Cf. similar copying in our own recent society, e.g. the hair styles of Jacqueline Kennedy and Princess Diana.

advertise that they too are part of authentic Roman society and, often, that they too have children to continue their line. Full-length family groups almost certainly post-date the Ara Pacis. One example in particular, a relief now in a fragmentary state in the Villa Doria Pamphili in Rome, is a new departure stylistically: made from marble, its interaction of the child with one of the two adults (presumably her mother) is striking (Fig. 9.5). She tugs at her mother's dress just in the manner of children on the Ara Pacis. There had been virtually no interaction between the figures in previous groups. As Kleiner says,[35] 'This gesture was invented by the creator of the Ara Pacis.' There is no precedent for it, Greek or Roman, and the relief is dated to the last decade of the first century BC. The bird in the child's hand is also new in Roman art, but not in Greek art. The number of children represented in funerary reliefs between 13 BC and AD 5 increases dramatically. Some of these continue the severe frontal style of earlier reliefs, e.g. C. Liuius Alexander and (probably) his wife and son,[36] but features are individualized and younger persons tend to be more up-to-date stylistically.

JULIO-CLAUDIANS

During the Julio-Claudian period the emperors were concerned with dynastic continuity and, overall, continuation of Augustus' official value system. When twins were born to Tiberius' son Drusus and his wife Julia Livia in AD 19 Tiberius paraded his joy and pride (Tacitus, *Annales* 2. 84). In AD 23 Drusus was allowed to issue a coin in his own name celebrating the twins. They were portrayed on coinage (the obverse) as emerging from cornucopiae on either side of a *caduceus* (Fig. 9.6).[37] Drusus' claims to the succession were at their height at this time (but Drusus and one of the twins were to die before the year was out). Germanicus and Elder Agrippina produced nine children and made much capital out of them, e.g. taking them on campaigns and provincial postings, and after Germanicus' death Agrippina involved them in the return of their father's ashes to Italy and then in his funeral procession.[38] When Claudius' son (Britannicus) was born in AD 41, soon after Claudius' accession, the emperor issued coinage celebrating Spes, the hope for a new age, as

---

[35] Kleiner (1985: 108–12). This relief is no. 66 in her 1977 collection. Cf. no. 65, from the Museo Nazionale, Rome. Kockel (1993: 152–3 and pl. 66*b*) adopts a dating earlier than Kleiner but without reasons.

[36] CIL 6. 21381; cf. 11146. Kockel (1993: 181–2 pl. 95*a*); Kleiner (1977: 233 no. 67).

[37] Sestertius: *RIC* 1². 97 no. 42.

[38] Augustus had already used these children to encourage others to become fathers: Suetonius, *Augustus* 34 re AD 9.

FIG. 9.5. Marble relief of child and two adults, Rome, 13 BC–AD 5.
(Villa Doria Pamphili.)

FIG. 9.6. Obverse of Roman coin (sestertius) of Drusus, son of Tiberius, AD 23. Drusus' twin sons emerging from cornucopiae.

a symbol of youth.[39] Claudius found a reason (Rome's 800th anniversary) to celebrate the Secular Games in AD 47, much less than a century since Augustus' celebration. Nero had no son, but his celebration of his infant daughter—at birth in AD 63 and after her premature death soon afterwards (Tacitus, *Annales* 15. 23)—was all the more touching for having no direct dynastic overtones.

Representations of children may be found in various forms of private art, especially that preserved at Pompeii, e.g. in wall-paintings and sculpture (Grant 1971: 162–3). The tondos of a boy and a girl on a doorway in the House of M. Lucretius Fronto (Fig. 9.7) cannot be taken to identify a children's bedroom (as in J. R. Clarke 1991: 161) but they surely indicate awareness of children in the house. References to children are also frequent in Pompeian inscriptions (Kepartová 1984).

The freedman taste for group reliefs belongs particularly to the Augustan period, but some of these reliefs continue into the Julio-Claudian period.[40] A trend away from friezes to altars can nevertheless be identified, and some altars commemorate individual children. The earliest funerary altar with portrait(s), that of Ti. Octauius

---

[39] *RIC* I². 118–19, 128–30 nos. 99, 115; Zanker (1988: fig. 190). Cf. Vespasian in AD 70: *RIC* 2. 63 no. 396 (sestertius), where 'SPES' is specified; and in AD 74/75, *RIC* 2. 41 no. 233 (gold and silver), where the same type is used in association with Domitian as *princeps iuuentutis*. Clark (1983: 83) discusses the association of Spes with Youth, especially the imperial heirs.

[40] See group M in Kockel (1993), where some experimentation (although clumsy) can be seen with interaction between members of groups.

FIG. 9.7. Tondos of a boy and a girl painted on walls of doorway of house in Pompeii, AD 45–79.

Diadumenus, previously thought to be from the second century AD, may be late Augustan or early Julio-Claudian.[41] The altar from Ostia of the 5-year-old A. Egrilius Magnus, portrayed with his pet goat (Fig. 9.8), is attributed by Kleiner to the middle of the first century AD.[42] Some statues of boys can be attributed to the Julio-Claudian period.[43] Trimalchio's wish to have a portrayal of a slave boy crying over a broken amphora depicted on his tomb suggests that such scenes—sentimental and focusing on children—were not unusual, especially in freedman culture.[44]

FLAVIANS

Vespasian was responsible for the appointment of Quintilian to a Chair of Education. Although Vespasian's interest seems to have

[41] Kleiner v. Boschung (1987: 975), in her review (1989b: 306), on the basis of 'portrait style, nomenclature, and other features'. In Vatican (Kleiner 1987a: no. 1).

[42] Kleiner (1987a: 12). Goette (1989: 460) labels it Trajanic, without explanation, but the nomenclature and the full form 'Dis Manibus' suggest an earlier date. The goat may have symbolic significance, associated with the after-life, but at one level it is part of the Roman fondness for pet animals on their funerary monuments.

[43] e.g. Gercke (1968: FK 6, 9, 10), all togate. This is now the preferred date for the bronze statue of a *camillus* in the Palazzo dei Conservatori in Rome, once pronounced pre-imperial by Helbig (1963–72: ii no. 1450 v. edn. of 1895–6).

[44] Petronius, *Satyricon* 70–1. Trimalchio's choice may be presented for the patronizing amusement of Petronius' circle. Trimalchio does seem to be crowding all the standard iconography onto his monument, e.g. a distribution scene and Fortuna with dove and dog. If Petronius' intention is mockery, this is consistent with the apparent absence of upper-class memorials of this kind.

FIG. 9.8. Altar of A. Egrilius Magnus, aged 5, with goat. Ostia, AD 50–60.

FIG. 9.9. Altar of Q. Sulpicius Maximus, aged about 11, as budding orator. Rome (Palazzo dei Conservatori), AD 94–5.

been in higher education, that of adolescent males, Quintilian wrote a treatise on education which emphasized the importance of infancy and childhood and which included much detailed and perceptive comment on these phases of life. Quintilian was interested in the education of both girls and boys, and the first monuments to young girls on their own of which I am aware are of the Flavian period.[45]

Domitian strengthened official support for oratorical education by providing opportunities in a new Capitoline festival for pre-adolescent boys to compete and show their prowess. An elaborate monument to Q. Sulpicius Maximus (Fig. 9.9) testifies to the 11-year-old's success in the poetry competition of AD 94 but also to his stress-related death resulting from efforts and achievements beyond his age.[46] One might be tempted to associate an interest in intellectual accomplishments and education scenes with the upper classes. The names, however, of the parents of Q. Sulpicius Maximus (Q. Sulpicius Eugramus and Licinia Ianuaria) do not have the indicators of freeborn status which their son's name does and they could well be ex-slaves. Education has in many cultures been an avenue for ambitious, upwardly mobile, and newly prosperous parents (especially migrants) to improve the standing of their children. Education scenes become frequent in biographical reliefs on *kline* monuments and sarcophagi from the second century.

Boys and girls would have performed in the ceremonies of the Secular Games which Domitian celebrated a century after Augustus' celebration. As emperor, Domitian celebrated in apotheosis scenes on the coinage the young son who had died in the previous decade.[47] This may have been the model for Regulus' extravagant mourning and commemoration of his own dead son. Pliny's severe condemnation of this (4. 2, 7) must have stemmed partly from the personal hostility between the two men, but in Pliny's criticism there seems also to be the view that free-standing statues were inappropriate for a child. Statues were still being erected in public places to prominent citizens, albeit needing the permission of the emperor, and these may have been seen as an honour appropriate to individual senators and members of the imperial family. This would be in the tradition of individual honorific commemoration of individual senators rather than funerary memorials for them with their families.

---

[45] Kleiner (1987a: no. 23) (an 8-year-old freeborn daughter of a man and his freedwoman wife); Gercke (1968: FM 26–8), two statues and a bust.

[46] Palazzo dei Conservatori, Rome; Kleiner (1987a: no. 45). CIL 6. 33976, IG 14. 2012.

[47] RIC 2. 179–80 nos. 209a, 213, AD 81–4: gold and silver. Cf. the bronze coin of the same period with mother-and-son scene, celebrating Domitia as the mother of the deified child: RIC 2. 209 nos. 440–1.

In Pliny's own circle there was difference of opinion about the appropriateness of different forms of commemoration and indeed whether any form of material memorial was appropriate (e.g. Pliny 9. 19). This would fit Cannon's argument (above) about class differences in display and commemoration. There seems also to be a gender difference within the upper classes. Women could not aspire to all the kinds of achievement advertised in men's honorific monuments (especially those of political and military life, although some women were notable financial benefactors in the public sphere). Thus the inscriptions for the wife and young daughter of Pliny's friend Minicius Fundanus record only personal, family details (*CIL* 6. 16631–2: Statoria M. f. Marcella and Minicia Marcella Fundani f.) (cf. Eck, Ch. 4 above). The epitaph gives the daughter's age as 12 years, 11 months and 7 days, whereas Pliny (5. 16) remembered her as being not quite 14 when she died. Minicius' own inscription, found this century, is honorific and of the *curriculum uitae* type, evincing nothing of family relations.[48]

THE SECOND CENTURY

The second century saw the development of a range of official and privately sponsored projects for the support of children and family life. Trajan fostered the concept of the birth of a new age[49] and made much of not accepting the title *pater patriae* until he was worthy of being his country's father. The *alimenta* scheme is one of the best-known elements of this period. There had already been private foundations which provided financial support for children on a local basis and Nerva may have conceived the official scheme at the end of the first century. Trajan developed the scheme in detail, providing farmers in various parts of Italy with loans, the interest on which was available to support boys and girls (legitimate and illegitimate) in each local area. The coinage which celebrated the *alimenta* scheme was diverse and continued over many years, developing from the concept of an imperial handout to a more generalized connection between children and the good of the country (especially *fecunditas*, agricultural prosperity, and *pietas*). The

---

[48] Found in Bosnia 1926: R. Syme, *Tacitus* (Oxford: 1958), 801 n. 3. Cf. Pliny's inscription on the baths at Comum (*CIL* 5. 5262) and the (much briefer) one planned by Verginius Rufus for his tomb (Pliny 6. 10).

[49] e.g. Pliny, *Panegyric*, including reference (s. 28) to a *congiarium* for children. Cf. references by Trajan to 'the spirit of our times' in correspondence with Pliny, e.g. Pliny 10. 97: 'nostri saeculi'; 10. 55: 'ex iustitia nostrorum temporum'.

scheme continued for much of the second century and variations such as the *puellae Faustinianae* (for girls, in honour of Antoninus Pius' wife Elder Faustina and then Marcus Aurelius' wife Younger Faustina) were developed. The iconography on Trajan's arch at Beneventum (dedicated AD 114) connected his concern for children and the prosperity of Italy, e.g. in the scene on the 'country' façade (the side facing away from Beneventum) where Trajan presents two children to Italia and Mars, and in the scene on the passageway of the arch where a group of children with their fathers receives largesse from Trajan, backed by four goddesses symbolizing the towns of Italy.[50]

Under Hadrian and the Antonines *felicitas temporum* and *fecunditas* were important motifs, to denote a happy and productive period. Coinage continued to give prominence to children, including the *puellae Faustinianae* on Antoninus Pius' gold and silver (Fig. 9.10).[51] Reliefs (now in the Villa Albani at Rome) of Marcus Aurelius' reign depicted two processions of girls (thirteen in each) who appear to be *puellae Faustinianae*: the two women presiding over the distribution scene are usually identified as Faustina the Younger and Lucilla (Fig. 9.11).[52]

This was a period of great legal activity in areas which might loosely be called 'human rights'. Slaves and women benefited from this and children received particular attention. A brief summary of these developments must suffice here to provide a context for the increased visual prominence of children and sensitivity to their representation. Hadrian restored the right of children to free birth (*ingenuitas*) if the mother was of free status at the time of their birth even if the father was a slave, cancelling the change introduced by Claudius, to the disadvantage of such children, in the *senatusconsultum Claudianum*. Hadrian similarly ruled on the status of children of a Roman citizen mother and a Latin father: the children were to be Roman citizens, not Latins. In matters of status the law gave children the benefit of doubt (e.g. children of slave-women whose manumission was in some way irregular or mistimed). Soldiers

---

[50] Kleiner (1992: 224–9 and fig. 190). In a recent paper Sarah Currie (1995) has analysed in depth the symbolism and function of these reliefs: 'The Empire of Adults: The Representation of Children on Trajan's Arch at Benevento', in a volume edited by J. Elsner (CUP). She discusses the politicization of children's bodies on the arch and on Trajan's column in Rome. She also points out that the arch contains the first known monumental representation of the Seasons in childish form, as *putti*; 'it was now the child's body rather than the woman's body that was the prime denoter of a perpetual and natural cycle'. I am grateful to Sarah Currie for allowing me to read a pre-publication copy of her paper.

[51] *RIC* 3. 74–5 nos. 397–9, after Elder Faustina's death in AD 141.

[52] Helbig[4] (1963–72: iv. 199–200, no. 3234); Reinach (1912: iii. 147).

FIG. 9.10. Reverse of Roman coin (aureus) of Antoninus Pius, AD 141–61. Distribution scene for *puellae Faustinianae*: emperor, parents, and daughters.

FIG. 9.11. Relief, Rome (Villa Albani), AD 164–80. Procession of girls (*puellae Faustinianae*) approaching empresses Younger Faustina and Lucilla who are represented in a distribution scene on a matching relief.

who were *filiifamilias* (not independent of their fathers) had had some property rights (the *peculium castrense*) since the time of Augustus. Under Hadrian the children of soldiers, although by definition illegitimate, were granted some access to their father's property. Illegitimate children[53] were admitted to birth registers from the time of Marcus Aurelius. In the same period, by the *senatusconsultum Orphitianum* of AD 178, illegitimate children as well as legitimate were given priority

---

[53] See Rawson (1989) on the variety of circumstances which could make children *spurii*.

in succession to their mother's estate. The *Digest* and other legal sources are full of discussions of the protection of children's property rights in a variety of situations. This may have been motivated partly by a concern to keep the succession within the *familia*, but a concern for children's welfare is also discernible. There were many safeguards for the property of not-yet-adult children (those in *tutela*) and Marcus Aurelius allocated a specific praetorship to be responsible for such children (SHA, *Marcus* 11).[54] Provisions for the proper maintenance of children (and mutual obligations between children and parents) received much attention from the Antonines. Antoninus Pius was prepared to consider the interests of the child (rather than the legal rights of the father) in deciding where the child should live and be raised after a divorce.

A second-century bust dedicated to a slave boy reflects something of this atmosphere (Fig. 9.12).[55] This sculpture, of considerable artistic merit and of not inconsiderable cost, was dedicated by a master to the slave who had been born and raised in his house (a *uerna*) and who died at the age of 2. The 'Isis curl' behind the right ear may indicate initiation into the cult of Isis or some form of apotheosis.

During the Trajanic period *kline* monuments developed: funerary couches, with a representation of the deceased, which often had a relief below. The life-cycle reliefs on these monuments reflect an increased interest in biographical narration in funerary art and are characterized by movement and interaction. Kampen (1981) believes that customers for the *kline* monuments tended to be *liberti* and non-élite people.

Among the earliest of these monuments is the one from the Via Portuensis,[56] showing several scenes in a child's life: birth, play, education. The birth scene is frequent, involving mother, infant, midwife, and sometimes other female attendants. The first bath is often part of this scene. Even if the inspiration for such scenes was the well-known representation of Dionysus' birth, their popularity now and their use in human rather than mythological contexts indicates a lively interest in the first stages of infancy and recognition of this phase in people's own lives.[57]

There are many other examples which can be cited. All indicate a close observation of the development of children and an interest

[54] On *impuberes* in the law see McWilliam (1990).
[55] Getty Museum 85. AA. 352. I am grateful to Marit Jentoft-Nilsen for kindness in providing access to this bust and to supporting literature.
[56] Now in Museo Nazionale, Rome; dated *c*.100 by Berczelly (1978: pl. 1).
[57] There appears to have been a developing taste for mythological scenes in private memorials which included children. The stuccoes in the Porta Maggiore basilica, probably late 1st cent., seem to be an example of this (Berczelly 1978): there are mythological subjects, initiation scenes, and education scenes (e.g. a *lectio*).

FIG. 9.12. Marble bust of slave boy, Rome, 2nd century AD. The home-born slave, Martialis, died aged 2; dedication apparently by his master.

in these phases. Some *kline* monuments commemorate a dead child.[58] Similar life-cycle scenes appear on sarcophagi as the second century develops.

A sarcophagus gave scope for decoration or narrative on all four sides and its lid. The increasing use of inhumation rather than cremation in Italy from the early second century AD (but especially from the end of that century) must have been inspired partly by the greater scope for pictorial representation of stages in a life. It is too early for Christian beliefs to be the stimulus. Indeed, sarcophagi might sometimes have been used as the receptacle of ash urns, thus retaining the dominant form of disposal of the dead but taking advantage of a new medium for visual display.

Even during the first two centuries, when cremation was the dominant form of burial, there may have been a preference for inhumation for children (H. J. Rose 1923). There is literary evidence for the inhumation of very young children (those whose permanent teeth had not yet grown: Elder Pliny, *NH* 7. 16. 72) because cremation would have consumed their whole bodies and not left the obligatory remains for concluding the funerary ritual. The excavation of a cemetery on the east coast of Italy (at Portorecanati, south of Ancona) has yielded skeletons of 19 babies or children amongst 53 inhumations in a total of 357 tombs (Capitanio 1974). There are, however, no inscriptions or visual representations of the dead to help us individualize them further. Nor can we establish how many of the cremations were those of children. Grave-goods in children's burials here include a bracelet, vases, jewellery, coins, lamps, nails, tools (e.g. a bodkin), scent-bottles, knuckle-bones.

On sarcophagi the scenes are sometimes of the early life of an adult who has died, sometimes the deceased was still a child. Of the sarcophagi for children,[59] one of the earliest is from Trajan's reign.[60] It includes scenes of a child riding in a carriage with his parents, learning to walk, playing with a pet goose, and finally taking another carriage ride which symbolizes the end of his life and some form of apotheosis. Although the whole set of scenes may be a metaphor for the child's life they surely also reflect real-life activities. A late second-century sarcophagus[61] has scenes of birth, education,

---

[58] e.g. a boy's monument from Verona: Goette (1989: pl. 23).

[59] Janet Huskinson, whose contribution follows in this chapter, has a book on children's sarcophagi ready for publication. I therefore deal very briefly with such material here.

[60] Now in Museo Nazionale, Rome. Berczelly (1978: 64). Cf. Helbig[4] (1963–72: iii. no. 2394).

[61] Museo Torlonia. Kampen (1981: 22 fig. 7); cf. Amedick (1991: pl. 55. 3). Cf. a similar one in Villa Doria Pamphili (Kampen 1981: 27 fig. 4).

230

FIG. 9.13. Sarcophagus, Rome (Museo Torlonia), late 2nd century AD. Single panel depicting scenes (from left) of deceased's first bath as infant, education, funeral, and apotheosis.

funeral, and apotheosis (Fig. 9.13). An otherwise unpublished example from Ostia (Berczelly 1978: pl. V*c* and *d*) shows, on the fragments remaining, a bath scene, a school scene, and a *declamatio*.[62]

A sarcophagus in the Getty Museum, dating from the latter half of Hadrian's reign (Eberle 1990), belonged to a child who was about 10 years old when he died (Fig. 9.14). The boy's bust appears on the main side: such portrait images on sarcophagi became more popular from the middle of the second century. Surrounding the bust are Erotes and griffins—symbolism particularly associated with children's memorials at this time. Griffins were the guardians of the underworld, the guides of souls (*psychopompes*), and the accompaniment of Erotes and torches suggested some form of apotheosis.[63] Cf. the (more explicit) apotheosis scene on the child's sarcophagus from Museo Torlonia, from the late second century,[64] mentioned above (Fig. 9.13). Apotheosis symbolism seems to be associated mainly with children but sometimes with women.

FIG. 9.14. Marble sarcophagus of boy aged about 10, *c.*AD 120–30. Bust of boy held by Erotes; griffins to the sides.

Other sarcophagi, which probably date from the second or third centuries but whose style does not provide a basis for more specific dating, show children (boys and girls) playing games,[65] parents

---

[62] Cf. such scenes on adults' sarcophagi, e.g. LA County Museum (Kampen 1981), Museo Archeologico, Florence (Berczelly 1978), Museo Nazionale, Rome (ibid.), Louvre (ibid.), the first three of which date from the latter half of the 2nd cent. and the last one dates from the first half of the 3rd cent.

[63] Cf. the use of the 'Isis curl' behind a child's ear, noted above.

[64] Kampen (1981: pl. 8 fig. 7 and pp. 53–4).

[65] Museo Chiaramonti, Vatican (Helbig[4] 1963–72: i. no. 309); British Museum, sarcophagus of Aemilius Daphnus (Walker 1985: no. 32).

mourning a girl's death[66] and what has been called 'the Young Poet' giving a reading of his work.[67]

Sarcophagi must have been comparatively expensive, but they were not necessarily the monopoly of the upper classes. Freedmen seem to have been active clients for these—as other—funerary monuments.[68] The upper classes seem not to have been interested in narrative, life-cycle reliefs.

CONCLUSION

We have seen some evidence of an early Italian interest in representations of infants and motherhood. Although Hellenistic Greek art had been experimenting with representations of children, no direct influence on Rome is obvious. The funerary inscriptions of early imperial Rome reveal a contrast between Latin and Greek memorializations of children, with Latin inscriptions favouring the very young far more than did the Greek (MacMullen 1982). Saller and Shaw have shown that 'the epigraphic habit' is a particular characteristic of Roman culture, especially its use for family memorials. As inscriptions and sculpture are so often associated on Roman memorials (for those who could afford this), it would not be surprising if there were also an iconographic habit which was applied to family memorials and which featured children prominently and sensitively.

[66] British Museum (Walker 1985: no. 40).   [67] Louvre (Berczelly 1978: IXa).
[68] Eberle (1990) says that the new bourgeoisie were adapting artistic forms of the imperial cult from Flavian times—altars, stelai, urns. See Kleiner (1988: 118–19).

Iconography: Another Perspective

COMMENT by JANET HUSKINSON

The perspective offered here, from a viewpoint in Roman funerary art of the later Empire, is complementary to that of the social historian given above. Both perspectives start from the belief that it is important to contextualize iconography by considering a full range of evidence as a whole. My own work on the decoration of children's sarcophagi from Rome often presents the need to distinguish artistic from social construct, since many of the varied images of children and childhood which these contain are conventionalized and are not accompanied by any reliable text. Some appear to have been shaped more by artistic factors, others more by social ideas, so that in order to arrive at a balanced assessment of the final image it is necessary to look at each of these influences in its own context. This is where an interdisciplinary approach is important.

The chapter above presents two main theses. First that there was a visible and sympathetically differentiated stage of childhood in art, which developed over the course of time; and second that in terms of social class there is an apparent imbalance in the distribution of representations (certainly in earlier periods), with a 'strikingly low' number that can be associated with the upper classes.

This comment will concentrate on the first of these themes. It is certainly the case that children regularly appear in Roman art from the late Republic onwards, and in ways which observe their differences from adults. However, there are some general qualifications to be made to this. Because Roman art is generally more interested in suggesting status rather than emotion, it can provide only quite limited evidence for changes in sentiment towards children; for instance it offers none of the insights into adults' feelings about them which emerge from passing references in literature and letters. Furthermore, some of the imagery which is used in art for children is so adult (see below) as to blur the demarcation between adult and child; and in early Christian art this practice acquires another perspective from the new ways of considering the child—especially metaphorical—which Christianity offered (Currie 1993; Huskinson 1993). (In fact some of the questions raised above for the earlier

Empire, about iconography as evidence for changes in sentiment and ideology to do with children, have general parallels in this later period where the work-out of new ideas combined with the emergence of a new artistic iconography.) The remarks below will be focused under two general headings: (1) the child as represented in a wider social context, versus the child as an individual, and (2) the child as defined in terms of some other figure, principally the adult. (These are obviously working distinctions, and the groups overlap.)

Some points of specification should be borne in mind when using the term 'the child'. These are gender, age—which is especially important here where its biological and social definitions may substantially differ, e.g. Kleiner (1987a: 47) recording 'children' in their 20s and 30s commemorated on funerary altars by their parents—and what one might describe as behavioural expectations. This last point can be neatly illustrated by the fact that in English the noun 'child' tends to be neutral about these, whereas its associated adjectives 'childlike' and 'childish' specify, judgementally, different modes, good and innocent versus immature and, often, anti-social. All of these things need to be unpacked from the word, because they colour the Roman iconography too.

THE CHILD INSIDE AND OUTSIDE THE SOCIAL GROUP

The major point in the first part of this chapter is that developments in the representation of the child should be set firmly in the historical context of society, that initially—certainly in the earlier Empire—they were stimulated by the needs and policies of the state, through dynastic art, legislation, literary treatment, and so forth, and that they came to be taken up by individual families, particularly by those whose future or upward mobility depended on investment in the child. We are lucky to have some well-defined material at this point, where visual image may often be matched with inscription, which may be associated with freedman families (Zanker 1975; Kleiner 1977, 1987a); but this may have skewed the picture, obscuring the number of possibly upper-class representations of children. Examples of this social group may be harder for us to spot due to the loss of much contextual evidence and the fact that so many individual portraits, for instance, tend to be identified with the children of the imperial family.

How do these representations relate to any chronological development in sentiment towards the child in society? My view is that they are most probably reflections of a growing interest, but that it may be wrong to promote them too far as evidence for it: they are few in relation to comparable evidence from other disciplines, hard to pin down in terms of any close chronological development within this early period, and rarely deal directly with affective themes. It is worth taking into account the degree to which children were visible in post-classical Greek art, as this must surely have influenced Roman representations at this time, even if indirectly (Garland 1985: 84–5).

Some examples have been given in the first part of the chapter which can be looked at in terms of interaction of the individual child with the group: first, the children on the Ara Pacis and on the relief in the Villa Doria Pamphili (Kleiner 1977: no. 66). Note how we, as viewers, are persuaded by the powerful iconographical factors of dress and invented gesture that these are little individuals, with their own identity and actions, although they are in fact completely subordinate to the group theme, just as (on the Ara Pacis) their childhood is subordinate to adult political needs.

Secondly, the children portrayed in funerary altars: although their commemoration is very much a family affair, the terms in which they are represented often show an acute appreciation of individual achievements and characteristics. Kleiner notes (1987a: 87–8) in her discussion of these altars the special prominence given to children, which is expressed not just in the motif of the infant prodigy but also in the relatively high number of representations which identify the child with some divinity. Both of these themes, interestingly, set the child outside the norms of his usual social group, and promote him as an individual to be beyond the reach, as it were, of his human family.

There seems to be a comparable development in the choice of mythological images that relate to the child. As mentioned above, the Aeneas group was a powerful Augustan image of the family unit—as to a lesser extent was the wolf, the *lupa Romana*, with the twins—(Dulière 1979: 153–4); but certainly on sarcophagi by the later second century it is the acts of individual heroes such as Achilles and Meleager (who was the most popular myth on child sarcophagi) which seem to have more to say. In this funerary context they function as a mythological model to human children and their families of the hero fated to die young: it is a model of individual life and destiny (Brilliant 1984: 134–52).

Finally, children on sarcophagi: despite this increased interest in the individual, there are various scenes which specifically depict children operating within their own social group. In games scenes, for instance, they play with their peers (displaying some 'childish' behaviour), in biographical events they appear in a family setting, while in the deathbed scenes they are surrounded by household and professional mourners. These *conclamatio* scenes are particularly significant for an understanding of how iconography reflects social ideas about the child, since they do not appear on adults' sarcophagi from Rome as they survive (Amedick 1991: 74). (Perhaps these too commemorate the role reversal suffered by bereaved parents who had to show this *pietas* towards their children: see Sigismund Nielsen, Ch. 8 above.)

THE CHILD DEFINED IN TERMS OF OTHERS

Although this primarily concerns the adult, one might also look at mythological paradigms (some are mentioned above), and also at cupids who in some scenes, especially when they are not consistently winged, are hard to differentiate from the human child. Is their timeless childhood what human children often had to miss . . . ?

The representation of the child in adult terms is a very important issue, which is central to the Ariès debate about whether or not childhood was a differentiated stage; and if visual material is to be used in this debate—as it should be—artistic and social factors need some sorting out.

The use of the adult as a yardstick for the child is primarily visible in the representation of appearance and of behaviour. It tends to set up two polarized constructions, both visible in art and also described in literary evidence, ancient and modern (Néraudau 1984: 91–8). One is of the child as innocent and as yet untainted by the ways of the adult world; the other takes this inexperience as *infirmitas* which must be remedied through the acquisition of adult social qualities.

When we look at artistic representations for these views they are apparent to rather discrepant degrees. Certainly many of the *genre* depictions of children, like the pieces from Pompeii in the first part of the chapter, portray children in their own terms and make the most of this appeal for decorative effect. But in funerary art evocations of childlike innocence are relatively few: on altars and sarcophagi they are found in some portraits of infants and lively youngsters, scenes of games and pets, and, as indirect allusions, in some of the cupid motifs (for some assorted examples see Amedick 1991: nos. 60, 141, 165, 261). Here again it is noticeable how different material can yield different results: epithets on epitaphs may commemorate the quality of *dulcis* (see Sigismund Nielsen, Ch. 8 above), but it is not immediately recognizable in many funerary portraits of children.

Instead they give the cumulative impression of the child portrayed in adult terms, with some adult attributes and according to adult social and intellectual qualities. The classic example of this is the so-called *puer-senex* motif, illustrated by the memorial of the prodigious young orator Q. Sulpicius Maximus (see Fig. 9.9), where the visual imagery is reinforced by text. Frequently the same values are simply suggested through an oratorical gesture or the attributes of scroll or scroll-box, although some sarcophagi treat the theme more extensively in scenes of *declamatio* or discourse with the Muses (e.g. Amedick 1991: no. 112). Some of this imagery may be retrospective, some prospective—the child as he was or as he would have been; some may refer to this world, some to the next. But with any of these readings it remains clear that adult standards still retain a strong grip on this image of the child; and this must qualify, to some extent, the view of childhood presented in art as a fully differentiated stage.

The general social relevance of these ideas is not hard to see; but when we consider some of its manifestations in art-historical terms the picture is not always clear.

One aspect of this is illustrated by the biographical sarcophagi. These are very instructive about the kind of episodes in which they show children—the first bath, perhaps in the presence of the Fates, the lesson—because they give us some sense of the value attached by society to the status of childhood and its different stages. But as Kampen (1981) showed, that value differs depending on whether the scenes appear on a sarcophagus made for an adult, which would then include subsequent episodes of adulthood, or on one made for a child, for whom life allowed no further significant events: the same episodes illustrate thwarted potential for the child, but the preface to fulfilment for the adult. The point is that context is all-important to the understanding of some of these images, since the compositions themselves are often capable of more than one reading.

A second complicating factor is the range of artistic conventions to do with physical appearance in its relation to age. One is a tendency to portray children as older than the age given in the related inscription. Babies may look like 5-year-olds and so on (e.g. Walker 1985: fig. 31 recut; Goette 1989).

More critically, there is the fact that Roman commemorative art used two radically different approaches to sizing, one naturalistic and the other symbolic which represented figures as larger or smaller according to status. This obviously makes it hard in some cases to 'spot the child'. The children on the Ara Pacis are naturalistically sized but on many funerary altars, for instance, they are not (e.g.

Kleiner 1987a: nos. 58, 68). Furthermore, it is clearly the case that artistic creations might respond to the shape and size of the space which they had to fill. Thus some adults appear squat and 'child-like' in the rather cramped space of sarcophagus lids (e.g. Amedick 1991: no. 272), urns, and altars (e.g. Sinn 1987: nos. 83, 545); in contrast, the tall thin space in the centre of a strigillated sarcophagus meant that any child depicted there inevitably stood up straight and formal as if in an adult pose (Amedick 1991: no. 110).

In sum, two powerful forces might be at work—artistic and social —in creating the iconography of the child, and it is not always so easy for us to assess their relative power and intentionality. It means that the viewer has to know how to decode the image in individual instances, particularly amongst the conventions of funerary and political art (which have provided most of our examples). Ultimately, though, the representation of a child is an adult construct, in terms of patron, artist, and viewer, which is why a multidisciplinary approach to it can be fruitful.

10

Familial Structures in Roman Italy: A Regional Approach

PAUL GALLIVAN and PETER WILKINS

Scholars have long recognized that for the social history of Rome the benefits to be gained from the use of the vast corpus of Latin inscriptions[1] are great. Great too, however, are the pitfalls associated with the extraction of evidence from these inscriptions.[2]

This chapter attempts to quantify some of the evidence relating to the family in Roman Italy during the early empire. The chronological limits of this study, therefore, are from the beginning of the reign of Augustus to the end of the reign of Diocletian, i.e. *c*.31 BC–*c*.AD 305. The data have been organized on a geographical basis. In the original project this was done according to which of the eleven Augustan regions of Italy the evidence belonged to. For the purposes of this chapter, the material has been grouped into four geographical areas—the 'regions' of the chapter's title. These areas, which do not include Regions I and X, for which results are not yet complete, are as follows:

South	(Regions II, III—Apulia, Calabria, Lucania, Bruttium)
South-Central	(Regions IV, V—Sabina, Samnium, Picenum)
North-Central	(Regions VI, VII, VIII—Umbria, Etruria, Gallia Cispadana)
North	(Regions IX, XI—Liguria, Transpadana)

This chapter incorporates results drawn from a much larger project which involves a full-scale study of the family in Roman Italy. This long-term project supported by the Australian Research Council began as a joint venture between the University of Tasmania (represented by Professor P. R. C. Weaver and Dr P. A. Gallivan) and the Australian National University (represented by Professor B. Rawson). Dr P. Wilkins has worked on the project as Research Fellow since its inception. The aim of the project has been to create a complete database for all known families of Roman Italy below senatorial class, but not including at this stage the evidence from Rome itself. In this chapter, Gallivan was chiefly responsible for discussing Tables 10.1–10.5; Wilkins for Tables 10.6–10.13.

[1] The number of these inscriptions has been variously estimated. The most recent estimate would place the number at about a quarter of a million; see further Saller and Shaw (1984*a*: 124 n. 1), citing earlier works; Shaw (1991: 66–7).

[2] We record here our debt to earlier studies by Professors Rawson and Weaver and also to more recent works such as those by Saller and Shaw (1984*a*: 124) and Parkin (1992).

The evidence has been drawn from as wide a range of sources as possible—literary, iconographic, and epigraphic—and entered on a database using the Oracle computer software program.[3] The method has been to catalogue all family relationships recorded in the evidence along with all data which have a bearing on questions of family size, gender balance, and the commemorative roles played by parents and children. The study concentrates on the structure usually termed the 'nuclear family', that is parents and their children.[4] For the purposes of this chapter, the term 'child' is used of any person regardless of age, for whom a parent or stepparent is attested. Furthermore, the term 'family' is held to include not only parents and children but also siblings for whom no parents are attested.[5]

The aim of this chapter, as stated above, is, first, to investigate the questions of family size and gender balance. This will be attempted by means of a quantitative overview of the available data. We shall then pass on to an analysis of the commemorative roles played by parents and children with a view to discovering what light this sheds on family structures from region to region.[6] Finally, we shall turn our attention to an anomalous but important group which we style 'children with missing parents', a group which includes siblings and grandchildren for whom no parent is known, as well as stepchildren and *alumni*. The tables quantifying the data to which we will henceforth refer are given in Appendix 1, following an explanation of the codes used therein.

We begin with a rapid quantitative overview of the data relating to the size of the families (Tables 10.1 and 10.2) and to gender balance (Tables 10.3 and 10.4).

---

[3] Thus for the epigraphic material not only were the volumes of the *Corpus Inscriptionum Latinarum* and *L'Année Epigraphique* utilized, but also a wide range of other epigraphic *corpora* as well as periodical articles and monographs on individual towns and regions and numerous other publications of related interest. It should be noted, in particular, that the epigraphic evidence used includes not only epitaphs but also other texts which identify family relationships such as ex-voto inscriptions, records of benefactions, and official decrees.

[4] The results of our study strongly support earlier conclusions that the nuclear family was the predominant family structure in Roman Italy during the first three centuries of the Christian era. See e.g. Rawson's Introduction in Rawson (1986*b*); Saller and Shaw (1984*a*: 124 n. 1); Shaw in Kertzer and Saller (1991: 72–3).

[5] Our researches show that siblings as a group make up approximately one-third of all the evidence for families with two or more children. They are therefore crucial for any analysis of family size and gender balance.

[6] For the purpose of reconstructing family size, most epitaphs are unsatisfactory, Roman commemorative practice varying enormously but tending to favour separate commemorations for each deceased child. In such dedications parents frequently commemorated a child without naming their other children as co-dedicands. This practice can be verified by the occasional preservation of two or more memorials to children of the same family. Discussion of these examples has been reserved for Appendix 2, 'Hidden Children'.

TABLE 10.1

This table summarizes the data for those families attested with children, some 4,335 in all. Because the dispersal of these families is uneven—about one-third occur in the North-Central area compared with only about one-fifth in the North; while each of the South and South-Central areas has about a quarter of the total number —percentages in the final right-hand column should be read vertically. All other percentages should be read horizontally. The left-hand column gives the geographical area with the Augustan regions recorded in brackets. Moving towards the right, the families are recorded according to the number of children they are known to have contained.

When we turn to the columns relating to size of families, it is immediately obvious that 90 per cent of all known families recorded two or fewer children—71 per cent had one and 19 per cent had two. Next, we turn to the regional breakdowns. In the South, 8/10 (79%) families are attested with one child; in the South-Central region this figure is 7/10 (71%), in the North-Central region 7/10 (69%) and in the North just under 7/10 (67%). There is a problem with the figures for the two northern regions, however. This is because the number of families is inflated by those children whose parents are known only by Etruscan or peregrine modes of filiation. In what follows, we have disregarded all such instances. The familial structure of parents with one child in the South is considerably more common than the same familial structure in the North. Thus 79 per cent in the South compared to 68 per cent in the North-Central and 67 per cent in the North. In the case of families with two children, regional variation does not seem to have been so great—the exception in this category is the South with 16 per cent, whereas other regions all show about 20 per cent of their totals.

The next column (? 2+ children) incorporates all those who are simply termed *filii* without further identification. Except in so far as they are distinct from single-child families, little of value can be said about them.

Finally, let us look at families with three or more children who account for 7.6 per cent of our total sample. These families will be examined in more detail in Table 10.2, but for the moment we limit ourselves to the following observations, namely that the evidence suggests that larger families become more common as you move north. Thus 3.5 per cent in the South, 7 per cent in the South-Central, 8 per cent in the North-Central but 12 per cent in the North. Families with four or more children are a subdivision of the three-or-more group and have, therefore, not been added into the total. We will return to this group for more detailed comment later on.

TABLE 10.2

This table lists all the families known to have had two or more children. We will concentrate on the left-hand side of the table since the data recorded on the right-hand side have been included only for the sake of completeness and are useful only in establishing minimum family size.

The most obvious conclusion to be drawn from this table is that large families were but rarely recorded. (The largest one we have come across so far is a slave family containing ten children at Saepinum in Region IV, recorded in *CIL* 9. 2485.) The proportion of families with two children decreases from South to North, that of those with three children increases slightly from South to North while the proportion of those with four children noticeably increases from South to North.

We turn now to Tables 10.3, 10.4, and 10.5 which detail the evidence for the gender ratios of children. Table 10.3 catalogues families with children of one sex only and Table 10.4 families with children of both sexes. Table 10.5 compares the data from Tables 10.3 and 10.4 with respect to the frequency of both family structures according to the number of children.

TABLE 10.3

Perhaps the most obvious (and not altogether surprising) fact from a first reading is that families with boys outnumber those with girls. Throughout Italy the overall ratio is roughly 7 : 3. There is some slight regional variation evident in the totals columns for boys and girls, but it is too slight to require detailed discussion. Comparison of familial structures on a gender basis and by region reveals that in the South and South-Central areas the ratio of families with a single son to those with a single daughter is 2 : 1, in the North-Central area it is 7 : 3, and in the North it is just under 2 : 1. In a comparison of families with two boys and those with two girls, we find that in the South the ratio is 8 : 1, in the South-Central area it is 5 : 1, in the North-Central area 5 : 1, but in the North it is 13 : 1. Comparing families with three boys to families with three girls, the ratios are: in the South 6 : 1, in the South-Central area 3 : 1, in the North-Central area 10 : 1, and in the North 13 : 1.

TABLE 10.4

This table deals with families which have children of both sexes. Once more the imbalance between male and female children can be seen, especially when attention is directed to those families which have three children or more. Families with two sons and a daughter compare with two daughters and a son in the following ratios: in the South 3 : 1, in the South-Central area 7 : 3, in the North-Central area just under 7 : 3, and in the North 3 : 2. The figure for the North is rather surprising, given the results we noted above in Table 10.3. Table 10.5 compares the frequency of the family structures analysed in Tables 10.3 and 10.4.

Our overall analysis of Tables 10.3–10.5 produces the following conclusions. The sex-imbalance favouring sons over daughters rises sharply when families containing one, two, three, and four boys are compared with those having the equivalent number of girls. The sex imbalance is most extreme in the North. On the other hand, a comparison of families with children of both sexes shows that the imbalance is at its lowest in the North. These variations should caution us against viewing the marked male dominance in families with larger number of children as being the product of parental manipulation of the sex ratio. In the North at least they are in accordance with the well-attested male commemorative dominance as dedicands by sons and brothers which far exceeds that of any other area. More will be said about this fact later. Secondly, all families with three or more children (it will be recalled that there was a pronounced imbalance of sons over daughters in families with three to five children) demonstrate an imbalance which rises progressively from 2 : 1 to 6 : 1 to 8 : 1. Thirdly, from Table 10.5 we conclude that commemorative practice and the early marriage of daughters so colours our evidence that the totals in our sample vary markedly from the biological norm. This norm for families with two children is an equal distribution of children of one sex and children of both sexes, and not more than 2 : 1 in favour of children of one sex as our figures show. Similarly, for families with three children, the distribution should favour those with children of both sexes by 2 : 1, not by a mere 10 per cent as in our sample.[7] The figures for the South come closest to 'normality' because of the higher proportion of daughters in both family types.

---

[7] For the normal biological distribution of boys to girls in families, cf. Russell (1948: 244).

TABLE 10.6

This table provides an overview of the gender of all family members as a background to the more limited—but for us more useful—perspective of family commemorations detailed in Tables 10.7 and 10.8. Single children appear on the left, multiple children on the right, and the columns distinguish between both parents, fathers, mothers, and parents of indeterminate sex.

The most common family unit recorded is that of one parent and one child, and in particular that of a father and son (17%). It should be observed, however, that when the totals of fathers and mothers of single children are adjusted to remove the pronounced skewing of parents whose identity is known by peregrine or Etruscan filiation modes in the North and North-Central areas, the distortion favouring fathers diminishes for sons (15% for fathers and 14% for mothers —cf. the unadjusted totals of 17% for fathers and 12% for mothers) and evaporates for daughters (5% for fathers and 5% for mothers—cf. unadjusted totals of 7% for fathers and 5% for mothers). The adjusted totals also illustrate a singular feature of the North, which is that this area records no bias favouring the mention of fathers and sons over mothers and sons (10% for fathers and 10% for mothers). Where a bias does favour the mention of fathers, it is not because more fathers than mothers commemorated their deceased sons. Sons are attested about twice as often as daughters (46% compared with 21%). This is true whether the parent is the father, the mother, or both together. Both parents are most common where multiple children are recorded (10%).

TABLE 10.7

This table illustrates the commemorative role of parents and children in families where only one child is known. Parents appear as dedicands at the left and as honorands at the right. The columns again distinguish between both parents, fathers, and mothers and are further subdivided according to whether the child was a son or a daughter. Persons of indeterminate sex are omitted.

Kleiner (1987*b*: 549) comments that 'more fathers than mothers were sole dedicands to their children by virtue of their greater access to funds'. This observation is not borne out by the Italian evidence. Table 10.7 indicates, if anything, a slight bias the other way, both in dedications to sons (14.2%, cf. 13.6%) and, more noticeably, to daughters (7%, cf. 6%). Mothers are likewise found commemorated more frequently than fathers by daughters (4%, cf. 3%)

and only marginally less frequently than fathers by sons (8.4%, cf. 8.8%). In the North, conspicuous for its very high proportion of mothers as honorands by both sons and daughters, sons commemorate their mothers almost twice as often as their fathers (16%, cf. 8.7%). The literary evidence compiled by Hallett to argue for the centrality of the father–daughter bond in Roman society—filiafocality, as she terms it—deserves Saller's scepticism[8] and finds no support from Italian epigraphy.

In an apparent inversion of the laws of nature, parents, whether acting together or separately, commemorate their children far more often than their children commemorate them (68%, cf. 32%). In the North, however, the reverse is true for all except fathers (47%, cf. 53%), and their prevalence as dedicands falls well below par (11% and 4%). This same contrast between the North and other Italian regions—in this case between Region XI and Latium—can be seen in Table II of Saller and Shaw's important article (1984a), quantifying family relationships from tombstones, although they decline to comment on it.[9] Instead, the authors focus on a similar contrast in the high ratio of child-to-parent dedications amongst senators in comparison to those of the lower orders in Rome. One of the reasons put forward to explain this may be of relevance here, namely the assumed preference of servile populations to produce children after manumission, and in consequence the reduced likelihood of such parents having free children of a sufficient age to commemorate them.[10] The high proportion of *ingenui* and *peregrini* in the North who lacked this incentive to delay child-rearing may therefore account for the greater ratio of parents as honorands. However, the validity of widespread post-manumission marriages in Italy may be questioned.[11] In the South-Central area, six marriages resulting in three or more children were those of slaves (including our largest family—that of ten children—from Saepinum)[12] compared with eight

---

[8] Saller (1986b: 354) review of Hallett (1984).

[9] Saller and Shaw (1984a: 148 n. 2). The percentage of parents as dedicands (i.e. the descending nuclear family) is 36% in Latium, cf. 21% in Region XI. The percentage of parents as honorands, however (i.e. the ascending nuclear family), is 14% in Latium, cf. 26% in Region XI.   [10] Ibid. 138.

[11] Cf. Rawson (1966) (for Rome), and see further below.

[12] CIL 9. 2485 (cited earlier). The largest family in Italy is that of Iulia Gemella of Puteoli who bore Philadelphus 18 children before dying aged 32 years and 5 months (CIL 10. 2597). If Iulia Gemella was a *liberta* as seems probable from her husband's single name—a Greek *cognomen*—at least some of her prodigious output is likely to have been born prior to manumission. The largest family on record is that of Eutychis of Tralles, who was survived by 20 children and had given birth to 30 (Elder Pliny, NH 7. 34). The largest family ever recorded is 69 children born to an anonymous Russian peasant woman in the eighteenth century (*The Guinness Book of Records* 1994: 61).

by *libertae*, of whom one had a slave husband and three children
with single names, indicating their birth prior to manumission.

Whether as dedicands or as honorands, the proportion of fathers
to mothers differs by only about 1 per cent.[13] Both parents acting
together are about 5–7 per cent more frequent than either fathers
or others as dedicands[14] but about 4 per cent less frequent as honorands.[15] In the North all parental subsets achieve virtual parity as
dedicands,[16] whilst fathers lag some 8–9 per cent behind mothers and
both parents as honorands.[17] Two fundamental differences thereby
emerge. First, in the North the custom of awaiting the death of both
parents before erecting a memorial was far more prevalent—in fact
treble the frequency of any other area.[18] Secondly, mothers were commemorated twice as often as fathers in the North.[19] The former suggests a stronger sense of family identity and filial obligation in the
North rather than a canny scheme to halve funeral costs. Even where
separate epitaphs were erected to parents, the high proportion devoted
to mothers is consistent with an enhanced code of family loyalty,
for which both Tacitus and Pliny offer anecdotal support.[20]

Sons occur about twice as often as daughters and this proportion
is little affected by the gender, number, or commemorative role of
parents.[21] The bias favouring sons as dedicands—a bias most visible
in the North[22]—was natural in the Roman environment. When Ulpian
discusses filial responsibility for seeing to the burial of the father, he
talks of sons, not daughters (*D.* 11. 7. 4). Daughters presumably intervened only when a brother was not available or was too young.
The low ratio of daughters as honorands we can attribute, with
Hopkins (1966: 261), to 'the low social estimation of females among
those who set up tombstones'. We can add that the sex imbalance

[13] Dedicands: fathers 14%; mothers 14%; honorands: fathers 8.8%; mothers 8.5%.
[14] Dedicands: both parents 26.5% (17.5% + 9%); fathers 19.8% (13.6% + 6.2%); mothers 21.4% (14.2% + 7.2%).
[15] Honorands: both parents 7.9% (5.9% + 2%); fathers 11.9% (8.8% + 3.1%); mothers 12.4% (8.4% + 4%).
[16] Dedicands: both parents 15.7% (10.9% + 4.8%); fathers 15.7% (11.3% + 4.4%); mothers 16.1% (10.9% + 5.2%).
[17] Honorands: both parents 19.6% (15.2% + 4.4%); fathers 11.7% (8.7% + 3%); mothers 21.3% (16.1% + 5.2%).
[18] North: 19.6% (15.2% + 4.4%); cf. South: 5% (3.2% + 1.8%); South-Central: 6.8% (5.1% + 1.7%); North-Central: 6.9% (5.3% + 1.6%).
[19] Mothers: 21.3% (16.1% + 5.2%); fathers: 11.7% (8.7% + 3%).
[20] Tacitus, *Historiae* 2. 13; Pliny 6. 24.
[21] Sons as dedicands: 23.1% (5.85% + 8.8% + 8.45%); cf. daughters: 9% (2% + 3% + 4%); sons as honorands: 45.4% (17.5% + 13.6% + 14.3%); cf. daughters: 22% (9% + 6% + 7%).
[22] North: sons as dedicands 40.01% (15.22% + 8.7% + 16.09%); cf. daughters 12.6% (4.4% + 3% + 5.2%); cf. South: 23% sons to 8% daughters; South-Central: 19% sons to 9% daughters; North-Central: 24% sons to 9% daughters.

was much less among children 20 and under (61%, cf. 68%), a testimony to the value placed upon all young children for whom age is recorded.[23] The ratio of daughters aged between 0 and 10 compared to all daughters for whom ages are recorded decreases exponentially from South to North.[24] The South likewise has the lowest imbalance of daughters in this decile (55%).[25] For females aged between 11 and 30, husbands were almost as likely as parents to be commemorators (47% to 53%),[26] and this also accounts for the bias favouring sons aged 20 and over as honorands, males on average marrying some nine years after females.[27] Husbands take over as commemorators from parents for females dying in their early twenties in all areas except the South-Central, where this process occurs in the late twenties—perhaps reflecting a later age of marriage here.[28] As Parkin (1992) observes with a similar survey taken by Shaw, not all those daughters of marriageable age to whom dedications were erected by parents need have been unmarried.[29] The fact that 36 per cent of all females aged between 21 and 30 are still commemorated by parents suggests that many will have been widowed or divorced, especially given the age gap between spouses.[30]

---

[23] Of the 1,004 children with usable ages, 701 (70%) are aged 20 or younger and 288 (27%) 21 and over. A further 15 (1.5%) of indeterminate sex are excluded from the calculations below. The ratio of sons to daughters in the 0–20 age cohort is 61% (430/701). For children aged 21 and over the ratio is considerably higher—75% (215/288)—due primarily to the fact that females in this age bracket tend to be commemorated by husbands. For the overall son–daughter ratio of 68% (2,011/2,939), cf. the totals of sons and daughters in Table 10.6. In general, the pattern of distribution by age cohort bears little or no resemblance to the model life-tables devised by Coale-Demeny, even as adjusted by Parkin (1992: 147–8) to suit the contingency of a probable average Roman life expectancy of about 25. The largest skewing is in the deficiency of infants, a long recognized phenomenon. No infant is recorded younger than three months and those under one year of age form only 1.3% of our sample (cf. Parkin's 26–30% in his tables 9–10). By contrast the 6–10-year-old cohort is massively overrepresented—5.14% (cf. Parkin's 3.3–3.8%)—as are those in their teens.
  There are two distinctive features of the North. First, the practice of recording ages is far less common (only 88 examples or 9% of the total of 1,004 children with usable ages). Secondly, the proportion of children aged 5 and under in the North is only 10% of the total (9/88) or approximately half that recorded for the other areas by this group (72/343 or 21% for the South, 58/281 or 21% for the South-Central, 68/292 or 23% for the North-Central).
[24] Daughters aged 0–10: S, 48% (57/120); SC, 39% (34/87); NC, 38% (40/105); N, 25% (8/32).
[25] Son–daughter ratio (age 0–10): S, 55% (71/128); SC, 64% (61/95); NC, 64% (70/110); N, 60% (12/20).
[26] Wives, cf. daughters (age 11–30): S, 47% (51/109); SC, 35% (28/79); NC, 54% (73/136); N, 49% (22/45); all areas, 47% (174/309).
[27] Parkin (1992: 135) puts the difference at 8–10 years.
[28] Wives, cf. daughters (age 11–30) for age cohorts 11–15, 16–20, 21–5, 26–30: S: 14.29%, 44.12%, 54.55%, 71.43%; SC: 13.33%, 33.33%, 45%, 71.43%; NC: 34.62%, 39.53%, 73.53%, 66.67%; N: 12.5%, 50%, 60%, 66.67%.
[29] Parkin (1992: 124) on Shaw (1987: 30–46).
[30] 36% (61/168, i.e. 40/101 at 21–5 and 21/67 at 26–30).

The format for the commemorative patterns of parents with multiple children in Table 10.8 is identical to that for Table 10.7, except that the children are no longer subdivided by sex. The chief distinction with Table 10.7 is that parents of each subset are now predominantly honorands not dedicands (66%, cf. 34%). This is especially true of the North where three-quarters of all parents are honorands (75%), with both parents being far better represented than single parents.[31]

TABLE 10.8

For reasons of space, Table 10.8 is a simplification of the actual commemorations. The fixed point is the role of the named parent (or parents). Thus each heading also includes instances where one or more children share the role of the named parent (or parents).[32] For families of three or more children these intricacies are of a special relevance to the North, where—uniquely—the most frequent commemorative pattern (30%) is that of a child dedicating to both parents and to two or more siblings. This practice, significantly, is especially prevalent amongst *ingenui* and *peregrini* who comprise 45 per cent and 17 per cent of all large families in the North.[33] In the other areas where the percentage of *ingenui* amongst large families is considerably less (23%, 20.5%, and 41% as one moves north) and that of *peregrini* non-existent, different commemorative trends predominate. Unlike the North, parents are most frequently commemorated individually, not together. In the South and North-Central areas, children club together to commemorate a parent. In the South-Central area one child dedicates to a parent and to two or more siblings.

An interesting aspect of the analysis of families with three or more children by status is the high concentration of large families of slave or ex-slave status in the South-Central area. The combined proportion of *serui* (15%), *liberti* (26%), and probable *liberti*—i.e. those individuals who possess a Latin *nomen* in conjunction with a Greek *cognomen*[34] and/or share the same *nomen* as their spouse (13%) comprises over half of all large families in the South-Central area

---

[31] Both parents 36%; cf. fathers 21%, mothers 18%.
[32] Similarly each heading involving a single parent commemorating or being commemorated by children also includes instances where the other parent shares the role of the children.
[33] Clearly, the assessment of Brunt (1971: 387), that the Roman freeborn population 'was markedly failing to reproduce itself', was far from true of *ingenui* in the North.
[34] For descendants of freedmen with names of this type, cf. Garnsey (1975: 172–7).

(54%). This proportion is over 20 per cent higher than the same status group in both the South (32%)[35] and the North-Central area (30.5%)[36] and over 40 per cent higher than in the North (13%).[37] It can be observed, moreover, that the proportion of the servile population in the South-Central area with three or more children is substantially higher than the overall representation of this same status group for all families with children from this area (54% (see above), cf. 42%).[38] If *seruae* were consciously postponing the starting of a family until after manumission, there might be some reflection of this in the South-Central area, with (*a*) its very large servile population and (*b*) the apparent later average age of marriage by females here than elsewhere, as suggested by the fact that it is in this area that husbands take over later than parents as dedicands to females. On the other hand, we have seen that slaves with large families are well represented in the South-Central area, as are *libertae* with at least some of their three or more children born prior to manumission.

As in Table 10.7, the overall distribution of fathers and mothers differs little, whether as dedicands or honorands, although there are wider swings from area to area. Thus in the North, fathers are twice as frequent as mothers as dedicands (13%, cf. 6.5%), but in the South-Central area it is the opposite (5%, cf. 11%). There is also considerable regional diversity in the proportion of both parents as dedicands,[39] although the pattern of distribution is similar for both tables.

The larger number of big families recorded in the North was not the product of colder nights, no television, and northern ingenuity. Family commemorations simply tended to be more inclusive in the North because of different cultural practices, children being more frequent as commemorators, especially to both parents. A stronger sense of family identity in the North can also be sensed in the virtual absence (only 2 out of 56 examples) of dedications by couples *sibi* (to themselves) which excluded children from a commemorative role.[40] Furthermore, over half (54%) of all commemorations in the

[35] S: *serui* (9%), *liberti* (14%), probable *liberti* (9%).

[36] NC: *liberti* (19%), probable *liberti* (12%).

[37] N: *serui* (5%), *liberti* (7%), probable *liberti* (1.7%).

[38] SC: families grouped according to status (excluding those of siblings) appear in the following proportions: *ingenui* 19%, servile 41% (*serui* 11%, *liberti* 16%, *serui/liberti* 1%, probable *liberti* 13%), others 39%.

[39] Both parents as dedicands form only 6% of the total of commemorations to or by multiple children in the North, cf. 25% in the South-Central.

[40] The distribution of dedications by couples *sibi* is as follows: S, 32% (18/56); SC, 43% (24/56); NC, 21% (12/56); and N, only 4% (2/56).

North involving large families were erected by one family member
to all the others, either—as seen above—a child to both parents and
to two or more siblings (30%) or a parent to a spouse and to three
or more children (24%). In these instances it is probable that the
epitaphs are a true reflection of the actual size of the family (excluding infants). By contrast, epitaphs of this sort are in a minority in
other areas (22% in the South, 13% in the South-Central area, and
17% in the North-Central area). The majority of epitaphs concerning large families from these areas are dedications to one family
member by the rest and cannot therefore be regarded as a complete
'family album', in so far as earlier dedications to other deceased family members may always be predicated. This is obviously even more
true when, as in most instances, all we possess is a single commemoration to or by one child. There is in fact some evidence for the
existence of 'hidden children' in Italy south of the Po which indicates
that it was by no means customary for siblings or even for both parents to commemorate a deceased child (see Appendix 2).

TABLE 10.9

This table quantifies the number of families for whom three or more
generations are known. Single grandchildren are subdivided by gender and distinguished from multiple grandchildren. The columns differentiate between grandchildren with both grandparents and those
with a grandfather or grandmother only. Great-grandchildren and
their descendants appear on the right. Only 7 per cent (316/4,335)
of all families record grandchildren.[41] As for children, the male/
female ratio of grandchildren favours males by more than 2 to 1
(48%, cf. 19%). Where paternal and maternal grandparents can
be distinguished, the former are more prevalent (63%), especially
for granddaughters (71%). It is clear from these figures that the alleged special bond of affection from the maternal or cognatic line
in Roman society, as argued by Hallett (1984) and Radcliffe-Brown
(see Saller, Ch. 1 above), cannot be substantiated. Similarly, Saller
observes that *auunculus* (maternal uncle) commemorations in *CIL*
6 are only half those of *patruus* (paternal uncle) commemorations.

Geographically the North has the lowest discrepancy between
paternal and maternal grandparents (55%), a feature which well

---

[41] When the 54 examples attested only by Etruscan or peregrine modes of filiation are
deducted, the percentage is reduced to 6 (262/4335).

accords with this area's greater frequency of commemoration of mothers by children.[42]

There are only two examples of great-grandparents recorded as being contemporaries of their great-grandchildren, C. Crispinius Hilarus of Faesulae with his eighteen great-grandchildren[43] and Sabina of Aequiculi with her two great-grandchildren.[44] Atilia Posilla of Placentia is commemorated together with her great-grandson and great-great-grandson by her grandson, the decurion M. Coelius Verus.[45]

TABLE 10.10

Table 10.9 serves chiefly as a background to Table 10.10, which enumerates the small number of orphans who commemorate or are commemorated by grandparents. These children constitute the first of four groups of 'dislocated' children who have lost one or both parents or who have been fostered as *alumni* by another family. The others comprise stepchildren (Table 10.11), *alumni* (Table 10.12) and siblings with no recorded parents (Table 10.13). For the sake of convenience they have been loosely classified under one heading, 'children with missing parents'.

In Table 10.10, the male/female percentage of grandparents as commemorators (64%)[46] does not differ greatly from that of parents to single children (68%).[47] One might expect on these grounds that the grandchildren commemorated were very young. In fact, although eight of the thirteen ages recorded are relatively young (five were between the age of 2 and 4 and three between 10 and 13), a further three are aged between 17 and 23, while two others—if they are to be believed—concern grandchildren aged 55 and 72! The ratio of

---

[42] The ratio of paternal to maternal grandparents in other areas is as follow: S, 77% (34/44); SC, 63% (22/35); NC, 66% (43/65); 61 uncertain cases and 10 cases where both sets of grandparents are known have been omitted from calculation.

[43] Elder Pliny, *NH* 7. 60—Hilarus sacrificed on the Capitol in the presence of his 8 children, 27 grandchildren, their 8 wives, and 18 great-grandchildren. For a modern equivalent, cf. *The Mercury* (Hobart), 30 Aug. 1994, p. 7 which reported that a Mrs Rene Standen of Geeveston, Tasmania, has 131 living descendants (cf. Hilarus' 53!), i.e. 11 children, 46 grandchildren, and 74 great-grandchildren (with another 4 on the way). For a record 824 descendants of an American, Samuel Mast, all of whom were alive at his death at 96, see *The Guinness Book of Records* (1994: 63). [44] *CIL* 9. 4151.

[45] *CIL* 11. 1224 = p. 1253. Only two other great-grandparents are commemorated in epitaphs. As with Atilia Posilla, it is the grandson who dedicates and the great-grandmother who is commemorated with her great-grandchildren (*CIL* 11. 2914*a* and 5. 6000*a*).

[46] 64% (23/36); the three dedications in which grandparents appear as both dedicands and honorands are omitted from calculation.

[47] 68% (see Table 10.7). The proportion of parent dedicands to single *and* multiple children is 61% (1,390/2,282).

grandsons to granddaughters as with that of sons to daughters is again more than 2 to 1 (41%, cf. 18%). In contrast to parents, where fathers and mothers commemorate children almost equally, grandfathers commemorate grandchildren twice as often as do grandmothers (36%, cf. 18%).[48] As honorands, however, grandparents and parents of both sexes are commemorated about evenly (15% cf. 13%).[49] For reasons we can only guess at, the distribution of epitaphs in Table 10.10 is markedly uneven, with 44 per cent for the South and only 10 per cent for the North.

TABLE 10.11

This provides statistics for stepchildren. The columns distinguish between children with a stepfather and a mother; a father and a stepmother; a stepfather only; a stepmother only; a stepparent of unknown sex; and those with no known parents. Although the total is small (65), there are a further 177 families for whom steprelationship is possible, but cannot be ascribed with certainty. The uncertainty generally arises from instances where a child's *nomen* differs from that of the father, but only perhaps as a result of manumission by a different patron or the child's illegitimacy. The actual numbers of stepchildren must have been considerable given the high mortality rate, the age difference between spouses and the incentive for widows to remarry in the *lex Iulia de maritandis ordinibus*. Once again the bias favouring the recording of male children is over 2 to 1 (62%, cf. 28%). Little should be made of the high ratio of stepfathers to stepmothers (15%, cf. 4%), which in half of all examples simply results from the ease with which stepfathers can be detected where their stepchildren are freeborn (*ingenui*). It is interesting, however, that stepchildren are almost four times as likely to be recorded when one of the commemorators is a biological parent (78%, cf. 22%).[50] This ratio is to some extent artificial as 22 per cent of stepchildren are described as *filii eius*, etc. and can only be detected by the presence of one biological parent, while another 10 per cent can be identified as stepchildren only by the presence of three or more parents. Nevertheless, even after subtraction of these examples, the ratio still remains high—3 to 1—and, given that the

---

[48] 36% (i.e. 26% + 10%); 18% (i.e. 10% + 8%).
[49] 15% (i.e. 13% + 2%); 13% (i.e. 5% + 8%).
[50] 78% (46/59). The six examples of stepchildren for whom no parents are known are omitted from the calculation.

ratio of stepchildren as dedicands and honorands is similar, perhaps suggests (*a*) that natural children were preferred as commemorators when available and (*b*) that stepchildren were less likely than natural children to be commemorated. On the other hand, it should be stressed that our sample is small and that many more stepchildren lie concealed, undifferentiated by nomenclature or the somewhat pejorative terms *priuignus, filiaster, filius eius*. The geographic distribution of stepchildren is relatively even.[51]

TABLE 10.12

This catalogues seventy-nine families recorded with *alumni* in the regions under consideration. The columns distinguish between those with two foster-parents and those with male foster-parents, female foster-parents, or foster-parents of unknown sex. The rows divide *alumni* from *alumnae*. Bellemore and Rawson (1990: 4) estimate that less than 0.5 per cent of the Italian epigraphic record attests *alumni*, a ratio less than half that of Rome. This estimate is, in fact, too low. From our wider epigraphic base another seventy-seven families with *alumni* can be added to their total of 161, although the proportion still falls well short of Rome's. Geographically the 238 attested families with *alumni* in Italy (besides Rome)[52] are primarily concentrated in Region I (136 or 57%) and particularly in the ports of Ostia (61 or 26%) and Puteoli (31 or 13%). For the remaining regions the distribution is as follows: II: 24 or 10 per cent; III: 3 or 1.3 per cent; IV: 9 or 3.8 per cent; V: 1 or 0.4 per cent; VI: 9 or 3.8 per cent; VII: 13 or 5.5 per cent; VIII: 13 or 5.5 per cent; IX: 3 or 1.3 per cent; X: 23 or 9.7 per cent; and XI: 4 or 1.7 per cent. The South-Central area and the North with only 4 per cent and 3 per cent respectively of all families with *alumni* are the most poorly represented, although it is from the South-Central area that the family with the largest number of *alumni* (4) derives.[53] The families with *alumni* in Table 10.12 for whom the following comments are reserved comprise only about one-third of the Italian total (79/238).

The male to female ratio for *alumni* in Table 10.12 is again more than 2 : 1 (64.5%, cf. 30%). Stepparents and foster-parents are analogous, in that the stepfather and male foster-parent are recorded

[51] On stepmothers and stepfathers in inscriptions, see now P. A. Watson (1995: 267–71).

[52] The actual number of *alumni* is 264+, with 26 families showing two or more *alumni*.

[53] Letta and D'Amato (1975: 355 n. 8). The dedication to L. Fruuius Symphorus, who died at 80, was set up by an *alumna* and three *alumni*, all Fruuii. For families with three *alumni*, cf. *AE* (1901), 170 (Puteoli), *CIL* 14. 5003, *AE* (1988), 189 (Ostia).

with more than treble the frequency of their female counterparts.[54] They differ significantly, however, in that stepparents are predominantly attested with spouses (78%),[55] foster-parents without (78%).[56] The greater affection of the biological parent has been postulated to explain why so many epitaphs involving stepchildren include them. The case of *alumni*, by contrast, whose epitaphs were overwhelmingly set up by male foster-parents acting without their spouses, can perhaps be attributed to the higher frequency of males in initiating foster relationships. Male foster-parents are most prevalent in the North (75% and 100% for *alumni* and *alumnae* respectively), the area where families with *alumni* are least represented (9%). As a proportion of all families for whom children are recorded, *alumni* are most represented in Brundisium (13%), Ravenna and Ariminum (5%), and Beneventum (4%). The fact that the first three of these towns were ports with large servile populations, many of whom prospered from trade, is probably significant, and we may compare the high proportion of *alumni* (7%) in two other major ports, Ostia and Puteoli.[57]

TABLE 10.13

This table concludes this survey by looking at the largest group of 'children with missing parents', namely siblings for whom no parents are known. The columns distinguish between dedications to other siblings by brothers, by sisters, by siblings of unknown sex, and by two or more siblings. Not all the 430 known are necessarily parentless, but there is a strong presumption that this is so for the 335 known from epitaphs. Comparison between two-children families with parents known and those which can be reconstructed only by the record of two siblings reveals remarkable consistency in the gender balance. For both, the proportion of families with two sons,

---

[54] Male foster-parents of *alumni* 57%, cf. 18%; stepfathers 15%, cf. 4% (see above). In Rome the discrepancy between male and female foster-parents is nowhere near as pronounced (55% male to 43% female). See Rawson (1986: 177). For Regions I and X, the ratio of male/female foster-parents as dedicands is about 2 to 1 (60 : 27 in I; 11 : 5. in X).

[55] See n. 50.   [56] 78%, i.e. 45 + 14 + 3 = 62/79.

[57] Another major port, Aquileia, records 10 families with *alumni*, or about 4% of all families with children, a proportion similar to that seen for Beneventum. Other towns with high concentrations of families with *alumni* are Tusculum with 5, Tibur with 4, and Velitrae with 3, or 8%, 3%, and 11% respectively of all families with children from these towns. Proximity to Rome and the numerous wealthy villas employing large staffs of slaves and freedmen are the most likely factors which account for these high ratios. For the value set upon *alumni* by the servile elements of towns cf. Bellemore and Rawson (1990: 16).

two daughters, and a son and a daughter is about 60 per cent, 9 per cent, and 31 per cent respectively, with all the variations below 2 per cent.[58] The even greater bias favouring sons over daughters in the North—a bias of over 90 per cent—is likewise reflected in both.[59] The commemorative bias favouring males was clearly not restricted to a parental value system.

In conclusion, our survey indicates great regional variations in Italian commemorative practices. This was particularly true of the North, where the slave and ex-slave population was far less represented and where the traditions and codes of family loyalty of *ingenui* and, to a lesser extent, *peregrini* tended to preserve the names of more family members on memorials than elsewhere. These memorials usually appear in the form of one family member dedicating to several others and may be taken as reasonably indicative of actual family size. Commemorations of a single family member, most commonly of a child, are the most frequently attested type of Italian memorial, and allow us only to deduce the minimum family size. The sex ratio of children of all types—including all those labelled as 'children with missing parents'—is remarkably constant, boys exceeding girls by a factor of more than 2 to 1. There is a very detectable bias in the commemoration of stepchildren by a stepparent in conjunction with a biological parent rather than by a stepparent only. Finally, *alumni* are three times as likely to be commemorated by a male foster-parent (*nutritor*) as opposed to a female, in contrast to biological children where both fathers and mothers commemorate them equally.

---

[58] Siblings: 2 sons (151/249 or 60%), 2 daughters (23/249 or 9%), a son and a daughter (45 + 30 = 75/249 or 30%). Children: 2 sons (469/787 or 60%), 2 daughters (72/787 or 9%), a son and a daughter (246/787 or 31%). See Tables 10.3, 10.4, and 10.5 for the latter figures.

[59] For children in the North, the male/female ratio for families with 2 children of the same sex is 116/125 or 93% (See Table 10.3).

Appendix 1. Tables

1. In all tables where the heading 'Area' is specified, the four areas (listed in the left-hand column) are:

S	South
SC	South-Central
NC	North-Central
N	North

2. Family codes are those used in the database, i.e.:

B	son
b	daughter
C	father
c	mother
D	brother
d	sister
E	grandfather
e	grandmother
F	grandson
f	granddaughter
M	stepfather
m	stepmother
N	stepson
n	stepdaughter
P	male foster-parent of *alumnus/alumna*
p	female foster-parent of *alumnus/alumna*
S	*alumnus*
s	*alumna*
—	families of siblings for whom no parents are known

Note: duplication of E, e, F, or f indicates the addition of another generation (e.g. EE = great-grandfather, EEE = great-great-grandfather.)

TABLE 10.1. *Families with children (1–10)*

Area	1 child	2 children	?(2+ children)	3+ children	4+ children	All children
S (II, III)						
no.	813	160	23	32	5	1,028
%	79.09	15.56	2.24	3.1	0.49	23.71
SC (IV, V)						
no.	716	212	22	57	15	1,007
%	71.1	21.05	2.18	5.66	1.49	23.23
NC (VI–VIII)						
no.	987*	277	80**	86	26	1,430
%	69.02	19.37	5.59	6.01	1.82	32.99
N (IX, XI)						
no.	583*	180	31	76	32	870
%	67.01	20.69	3.56	8.74	3.68	20.07
TOTAL						
no.	3,099	829	156	250	78	4,335
%	71.49	19.12	3.6	5.77	1.8	100

* The number is inflated by those whose parents are known only by filiation (after the mother in VII: 66 (50 from Clusium), and after the father in IX and XI: 206).

** The number is inflated by 34 groups of *fratres* from the alimentary charter of Veleia.

TABLE 10.2. *Families with multiple children (2+)*

Area	2	3	4	5	6-10	?(2+)	?(3+)	?(4+)	Total
S (II, III)									
no.	160	22	4	—	—	23	5	1	215
%	74.42	10.32	1.87	—	—	10.7	2.33	0.47	17.39
SC (IV, V)									
no.	212	35	6	4	4	22	7	1	291
%	72.85	12.03	2.06	1.37	1.37	7.56	2.41	0.34	23.54
NC (VI–VIII)									
no.	277	52	17	5	3	80*	8	1	443
%	62.53	11.74	3.84	1.13	0.68	18.06	1.81	0.23	36.84
N (IX, XI)									
no.	180	40	22	6	4	31	4	—	287
%	62.72	13.94	7.67	2.09	1.39	10.8	1.39	—	23.22
TOTAL									
no.	829	149	49	15	11	156	24	3	1,236
%	67.07	12.06	3.96	1.21	0.89	12.62	1.94	0.24	100

* The number is inflated by 34 groups of *fratres* from the alimentary charter of Veleia.

TABLE 10.3. *Families with children of one sex*

Area	B	B2	B3	B4	B5	B6	Total	b	b2	b3	b4	b2+	b3+	Total	B/b	Total
S (II, III)																
no.	528	76	6	2	—	—	612	244	10	1	—	—	—	255	41	867 (908)
%	60.9	8.77	0.69	0.23	—	—	70.59	28.14	1.15	0.12	—	—	—	29.41	4.52	24.28 (24.34)
SC (IV, V)																
no.	452	122	13	1	—	—	588	212	23	5	1	1	—	242	52	830 (882)
%	54.46	14.7	1.57	0.12	—	—	70.84	25.54	2.77	0.6	0.12	0.12	—	29.16	5.9	23.24 (23.64)
NC (VI-VIII)																
no.	662	155	22	5	3	1	848	275	30	2	—	3	2	312	50	1,160 (1,210)
%	57.07	13.36	1.9	0.43	0.26	0.09	73.1	23.71	2.59	0.17	—	0.26	0.17	26.9	4.13	32.48 (32.43)
N (IX, XI)																
no.	369	116	13	7	2	—	507	197	9	1	—	—	—	207	17	714 (731)
%	51.68	16.25	1.82	0.98	0.28	—	71.01	27.59	1.26	0.14	—	—	—	28.99	2.33	20 (19.6)
TOTAL																
no.	2,011	469	54	15	5	1	2,555	928	72	9	1	4	2	1,016	160	3,571 (3,731)
%	56.31	13.13	1.51	0.42	0.14	0.03	71.55	25.99	2.02	0.25	0.03	0.11	0.06	28.45	4.29	100 (100)

Notes: The totals in brackets include children of indeterminate sex (B/b).

All percentages (except those in the B/b column) are taken from the unbracketed totals.

Some numbers are inflated by those whose parents are known only by filiation (after the mother in VII and after the father in IX and XI).

NC: B (662 − 56 = 606): b (275 − 10 = 265)

N: B (369 − 113 = 156): b (197 − 91 = 106): B/b (17 − 2 = 15).

TABLE 10.4. *Families with children of both sexes*

Area	2		3		4			5			6		7	8	Total
	B&b	B_2&b	B&b_2	B_3&b	B_2&b_2	B&b_3	B_4&b	B_3&b_2	B_2&b_3	B_4&b_2	B_3&b_3	B&b_5	B_3&b_4	B_6&b_2	
S (II, III)															
no.	65	10	3	1	1	—	—	—	—	—	—	—	—	—	80
%	81.25	12.5	3.75	1.25	1.25	—	—	—	—	—	—	—	—	—	21.56
SC (IV, V)															
no.	52	12	5	2	2	—	1	2	1	2	—	—	1	—	80
%	65	15	6.25	2.5	2.5	—	1.25	2.5	1.25	2.5	—	—	1.25	—	21.56
NC (VI–VIII)															
no.	81	16	7	8	3	1	—	1	—	1	—	—	—	1	119
%	68.07	13.45	5.89	6.72	2.52	0.84	—	0.84	—	0.84	—	—	—	0.84	32.08
N (IX, XI)															
no.	48	14	9	9	3	2	1	3	—	—	2	1	—	—	92
%	52.17	15.22	9.78	9.78	3.26	2.17	1.09	3.26	—	—	2.17	1.09	—	—	24.8
TOTAL															
no.	246	52	24	20	9	3	2	6	1	3	2	1	1	1	371
%	66.31	14.02	6.47	5.39	2.43	0.81	0.54	1.62	0.27	0.81	0.54	0.27	0.27	0.27	100

Note: The following 17 examples are excluded: B_2+ & b (SC-4, NC, N); B & b_2+(SC-2); B_2 & b_2+(S, SC, NC); B_3 & b_3+(SC); B & b_3+(SC, NC, N); B_3 & b B/b (NC & N-2); B_3 & b_2 & B/b (NC); B_3 & b_2 & b_2 & B/b (N).

TABLE 10.5. *Comparison of Tables 10.3 and 10.4*

Area and family structure		2 children	3 children	4 children	5 children	6 children	Total
S (II, III)							
Single sex	no.	86	7	2	—	—	95
	%	56.95	35	50	—	—	54.29
Both sexes	no.	65	13	2	—	—	80
	%	43.05	65	50	—	—	45.71
Total	no.	151	20	4	—	—	175
	%	100	100	100	—	—	100
SC (IV, V)							
Single sex	no.	145	18	2	—	—	165
	%	73.6	51.43	33.33	—	—	67.62
Both sexes	no.	52	17	4	4	2	79
	%	26.4	48.57	66.67	100	100	32.38
Total	no.	197	35	6	4	2	244
	%	100	100	100	100	100	100
NC (VI–VIII)							
Single sex	no.	185	24	5	3	1	218
	%	69.55	51.06	29.41	75	50	64.88

Both sexes no.	81	23	12	1	1	118
%	30.45	48.94	70.59	25	50	35.12
Total no.	266	47	17	4	2	336
%	100	100	100	100	100	100
N (IX, XI)						
Single sex no.	125	14	7	2	—	148
%	72.25	37.84	33.33	33.33	—	61.67
Both sexes no.	48	23	14	4	3	92
%	27.75	62.16	66.67	66.67	100	38.33
Total no.	173	37	21	6	3	240
%	100	100	100	100	100	100
TOTAL						
Single sex no.	541	63	16	5	1	626
%	68.74	45.32	33.33	35.71	14.29	62.91
Both sexes no.	246	76	32	9	6	369
%	31.26	54.68	66.67	64.29	85.71	37.09
Total no.	787	139	48	14	7	995
%	100	100	100	100	100	100

TABLE 10.6. Gender of parents

Area		1 son					1 daughter					1 son/daughter					2+ children						GRAND TOTAL
		C&c	C	c	C/c	Total	C&c	C	c	C/c	Total	C&c	C	c	C/c	Total	C&c	C	c	C/c	—	Total	Total
S (II, III)	no.	177	208	137	6	528	91	67	80	6	244	6	18	16	1	41	64	37	29	—	85	215	1,028
	%	17.22	20.23	13.33	0.58	51.36	8.86	6.52	7.78	0.58	23.74	0.58	1.75	1.56	0.1	3.99	6.23	3.6	2.82	—	8.27	10.91	23.71
SC (IV, V)	no.	207	123	112	10	452	100	52	48	12	212	20	15	17	—	52	110	39	43	2	97	291	1,007
	%	20.56	12.21	11.12	1	44.89	9.93	5.16	4.77	1.2	21.05	1.99	1.49	1.69	—	5.16	10.92	3.89	4.27	0.2	9.63	28.9	23.23
NC (VI-VIII)	no.	227	224	196	15	662	125	74	75	1	275	15	16	19	—	50	145	62	55	3	178	443	1,430
	%	15.87	15.67	13.71	1.05	46.29	8.74	5.17	5.24	0.07	19.23	1.05	1.12	1.33	—	3.5	10.14	4.34	3.85	0.21	12.45	30.98	32.99
N (IX, XI)	no.	122	179	65	3	369	53	113	28	3	197	8	4	5	—	17	124	51	37	5	70	287	870
	%	14.02	20.57	7.47	0.34	42.41	6.09	12.99	3.22	0.34	22.64	0.92	0.46	0.57	—	1.95	14.25	5.86	4.25	0.57	8.05	32.99	20.07
TOTAL	no.	733	734	510	34	2,011	369	306	231	22	928	49	53	57	1	160	443	189	164	10	430	1,236	4,335
	%	16.91	16.93	11.76	0.78	46.39	8.51	7.06	5.33	0.51	21.41	1.13	1.22	1.31	0.02	3.69	10.22	4.36	3.78	0.23	9.92	28.51	100

Note: Some numbers are inflated by those whose parents are known only by filiation (after the mother in VII and after the father in IX and XI).

NC: 1 son (c) (196 − 56 = 140); 1 daughter (c) (75 − 10 = 65)

N: 1 son (C) (179 − 113 = 66); 1 daughter (C) (113 − 91 = 22); 1 son/daughter (C) (4 − 2 = 2)

TABLE 10.7. *Parents of single children*

Area	Parent as dedi-and							Parent as honorand							GRAND TOTAL
	C&c-B	C&c-b	C-B	C-b	c-B	c-b	Total	B-C&c	b-C&c	B-C	b-C	B-c	b-c	Total	
S (II, III)															
no.	93	46	89	42	87	54	411	18	10	50	12	38	22	150	561
%	16.58	8.2	15.86	7.49	15.51	9.63	73.26	3.21	1.78	8.91	2.14	6.77	3.92	26.74	30.98
SC (IV, V)															
no.	105	57	54	27	67	26	336	24	8	36	17	29	18	132	468
%	22.44	12.18	11.54	5.77	14.32	5.56	71.79	5.13	1.71	7.69	3.63	6.2	3.85	28.21	25.84
NC (VI–VIII)															
no.	94	50	78	33	79	38	372	29	9	53	20	49	20	180	552
%	17.03	9.06	14.13	5.98	14.31	6.88	67.39	5.25	1.63	9.6	3.6	8.88	3.6	32.61	30.48
N (IX, XI)															
no.	25	11	26	10	25	12	109	35	10	20	7	37	12	121	230
%	10.87	4.78	11.3	4.35	10.87	5.22	47.39	15.22	4.35	8.7	3.04	16.09	5.22	52.61	12.7
TOTAL															
no.	317	164	247	112	258	130	1,228	106	37	159	56	153	72	583	1,811
%	17.5	9.06	13.64	6.18	14.25	7.18	67.81	5.85	2.04	8.78	3.09	8.45	3.98	32.19	100

TABLE 10.8. *Parents of multiple children (2+)*

Area	Parent as dedicand				Parent as honorand				GRAND TOTAL
	C&c–B/b2(+)	C–B/b2(+)	c–B/b2(+)	Total	B/b2(+)–C&c	B/b2(+)–C	B/b2(+)–c	Total	
S (II, III)									
no.	5	9	11	25	13	22	15	50	75
%	6.67	12	14.67	33.33	17.33	29.33	20	66.67	15.92
SC (IV, V)									
no.	29	6	13	48	22	17	30	69	117
%	24.79	5.13	11.11	41.03	18.8	14.53	25.64	58.97	24.84
NC (VI–VIII)									
no.	26	15	17	58	33	38	26	97	155
%	16.77	9.68	10.97	37.42	21.29	24.52	16.77	62.58	32.91
N (IX, XI)									
no.	7	16	8	31	45	26	22	93	124
%	5.65	12.9	6.45	25	36.29	20.97	17.74	75	26.33
TOTAL									
no.	67	46	49	162	114	103	92	309	471
%	14.22	9.77	10.4	34.39	24.2	21.87	19.53	65.61	100

TABLE 10.9. All grandchildren and great-grandchildren

Area	1 grandson				1 granddaughter					2(+) grandchildren				GRAND TOTAL	Great-grandchildren			
	E&e	E	e	Total	E&e	E	e	E/e	Total	E&e	E	e	Total		EE	EEE	EEEE	EEEEE
S (II, III)																		
no.	6(1)	20	11(1)	37(2)	2	8	4	1	15	6	7	1	14	66	3	2	1	—
%	9.09	30.3	16.67	56.06	3.03	12.12	6.06	1.52	22.73	9.09	10.61	1.52	21.21	20.89	50	33.3	16.67	—
SC (IV, V)																		
no.	9(1)	9(1)	6	24(2)	5	4	5	—	14	5	3	3	11	49	6	—	1	1
%	18.37	18.37	12.24	48.98	10.2	8.16	10.2	—	28.57	10.2	6.12	6.12	22.45	15.51	75	—	12.5	12
NC (VI–VIII)																		
no.	11	10(2)	18	39(2)	2	9	5	—	16	11	9	7	27	82	5	1	—	—
%	13.41	12.2	21.95	47.56	2.44	10.98	6.1	—	19.51	13.41	10.98	8.54	32.93	25.95	83.33	16.67	—	—
N (IX, XI)																		
no.	11	30	11	52	2	10	3	—	15	13	36	3	52	119	7	—	—	—
%	9.24	25.21	9.24	43.7	1.68	8.4	2.52	—	12.61	10.92	30.25	2.52	43.7	37.66	100	—	—	—
TOTAL																		
no.	37(2)	69(3)	46(1)	152(6)	11	31	17	1	60	35	55	14	104	316	21	3	2	1
%	11.71	21.84	14.56	48.1	3.48	9.81	5.38	0.32	18.99	11.08	17.41	4.43	32.91	100	77.78	11.11	7.41	3

Notes: Grandchildren of uncertain sex are counted as grandsons in the totals. They are distinguished by parentheses.
Great-grandparents include 2 couples (SC & NC) and another 2 great-grandmothers (NC & N). Great-great-grandparents include one great-great-grandmother (NC).
Some numbers are inflated by those whose parents are known only by filiation (after the mother in VII and after the father in IX and XI).

NC: 1 grandson (e) (18 – 2 = 16)
N: 1 grandson (E) (30 – 21 = 9); 1 granddaughter (E) (10 – 5 = 5); 2(+) grandchildren (E) (36 – 26 = 10)

TABLE 10.10. *Epitaphs involving only grandparents and grandchildren*

Area	Grandparent(s) dedicand(s)							Grandparent(s) honorand(s)							Grandparents either		GRAND TOTAL
	to grandson				to granddaughter			by grandson				by granddaughter			F	f	
	E&e	E	e	Total	E	e	Total	E&e	E	e	Total	E	e	Total	E&e	E&e	
S (II, III)																	
no.	1	5	1	7	3	1	4	1	2	2	5	—	—	—	1	—	17
%	5.88	29.41	5.88	41.17	17.65	5.88	23.53	5.88	11.76	11.76	29.41	—	—	—	5.88	—	43.59
SC (IV, V)																	
no.	—	1	1	2	1	—	1	—	1	—	1	1	2	3	—	2	9
%	—	11.11	11.11	22.22	11.11	—	11.11	—	11.11	—	11.11	11.11	22.22	33.33	—	22.22	23.08
NC (VI–VIII)																	
no.	1	2	2	5	—	2	2	—	1	—	1	—	1	1	—	—	9
%	11.11	22.22	22.22	55.55	—	22.22	22.22	—	11.11	—	11.11	—	11.11	11.11	—	—	23.08
N (IX, XI)																	
no.	—	2	—	2	—	—	—	1	1	—	2	—	—	—	—	—	4
%	—	50	—	50	—	—	—	25	25	—	50	—	—	—	—	—	10.26
TOTAL																	
no.	2	10	4	16	4	3	7	2	5	2	9	1	3	4	1	2	39
%	5.13	25.64	10.26	41.03	10.26	7.89	17.95	5.13	12.82	5.13	23.08	2.56	7.69	10.26	2.56	5.13	100

Note: Two examples of *nepotes* are included as grandsons:
1. F & f — E (S)
2. F2+ — E (N)

Table 10.11. *Stepchildren*

Area		M&c	C&m	M	m	M/m	—	TOTAL
S (II, III)								
N	no.	1	4	3	—	—	—	8
	%	12.5	50	37.5	—	—	—	12.31
n	no.	3	1	3	—	1	—	8
	%	37.5	12.5	37.5	—	12.5	—	12.31
N/n	no.	—	—	—	1	—	2	3
	%	—	—	—	33.33	—	66.67	4.62
Total	no.	4	5	6	1	1	2	19
	%	21.05	26.32	31.58	5.26	5.26	10.53	29.23
SC (IV, V)								
N	no.	8	—	1	—	—	—	9
	%	88.89	—	11.11	—	—	—	13.85
n	no.	1	1	1	—	—	—	3
	%	33.33	33.33	33.33	—	—	—	4.62
Total	no.	9	1	2	—	—	—	12
	%	75	8.33	16.67	—	—	—	18.46
NC (VI–VIII)								
N	no.	7	1	1	—	—	1	10
	%	70	10	10	—	—	10	15.39
N/n	no.	1	—	—	—	—	3	4
	%	25	—	—	—	—	75	6.15
Total	no.	8	1	1	—	—	4	14
	%	57.14	7.14	7.14	—	—	28.57	21.54
N (IX, XI)								
N	no.	7	4	1	1	—	—	13
	%	53.85	30.77	7.69	7.69	—	—	20
n	no.	4	3	—	—	—	—	7
	%	57.14	42.86	—	—	—	—	10.77
Total	no.	11	7	1	1	—	—	20
	%	55	35	5	5	—	—	30.77
TOTAL								
N	no.	23	9	6	1	—	1	40
	%	57.5	22.5	15	2.5	—	2.5	61.54
n	no.	8	5	4	—	1	—	18
	%	44.44	27.78	22.22	—	5.56	—	27.69
N/n	no.	1	—	—	1	—	5	7
	%	1.54	—	—	1.54	—	7.69	10.77
Total	no.	32	14	10	2	1	6	65
	%	49.23	21.54	15.38	3.77	1.54	9.23	100

TABLE 10.12. Alumni

Area Alumnus/a		P&p	P	p	P/p	TOTAL
S (II, III)						
S	no.	3	13	3	—	19
	%	15.79	68.42	15.79	—	24.05
s	no.	2	3	1	1	7
	%	28.57	42.86	14.29	14.29	8.86
S/s	no.	—	—	—	1	1
	%	—	—	—	100	1.27
Total	no.	5	16	4	2	27
	%	18.52	59.26	14.81	7.41	34.18
SC (IV, V)						
S	no.	—	3	1	—	4
	%	—	75	25	—	5.06
s	no.	1	3	1	—	5
	%	20	60	20	—	6.33
S&s	no.	—	—	1	—	1
	%	—	—	100	—	1.27
Total	no.	1	6	3	—	10
	%	10	60	30	—	12.66
NC (VI–VIII)						
S	no.	8	12	4	—	24
	%	33.33	50	16.67	—	30.38
s	no.	3	5	1	—	9
	%	33.33	55.56	11.11	—	11.39
S/s	no.	—	—	—	1	1
	%	—	—	—	100	1.27
S&s	no.	—	—	1	—	1
	%	—	—	100	—	1.27
Total	no.	11	17	6	1	35
	%	31.43	48.57	17.14	2.86	44.3
N (IX, XI)						
S	no.	—	3	1	—	4
	%	—	75	25	—	5.06
s	no.	—	3	—	—	3
	%	—	100	—	—	3.8
Total	no.	—	6	1	—	7
	%	—	85.71	14.29	—	8.86
TOTAL						
S	no.	11	31	9	—	51
	%	21.57	60.78	17.65	—	64.56
s	no.	6	14	3	1	24
	%	25	58.33	12.5	4.17	30.38
S/s, S&s	no.	—	—	2	2	4
	%	—	—	2.53	2.53	5.06
Total	no.	17	45	14	3	79
	%	21.52	56.96	17.72	3.8	100

Notes: The following multiple *alumni/alumnae* are included in the total: S2—IV (P), IX (P); s2—IV (p); S2+—VI (P&p); S&s—VIII (p): S3&s—IV(p). Four uncertain *alumni* are excluded: NC—3; N—1. Note the concentration of *alumni* in 4 towns: S (Brundisium—8), Beneventum—7); NC (Ravenna—5, Ariminum—3).

TABLE 10.13. *Siblings*

Area		D-D	D-d	D-D/d	D-D/d(2+)	d-d	d-D	d-D/d(2+)	D/d-D	D/d-d	D/d-D/d2(+)	D/d2(+)-D	D/d2(+)-d	D/d2(+)-D/d2(+)	Other	TOTAL
S (II, III)	no.	32	14	—	3	3	10	—	6	—	2	2	1	—	12	85
	%	37.65	16.47	—	3.53	3.53	11.76	—	7.06	—	2.35	2.35	1.18	—	14.12	19.77
SC (IV, V)	no.	37	7	6	2	7	7	4	3	2	—	3	2	2	15	97
	%	38.14	7.22	6.19	2.06	7.22	7.22	4.12	3.09	2.06	—	3.09	2.06	2.06	15.46	22.56
NC (VI–VIII)	no.	54	17	1	4	12	10	—	4	2	1	16	4	—	53	178
	%	30.34	9.56	0.56	2.25	6.74	5.62	—	2.25	1.12	0.56	8.99	2.25	—	29.78	41.4
N (IX, XI)	no.	28	7	—	6	1	3	1	3	—	2	1	3	—	15	70
	%	40	10	—	8.57	1.43	4.29	1.43	4.29	—	2.86	1.43	4.29	—	21.43	16.3
TOTAL	no.	151	45	7	15	23	30	5	16	4	5	22	10	2	95	430
	%	35.12	10.47	1.63	3.49	5.35	6.98	1.16	3.72	0.93	1.16	5.12	2.33	0.47	22.09	100

Appendix 2. Hidden Children

PETER WILKINS

For a small number of families, the existence of more than one memorial allows us to observe the exclusion of children as dedicands with their parents to a brother or sister. Alternatively, as in the first four examples which follow, children are mentioned as existing in the text of an epitaph but do not act as dedicands.

1. *CIL* 11. 4311: Interamna Nahars (VI)

> D(is) M(anibus). | L(ucio) Valerio | Magno | L(ucius) Valerius | Euaristus et | Mu[rri]a Amplilata [fili]o piissimo. | Tu quicumq(ue) legi[s ti]tulum | (nostrum) nomenq(ue) requiris, | aspice quo fata raptus mih[i] | spiritus or[e] est: | nonus ab incepto currebat | (mihi) tem[po]ris annus, | dum subito incautus fratri | succurrere tendo, | me rota sublapsum pressit | [– | –]us mihi | [uita?] sub au[ras].

In the first example a son is mentioned only in the context of a tragic accident which befell his 9-year-old brother. He himself does not appear as dedicand, although the text is admittedly lacunose.

2. *AE* 1976, 188 = 1978, 282: Histonium (IV)

> D(is) [M(anibus)] s(acrum). | Splatt[iae Co]rnelianae, | quae [uix(it) a]nn(is) XX m(ensibus) | II d(iebus) XI, matre atque | fratribus quod a[mauit] | ut ante lege debuit | quam filia. Mindia | Tyche mater fil(iae) dulc(issimae) | et pientissimae et sibi f(ecit).

The brothers of Splattia Corneliana, despite her attested affection for them, do not set up the memorial to her. Her mother, Mindia Tyche, sets up the memorial to her daughter and to herself, but not to her sons. Had the sons died previously or were they married (and commemoration left to their wives and/or children)?

3. *AE* 1985, 355: Ricina (V)

> D(is) M(anibus) | Herennia L(ucii) f(ilia) Ceruilla | uxor uixi annis XVIII et | diem tricesimum. | Liberis tribus relictis, | uita(m) finiui dolens. | Co(n)iux karus ut memoriae | posuit hoc uiuos mihi, | ut prodesset in suppre|mis talem titulum | consequi. C(aius) Carrenas | Verecundus coniugi | incomparabili b(ene) m(erenti).

Although Herennia Cervilla is described as being survived by three children, they do not act as co-dedicands in the memorial set up to her by their father C. Carrenas Verecundus. Her age at death (18) suggests that this may have been because the children were so young.

4. *CIL* 11. 4364: Ameria (VI)

> D(is) M(anibus) | Iuliae Doridi | Sex(tus) Restianus Sex(ti) f(ilius) | Clu(stumina) Iustus ueteɪ(anus) Aug(usti) | et decurio coniugi | carissimae cum | qua uixsit an(nis) XVI | dulcissim(a)e annu(m) | autem XXX agens | decessit reliclltis liberis sulperstitibus IIII. | C(oniugi) b(ene) m(erenti) f(ecit).

The memorial to Iulia Doris by her husband Sex. Restianus Iustus is very similar to example (3), except that she is survived by four children and not three. Once again the young age of the children may account for their absence as dedicands (Iulia Doris died at 30 and was married for only 16 years, i.e. the eldest would have been 15 at most).

5*a*. *CIL* 11. 5772: Sentinum (VI)

> D(is) M(anibus) | Aur(eliae) Florenlti(a)e fil(iae), Aur(elius) Fllorinus palter u(eteranus) c(ohortis) [I pr(a)eto(riae) | bene] merite polsuit. Vix(it) a(nnis) XXVII.

5*b*. *AE* 1981, 322: Sentinum (VI)

> D(is) M(anibus) | C(aio) Aurelio Florino | u[e]t(erano) Aug(usti), Aurelia | Velrina co(n)iugi, cum qulo uixit an(nis) L, Aurelius | Herculanus patri pio belne merenti hered(es) posu(e)r(unt).

In the first dedication—to Aurelia Florentia by her father Aurelius Florinus —Florinus' wife and son do not act as co-dedicands. That they were alive at the time of this dedication is made clear by the second dedication in which they erect a memorial to Florinus himself. His wife, Aurelia Verina, describes herself as having been married to him for 50 years. The age at death of the daughter Aurelia Florentia (27 years) makes it certain that the son Aurelius Herculanus was alive when her memorial was set up.

6*a*. *CIL* 11. 5780: Sentinum (VI)

> D(is) M(anibus) | Quintae | C(aius) Graecinius | Verinus pater | et C(aius) Graecinius | Primitiuos | contub(ernali) optum(a)e. | Vix(it) ann(is) XXIII | mens(ibus) V d(iebus) XII.

6*b*. *CIL* 11. 5779: Sentinum (VI)

> D(is) M(anibus) | Graeciniae | Tyche C(aius) Graecinius | Ver(i)nus con(iugi) quicu(m) | uix(it) an(nis) LIII. | Graecinius Seuelrus et Primitius | m(atri) b(ene) m(erenti).

These dedications—also from Sentinum—are similar to those in example 5. The first memorial to Quinta was erected by her father C. Graecinius Verinus and her husband C. Graecinius Primitiuos. The second memorial is to Graecina Tyche the wife of C. Graecinius Verinus who is said to have been married to him for 53 years. Verinus erected the memorial together with his two sons Graecinius Severus and Primitius. Graecinia Tyche was either a freedwoman of her husband's or was manumitted by the same patron as manumitted her husband and son-in-law. This is suggested (*a*) by her name, which combines a Latin *nomen* with a Greek cognomen and (*b*) by the fact that two of her children have single names (Quinta and Primitius) and were presumably slaves born prior to her manumission, while a third (Graecinius Seuerus) appears to have been born afterwards. Although younger, Seuerus' name precedes his brother Primitius' by virtue of his status (see Flory 1984: 216–24; cf. also Rawson 1986: 184–5, on the order of names of *alumni*). The dedication to Quinta probably pre-dates that to her mother, i.e. neither her mother nor her two brothers acted as joint dedicands although alive at the time.

7*a. AE* 1975, 317: Marsi Marruvium (IV)

> D(is M(anibus) s(acrum). (Publio) Ostori|o Vitali|oni, seuir(o) | Aug(ustali) qui | uicxit (sic) ann(is) XXIII, | Ostoria | Vitalis | filio dul|cissimo | p(osuit).

7*b. AE* 1975, 318: Marsi Marruvium (IV)

> D(is) M(anibus) s(acrum). | Ostoria | Vitalis, | uix(it) an(nis) L | sene macula, | Claudius | Campanus | co(n)iugi san(c)tis|sim(a)e | et Felis (sic) matri b(ene) m(erenti) p(osuerunt).

In examples 5 and 6 it was seen that a mother (as well as her son or sons) could be absent from a dedication to her daughter. In example 7*a*, con-versely, the father Claudius Campanus does not participate with his wife Ostoria Vitalis in the dedication to their son P. Ostorius Vitalio. That he was alive at the time is certain by the marriage span of 50 years which is cited on the epitaph he erected to his wife, together with their son Felix. The age of P. Ostorius Vitalio at his death (23 years) suggests that Felix was also alive at the time of the first dedication. This would certainly be so if, as seems probable by Felix' single name, he was born prior to his mother's manumission and his brother, P. Ostorius Vitalio, after it.

8*a. CIL* 9. 1640: Beneventum (II)

> Verzobio | C(aio) Caelio | C(ai) f(ilio) St(ellatina) Bassaeo | Donato, | pr(aetori) Cer(eris) i(ure) d(icundo), q(uin)q(uennali), | adlect(o) in ord(inem) | dec(urionum), eq(uo) R(omano), | C(aius) Caelius Dona|tus et Bassaea Ianuaria parent(es). | L(oco) d(ato) d(ecreto) d(ecurionum).

8*b. CIL* 9. 1641: Beneventum (II)

> Nauigi | C(aio) Caelio | C(ai) f(ilio) St(ellatina) Bassaeo | Procillio Faus|tino, pr(aetori) Cer(eris) i(ure) d(icundo), q(uin)q(uennali), | adlect(o) in ord(inem) dec(urionum), | eq(uo) Rom(ano), | C(aius) Caelius Dona|tus et Bassaea Ianuaria parent(es). | L(oco) d(ato) d(ecreto) d(ecurionum).

In both the examples above, the parents C. Caelius Donatus and Bassaea Ianuaria set up inscriptions of identical format to sons with identical careers. Their municipal careers and the official consent granted for the memor-ials makes it highly probable that statues to the two youths were erected together in a public place. (The text of *CIL* 9. 1641 is described as being inscribed upon a 'basis ingens'.) It is uncertain whether the inscriptions served as epitaphs and if so whether the two brothers died at a similar age.

9a. CIL 9. 3113: Sulmo (IV)

> D(is) M(anibus) s(acrum). | Matino | M(arcus) Arruntius | Is(s)us et | Arruntia | Asia | parentes | filio optimo | et pientissimo | p(osuerunt).

9b. AE 1986, 204: Canusium (II)

> D(is) M(anibus) | M(arco) Arrun|tio Asiati|co u(ixit) an(nis) XXII, | M(arcus) Arruntius Issus et Arrun|tia Asia paren|tes filio b(ene) m(erenti) | f(ecerunt).

As with example 8, the two texts above concern separate dedications by parents to two sons. There are, however, distinct differences between the two cases. In example 9 the inscriptions are clearly identified as epitaphs, the format and even the provenance of the texts is different, and the status of the children differs. M. Arruntius Issus and his wife Arruntia Asia are clearly *colliberti* (note the Asiatic place-names as *cognomina*) and their first son Matinus a slave. Their other son M. Arruntius Asiaticus was born after his mother's manumission and the detail of his age perhaps indicates pride in his higher status.

10a. CIL 9. 5920: Ancona (V)

> D(is) M(anibus) | M(arco) Gratio Co|ronario, qui | in mare ui tem|pestatis deces(sit), | Scaefia Calliope, | coniugi optimo | et Scaefiae Ter|tullae filiae d|ulcissimae, qu(a)e | uixit annum d(iebus) XIII, | b(ene) m(erenti).

10b. CIL 9. 5929: Ancona (V)

> [–] VIII d(iebus) XV, | Scaepia (sic) | Calliope | mater | b(ene) m(erenti).

10c. CIL 9. 5929: Ancona (V)

> D(is) M(anibus) | Sc(a)efi(a)e | Restut(a)e | Sc(a)efia | Calliope | soror | b(ene) m(erenti).

In the first inscription Scaefia Calliope dedicates an epitaph to her husband M. Gratius Coronarius who had drowned at sea during a storm and to her 1-year-old daughter. In the two following epitaphs Scaefia Calliope dedicates to another child (absent from the first text) and to her sister.

11a. CIL 9. 5373: Cupra Maritima (V)

> Publicio | Optato VIII uir(o) | Quintilia Procilla | uxor | bene merenti | uiro | l(ibens) m(erito) p(osuit) | ossa.

11b. CIL 9. 5303: Cupra Maritima (V)

> [–| L.] Publicio L. f. Ve[l(ina)] | Consultino | equo publico, iudi|ci selecto decuri(i)s | quinque Procilla | mater.

11c. CIL 9. 5304: Cupra Maritima (V)

> Publiciae L. f. | Bassillae filiae | Procilla mater.

The chronological order of these inscriptions, as with example 10, is based on the assumption that the father did not act as co-dedicand with his wife to his children (10*b*, 11*b*, 11*c*) because he predeceased them (10*a*, 11*a*). Although this is the most probable chain of events, example 7 shows that this need not have been so. In all three texts Quintilia Procilla (who curiously calls herself simply Procilla on the two dedications to her children) is the dedicand. Those commemorated are her husband (L.) Publicius Optatus, her son L. Publicius Consultinus and her daughter Publicia Bassilla. If the chronological sequence is correct and her children were alive at the time of their father's death, neither participated in commemorating him. For that matter, the child who died first was not commemorated by the other, although there exists some doubt—as in example 8—whether the memorials to the children are epitaphs or statues erected in their honour.

12*a*. *CIL* 11. 6575: Sassina (VI)

> D(is) M(anibus) | C(ai) Sabini Valeriani uixit | ann(is) XVII m(ensibus)
> VII diebus XVI | Sabinia Iustina mater et Sabi|nius Victorinus auonculus.

12*b*. *CIL* 11. 6576: Sassina (VI)

> [–]ctus [matri? | dul]cissim(a)e et | [Sa]binius Vic|[tori]nus sorori |
> [sa]nctissim(a)e.

Some doubt occurs in this and the following three examples as to the identity of persons involved in the text. In the first text above, Sabinia Iustina (together with her brother Sabinius Victorinus) commemorates her son C. Sabinius Valerianus. In the second text Sabinia Iustina (or another sister?) is herself commemorated either by another son—who did not commemorate his brother in the first text—or by a husband, together with Sabinius Victorinus. The reading *matri* is suggested by *CIL* and considered a more probable reading than *uxori* by Hanne Sigismund Nielsen, for whose comments I am grateful. On the epithet *dulcissimus/a*, see Ch. 8 above.

13*a*. *CIL* 10. 424: Valva (III)

> Allidiae C(ai) f(iliae) St[atu]|tae matri [–].

13*b*. *CIL* 10. 446: Valva (III)

> Allidiae | C(ai) f(iliae) | Statutae et | C(aio) Spedio Atimeto | Augustal(i)
> | C(aius) Spedius Asiaticus | optimis parentib(us).

The death of Allidia Statuta is commemorated twice by her children. The second commemoration occurred at the time of her husband's death, the dedicand being their son C. Spedius Asiaticus. It is unclear whether the dedicand of the first text was the same son or whether other children who died in the interim between the two texts were co-dedicands. Presumably her husband erected a separate (or adjoining) epitaph on the same occasion.

14*a*. *CIL* 9. 5471: Falerio (V)

> D(is) M(anibus) | Caeciliae Erotices | uixit annis XI dieb(us) XXX |
> Caecili(i) Eroticus et | Romana parentes.

14*b*. *CIL* 9. 5470: Falerio (V)

> [D(is) M(anibus)] Q. Caecili Ero[tici] | uixit an(nis) XXXXII [–] |
> Caecilius Chres[t]u[s] | liberto incomparalbili et Caecilia Romalna,
> cum qua uix(it) ann(is) XXV m(ensibus) VII sine querella, | hic
> post mortem filiae su[ae] septimo mense decessit.

In the first epitaph Caecilia Erotice is commemorated by her parents Caecilius Eroticus and Caecilia Romana. In the second epitaph it is the father
Caecilius Eroticus who is commemorated—by his patron and his wife—
and it is stated that he died seven months after his daughter. Although it
is highly probable that the daughter is identical to Caecilia Erotice, we
cannot be certain. If this identification is correct, Caecilia Erotice was probably born after the manumission of both parents, as her father was above
the legal minimum age required for manumission of 30 (i.e. his age at
death of 42–44 less his daughter's age at death of 11).

15*a*. *CIL* 11. 6738: Ravenna (VIII)

> [–]n exi[– | –]en Aegr? [– | F]undaniu[s | Te]rentianu[s | et] Val(eria)
> Cal(l)iste | [fili]o dulciss[imo –].

15*b*. *CIL* 11. 6755: Ravenna (VIII)

> [–an]n(is) XXIII mens(ibus) V [– | – Ca]lliste mater et sibi et c[– | post
> co]nditos q(ui) s(upra) s(cripti) s(unt) si q(uis) aperier(it) ha[nc arcam
> ?, | poen]ae nom[i]n(e) in(feret?) fisco Caes(aris) [–].

If Val(eria) Cal(l)iste of the first text is the same as the [– Ca]lliste of the
second—a possibility mooted by *CIL*—the child commemorated in each
text cannot be the same. The son in the first text is commemorated by
Valeria Calliste and her husband, the child in the second (whose sex is
unknown) by Calliste alone and the memorial is to herself (*sibi*) as well.
The husband, in other words, has presumably died or divorced Calliste in
the interim between the two texts. The second child whose age at death
(23) suggests that he was alive when the memorial to his brother was
erected did not commemorate him with his parents.

16*a*. *CIL* 11. 6350: Pisaurum (VI)

> D(is) M(anibus) | Sueto Marcellin(us) | militauit | an(nos) VI m(enses)
> VIII, | tes(serarius) an(nos) II m(enses) XI, | eq(ues) an(nos) II m(enses)
> VIIII d(ies) X. | Posuerunt fratres, | curant(e) Salena | Paulina mat(re),
> | Sueto Crispin(us) et | Sueto Paulin(us) eu(ocatus) Au[g(usti)], | Sueto
> Augyrin(us) m(iles) c(ohortis) IIII pr(aetoriae), Sueto Iustus.

16*b*. *CIL* 11. 6281: Fanum Fortunae (VI)

> D(is) M(anibus) | Sal[e]n(a)e Paulin[(a)e] | posuit Sueto Iusltus matri
> piissim(ae) | uniuir[(ae)] astros[(a)e] | quei fato [e]x filis quinlque superaui
> uixit anlnis LXXVIII dies LVI.

The final example is particularly interesting. In this case the children are not
'hidden', as all five sons in the family are mentioned in both texts (although

four are unnamed in the second). The example is included because it is one of the rare instances where we can be reasonably certain that all the children who survived infancy are recorded. In the first text the soldier Sueto Marcellus is commemorated by his mother and four brothers, two of whom were also soldiers. In the second text, one of the brothers, Sueto Iustus, describes himself in a memorial to his 78-year-old mother as the only child of five whom fate allowed to survive. The interval between the two epitaphs—during which the three other brothers died—is about 20–35 years (i.e. his mother's 78 years less about 26 years for Marcellinus—assuming that he began his six years of military service at about 20—which would place Marcellinus' birth at a time when his mother was between 17 and 32).

II

Perceptions of Domestic Space in Roman Italy

LISA NEVETT

The wealth of the material evidence uncovered at Pompeii, Herculaneum, and Ostia offers an almost unparalleled opportunity to explore
the domestic life of a past society through archaeological evidence.
Indeed, Pompeii has sometimes been held up by archaeologists working on other societies as the site that exemplifies their ideals in terms
of the manner of its destruction and the exceptional standard of
preservation (the 'Pompeii premise', cf. Allison 1992a: *passim*). Yet
despite all the advantages offered by this material, in many ways it
has yet to be exploited to its full potential, and, in particular, our
knowledge of patterns of activity within individual dwellings remains surprisingly poor, even for the *atrium* house, which has been
the subject of the most extensive research. In this chapter it is argued
that, in conjunction with study of the archaeological evidence, an
alternative approach to the use of literary sources for activity in the
Roman household in general, and in urban houses in particular, can
help us to construct a clearer and more detailed picture of Roman
attitudes to spatial organization and of some of the factors that helped
to shape domestic space in different types of dwelling.

INTRODUCTION: APPROACHES TO THE ROMAN HOUSE

Out of the huge volume of past research that has been carried out
into the houses of Pompeii, Herculaneum, and Ostia, the majority

I wish to thank Professor Beryl Rawson very much for inviting me to contribute this paper
and for making it possible for me to attend the conference. I also wish to thank Todd
Whitelaw for his help and support, together with everyone else who has discussed with me
both Roman and Greek houses and the topic of domestic space more generally, both at the
conference and elsewhere; their suggestions have helped to shape my own perceptions of
Roman houses, although I naturally take responsibility for any weaknesses in my argument.
Finally, I should like to acknowledge the financial support of the British Academy which
funded the research and writing of this paper as part of a Post-doctoral Fellowship, and of
the Australian National University which granted me a Visiting Fellowship enabling me to
attend the conference.

of work has centred on the nature of the house as a physical entity, and the questions that have been asked have often tended to derive from the manner in which space itself was constituted, rather than from an interest in the implications that particular patterns of organization may have had for spatial, and ultimately for social, behaviour.[1] Attention paid to the interior of the houses has usually concentrated on the nature of architectural, painted, and mosaic decoration.

This work provides a solid base of evidence from which to explore the Roman house, but it exploits only a part of the total potential of the archaeological remains. In particular, the types and distributions of artefacts within the domestic context have generally not been of interest (Dwyer 1982: 15; Allison 1993: 3), so that conclusions about the activities that were carried out in different rooms have been largely dependent on architectural information.

Houses in general can be an invaluable source of information not only about architecture and decoration, but also about a range of aspects of the society within which they are created and inhabited. This is demonstrated by studies of domestic organization, which have taken place in a variety of contexts, and have looked at spatial behaviour in societies ranging from prehistory to the present day.[2] In general terms these studies have emphasized the fact that the form and use of domestic space is influenced not only by the environmental and the economic context in which a particular household is located, but also by the patterns of social interaction taking place within the house: the organization of household space is shaped by the necessity to provide an atmosphere and setting that will facilitate particular patterns of behaviour, and at the same time the spatial structuring of the household in turn acts as an influence on the organization of the activity taking place within. In short, a dialectical relationship exists between social and spatial behaviour, and this offers the possibility of exploring some aspects of social relations using the physical evidence of the domestic context. With respect to archaeological material, this means that, by looking at the way in which space was used in the house, it should be possible to explore at least some aspects of the relationships that took place within that setting.

---

[1] So, for instance, evolutionary typologies of excavated house-plans have been constructed (e.g. Carrington 1933; Graham 1966; Wistrand 1970; De Albentiis 1990), sometimes invoking concepts such as the 'rise' and 'decline' of domestic architecture and decoration (e.g. Van Aken 1949: 242). Similar developmental trajectories have been formulated to explain the rise of the apartment and the differences between accommodation provided at Pompeii and that found at Ostia (e.g. Harsh 1935).

[2] A summary of recent work is given in Lawrence and Low (1990); examples of archaeological applications of this kind of work are included in Kent (ed.) (1990).

A second important factor emphasized by ethnographic studies of the use of social space is that very diverse patterns of spatial behaviour are found in different societies, and these also tend to be radically different from our own. This means that in order to study effectively spatial behaviour in other societies, we need to try to lay aside our own preconceptions about the principles that are used when dividing up living space, about which different activities may be performed in the same space, about the manner in which public and private spaces are constituted, about which individuals may or may not enter particular spaces, and so on.

In the context of Roman Italy the potential of the house as a source of information about social life has begun to be explored, particularly the relationship between public and private spheres within the house (e.g. Coarelli 1983). One of the most notable proponents of this kind of approach, Wallace-Hadrill (1988; 1990; 1991*a*; 1991*b*; 1994), has stressed his concern 'to understand the social patterns which dictated the structure and decoration of the Roman house' (Wallace-Hadrill 1988: 96). Such work has contributed to our understanding of the role of social relationships, and in particular patronage, in the organization of the *atrium* house. Nevertheless, other influences over spatial organization remain unclear, and there are few other recent studies that have recognized the importance of the house as a source of information about domestic organization and social relations in its own right.

Even where efforts have been made to reconstruct spatial and social behaviour, the conclusions drawn have often failed to take full account of the possible differences between Roman spatial behaviour and our own, and interpretations have been strongly influenced by modern, Western preconceptions. This is a difficulty which has been acknowledged in the context of various different areas of Pompeian studies (cf. Andreau 1973: 231; Wallace-Hadrill 1991*a*: 250–64), including the study of houses (J. R. Clarke 1991: p. xxiv). Nevertheless, it has proved difficult to set aside assumptions that are deeply ingrained within the tradition of previous scholarship. Unfortunately, if we fail to be aware of our preconceived ideas and the manner in which they can influence our interpretation of behaviour in the past, then we will fall into the trap of trying to visualize Roman behaviour merely through our own eyes, and of creating a Roman house populated with twentieth-century Western occupants and which will tell us little about the ancient Roman view. Thus, we should be aware of the problems involved in using words such as *cubiculum* as bedroom and *culina* as kitchen, since this kind of translation encourages us to ignore the possibility that there may have been fundamental differences between the way in which such spaces are used in modern Western houses, and the way in which they would have functioned in the past. Instead, we need to try to build up an understanding of the kind of significance these spaces held in Roman culture, in both symbolic and behavioural terms.

In short, then, the requirements of an awareness of the potential of the archaeological evidence and a willingness to set aside ethnocentric assumptions, which the ethnographic and sociological work suggests must be fulfilled for a maximum understanding of the domestic context to be developed, are often not operating in the analysis of the houses of Roman Italy.[3] This means that despite the volume of previous research our comprehension of the roles of some of the spaces is often vague and contradictory, and this in turn affects our interpretation of behaviour within the house as a whole.

The effects of these problems can be illustrated with reference to a recent study, Richardson's treatment of the architecture of Pompeii (Richardson 1988), in which private houses are given considerable attention. Alongside the customary terminology that is used to describe the different parts of the house, assumptions are also made about the activities carried out in particular spaces in some of the houses discussed. The basis for attributing functions to particular rooms is not made explicit.

A specific example is Richardson's description of one of the rooms in the Casa delle Nozze d'Argento: 'The pavement has a patterned sill panel, and a place for a couch is marked off from the rest against the back wall . . . Too richly decorated and too open to be the bedchamber it first appears to be, the room must have been a dining room for ladies' (Richardson 1988: 156–7). This passage exemplifies both the major problems discussed above. The reason for Richardson's first suggestion, that the room may have been a bedroom, is not stated, although it is presumably related to the presence of an area that appears to be designed to take a bed. In ruling out this interpretation, he cites as his reason the fact that a bedroom would not be highly decorated, and would be more enclosed, although no support for this assumption is offered. To the modern reader the use of the word 'bedchamber' immediately implies a room for sleeping. Presumably Richardson is relying on his own expectations, first, of what a room with a bed is for (in modern Western society it is generally for sleeping in) and, second, of what

---

[3] Studies of other areas of the Roman world have, however, tried to overcome this difficulty: see e.g. Smith's and Clarke's analyses of the organization of Romano-British villas (J. T. Smith 1987; S. Clarke 1990), or Thébert's work on Roman North Africa (Thébert 1987).

other characteristics it might be expected to have (privacy, and simplicity because it would not be expected to play any role in public display). In concluding, finally, that the room was for women to eat in, there is again no concrete evidence offered, but presumably Richardson is relying on the fact that similar rooms in this context are usually identified as dining-rooms, and he brings in separate dining facilities for women to explain the fact that there was more than one, something that again would not necessarily be expected in the context of an average twentieth-century Western private house. In short, the identification of the purpose of this room rests upon a variety of preconceptions derived, first, from the author's own cultural context, and, second, from previous scholarship, which itself is frequently reliant on ethnocentric assumptions.

Such problems illustrate the need to adopt an approach to the interpretation of the archaeology that is less influenced by the weight of previous scholarship, which, although useful, can be instrumental in discouraging us from being more critical of some of our interpretations. We must also try to put aside some of our own assumptions about behaviour and aesthetics that may be shaping our own interpretations; where possible we must replace them with something the Romans may have recognized.

One aid to achieving at least a partial view of domestic space from a Roman perspective is through the surviving textual evidence. Although individual authors are sometimes quoted in connection with domestic organization, a more systematic review will provide a broader picture, and the examination of a large sample of different sources will be less affected by the problems that are involved with making use of individual texts.

LITERARY EVIDENCE FOR ROMAN PERCEPTIONS OF HOUSEHOLD SPACE

In the past, literary evidence has frequently tended to be dominant in reconstructing the Roman household. Although I have argued above for more awareness of the importance of archaeological material as a source of information about Roman domestic life, it would be foolish to ignore the literary evidence, which can provide a rich background for our interpretation of the archaeology, and give us insights into how the Romans themselves may have viewed their domestic environment. The existence of such sources gives students of Roman Italy an immense advantage, both over those studying areas of the empire that do not have such a rich literary record and over prehistorians, for whom such material is totally lacking. Para-doxically, however, the very wealth of this material has led to an unsystematic approach, in which it has tended to be used anecdotally to support individual points, rather than to sketch a broader picture of Roman attitudes to domestic space.[4] The aim of the remainder of this chapter is to create such a sketch. First, however, it is necessary to consider some of the characteristics of the literature, and how these may affect its interpretation.

Long descriptions of the organization of houses are somewhat limited in number and are of variable utility: the instructions of Vitruvius are often quoted, suggesting modes of interior decoration (Bk. 7) and how different types of *atrium* are designed (Bk. 6). Some of the spaces of the house, and the manner in which they are organ-ized, are also mentioned by Quintilian, who suggests that the pattern of spatial organization could be used as a mnemonic for memorizing speeches (Quintilian 11. 2. 20–4). Varro gives details of the objects that he says used to be found in the *atrium* and other rooms, within his memory, although they had disappeared by the time he was writ-ing (*De lingua Latina*, Bk. 5). The agricultural texts of Cato, Varro, and Columella also include descriptions of working farms, and the kinds of considerations that influence their layout. In addition to these generalized sets of instructions on how domestic space should be organized, there are also several descriptions of specific houses in the letters of Pliny (1. 3; 2. 17; 5. 6) and Cicero (*Q. fr.* 3. 1), which give details of the layout and of the features that were favoured. The fictional house of Trimalchio can perhaps also come into this category (Petronius, *Satyricon*), although it presents more difficult problems for interpretation. Finally, Justinian's *Digest* covers laws that describe specific situations, including a detailed inventory of the inhabitants and contents of a farmhouse (*D.* 33. 7–10).

These various forms of literary evidence carry with them their own problems as sources of information about the interiors of Ro-man houses (Bek 1980: 164). An obvious prime consideration is that they represent a variety of different genres, which are each associ-ated with their own styles and conventions. No individual work can be seen as a straight 'reflection' of society; rather each is a creation both of literary practice and of the perceptions of a given individual, the author. At the same time, however, these works must all represent

---

[4] An exception is the work of Bek (1980; 1983), but this has focused on the aesthetic rather than the social and practical aspects of Roman domestic architecture. A successful analysis of the literary sources is Hermansen's treatment of the evidence for apartment living (1981: 17–49).

interpretations of a single society, within which all the authors were operating. For the purposes of the present discussion it is the underlying patterns rather than the accuracy of individual observations which are important, since those patterns offer clues to general perceptions of domestic space.

It is to be hoped that by constructing a composite picture, rather than relying on only one or two sources, any difficulties pertaining to an individual author or passage will become insignificant; nevertheless, an important distinction should be noted. Those texts that describe the organization of specific individual structures are obviously limited in their application: clearly they are insufficient in number to provide a sample from which to generalize, and many of the features to which they refer, such as the relationship of the different rooms to each other, or the leisure facilities that are provided, are likely to have varied from house to house. In contrast, the more generalized sources such as Vitruvius and the agricultural authors can be expected to be more broadly relevant since they are offering general guidelines about the organization of houses. It should be noted, however, that such guidelines were not necessarily followed, and there are some excavated houses where even Vitruvius' basic guidelines have not been observed (J. R. Clarke 1992: 14). Bearing this in mind, it is important to recognize which questions will be most fruitfully asked of these texts: details such as the relationship of different rooms to each other are likely to have varied considerably from house to house, as the archaeological material from Campania has shown. A composite picture, produced by combining different elements of these various texts, should offer an impression, not of the appearance of any individual house or of the use of any one space, but of the ways in which concepts such as privacy operated in Roman houses, of the kinds of priorities involved in the organization of domestic space in different types of dwelling, and of the way in which various activities were organized in relation to each other.

The likely scope of the resulting picture should also be noted: from what is known of the biographies of the various authors, they generally seem to be from wealthier backgrounds, and in this sense they represent only a limited sector of the population. When comparing the expectations expressed by these individuals with the archaeological material, there has not always been agreement as to what clientele any one structure was meant to cater for (Wallace-Hadrill 1991a), and this is especially a difficulty with interpreting the remains of apartment blocks. Further biases also exist since the texts represent only adult male views, and the perceptions and concerns of female family members, of minors, and also of household servants or slaves, are all excluded. There are, then, many aspects of Roman domestic life, and many viewpoints on the subject, to which the literary sources will never offer access, and for the most part the models derived from them will necessarily be incomplete. Nevertheless, however biased and limited the literary sources are, they do at least provide a glimpse into the way in which domestic space may have been perceived by some of the population, some of the time.

An examination of large amounts of textual material, mainly covering the first century BC to first century AD, but also including earlier and later works and taking into account passing references to households as well as detailed descriptions, will allow a more detailed and complex picture to be constructed than any individual text on its own.

ROMAN HOUSES AS SETTINGS FOR SOCIAL RELATIONS

Since the authors of most of the literary works can be assumed to have been from the wealthier end of the socio-economic scale, many of those which survive are likely to refer to the larger town houses. In some cases, however, they are talking about a country villa or farm, and in the *Digest* many of the situations discussed seem to have occurred within multiple dwellings. Vitruvius (6. 5. 1) suggests that there were important contrasts between the homes of different members of society in terms of the facilities provided and the way in which space was organized. Differences also seem to have existed between houses constructed in the city and those that lay in the country and that served different purposes (ibid. 6. 5. 3; D. 50. 16. 198, Ulpian). So it seems that at least some Romans had definite ideas about exactly what kind of house was appropriate in what circumstances, and it was taken for granted not only that houses should be designed to be suitable for their occupants, but also that they should vary according to their context. Separate treatment of the various types will allow the precise nature of these differences to be explored, and should at the same time offer an indication of whether there may none the less have been common influences on spatial organization and shared elements in spatial perception.

1. *Town Houses*

The town house is the type for which most information is available. Although many of the details must have varied, a basic framework for understanding the terms used for different parts of the house is provided by Vitruvius' description of a house that has a *cauum aedium* or *atrium* (6. 3. 1) around which are located *triclinia* and *hibernacula* (6. 3. 2) whilst on either side are *alae* (6. 3. 4). *Tablinum* and peristyle are also mentioned (6. 3. 5 and 6. 3. 7). Although suggestions are made about the proportions of the different rooms to each other, their spatial relationships are not made explicit, and our ability to visualize the *atrium* house depends on our ability to use Vitruvius' descriptions in conjunction with excavated evidence. The difficulties encountered in reconstructing Vitruvius' house before the excavation of archaeological examples (Weiskittel 1979: 25–7) serve to emphasize the ambiguities in the textual evidence, which make it difficult and dangerous to identify areas of the house found in the archaeology with the labels used by the Latin authors. Furthermore, although Vitruvius also outlines a range of other apartments (6. 4. 1–2), the number of types mentioned is very small in comparison with the variety that occur in many other textual sources. Nevertheless, this description, together with the excavated houses from Campania, has given us the traditional picture of the *atrium* house.

From a wider consideration of the literary sources, two underlying factors emerge as having been particularly characteristic features: first, a range of symbolic elements established and reinforced the identity of the occupants of the house and their relationship with the world around them; secondly, a range of practical requirements meant that the organization of space was flexible and could constantly readapt to the changing needs of different social situations and, in particular, to seasonal changes in weather.

Symbolism attached both to the house as a whole and to many of its individual spaces. The strength of the ties between a family and its physical home is demonstrated by the fact that the theme of separation of the family from its home as a catastrophic event is a theme of exiles (e.g. Cicero, *Philippics* 12. 14. 8–10). The *Penates* watched over the house as a whole, and Cicero frequently uses them as a symbol or metaphor for it (e.g. *Pro Quinctio* 83. 6, *Pro Roscio Amerino* 23. 5, *Pro Rege Deiotaro* 8. 14, *Philippics* 12. 14. 9). Different gods are mentioned as being responsible for various elements of the domestic environment: the *Penates* seem to have been especially associated with the back parts (*penetrales*) of the house (Servius, *Ad Aeneid.* 3. 12), in particular the kitchen area (ibid. 2. 469) or the hearth (ibid. 3. 134). The hearth could also symbolize home (Terence, *Eunuch.* 815; Apuleius, *Metamorphoses* 2. 7). The transition between the street and the house was marked by the *uestibulum*, which according to some authors actually lay in front of the front door (Aulus Gellius pr. 16; Varro, *De lingua Latina* 7.

8. 1). This was also a sacred area (Cicero, *De haruspicum responso* 31. 8) associated with Vesta (Servius 2. 468), and it was also associated with patronage as an area where clients would gather (Cicero, *Att.* 4. 3. 5; Statius, *Siluae* 4. 4. 42).

The house had to be suitable for its owners both in symbolic and practical terms, so that those members of society who had positions in public life needed elaborate rooms such as *atria* (Vitruvius 6. 5. 2; Suetonius, *Vita Iuuenalis* 12) where guests could be received (Seneca, *Dialogues* 6. 10. 1; Velleius Paterculus 2. 14. 1; Ovid, *Metamorphoses* 5. 3). The *atrium* was expected to impress these visitors (Lucan 10. 119), and the effect was enhanced through statues (Apuleius, *Metamorphoses* 6. 20; Suetonius, *Gaius* 41. 2; Valerius Maximus 5. 8. 3) and wax images (Ovid, *Amores* 1. 8. 65 and *Fasti* 1. 591; Elder Pliny, *NH* 35. 5; Seneca, *Dialogues* 11. 14. 3). In the *tablinum* or *tabulina*, which is described as being next door to the *atrium* (Festus 356. 67), Elder Pliny records manuscripts noting the careers of the ancestors of the *paterfamilias* (*NH* 35. 7. 1), which would presumably have enhanced the role of the house as a symbol of the continuity of the family as a whole.

The importance of entertaining guests and of projecting a good impression of the household is underlined by the lavish nature of some of the recorded occasions; feasts could allegedly involve the use of gold and silver vessels (Curtius 8. 12. 16; Sallust, *Histories* frag. 2. 86. 1; SHA, *Heliogabulus* 29. 4–5) and also couches covered with gold, silver, and bronze (Horace, *Satires* 2. 6. 11, *Epistles* 1. 5. 1; Livy 39. 6. 7; Martial 3. 82. 6).

A constant theme of a variety of writers over a long period is that, for various reasons, different spaces were flexible in terms of the uses to which they could be put. This may be what is reflected in references to the *atrium* which suggest that in addition to this role as a reception area it also fulfilled a range of other functions, although it is not entirely clear whether these sources refer to the contemporary house, or only to some (possibly mythical) past pattern of behaviour: Valerius Maximus (3. 1. 2) records use of the *atrium* as a place to sit, whilst elsewhere it is recorded as a place for eating (Servius 1. 637; 726 (quoting Cato); Ovid, *Metamorphoses* 4. 763). The traditional explanation for the name of the *atrium* is also attributed by some authors to the fact that this was originally where the main hearth of the house was located (so turning the roof black—*ater*) (Varro, *De lingua Latina* 161; Servius 1. 726).

Several different activities are also mentioned in connection with the *cubiculum*: the word is often translated as bedroom, and there are numerous references to suggest that it could indeed contain a *lectus* (for example Cicero, *Tusculan Disputations* 5. 59. 5; Martial 14. 39. 1; [Quintilian], *Declamationes Minores* 347. 6; Suetonius, *Nero* 22. 2; Valerius Maximus 6. 8. 6; in a rural context, also Pliny 3. 7. 4). In some cases this room does seem to have been used for sleeping (Cicero, *Pro Rege Deiotaro* 129; Quintilian 4. 2. 72, and, again in a rural context, Pliny 5. 6. 21; 2. 17. 22). Nevertheless, it also seems to have been a suitable location for receiving friends, clients, or business associates (Apuleius, *Metamorphoses* 1. 23; Cicero, *Pro Scaur.* 26. 4; in a rural context, also Pliny 5. 1. 6; 5. 3. 11). Occasionally the term *cubiculum* is qualified by a further descriptive word: Elder Pliny refers explicitly to the *cubiculum dormitorium* (*NH* 30. 52), and in a rural context Younger Pliny makes reference to a *cubiculum diurnum* (3. 1. 1).

Such qualification of the term *cubiculum* suggests that in at least some cases the term may have been used in a generic sense, perhaps describing a smallish room containing a couch, rather than being linked with any specific activity. Thus there may have been a variety of *cubicula* used for different purposes. (There are other examples of words that seem to be used in this manner, for instance *cella* and *diaeta*, both of which seem to mean room in a general way and appear in the context of a variety of different activities.) Nevertheless, this need not have been so in all cases and it is also possible that, contrary to modern Western practice, there were no inhibitions about entering someone else's sleeping accommodation, and that some of these rooms were used both for sleeping, for receiving selected visitors, and perhaps also for other purposes not attested by the literary sources.

The *cubiculum* is not the only room to have been furnished with couches: in addition to the obvious example of the *triclinium*, couches could also be used for general relaxation such as reading (Fronto, *Letters* 4. 5. 2), in locations such as the *exedra* (Cicero, *De oratore* 3. 17. 8). It seems that at least some of these rooms were duplicated so that different ones could be used in different circumstances, as with Vitruvius' *triclinium cotidianum* (Vitruvius 6. 7. 2). One of the particular reasons for changing the use of a specific space, which recurs frequently in the texts, is the necessity to adapt to the different seasons. Despite the availability of hypocaust heating systems (which are mentioned occasionally, for example Pliny 2. 17. 23, in a villa context), various authors imply that it was normal practice for activities to take place in different parts of the house at different times of the year, in order to buffer against the effects of hot summer sunshine or of cold winter winds. This is reflected in references to dining in different places (Varro, *De re rustica* 29. 1) and the use of different *triclinia* (Varro, *De lingua Latina* 8. 29. 4; Vitruvius 6. 4. 1, 2; 7. 4. 4). It also seems to have been true of the *cubiculum* (Cicero, *Q. fr.* 3. 1. 2; Columella 1. 6. 1–2, in the context of a farm).

This flexible approach to the use of space may have encouraged the construction of a variety of suites that could be brought in and out of use as the season dictated. In an urban setting, however, the area available would have been limited, and it would have been used more efficiently if rooms with different functions were exchanged. This would have discouraged the use of much permanent furniture with specialized function which could not be relocated as necessary.

2. *Villas*

Rural dwellings seem to have varied both in scale and in primary function. It seems reasonably clear that authors such as Pliny and Cicero are referring to villas, of which an important role was as a setting for relaxation. There can be more doubt about the sort of establishment planned by Columella, Cato, and Varro: the attention paid to the agricultural arrangements suggests a serious intention to farm, implying that these authors are concerned with establishments whose major function is farming. These authors are therefore treated separately below.

Fewer references are available for the villa than for the town house, and, in addition, many of those which we do have describe specific examples rather than making general statements. For these reasons our picture of this form of establishment is sketchier than for the town house, although some features emerge as being common to both.

Vitruvius (6. 5. 3) says that the organization of space in the country house was different from that in the *atrium* house in that the positions of the peristyle and *atrium* are reversed. Any specific suggestions on the particular symbolism of different areas within the *uilla urbana* are, however, lacking. Nevertheless, some of the flexibility in spatial organization noted in relation to the town house is also apparent in descriptions of various villas. The *cubiculum* seems to have had a similar range of uses in the country to those mentioned in the context of town houses (see above). Pliny also suggests that a single room could serve either as a large *cubiculum* or a moderately-sized *cenatio* (2. 17. 10). This provision of a variety of spaces to accommodate different situations was extended to the use of several *triclinia* to suit larger and smaller dinner parties (ibid. 1. 3. 1). As in the town house, the changing seasons also often seem to have required relocation of some activities. Pliny's *hibernaculum* (ibid. 2. 17. 7) was perhaps used primarily during winter suggesting that different suites of rooms may have been brought in and out of use at different times of year.

3. Rural Farms

In this form of establishment, there is some evidence for the importance of symbolic elements, similar to those that are mentioned above in the context of the town house. Nevertheless, the main factors which are recorded by the agricultural authors are the practical requirements of a working farm.

Ritual on the farm is mentioned by Columella, in connection with the *Penates*. These are referred to above with respect to the town house as having been associated with the service areas, but in Columella's description they are especially associated with the master (12 pr. 7; 1. 8. 20).

The practical necessities of construction are a more frequent topic: the hearth, which in the urban context was a symbol of the house itself, played a vital role in the life of the farm as the location both of cooking and also of eating (Cato, *De agri cultura* 76; Columella 11. 1. 19). These activities may have taken place at a fixed hearth, integral to the farm building (as described by Cato, ibid. 76. 2), although portable braziers were also known (10. 4, 11. 5). The *culina*, where the farm workers seem to have eaten (Varro, *De re rustica* 1. 13. 2), was recommended to be located for ease of access. Vitruvius suggests that in a farm the *balnearium* should be located beside the kitchen (6. 6. 2), which would have made supplying water easier, and may also have provided heat for hot water from the cooking fires within the kitchen, although Columella implies that the oven was not always in the same location as the kitchen itself (8. 3. 1).

The organization of the livestock accommodation in relation to the house is also important and particular animals are recommended to be placed in specific locations. Poultry, for example, were to be kept close to the kitchen because the smoke was thought to be good for them (Columella 2. 14. 7), whilst separate summer and winter stables were recommended for cattle (ibid. 1. 6. 4). The quarters of the farm personnel were located so as to provide ready access to their charges (ibid. 1. 6. 8).

We should not expect that these instructions would necessarily have been followed, but they do offer some picture of the kinds of priorities which may have been involved in organizing the different spaces and activities within a house of this type.

4. Multiple Dwellings

Although Seneca mentions that he lived in an apartment above a bath house (*Letters* 56), and Martial and Juvenal seem to have lived in apartments (Martial 1. 117. 7; Juvenal 3), the number of clear and detailed references to this form of accommodation is limited. Our main source of information is therefore Justinian's *Digest*, which gives us some ideas of the general conceptualization of space, even if the cases discussed represent uncommon exceptions rather than general forms of behaviour.

The term *cenaculum* or *caenaculum* seems, in some instances at least, to designate a dwelling unit (e.g. *D.* 39. 2. 43. 1, Alfenus Varus; 39. 5. 27. pr., Papinian) which could be occupied by a number of different people (e.g. ibid. 9. 3. 1. 10, 9. 3. 5. 2, Ulpian; 19. 2. 27, Alfenus), although the fact is that its name implies some connection with dining (an explanation for its origins given by ancient writers, e.g. Varro, *De lingua Latina* 5. 162). Both the *Digest* and Petronius suggest that it could be rented (*D.* 13. 7. 11. 5, Ulpian; Petronius, *Satyricon* 38. 10). At least some of these apartments seem to have been located on upper floors (Apuleius, *Metamorphoses* 9. 40; *D.* 44. 7. 5. 5, Gaius), sometimes with their own entrances (Livy 39. 14. 2).

The kind of accommodation provided in such a building is unclear from the literary sources, but the archaeological examples show that it must have varied considerably. There is at least one instance mentioned in the *Digest* where the space of the apartment seems to have been internally subdivided, and an *exedra* and *cubiculum* are noted separately (*D.* 9. 3. 5. pr., Ulpian). Because of the small number of references, however, our main source of information on this type of dwelling must remain the archaeological record, and the paucity of written material together with the lack of evidence relating to the contents of individual rooms in such buildings leaves us with very little evidence as to the manner in which space was used, and even the numbers of co-residential units such structures may have contained.

CONCLUSIONS: ARCHAEOLOGICAL IMPLICATIONS OF THIS STUDY

The aim of this analysis has been to look in detail at the use of space in different types of Roman dwelling through the contemporary literary sources. I have used this information to outline some of the kinds of factors which may have influenced the organization and perception of different forms of domestic space in Roman Italy. In this final section, I summarize the main points arising from the literary analysis and make some brief suggestions about its implications for studies of the archaeological remains of Roman dwelling spaces.

With the exception of the multiple dwelling, it has been possible to use the literary evidence to create an impression of some of the considerations which may have been perceived as being influential in the organization of space. In the town houses, there seems to have been a strong symbolic element, which has previously been a focus for discussion (e.g. Saller 1984: 349–53; Wallace-Hadrill 1988; Dwyer 1991: 26–7; J. R. Clarke 1992: 1–12). In addition, a powerful role also seems to have been played by practical factors, particularly the very different conditions prevailing in summer and winter, which meant that space may not have been defined rigidly but may have changed usage in different seasons. Thus there may have been a tension between the formality of the main core of the house and the flexibility provided by the remaining areas.

In the context of villas there is no evidence for the kind of symbolism attached to the town house, suggesting that these houses may have played a less public role than their urban counterparts: perhaps they constituted relatively private structures that were used for leisure and for entertaining friends, but which would not have been so closely involved with the formal patron–client relations that have often been seen as a determining element of the architecture and decorations of the *atrium* house. As some of the individual texts suggest, the primary concern of the owners of the villas seems to have been with comfort, so that adaptation to the changing seasons becomes an element of primary importance, and the significance of many of the symbolic elements of the *atrium* house would have been reduced.

In the case of the farm, the main influence seems to have been the practical requirements of an agricultural installation. In this instance, though, the primary concern is not to buffer against the effects of seasonal changes in weather in order to give a more comfortable living environment. Instead, the authors concentrate on the productive role of the establishment, and making the farm functional as a centre for the agricultural operations is paramount. One important point that is unclear is whether these characteristics are the result of the orientation of the sources themselves, which are geared to giving practical information. Indeed, it is possible that this and the villa category could represent two different aspects of a single form of establishment, which provided leisure facilities for the owner, but which was also equipped with a working farm to keep the household

supplied, and perhaps also to provide a surplus for sale or for usage
in the town house. Such an interpretation is supported by a passage
by Columella (1. 6. 1), who describes the rural villa as being composed of different functional units, namely the *uilla urbana, uilla
rustica*, and *uilla fructuaria*. It seems possible, then, that in at least
some cases villa and farm would be part of a single establishment.

With respect to multiple dwellings, the fact that relatively little is
known from the literary sources is reflected in the attempts which
have been made to adapt the terminology of the *atrium* house in
order to describe excavated buildings of this kind (e.g. Packer 1971:
5–19). The problems with this approach have already been pointed
out (Hermansen 1981: 17–24) and it can only be unhelpful in that it
encourages false images of the organization of activities which may
have been carried out in such spaces, when in truth almost nothing
is known about the social units that would have occupied such structures, the size of individual dwelling units, or the patterns of behaviour within those units. What information we do have has come
largely from detailed analysis of the archaeological evidence (e.g.
Felletti Maj 1960; Meiggs 1973: 238–52), even where the literary
material is used, as in Hermansen's excellent study (Hermansen 1981:
24–49). A valuable area for future work would be the detailed study
of finds in addition to architecture, so that the distribution of different activities may be reconstructed in detail.

Within the scope of this chapter it has not been possible to look
in detail at specific archaeological examples of these dwelling types
in the light of the literary information. Nevertheless, various points
have emerged as being of significance in an archaeological context.
A first thing to notice is that the number of useful literary references
is smaller than one might perhaps have anticipated, so that there are
relatively few sources referring to any single household space or activity. This means that it is not possible to attempt any chronological
division of the sources, and it also reinforces the point made above,
that the literary material is likely to represent only a restricted view
of the total range of activity which would have taken place. These
limitations serve to emphasize the importance of archaeology as a
source of information about Roman households, since it gives us relatively large, often well-dated samples for analysis, and offers a range
of activities which have been selected through a different set of processes (that is, through the effects of preservation and excavation
rather than by the observation of a specific group of individuals).

A second point to note is that, although Latin terms are frequently
employed to identify different spaces within excavated houses, the result has not always been very useful. It has already been noted that

the ancient use of at least some of these terms was not itself consistent (Downey 1946: 26). On the basis of the present analysis it can be argued that the usage of different household spaces is unlikely to have been as rigidly defined as we have sometimes assumed. I have already stressed the fact that the sheer volume of excavated material has made it difficult to obtain information on the precise nature of the objects found in the rooms of different houses. Where the finds from rooms have been examined, they have sometimes been at odds with what has been assumed to have been the primary role of the room in which they were found. For example, both *atrium* and *cubiculum* sometimes seem to have served as storage areas (Dwyer 1979: 60; 1982: 115; 1991: 28 and n. 19; Allison 1993: 4–6). Nevertheless, the literary material suggests that we should not be surprised to find a range of material within a single room, and also that we should be prepared to accept evidence of combinations of uses of a single space that would not normally occur in a modern, Western house, such as sleeping and entertaining visitors in the same room at different times.

This material also raises questions about the manner in which space was defined: in our own society, the main purpose of a room is normally clear from the manner in which it is furnished. In the Roman context, however, the range of possible furniture seems to have been more limited, and the activities being performed in the space at any one time may have represented an important element of spatial definition. Thus individual spaces which may normally have hosted differing ranges of activity may have been furnished in similar ways. For archaeologists this will make interpretation difficult, especially in the absence of detailed information about small finds. One avenue of approach which has already been used to draw conclusions about the use of space is study of decorative schemes (e.g. J. R. Clarke 1991). An awareness of the fact that a room may have served a variety of different purposes may help to inform interpretation of the more complex decorative schemes, which may have been created to provide a backdrop to a range of different social situations.

These features of spatial behaviour should also remind us that concepts such as privacy tend to be culturally specific and are likely to have been very different in the Roman world from our own, and there are further features which also serve to emphasize the 'otherness' of the Roman house. For instance, a notable absence from all the literary descriptions is the notion of personalized space: there is virtually nothing to suggest that individual household members would have had their own rooms, and this ties in not only with the changing use of different spaces, but also with the idea that, although certain parts of the house could not be entered without invitation (Vitruvius 6. 5. 1), the wealthy town house was as a whole a much more public area than it is in our own culture (Wallace-Hadrill 1988: esp. 55–6; Elsner 1995: 76–7).

In conclusion, it must be emphasized that all the literary sources reflect different individual and highly selective perceptions of the Roman house. We cannot expect them to be comprehensive, nor can we hope that they would represent the experience of every Roman, or even of every upper-class male. We should also be unsurprised if they do not agree with one another. Nevertheless, they do offer an insight into the kinds of issues that may have been important in shaping the domestic environment in different contexts, and they help us to challenge our own preconceptions about what it may have meant to construct and live in these types of housing. Such a step should be of assistance when more detailed studies come to be undertaken of the distribution of material in archaeological contexts.[5]

---

[5] The editions of the ancient texts referred to are those used by the Harvard University *Thesaurus Linguae Latinae* database. For economy of space I have not listed them all separately here.

12

Repopulating the Roman House

MICHELE GEORGE

Recent scholarship by both archaeologists and social historians has attempted to give a spatial dimension to Roman social relations in the domestic context. Studies of the domestic architecture of Italy and of imperial North Africa in particular have demonstrated how the Roman house displayed the social status of its owner, the *paterfamilias* (Thébert 1987: 313–409; J. R. Clarke 1991; Wallace-Hadrill 1994). The *domus* was at once a reflection of social position and a facilitator of it, providing the Roman élite with a variety of suitable spaces for the demands which the *clientela* system made on patrons. However, the *paterfamilias* did not live alone; on the contrary, it is clear that the Roman élite household was a full one (Saller 1984; Gardner and Wiedemann 1991). In addition to members of the nuclear family, other residents might have included such dependants as clients, *alumni*, and perhaps elderly parents. There were also *liberti* and the servile *familia*, who had menial and important responsibilities, from maintenance of the house to child-care. In many cases industrial or commercial areas were integrated into the fabric of the house, showing that such activities could take place in close proximity to domestic life (Wallace-Hadrill 1994: ch. 6; Thébert 1987; La Torre 1988). Although written sources inform us of the presence of other inhabitants, extant archaeological evidence for domestic architecture reveals little about how household life was conducted; it is most informative about only one resident, the *paterfamilias*, and about the reception of guests. The Roman house did not merely reflect status; as the setting for the constant re-enactment of social roles, the house served as a physical reminder of the social hierarchy, to visitor and occupant alike. The social study of the Roman house has thus far emphasized the message and impact of the house on the visitor, and in particular on how the spatial hierarchies of the *domus*

I would like to thank Keith Bradley, Katherine Dunbabin, George Paul, and Leslie Shumka, as well as all the participants at the Canberra conference, especially Beryl Rawson, Lisa Nevett, and Pim Allison. The writing of this paper was supported by the Social Sciences and Humanities Research Council of Canada and the Arts Research Board of McMaster University, whose help is gratefully acknowledged.

helped control access to guests of different rank. In this chapter I
would like to consider the consequences of such hierarchies on the
occupants, and how the house absorbed and accommodated both
its inhabitants and guests.

OCCUPANT AND VISITOR

The public character of the Roman house is well known from
ancient literature, which portrays the *domus* as the arena for a wide
range of social and business activities. In a well-known passage
Vitruvius (6. 5. 1) records that men with particular social roles required appropriate spaces in order to conduct business in their homes;
hence, Roman bankers and tax-collectors needed houses which were
large and secure, and orators houses with enough space to seat their
audiences. Above all, men in high political office required the wid-
est range of rooms and spaces: lofty vestibules, *atria*, peristyles, and
porticoes, as well as libraries and basilicas. Vitruvius goes further to
characterize certain areas of the house, such as the *atrium* and peristyle, as open to everybody, while access to others, such as *triclinia*
and *cubicula*, required an invitation. Because a conspicuous distinction between public and private exists in our own culture, in which
the house is valued as a retreat from the outside world, the combination of the two in the Roman context seems to us an incongruity,
if not an impossibility. From the modern perspective, it is difficult
to understand how the nuclear family could flourish in such circumstances, or how bonds of affection or a familial identity be forged.
Early studies of the Roman house identified a clear separation between public and private areas, leading to a characterization of the
atrium as public, intended for the reception of visitors, and the peristyle as private, reserved for the nuclear family (Marquardt and Mau
1886: 247; Crema 1959: 112; cf. J. R. Clarke 1991: 12). Yet, the
combination of *negotium* and family life was normal in the élite
Roman house. The traditional antithesis of public and private fails
to characterize adequately Roman domestic space because here the
two were apposite rather than opposite. The house was at once the
domus frequentata and a *sanctum perfugium*, and stressing a dichotomy between the two creates a disproportionate separation that
does not accurately reflect the Roman context.[1] In fact, the interface

---

[1] For the *domus frequentata*, see Seneca, *Letters* 21. 6; also Tacitus, *Dialogus* 6, 11; Cicero,
Att. 1. 18. 1; 2. 22. 3; *Fam.* 9. 20. 3. For the *domus* as a refuge, see Cicero, *In Catilinam* 4.
2; *In Vatinium* 22; *De domo sua* 109; also D. 2. 4. 18, Gaius; 50. 17. 103, Paulus (which
records that it was illegal to seize a man from within his own home). See Thébert (1987)
passim, but esp. 319–23; also Dunbabin (1995: 165–76).

between occupants and visitors provides a useful point of departure for examining spatial use by both groups.[2]

DOMESTIC ARCHITECTURE AND THE ROMAN FAMILY

Efforts to establish permanent divisions in spatial organization in the Roman house meet with difficulty for several reasons. Relative to other aspects of Roman life, written sources describing daily activities within the house are less than plentiful, and most depictions only incidentally include valuable references to family members.[3] Like textual evidence, archaeology provides at best a skewed window on the ancient world. The vagaries of preservation supply disparate pieces of material culture which must be ordered and interpreted to be understood. Moreover, each kind of evidence has its own potential as a source of information. Although domestic architecture permits a view of household life which texts cannot, it has its own limitations. This is partly due to the nature of the subject as a whole, and partly due to the nature of the Roman house in particular. All domestic architecture is socially constructed, and to some degree reflects the society which created it. Yet the physical structure of the house, stripped of its contents, can give only broad indications of social values.[4] It was an inhabited space, and much of the texture of daily life is lost without those inhabitants and their possessions. Most importantly, spatial use is governed by rules of behaviour which were culturally ingrained and understood; they are not all revealed in the architectural evidence. Without the occupants themselves, or substantial information about how they regarded and used different areas within the house, the most important dimension in decoding the use of space is missing. In the Roman house especially the dominance of the *paterfamilias* accurately reflected his position at the apex of the social pyramid, and his authority over the members of the household.[5] In arrangement and decoration the house proclaimed

---

[2] Practical concerns, such as climate and building materials, also play a role. See the articles in Kent (1990) and Nevett, Ch. 11 above.

[3] The archaeological material in this chapter is limited to the élite house, because it is in these houses that the largest households existed, what Wallace-Hadrill, borrowing from Philippe Ariès, has termed the 'big house'. It is in these houses that one might look first for distinctions in spatial use, because there is simply more space to consider. I omit therefore the corpus of poorer or utilitarian housing from this discussion.

[4] The theoretical framework for domestic architecture as an active rather than passive social element was pioneered by Bourdieu (1973).

[5] In paralleling personal and political power, Seneca (*De ira* 3. 35) lists the *matrona, cliens, libertus*, and *seruus* as falling under the control of the *paterfamilias* in his own home.

the owner's power and prestige, and in so doing hid the presence of its other inhabitants.

The multiplicity of functions performed in the Roman house and the range of people involved in them demanded that spatial use be highly flexible. In such a house, permanently fixed room functions can be a hindrance rather than an advantage. Certain practical considerations did result in areas with a permanent function, e.g. kitchens with fixed hearths, and baths and latrines with drainage facilities. More specific identifications of room function are difficult to obtain from the physical evidence, however. Elements such as decoration, accoutrements such as curtains, and objects such as furniture or utensils are crucial factors in the use of domestic space. Since they served practical functions, they can be helpful indicators of spatial use and, if the function of a room can be determined, then some idea of who used it can also be reached.[6] In most cases, however, room function in Roman houses is difficult to determine with absolute certainty. Artefacts such as vessels or utensils are the most obvious potential aids, if it is assumed that the find-spot of an object is a valid indicator of a room's function. However, artefact studies have shown that this is very often not the case (Allison 1992a, and Ch. 13 below). Moreover, outside of Campania artefacts in Roman houses are in relatively short supply, and the crude excavation practices of the past have destroyed much potentially useful evidence. Room decoration can be another clue to function, since it is reasonable to assume that well-decorated rooms are more significant than poorly decorated rooms, and might therefore have had greater importance. But this too is not necessarily always the case.[7] Rooms with pavements that mark off an area for furniture such as couches can be considered *triclinia* or *cubicula*, but such pavements can point only to primary function, and do not necessarily exclude others. This is especially true in houses of average size. That the élite house did have some degree of specialization in room function is clear from textual sources;[8] however, those distinctions are not often obvious from the archaeological evidence, nor can they be taken as exclusive. The mobility of Roman furnishings and a ready slave labour supply meant that activities could

---

[6] For the role of such objects as 'cues' to behaviour, and for the relationship between behaviour and environment, see Rapoport (1990).

[7] e.g. the rooms in Pliny's Tuscan villa which are generally used by his slaves and freedmen, but which could also be used by guests (2. 17. 9).

[8] Textual sources reveal that in both houses and villas room use was adjusted according to seasonal and diurnal changes: in houses, Vitruvius 6. 4; in villas, differences in temperature or lighting according to changes in seasons (Pliny 2. 17. 10, 13, 17; 5. 6. 29, 30), and differences in the time of day (id. 2. 17. 6, 8, 17–19, 23; 5. 6. 15, 31) appear to indicate adaptations in spatial use. See also Wallace-Hadrill (1994: 52–7).

have shifted as necessary.[9] Thus, for a variety of reasons the function of many rooms defies identification.[10]

The problems in locating household members in the physical house and in defining their use of domestic space are not insignificant. The multivalence of the Roman house allowed it to serve both its residents and its guests simultaneously, and the spatial hierarchies which were designed to restrict access to guests of different rank and to control their mobility did have consequences for residents. Any attempt to determine distinctions in spatial use by occupants and visitors must be acknowledged as conjectural in nature, because of the inherent limitations of the evidence; nevertheless, speculation is still enlightening.

THE *ATRIUM*-PERISTYLE HOUSE

The Atrium

The major social events in the élite household were the *salutatio*, the morning social call, and the *cena*, the dinner party. The latter has received recent attention by scholars, who have tried to read social values in the forms and rituals of dining (Slater 1991). Archaeologists too have noted the increased significance of the *triclinium*, and its emergence as the focal point in the imperial period (Dunbabin 1991; Ellis 1991). The *cena* took place in *triclinia*, and other rooms were used for the reception of important guests and for social and business affairs, as Vitruvius indicates. Less has been written on the mechanics of the *salutatio*. Texts record that it was a daily event in the élite home which took place in the morning and involved the influx of numerous visitors into the house, both clients visiting their patrons and acquaintances of similar status seeking advice or favours.[11] As the setting for the *salutatio* the *atrium* is depicted as public and formal in function; here too the ancestral *imagines* and genealogies were displayed.[12] But the *atrium* was important for the

---

[9] Note Pliny's comment on the suburban villa of Caninius Rufus: 'quid triclinia illa popularia illa paucorum, quid cubicula diurna nocturna' (1. 3. 1), and the room in the Tuscan villa which he describes as 'uel cubiculum grande uel modica cenatio' (2. 17. 10). Cf. Petronius, *Satyricon* 68, where slaves change the tables in Trimalchio's *triclinium*.

[10] For the complexities and discrepancies of the terminology of rooms and room function, see Nevett, Ch. 11 above.

[11] Marquardt and Mau (1886: 259–63); A. von Premerstein, 'Clientes', *RE* 4. 23–55; Saller (1982: 11, 61–2, 128–9).

[12] Markers of the *salutatio* include benches which might have been used for waiting visitors located outside the house, e.g. at Pompeii the House of M. Epidius Rufus (XI 1. 20), and at Herculaneum the House of the Gem and the House of the Relief of Telephus (Insula Orient. 1. 2, 1. 2), among others; see Dwyer (1991: 27–9). For the *imagines* in the *atrium*, see Polybius 6. 53; Elder Pliny, *NH* 35. 6–7; Vitruvius 6. 3. 6. For the tokens of status erected on the lintels of doors, see Wiseman (1987: 393–413).

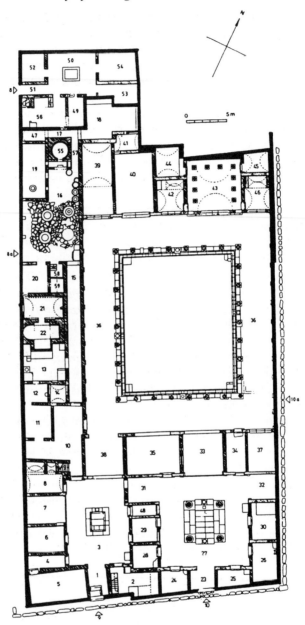

FIG. 12.1. House of the Labyrinth, Pompeii, 1st century AD.

household as well, on both a literal and symbolic level. Several key rites of passage in family life traditionally took place in the *atrium*, and it was in the *atrium* that the household gods were worshipped (Marquardt and Mau 1886: 228–36; J. R. Clarke 1991: 2–12). The *atrium* was therefore the focus of the Republican house for both occupant and visitor. The whereabouts of the rest of the household during the *salutatio* is not clear from textual evidence; *liberti*, when part of the household, assisted the master in the reception of guests, as did appropriate slaves. There is nothing to suggest that the *matrona*'s presence was required at the *salutatio*, and it seems that she saw to her own domestic responsibilities while her husband took care of his.[13]

In his discussion of Pompeian houses Wallace-Hadrill (1994: Chs. 2, 3) has noted the variety of markers which signalled to guests the division of space according to social distinctions. These markers range from the obvious, such as room arrangement, to the more subtle, such as differences in wall and floor decoration. Other indicators might include definitive physical barriers, such as doors, or somewhat more permeable obstacles such as curtains.[14] But such mechanisms of access did not only help to maintain distinctions between guests of different rank; they probably also enabled the separation of visitor and occupant. This was especially important in an *atrium* house that lacked a peristyle and therefore had limited space for the family to use. As the central space in the Pompeian house in the Republican period, the *atrium* was by necessity the location for diverse activities. The arrangement of the *atrium* house itself indicated to the visitor which rooms were of restricted entry, and which were not. In most Pompeian *atrium* houses a clear visual axis is established from the moment a visitor enters. This axis, which can be seen in the House of the Labyrinth (VI 11, 10, Fig. 12.1), focuses the visitor's attention on the rooms directly opposite the door. This includes the *tablinum*, traditionally the office of the *paterfamilias*, which was set at the end of the *atrium*'s axis opposite the entrance, and the *alae*, rooms which flank the *tablinum* and have a wide opening to the *atrium* without a door. Much has been made of the importance of this visual axis in the Roman house as an architectural manifestation of the

---

[13] Cornelius Nepos (*Praefatio* to *Lives of Foreign Generals* 6–8) describes Roman women, in contrast to their Greek counterparts, as comfortably present in the front part of the house, that is, in the *atrium*, where they would come in contact with visitors from outside the household. Nepos does not refer specifically to the *salutatio*, but it may be inferred from his comments that women moved freely throughout the house despite the presence of visitors. For the *matrona*'s reception of guests, see Treggiari (1991: 420–4).

[14] For doors and curtains: Seneca, *Letters* 80. 1; Martial 1. 34.

patriarch's power.[15] But I would suggest that the effect is twofold. The accentuation of the *tablinum* marginalizes the side-rooms, and in detracting attention accords them greater isolation. Members of the household could thus have enjoyed their privacy at the same time as guests were visiting. Doors, as indicated by marks of the door hinges (*cardines*) in threshold blocks, were common to rooms off *atria* at Pompeii.[16] The advantage of doors and curtains is that, although fixed, they are flexible, and can be opened, closed, or left ajar. This adaptability granted control over privacy.[17] Slaves too, such as door-keepers (*ostiarii*), could act as human barriers, both directing the flow of traffic and ensuring that only invited guests were admitted to restricted areas, according to the orders of the host.[18] This practice was not merely good manners, but also served as an effective control tactic, and made certain that the right visitors ended up in the right parts of the house. In this way women, children, and servile staff could be in the rooms off the *atrium*, engaged in domestic activities, without disturbing the *paterfamilias* at his social obligations, or being disturbed themselves. It is likely too that physical obstacles were only complementary to the rules of social behaviour; etiquette dictated the conduct of visitors within the house, and most guests probably did not seek out areas that were not intended for them. Temporal distinctions also allowed other residents to use the *atrium* at times of the day when guests were not being received. The image of Livy's Lucretia who weaves in the *atrium* at night while Collatinus is away, and the children in *Aeneid* 7 who play with tops in *uacua* (empty) *atria*, demonstrate its use for household activities when formal functions were not in progress (Livy 1. 57; Vergil, *Aeneid* 7. 379).[19]

Secondary Atria

Another architectural strategy for the accommodation of occupant and visitor within the house is the creation of a second *atrium* or court. At Pompeii there are a number of double *atrium* houses

[15] J. R. Clarke (1991: 2–6); Wallace-Hadrill (1994: 44–5). For visual axes in both the *tablinum* and peristyle: Drerup (1959: 145–74).

[16] e.g. as indicated in the large *atrium* of the House of the Labyrinth (Fig. 12.1). Such rooms are closer to the front door, and both permanent barriers and greater security were required. For locks found in Pompeian *atria*, see Dwyer (1991: 28). Plautus (*Miles gloriosus* 159, 287, 340) refers to people spying on the interior of the house through the *impluuium*.

[17] Doors are closed to create privacy and security, e.g. Petronius, *Satyricon* 94; Apuleius, *Metamorphoses* 1. 11, 14, 15; 2. 24, 30; 3. 15; 9. 2, 30; 10. 20.

[18] Petronius, *Satyricon* 30; Wallace-Hadrill (1994: 39).

[19] Artefactual evidence suggests that weaving did take place in Pompeian *atria*, although it was not limited to that part of the house, nor is it clear whether it was done by free or servile women. See Allison, Ch. 13 below.

which originated in the second century BC (Lauter 1975: 149; Strocka 1991: 66 n. 60; Seiler 1992: 89). The first of these appear to have been built with two *atria* from the outset, while in later examples a second *atrium* from a neighbouring house is added to a single-*atrium* house. The best-known example of a double-*atrium* house is the House of the Faun (VI 12, 2, Fig. 12.2), in which the grand, conservatively decorated Tuscan *atrium* is flanked by a smaller tetra-style *atrium*. The two *atria* create two almost separate tracts within the house. The Tuscan *atrium* is entered by a large door, with the entry passage (*fauces*) elaborately stuccoed and painted. Behind it lay the sets of mosaic pavements from the house, the Alexander mosaic, and other smaller but equally finely made genre scenes. Smaller, less decorated rooms open off the tetrastyle *atrium*, and behind it are the service areas of the house—the kitchen, baths, and a stairway to an upper storey. A similar arrangement of double *atria*, with decorated rooms off the large *atrium* and smaller rooms and pos-sible service tract off the smaller *atrium*, occur in the House of the Labyrinth (Fig. 12.1), the House of the Centenary, and the House of Obellius Firmus, to mention only a few.[20] Numerous other houses have a second *atrium* or peristyle in another position, such as off the back or side of the house, the apparent result of expansion by expropriation of a neighbouring property. In some cases distinc-tions between two *atria* are reasonably clear, as in the House of M. Lucretius (IX 3, 3), while in others it is difficult to determine if one *atrium* had greater status than another.[21] It may be that these smaller *atria* and courts permitted the rest of the household to con-tinue their domestic lives unimpeded while the *paterfamilias* received guests.[22] A. Maiuri identified several small courts as *gynaeconites*, or women's quarters, in imitation of areas so identified in Greek domestic architecture.[23] He characterizes the small court in the House of the Vettii (Fig. 12.3–*s, t, u*) as 'closed, intimate, and elegant' and

[20] Lauter (1975: 149 n. 6) mentions unpublished examples at Paestum (Poseidonia) and Vulci, and calls the double-*atrium* house 'ein fester Typ' in Campania.

[21] e.g. the House of P. Vedius Siricus (VII 1, 47), which has decorated rooms off both its *atria* (Overbeck and Mau 1884: fig. 171; House of M. Lucretius, fig. 170). How, for ex-ample, does one untangle the spatial hierarchies of an agglomeration such as the House of the Citharist (I 4, 5. 25), with its three full peristyles? (For a plan, see Overbeck and Mau 1884: fig. 179.)

[22] For this view, see Mau (1908: 241). Back entrances are also common in large houses in Pompeii and must have allowed members of the household to come and go without using the more imposing front doors. Cf. Seneca, *De breuitate* 14. 4, in which he castigates the *patroni* of his time for maltreating their clients by not bothering to get out of bed for the morning call, or by escaping a crowded *atrium* via a back door.

[23] Maiuri (1954) believed secondary *atria* such as those in the House of the Faun were used as guest suites. For women's quarters in Greek houses, see Mylonas (1946). For a new per-spective on the Greek evidence, see Nevett (1994).

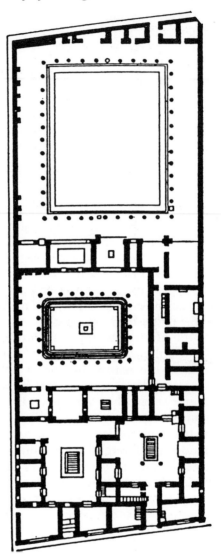

FIG. 12.2. House of the Faun, Pompeii, 1st century AD.

therefore appropriate for the mistress and other women in the house
(Maiuri 1954: 456: cf. J. R. Clarke 1991: 208, 221). However, as
Wallace-Hadrill points out (1994: 58), it is these very same features
which make this suite particularly suitable for the reception of the
most privileged guests. Gender differences of this magnitude do not
seem compatible with women's roles in Roman society as they are

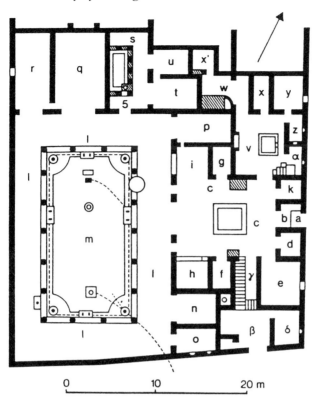

FIG. 12.3. House of the Vettii, Pompeii, 1st century AD.

currently understood, and although customs in behaviour probably did occur along gender lines, they cannot be identified securely in the architectural evidence. Alternatively, H. Lauter sees double *atria* as an emulation of Hellenistic luxury in domestic architecture, rather than as an adoption of Greek social practice in spatial use.[24] Rather than indicating sharp gender distinctions in spatial use, then, these *atria* and courts demonstrate the different gradients of space necessary in the Roman house, and the desire to separate different groups in the *domus*, probably occupant from visitor, but also perhaps occupants of different rank from each other. A desire for some distance between occupant and visitor should not be read as an enforced segregation of the household from the public sphere, but rather as a *modus vivendi* for the occupants of the house, and for all domestic

[24] Hellenistic 'Raumluxus', as evidenced by vast peristyles as well as double *atria* (Lauter 1975).

activity. Separate *atria* and courts must have presented a range of choices for both reception and domestic activities, but the subtleties of these choices and how they were worked out are largely lost to us. They were clearly limited to the wealthiest of élite householders, which suggests that most households had other, less tangible methods of creating privacy.[25]

The Peristyle

In the second century BC household activities adapted to include the porticoes and peristyles which were added to the Republican *atrium* in the Campanian house. That the peristyle was not intended as a secluded area for the family, as earlier generations of scholars believed, is now generally accepted. The incorporation of columns into the *domus* was part of a larger movement to embellish the private context with decorative forms which were either derived from or identified with public architecture. Although most obviously illustrated by the appearance of peristyles, the trend also saw the creation of columnar *atria*, colonnaded reception rooms, and the addition of elaborate pediments over doors. First and especially Second Style Pompeian wall-paintings, with their imitation of lavish marble facings and vistas of complex urban architecture, are part of this effort to imitate public space and monumentalize domestic interiors. It seems unlikely that peristyles were limited to use by household members, and it is more reasonable to assume that *atrium* and peristyle were used by both groups, and that rooms off the peristyle became the location for the reception of privileged guests as well as for domestic affairs (Thébert 1987: 357–78; Ellis 1991). The distinction between the two is then rather of gradients of space depending on status, rather than a sharp polarity of public and private. The peristyle in the House of the Labyrinth (Fig. 12.1), with its colonnaded *oecus* (no. 43) and its adjacent decorated *cubicula* (nos. 42–6), are good examples of this. The architectural arrangement creates a suite of

---

[25] Rooms of various purpose were probably located on upper storeys, and would have been suitably distant from the action of the *salutatio*. Although they were fairly common at Pompeii, as indicated by the number of stairwells, they do not survive in adequate condition to provide conclusive information. It should not be assumed that rooms in upper storeys were necessarily insignificant or unsuitable for entertaining, however. Some had well-decorated rooms which overlooked the *atrium* or peristyle; cf. Pliny 2. 17. 12–13, where he describes a *cenatio*, *diaetae*, and *triclinium* located on upper storeys. For bedrooms in upper storeys, cf. Petronius, *Satyricon* 77; Apuleius, *Metamorphoses* 4. 12. It is also frequently impossible to ascertain if an upper storey was occupied by the ground-floor residents or was rented out to a tenant; see Wallace-Hadrill (1994: 105–10); Sutherland (1989).

well-decorated rooms which were probably used for reception.[26] The increased size of the *atrium*-peristyle house gave more choice for both domestic and reception activities, and temporal alternation in room function probably facilitated this. The architectural change can be seen in its incipient form in Campania in examples such as the House of the Vettii at Pompeii (Fig. 12.3) and the House of the Stags at Herculaneum. Examples of the more developed peristyle plan are found in provincial domestic architecture, notably in North Africa.

THE CENTRAL PERISTYLE PLAN

In a peristyle house areas or suites of rooms off a peristyle are more easily made discrete from one another than rooms off an *atrium*. In the Pompeian peristyle rooms open off only one or two sides, while in the more elaborated central peristyle plan, such as the houses of Acholla and Volubilis in North Africa (Figs. 12.4–5), rooms open off four sides of the peristyle.[27] Access to rooms off the peristyle could be controlled using similar techniques as in the *atrium*, but there are subtle differences between the two. Although both *atrium* and peristyle provide light and air to surrounding rooms, as an architectural form the peristyle is a more articulated space than the *atrium*. It is the portico which provides the crucial difference from the *atrium*, since it more closely directs the flow of traffic and more easily permits the creation of distinctions between rooms. This is achieved in a variety of ways, such as variations in the portico pavement, with the insertion of different or more elaborate motifs in front of significant rooms or their thresholds. Wide doorways or tripartite entrances also aggrandize important rooms, and changes to the peristyle, such as the placement of columns and basins in front of significant rooms or the addition of other decorative features, can also enhance this effect.[28] In the central peristyle plan, rooms of different function can be separated by both the portico and the expanse of the garden or court as well as by doors or curtains. In several houses at Volubilis distance and an axial arrangement separate reception rooms and

---

[26] The *cubicula* may also have been used for sleeping; see Nevett, Ch. 11 above. See also Pliny's description of his Laurentine villa (2. 17), in which a *cubiculum* is also beside a *triclinium*.

[27] Peristyles with rooms off four sides can be found at Pompeii, e.g. the House of Menander (I 10, 4), but they are exceptional.

[28] e.g. the addition of *oscilla* (marble discs) (see Seiler 1992: 130–1), or the creation of a 'Rhodian' peristyle (Vitruvius 6. 7. 3), in which one side of the peristyle is at a higher level; the best preserved example is in the House of the Silver Wedding (V 2, 1) at Pompeii.

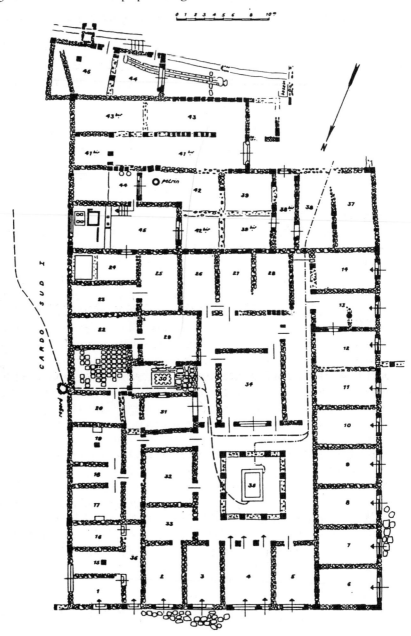

FIG. 12.4. House of the Gold Coins, Volubilis, North Africa.

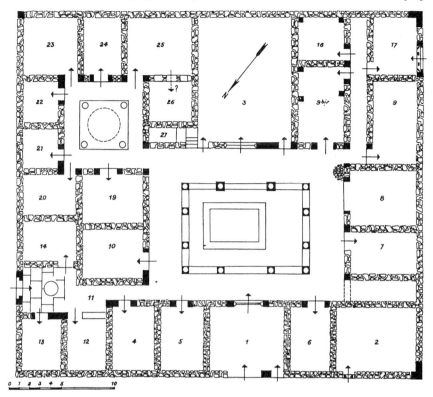

FIG. 12.5. House of the Large Pilasters, Volubilis, North Africa.

give them greater status. In the House of the Gold Coins at Volubilis (Fig. 12.4), for example, the large reception room (no. 34) off the peristyle is surrounded by corridors which isolate it from the other rooms.[29] As in the *atrium* house, however, a secondary consequence of this was greater isolation for other rooms off the porticoes, rooms which could have been used by household members in greater privacy.

In several other respects North African houses differ from those of Campania. The traditional *fauces* or entrance of the Pompeian house was here replaced by a vestibule, which appears to have functioned as an antechamber to the peristyle. In some Pompeian *atrium*-peristyle houses the *atrium* may already have assumed this subordinate

[29] Similarly, in the House of the Labours of Hercules and the House of Flavius Germanus corridors flank the reception room and separate it from surrounding rooms (Étienne 1960: pl. IV, V). In the House of Neptune at Acholla two unpaved areas which flank the reception room and are identified as courts or gardens separate it from two *cubiculum* suites; Gozlan and Bourgeois (1992: 6; plan I, nos. XXVIII, XXXIV).

position; certainly the arrangement of the House of the Vettii (Fig. 12.3) suggests this.[30] In the House of the Triumph of Neptune at Acholla there was an entrance vestibule with benches along three walls for waiting visitors, and in the House of Asinius Rufus at the same site the largest room found thus far forms what appears to be an entrance vestibule, which may have served as a waiting-room for visitors to the house.[31] The benches outside the Campanian house are thus incorporated into the first room of these houses.[32] In North Africa vestibules appear to have provided an additional spatial gradient within the house, another device to control access to the interior; reception activities previously carried out in the *atrium* were thus shifted to the rooms off the peristyle. Corridors too, uncommon at Pompeii, are used in many North African houses to join different parts of the house while still maintaining a degree of separation between them. There are also suites of rooms accessible by corridors which run off the peristyle; for example, the two *cubiculum* suites which flank the reception room in the House of the Triumph of Neptune and the four rooms in the south-west corner of the House of the Large Pilasters (Fig. 12.5: nos. 9, 9*bis*, 16, 17).[33] At Volubilis in particular there are also small courts, sometimes placed near service areas such as kitchens and latrines, usually off a secondary entrance.[34] These *atriola*, as R. Étienne labelled them, are at a distance from the peristyle and its reception rooms, and in many cases

---

[30] Dwyer (1991) argues against the decline of the *atrium* at Pompeii.

[31] For the House of the Triumph of Neptune, see Gozlan and Bourgeois (1992: plan I, no. I). The vestibule in the House of Asinius Rufus opens directly off the street and has pilasters which form a monumentalized, porticoed doorway into the interior of the house. An inscribed *cippus* placed beside one of the pilasters announced to visitors that Asinius Rufus had attained the consulship in AD 184 (Gozlan 1994: 163–72, fig. 2, room I). On vestibules in North African houses, see Thébert (1987: 355–6, 358–60).

[32] See the observation of Aulus Gellius (16. 5), who records that by the 2nd cent. AD *uestibulum* was used to designate 'partem domus primorem, quam uulgus *atrium* vocat'; *uestibulum*, he adds, traditionally refers to an intermediary area between house and street, where those intending to pay a call on the master ('qui dominum eius domus salutatum uenerant') had to wait until they were admitted. Tertullian (*De poenitentia* 11. 4–5) talks of the 'atria' of political candidates thronged with visitors. Since the *atrium* as we see it in Pompeii seems to have been long out of fashion by his time, the term must refer to another kind of architectural form, perhaps the vestibules we see in North Africa, or alternatively Tertullian uses it metaphorically.

[33] For the House of the Triumph of Neptune, see Gozlan and Bourgeois (1992: plan I, nos. XXIII–XXVII and nos. XXIX–XXXIII); also Dunbabin (1995).

[34] e.g. Figs. 12.4 and 5; also House west of the governor's palace, House of the Marble Bacchus, House of the Nereids, House of the Train of Venus (Étienne 1960: pls. VIII, XI, XIV, XVII). In numerous houses at both Pompeii and in North Africa there are rear entrances, which often lead directly to kitchens or stables or to commercial operations. Clearly some separation was desired between practical activities and hospitality. It is impossible to ascertain precisely who in the household used these areas, but presumably slaves and freedmen regularly had chores here.

are accessible down narrow corridors. As Thébert points out, in these houses peristyles and corridors simultaneously 'carve up' the interior as they integrate parts of the house by giving them autonomous access and a degree of separation from one another (Thébert 1987: 387). This separation operated for both public and private functions, and afforded the flexibility needed to accommodate both kinds of activities.

The social significance of these differences between the Pompeian and North African *domus* is difficult to establish. It has been suggested that the greater articulation of the latter—the use of vestibules, corridors, peristyles, secondary courts, and suites of rooms —demonstrates an increased hierarchization of domestic space, the result of greater social distinctions, or of still more public functions occurring in the house with a concomitant need for privacy, all of which reflect contemporary social change (Ellis 1991). From the typological perspective, similarities do exist in some houses in the Iberian peninsula, as at Conimbriga in modern Portugal, where there are secondary courts and peristyles off large elaborate central peristyles.[35] At late imperial Ostia, however, where houses with central arcaded courts resemble the North African central peristyle plan, there are none of the separate courts or suites seen in North Africa (Becatti 1948; Boersma 1985). Houses in southern Gaul offer other distinctive internal arrangements.[36] The Houses of Vaison-la-Romaine, Roman Vasio, show the use of porticoes and peristyles in a variety of ways, some approximating the central peristyle plan, others with more varied organization. At Saint-Romain-en-Gal, a residential suburb of Vienne, Roman Vienna, outside Lyons, houses are similarly distinctive, with porticoes and elaborately watered gardens the main common feature. In these houses rooms do not generally open off the sides of the peristyle garden, but rather are placed in units to one side of them. The result is an alternation between groupings of rooms and porticoed garden, set side-by-side rather than in the more circular arrangement as in Campania, North Africa, or the Iberian peninsula.

These differences illustrate the diversity in domestic architecture in the imperial period, and the subsequent difficulty in relating social changes to the varying house typologies which occur. The

[35] Although yet to be studied, they are dated to the Severan period by their pavements and so are contemporary with the North African evidence. See de Alarcão and Étienne (1981: 67–80). See also Italica in Spain, where the House of the Exedra and the House of the Birds have similar subsidiary courts. For these and other Romano-Spanish houses, see Balil (1974).

[36] Vaison-la-Romaine: Goudineau (1979). Saint-Romain-en-Gal: Le Glay (1981); Delaval and Savay-Guerraz (1992).

identification of an increased social hierarchization in Roman society on the basis of a group of North African houses neglects to explain houses which do not share these characteristics, whether in other western provinces or indeed in North Africa itself.[37] A better understanding of regional and chronological distinctions in house typology and development throughout the empire would certainly clarify the picture. However, the lack of consistency already apparent weakens the argument for widespread cultural changes, and raises the possibility that they represent regional tendencies. Differences in house typology throughout the empire present much fodder for the architectural historian, but they unfortunately contribute little to clarifying spatial use by the household or guest in these varied settings. There may well have been subtleties of articulation in spatial use in the Pompeian house which correspond in some fashion to North African houses, but which elude us because they were rooted in behaviour, and were not manifested in structural ways.

FREEDMEN AND SLAVES

As well as the nuclear family, freedmen and slaves formed two distinct groups within the élite house. Locating quarters for these members of the household is fraught with difficulty.[38] Most extant houses were simply too small to have separate areas for servants, of free or servile status. They may have been housed in upper storeys, or simply have slept in a convenient corner or in the same room as their master.[39] It is also impossible to discern legal status from architectural evidence, and therefore to identify with certainty freed from servile.[40] Service areas such as kitchens or stables in a big house were clearly used by slaves. Many Pompeian kitchens have *lararia*, while other shrines were located in the *atrium* and peristyle. These latter *lararia* may have been used mainly by the master and his family, while those

[37] Much work needs to be done in North Africa to determine if this is a regional pattern or reflects individual urban preferences. For a survey of the published plans of North African houses, see Rebuffat (1969/71).   [38] George (forthcoming); Bradley (1994: 84–6).
[39] D. 29. 5. 14, Maecianus; Apuleius, *Metamorphoses* 2. 15, where slaves sleep on pallets outside the door; Pliny 7. 27. 12, where two freedmen who are brothers share a bedroom. In the same letter Pliny refers to a slave boy who sleeps 'in paedagogio mixtus pluribus'; it is not clear whether a *paedagogium* is an area of the house or merely a single room (7. 27. 13). For slave quarters in houses at Rome: Carandini (1988: 359–87). For slaves inhabiting tombs: D. 47. 12. 3. 11, Ulpian. For archaeological evidence of slave quarters in villas, see Carandini (1985); Rossiter (1978: 40–8).
[40] Maiuri (1933: 186–220) identified a small suite of rooms as the dwelling of the procurator in the House of Menander.

in the kitchens may have been primarily intended for servile use, indicating status distinctions in domestic worship with corresponding differences in spatial use.[41] In any analysis of the Roman élite house, the omnipresence of slaves should be taken into account, and so even though the architecture hides them they can be seen throughout the house by their tasks. We must therefore place *nutrices* and *paedagogi* with their young charges (Tacitus, *Dialogus* 28), maids with their mistresses (*D.* 29. 5. 1. 28, Ulpian), servile attendants engaged in all manner of practical and managerial tasks. The development of slave families is also problematic.[42] In large houses separate suites for slaves with considerable responsibilities may have been usual. However, in houses of average size this would have been impossible, and here slave families must have evolved despite proximity to the free household, and in a cultural context with notions of intimacy and personal space which were different from our own.

PERSONAL PRIVACY

The certain existence of servile family units in the face of the paucity of evidence for slave quarters suggests the daily compromises in the use of space that must have existed between different groups of occupants within the house. The same factors which distinguished access to guests of different rank, and separated visitor from occupant, could separate occupants from each other. Doors, windows equipped with shutters, and curtains could be used to close off rooms or areas for use by different members of the household, and temporal differences in spatial use allowed individuals or groups to occupy the same domestic area. Pliny's letters about his villas provide useful insights into this aspect of shared domestic space.[43] Pliny's descriptions of his villas cannot be taken as exact parallels for spatial use

[41] Differences exist between scenes painted on shrines in kitchens and work areas, and those in *atria* and peristyles, the latter tending to depict the *penates*, the former more commonly the *Lares* and the *Genius*. This cult was primarily the duty of freedmen and slaves, while the worship of the Penates was in the hand of the *paterfamilias* himself. Of particular interest is the *lararium* painting in the kitchen of house I 13. 2, which may represent the *paterfamilias*, *matrona*, and the servile *familia* attending a sacrifice to the domestic *Lares*. See Fröhlich (1991: 178–9, 261).   [42] For slave families, see Bradley (1987: 47–80).
[43] The descriptions of Pliny's villas are included in this discussion because they are invaluable sources of information about spatial use in the *pars urbana* of villas. Although differences in scale between villa and *domus* were often substantial, Pliny's observations constitute one of the few sources for attitudes towards privacy, and as such should not be ignored. Cato, Varro, and Columella have been omitted for the sake of brevity and because they centre on the *uilla rustica*.

in the town house, and that his villas were significantly larger is understood. Indeed, Pliny describes a unique privacy in his villas which he says is impossible to obtain anywhere else, mostly due to the absence of throngs of visitors. However, the size of the villa is not the only reason Pliny gains privacy. Throughout the description Pliny notes the presence of doors and windows with shutters, by which he can control the view and the internal room temperature.[44] But it is apparent that doors and shutters also provided seclusion from other members of the household. A *cubiculum* is separated from the peristyle garden by a narrow passageway, which helps to muffle the sounds of nature and the voices of slave children; here too shutters help in the creation of privacy and quiet.[45] Pliny seems to delight in the effect of absolute retreat from his household and indeed the rest of his house.[46] Through the room's arrangement and shutters Pliny is neither disturbed while he works, nor does he hinder the celebrations of his slave *familia*. Similar attention to privacy is shown in the description of his Tuscan villa, where there are other *cubicula* which provide a retreat from the surrounding environment.[47] The descriptions of Pliny reveal both how different groups within the villa cohabited and obtained some measure of separation from each other, as well as the high value placed on personal privacy. They also demonstrate how, even in a spacious villa, physical barriers such as doors were required to accomplish this. In the urban *domus* such privacy was apparently much more difficult to achieve and must have necessitated greater concessions on the part of residents. A similar understanding between occupant and visitor allowed the latter into the house without disrupting regular domestic life. The features outlined above, from structural elements such as doors to aspects of broader influence such as hierarchical arrangement, controlled access, and temporal differences in spatial use by various household members permitted the accommodation of occupant and visitor. An awareness of appropriate behaviour by both groups was probably a decisive factor in this mutual compromise which enabled the successful operation of the house, but this seems unfortunately irretrievable from extant evidence.

[44] For controlling views: Pliny 2. 17. 5, 16; 5. 6. 19, 29, 38. For room temperature and breezes: 2. 17. 16, 29.   [45] Ibid. 2. 17. 22–4.

[46] Ibid. 2. 17. 24: 'in hanc ego diaetam cum me recepi, abesse mihi etiam a uilla mea uideor, magnamque eius uoluptatem . . . capio'. In 1. 3. 3 Pliny exhorts Caninius Rufus to withdraw to his suburban villa 'in alto isto pinguique secessu'.

[47] There is another *cubiculum* in this villa 'quod diem clamorem sonum excludit'; but this room is next to a 'cenatio cotidiana amicorum' (5. 6. 21). Presumably, the *cubiculum* was only quiet when the *cenatio* was not being used—another example of temporal differences in room use. Cf. the villa of Sidonius Apollinaris in 5th-cent. Gaul (*Letters* 2. 2. 10).

CONCLUSION

Residents can be found in the house both along points of intersection with visitors, and separate from them. As a product of Roman culture the house was itself an agent in the reiteration of status distinctions, and thus perpetuated the social hierarchy; just as the individual identities of family members were dwarfed by the identity of the patriarch, so their activities in the house itself were subordinated to his needs. In its versatility the Roman house mirrors the heterogeneous population which used it, from the nuclear family to the servile *familia*, and the guests who frequented its doors. Domestic architecture, like written sources, artefacts, and interior decoration, provides clues, but does not fully solve the puzzle, because not all aspects of social practice are reflected in it. To repopulate the house with its invisible occupants it is necessary to characterize as fully as possible, through an integration of text and archaeology, the activities of all household members and guests. A rereading of the textual evidence which takes into consideration the occupant as often as it does the guest might suggest new lines of enquiry. Likewise, a thorough comparison between houses in different parts of the empire might clarify features which are merely local characteristics, and allow the identification of wider shifts in cultural attitudes towards hospitality and spatial use by guests. Such discoveries, even if tentative in nature, would in turn have consequences for our perception of residents and their behaviour in the house. Potential areas of investigation such as these would help to define the evanescent presence of household members, to foster an insight into their use of domestic space, and to help position them within the *domus*. It will not fix them in any room or place, however, for it is the particular genius of the Roman house that such a diversity of activities could occur within one architectural setting, and it is that characteristic which makes an analysis of the *domus* a formidable task.

13

Artefact Distribution and Spatial Function in Pompeian Houses

PENELOPE ALLISON

INTRODUCTION

Research into spatial function of Roman houses has recently become very active. In many studies, when an illustration is needed to validate a textual anecdote, the investigator, usually a historian, will search for an example from a site such as Pompeii. Conversely, other investigators, usually archaeologists, will often scan the texts for an anecdote which may help explain the arrangement of architectural features of an excavated site. It is often difficult to test the appropriateness of such approaches. However, given current wariness of generalizations based on the presumed existence of an example, be it textual or archaeological, such haphazard methodology not only seems unscholarly but can be shown to be a restricted use of the available sources.

As investigators of past activity, archaeologists and ancient historians will never be able to carry out the kind of sampling employed in the experimental sciences. Because they are not dealing with matters of life and death, they also are unlikely to do any particular physical harm to anyone by building up generalizations in this manner. However, while speculation is an aspect which can lead to innovation in ancient history and archaeology, such methodologies can also mislead those who use this material for other purposes. Generalizations and assumptions are often taken as well-researched, known phenomena by anthropologists, architects, modern historians, philosophers, etc. who use aspects of the Greek and Roman world to

The results presented here formed part of my doctoral thesis (Allison 1992b). I am grateful to Prof. Baldassare Conticello, Dr Antonio Varone, Dr Antonio d'Ambrosio, and all the staff of the Soprintendenza archeologica di Pompei for the permission and facilities to carry out this Pompeian research. I wish to offer special thanks to the staff of the magazzino archeologico, Sig. Luigi Matrone, Sig. Franco Striano, and Sig. Ciro Sicigniano for their assistance with the archives. I am also particularly grateful to Ass. Prof. Roland Fletcher who, as my thesis supervisor, offered much useful advice on spatial analysis, and to Dr Peter Brennan for reading a draft of this paper and for offering very valuable comments.

explain or validate their own theories. These generalizations can eventually reach the public domain in a fantastic form which bears little relationship to the information that can be justifiably gleaned from the very limited original data.

To ensure that work is presented in as objective a form as possible, more rigorous methods for assembling all the available data should first be developed, and then each class of data and the relationships between them assessed. I believe it is possible to go a lot further towards a more rigorous investigation and use of archaeological data and consequently a more precise comprehension of the use of spaces in Roman houses. Through a more stringent assessment of the relationship of these data to textual data a more wholistic and reliable understanding of Roman domestic life can be developed.

INVESTIGATIONS OF SPATIAL FUNCTION

To date, scholars have employed textual, structural, and decorative evidence to glean from them information on the use of Roman domestic space. The first class of evidence, the textual, is usually the domain of ancient historians, the latter two, of archaeologists—or more specifically architectural and art historians. The combination of these classes of evidence, by all the above specialists, has been used to provide a wealth of generalized information about the domestic life in the Roman world.

I have elsewhere outlined these classes of evidence and discussed the appropriateness of the current methods for combining them to produce an understanding of Roman domestic life (esp. Allison 1992*b*: 5–20; 1993: 4–8). I will, therefore, not elaborate on this here but will add a few further points.

The works of Vitruvius, Varro, and Pliny have been instrumental in providing information on the names, and sometimes the uses, of spaces in Roman houses. However, little attention has been paid, by those employing these works to this end, to the purposes for which each was written. None of these works was actually intended as a description of Roman domestic life. Vitruvius was an academic architect with ideas and prerequisites about how to build the best Roman houses. To my knowledge he has never actually been credited with building one. Pliny, famed for his writing skills rather than architectural interest, was describing his luxurious villa at Laurentum (2. 17), using terminology and phraseology which he hoped would entice his friend Gallus to visit him there. In the light of such objectives (cf. Drummer: n.d.), attempts to reconstruct the plan of Pliny's villa (cf. Pinon *et al.* 1982: 104–42) would seem fruitless. Varro was concerned with the derivations of Latin words. He writes explicitly about how rooms acquired their names but gives little insight into how so-named rooms might have been used in his day. For example, while rooms around an *atrium* may have continued to be called *cubicula*, *penaria*, or *cenacula* in Varro's day, these names may have had little bearing on their function at that time.

Andrew Wallace-Hadrill, on the institution of patronage (1989: 9), has noted that ancient historians and literary critics are rather cavalier in their treatment of each others' textual data. However, comparable caution is not witnessed when using texts such as the above to gain an insight into the use of space in Roman houses. Still less caution has been taken when using these names for excavated spaces (cf. Wallace-Hadrill 1988: 48), or employing anecdotal information from various other ancient authors to elucidate the activities which might have taken place in such spaces. It is this very combination of architectural and textual remains, in a loose and unproblematic association with modern analogy, that is presenting the impression that we are very familiar with Roman domestic life. This is an oversimplification of the relationship between diverse forms of data.

It might be argued that I am being rather pedantic here and that the only way to gain the objective sought is to become involved in such combinations of diverse evidence. The Roman world, perhaps more so than any other ancient culture, is very rich in its textual and architectural remains. This very richness, both qualitatively and quantitatively, is providing us with more data than we feel we can cope with. Hence, it is instrumental in the production of this too-familiar view of Roman domestic life. And probably because we have such a wealth of textual and architectural material, which can be continuously reworked by different scholars from different perspectives, the archaeological material—the material on archaeological sites which is excavated out of its architectural contexts and used for specialist studies of pottery, glass, metal, etc.—has largely been ignored. To include a contextual study of all this would only bring further complications to an already complex area of study.

However, I feel that this is a gross oversight and a limitation of the available evidence, particularly if we are indeed concerned with the organization of space in a Roman house and with how the different types of inhabitants used that space. The textual information we often employ should be treated with more caution; not only is it largely written under other agendas, but it is also written by a predominantly aristocratic male élite with little concern for the majority of the occupants of a house.

A similar criticism might be levelled at the use of architectural remains to explain household activity. Vitruvius should help to make us only too aware that buildings tend to be constructed within strict, often very traditional, parameters. However, while there will always be a certain amount of traditional use of space in such structures, social change and fashion will often move too quickly for the time that it is possible, or desirable, to knock down and rebuild buildings. I would, therefore, argue that, while the extant architecture of a Roman house will give us an insight into how the architect, or the architectural tradition, intended such a building to function, such use is likely to change considerably over time. We need only look around at our own reuse of, for example, nineteenth-century houses to see how rapidly such functional change can occur without altering a building's structure.

Thus, studies which use a combination of textual and architectural evidence to assess the use of space in Roman houses are not only limited but run the risk of producing a prescriptive, architectural history rather than a truly social history.

POMPEIAN HOUSE CONTENTS

To obtain a more precise understanding of the spatial function in Roman houses, and particularly its more dynamic concepts, we need to look more carefully at the contents, including the fixtures, of excavated houses. Unfortunately, the current state of investigation of most Roman domestic sites prohibits the possibility of using Roman house contents, in general, to establish any possible universals concerning spatial function. However, it has been possible to carry out such an investigation for Pompeii, bearing in mind that the results, at this stage, are applicable only to Pompeii.[1]

For the purposes of this chapter, I propose to treat Pompeii as a prehistoric site. I hope that this will not only illustrate a methodology by which archaeological material from the domestic sphere can be analysed, but also highlight the complexities of the relationships between textual, architectural, and archaeological data. Only when the relationship between the architectural plan and the use of space in Pompeian houses is more fully comprehended in this manner will it be appropriate to treat Pompeii as a historic site, using written texts to elucidate the historical nature of thus identified social patterning.

---

[1] My current research project is to set up databases of other Roman and Etruscan settlement sites so that the distribution of their house contents can also be so examined.

First, I shall briefly summarize the methodology and theoretical framework for my analysis of the contents of thirty *atrium* houses from Pompeii.[2] I shall then present some of the results which illustrate the difficulty of identifying family behaviour or of isolating individual family members in the archaeological record. By using the word *atrium* I would seem to have already taken this study out of the realm of prehistory. However, I shall continue to use such terms (e.g. also *cubiculum*, *tablinum*) as conventional architectural terms, applicable to an identified space in a Pompeian house. I do not intend to add any further meaning to these terms, as used in Roman texts. It should be stressed that these terms, which are now well entrenched in the literature on this subject, are used so that the reader can identify which spaces are being referred to, and not for the purpose of any functional interpretation.

DATA COLLECTION AND INTERPRETIVE PROCEDURE

List of Pompeian houses in the sample:

Casa del Sacello Iliaco (I 6, 4)
House I 6, 8–9
Casa di P. Quadretti Teatrali
 (I 6, 11)
Casa di Stallius Eros (I 6,
 13)
Casa dei Ceii (I 6, 15)
Casa del Sacerdos Amandus
 (I 7, 7)
Casa dell'Efebo (I 7, 10–12)
House I 7, 19
Casa del Menandro (I 10, 4)
Casa del Fabbro (I 10, 7)
House I 10, 8
Casa degli Amanti (I 10, 11)
Casa della Venere in Bikini
 (I 11, 6)
Casa di Trebius Valens (III
 2, 1)
Casa delle Nozze d'Argento
 (V 2, i)

Casa di M. Lucretius Fronto
 (V 4, a)
Casa dei Vettii (VI 15, 1)
House VI 15, 5
Casa del Principe di Napoli
 (VI 15, 8)
Casa degli Amorini Dorati
 (VI 16, 7)
Casa della Ara Massima (VI
 16, 15)
House VI 16, 26
House VIII 2, 14–16
House VIII 2, 26
House VIII 2, 28
House VIII 2, 29–30
House VIII 2, 34
Casa di Giuseppe II (VIII 2,
 39)
House VIII 5, 9
Casa di Iulius Polybius (XI
 13, 1–3)

---

[2] For further detail see Allison (1992*b*: 21–39); Allison (forthcoming).

The choice of the individual Pompeian houses in this sample is dictated by the availability and quality of excavation documentation. Throughout the nineteenth century and until the 1950s, the excavators tended to concentrate their efforts and attentions on the largest houses, ascribed to the upper-middle and upper classes, which might produce more art-works and finds of precious materials. For such houses, exclusively *atrium* houses, the archaeological context and finds provenances have generally been more carefully described in the available documentation than they have for smaller dwellings and commercial buildings. The recorders have also concentrated on the houses which had the most complete assemblages and the best-preserved paintings. Consequently the best-documented houses are likely to be those which may have been fully functioning as domestic, and possibly also commercial/industrial, establishments at the time of the eruption.

A sample of thirty *atrium* houses constitutes a relatively homogeneous architectural group. Each house has its own street entrance and can be seen to be an architectural and functional entity. Also, certain architectural room types occur in each, or most of the houses. With the exception of the Casa della Ara Massima, each house has a garden courtyard, usually peristyled or pseudo-peristyled. The sample includes most types of *atrium* houses (cf. E. M. Evans 1984) which range, in ground-floor area, from approx. 300 sq.m. for the Casa di Stallius Eros to approx. 2,000 sq.m. for the Casa del Menandro.

The sample covers three geographical areas of the town (Fig. 13.1): fifteen houses are in Regions I, III, and IX along the Via dell'Abbondanza, in the eastern quarter; eight are in Regions V and VI in the central northern area; and seven in Region VIII in the south-west quarter. These areas equate roughly to three excavation periods. The houses in the first area constitute the best-documented group, excavated mainly in the 1920s and 1930s with one house, the Casa della Venere in Bikini excavated in the 1950s. One house in this area, the Casa di Iulius Polybius, was excavated in the 1960s and 1970s. The other three houses from Regions I and III and all eight houses from Regions V and VI were excavated between 1890 and 1915. The houses in Region VIII were largely excavated between 1880 and 1890, with some earlier documented exploration in 1767 and 1862. For each period, the excavation techniques have a bearing on the usefulness and reliability of the data (cf. Mouritsen 1988: 49).

The main available documentary sources for information on the excavation of these houses are: the excavation reports, published in

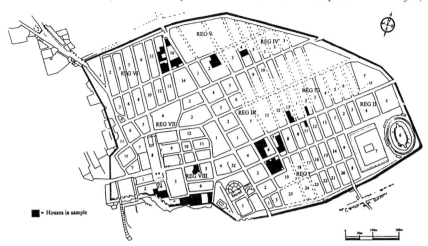

FIG. 13.1. Plan of Pompeii, showing distribution of houses in sample.

the *Notizie degli Scavi di Antichità*; the unpublished 'Giornali degli Scavi', held in the Pompeii archive; and the inventory of the finds brought from the excavation to the Pompeii storerooms. For the houses excavated in the 1880s and 1890s, August Mau also published a separate report in the *Bulletino dell'Istituto di Corrispondenza Archeologica*. The excavation notes compiled by Giuseppe Fiorelli in *Pompeianarum Antiquitatum Historia* provide information on exploration prior to 1860. The extant houses themselves, with fixtures and excavated material not removed to the storerooms but which corresponds to the finds recorded in the 'Giornali degli Scavi' (e.g. uninscribed amphorae, building material, stone furniture, and plaster casts), are another source of information.

The 'Giornali degli Scavi' follow the day-to-day excavations and are potentially the least interpreted source. The inventory of finds was written up after the 'Giornali degli Scavi', usually copying directly, but not always precisely, from the latter and only including those finds which were kept in the storerooms. The earliest published reports in the *Notizie degli Scavi*, from 1876, consist of a direct publication of the daily notes in the 'Giornali degli Scavi'. However, from the 1920s these publications consisted of a synthesis and an interpretation of the excavation, with the finds' information relegated to a list of what were considered the more notable finds, imprecisely provenanced, at the end of the publication of each house. This list was taken from the inventory and incorporated many of its errors.

This is a brief summary of availability of the excavation information on Pompeian house contents. A great deal of material, especially organic material, has undoubtedly gone unrecorded. This is particularly true of the earliest excavations, but even the later ones, such as those immediately after World War II, were not always very carefully executed. Therefore, to extract information on Pompeian house contents has been an exercise in gleaning information from less than perfect data. However, this does not mean that Pompeian house contents are unusable for studying the use of domestic space and that, as has always been the case, they should be rejected (cf. Allison 1992a). Rather, it has meant that a large sample was required to identify consistent patterns which could take into account these limitations and imperfections because, even with these limitations, Pompeii still provides a wealth of archaeological detail and varieties of evidence, surpassing those of other Roman settlement excavations, and probably of almost all other settlement sites in the world.

Thus, the sources above were used to compile a house-by-house and room-by-room database of these finds. By forming a computer database with some 8,000 entries it was possible to organize this material to facilitate the search for meaningful patterns of distribution. It cannot be assumed, however, that patterns so identified will immediately produce information on spatial function under some concept of normal living conditions. Despite the popular view of the frozen moment (e.g. Will 1979: 34) and the 'Pompeii Premise' of the new archaeologists (e.g. Schiffer 1985), it is apparent that many of the distribution patterns witnessed for the contents of these Pompeian houses were the results either of the abandonment processes before and during the AD 79 eruption (cf. Allison 1992b: 86–97; 1995a) or of disturbance between this eruption and the documented excavations (Allison 1992b: 37–9).

Nevertheless, it was possible to isolate patterns of conformity between specific room types and contents which it seemed feasible to attribute to habitual room use in Pompeii. As mentioned above, the traditional textual nomenclature will not be used to indicate room type. Rather, room type is based on architectural phenomena, the traditional names included in parentheses for ease of identification. The rooms in the sample have been divided into twenty-one types based on: location, relative to the *atrium*/peristyle complex; size, relative to house size; through-routes; and functions defined by fixtures (e.g. hearths, water catchment pool, etc.). Some of these are further subdivided according to whether or not their walls had extant painted decoration:

1. Main entranceway (vestibules/*fauces*)
2. Room leading directly off main entranceway
3. Covered forecourt (*atrium*)
4. Small closed room off covered forecourt (*cubiculum*)
5. Open room off covered forecourt (*ala*)
6. Medium/large room off covered forecourt (*triclinium*)
7. Open room leading to garden (*tablinum*)
8. Long, narrow internal corridor
9. Main garden or peristyle (also terraces)
10. Medium/large closed room (off garden without view) (*triclinium*)
11. Medium/large open room (off garden with view) (*oecus/exedra*)
12. Small closed room off garden
13. Small open room off garden
14. Room with cooking hearth (or associated room)
15. Latrine (entire room)
16. Service areas outside the *atrium*/peristyle complex
17. Stairway
18. Back entrance/service court or secondary gardens
19. Room at front of house open to street (shop)
20. Bath area
21. Upper storey

While the patterns of what constitutes habitual behaviour should have some consistency, it is to be borne in mind that considerable variability is likely to exist from house to house, particularly considering the range of house sizes and their numbers of rooms or internal spaces. This variability may be related both to the social status of the household and to the cycle of domestic change. Built into assessments of patterns of normality are a number of assumptions. In the first instance, while it is not always possible to ascertain the precise functions of particular artefacts or assemblages, general distinctions can be made between domestic material that is luxury (e.g. decorated bronze and silver vessels, cf. Fig. 13.2), and utilitarian (e.g. pottery, glass, and non-decorated bronze vessels, cf. Fig. 13.3); between objects which are seemingly more public (e.g. large-scale sculpture and marble furniture, cf. e.g. Jashemski 1979: fig. 200; Strocka 1984: 61; Maiuri 1929: 394 fig. 22) and those which appear to be more personal or private (e.g. small luxury items, toilet items, and items of apparel, cf. Fig. 13.4); and between material that is utilitarian domestic and commercial/industrial (e.g. building material, agricultural equipment, cf. Fig. 13.5). It is assumed that a room with lavishly painted decoration was intended for a formal rather than a utilitarian function. Such a room would not generally have been

FIG. 13.2. (*left*) Luxury domestic material, and FIG. 13.3. (*right*) Utilitarian domestic material, all from Casa del Menandro, Pompeii, 1st century AD.

intended for commercial/industrial activities or for the storing of construction or utilitarian materials.

Large heavy objects which are less easily moved than others (e.g. furniture such as cupboards and large chests) are less likely to be relocated in periods of abrupt disruption and are, therefore, the most useful for a study which assesses habitual room use. Extensive collections of smaller, more mobile, or losable items are also more relevant than isolated finds of small objects. While artefact assemblages only indicate final room use (which may—but need not be— that during the actual AD 79 eruption), the predominant patterns across the sample of more permanent items, or of particular collections, ought to provide information on the habitual use of a particular room type.

On the other hand, small objects (e.g. coins, buttons, beads) are likely to move or be moved during volcanic deposition, and during a disaster valuables may be moved from locations considered dangerous, or taken by fugitives. Unless significant patterns of this type of material are isolated they are not particularly useful in a study of spatial function under normal living conditions. Utilitarian artefacts might not be expected to be moved under hazardous conditions.

Absence is especially problematic for this study. While it is well known that the volcanic environment in which Pompeii was buried

FIG. 13.4. (*left*) Personal/private material, Casa del Menandro, Pompeii, 1st century AD.

FIG. 13.5. Commercial/industrial material, Casa del Menandro, Pompeii, 1st century AD.

preserved most material, including some organic, and left cavities to indicate the existence of other organic artefacts, much was either not recorded or possibly even removed after the eruption. Of particular importance is the absence of traces of wooden furniture. However, given the interest in metal remains (Allison 1992*b*: 24), the evidence provided in room HH in the Casa di Iulius Polybius, where beds of simple wooden slats were joined with nails (Oliva n.d.: VIII 58, 69), and the reconstructed cupboard in the *atrium* of the Casa dei Ceii, during excavations in 1914, it might be assumed that the complete absence of recorded finds, particularly in houses excavated this century, indicates that the room in question was empty at the time of the eruption.

Rooms which show evidence of post-eruption disturbance tended not to be completely devoid of finds, the looters having little interest in metal fragments, pottery, or glass (Allison 1992*b*: 37–9). Therefore, consistent patterns of absence can be regarded as significant (cf. Ross 1982: 99 on absence of evidence as evidence of absence: though of sites rather than artefacts in her case).

The lack of recording of organic material has also prohibited an assessment of whether containers were full or empty at the time of the eruption. There are only a few recorded instances of organic contents inside vessels which are actually diagnostic of whether these containers were in use. In general, the presence of the containers themselves, rather than organic contents, has been considered as evidence of use.

Analogies with our own and other societies may assist towards a comprehension of location and dislocation, or expected and accepted 'normal' behaviour, but this approach needs to be treated with some caution (cf. Kent 1990: 5–6). Nevertheless, it might be assumed that certain assemblages are 'normally' related and others are not. Attempts are made to break free of the assumption that a serviced, pre-industrial house would be more orderly than a contemporary urban dwelling. Such an assumption, which has pervaded studies of Pompeian living conditions (e.g. Maiuri 1933; McKay 1977: 30–1), can be seen as an inheritance from the nineteenth- and early twentieth-century excavators, who perceived the Pompeian houses as comparable to their own serviced establishments, leaving us with the illusion that we have a good understanding of the organization and normal living conditions in a Roman house. The fact that it has always been possible actually to enter Pompeian houses, but that they have been left devoid of all but a few selected contents, may be seen to contribute to this perspective. An investigator has been able to visit the empty shell but has drawn on his or her own resources to conceptualize it as a functioning establishment (cf. Wallace-Hadrill 1988: 63; J. R. Clarke 1991: 1–12).

Traces of a late twentieth-century model must, irrevocably, pervade my own work. For example, separation of industrial material from domestic may be misleading for a pre-industrial society. But I have at least attempted to be cognizant of my own prejudices. By using the available material evidence, this study has the potential to be less subjective than previous works. I hope that it also has greater comparative breadth, is less ethnocentric, and is not so overburdened with its own assumptions about living standards.

ROOM TYPES AND THEIR ASSEMBLAGES

The following is a list of the twenty-one room types and their assemblages. There is not the space here to give full details (cf. Allison 1992*b*). But I will provide a brief summary of the kinds of assemblages found in them.[3]

1. Main entranceway (*fauces/uestibulum*). As might be expected these corridors were generally devoid of finds, save door-fittings. Of the thirty houses in the sample only eight had fixed masonry benches outside the main entranceway, e.g. Casa dei Ceii (Michel 1990: fig. 59). These seats are thus relatively infrequent in this sample which consists of the larger, and presumably more noble, Pompeian houses. In addition, they are not concentrated in the largest and most elaborate houses within the sample.

2. Room leading directly off main entranceway. There were only nine such rooms in the sample. Their assemblages were fairly utilitarian domestic, possibly commercial/industrial. One had shelving suggesting a storeroom. The masonry seat in another was the only indication that any of these rooms may have had a formal function. All but room 2 of the Casa del Fabbro, which was a little further into the house than other rooms in this type, were devoid of painted decoration. This latter room also had finds which were of a less utilitarian domestic, possibly personal, character than other rooms of this type.

3. Covered forecourt (*atrium*). Because of the nature of the sample chosen for this study, each house has at least one covered forecourt (*atrium*) and five houses have two, making a total of thirty-five in the sample.[4] Aside from the central catchment pool (*impluuium*), household shrines (*lararia*), either in the form of an *aedicula*, a painting of household deities on the wall, or a combination of these, were the most frequent fixture to be found in these forecourts. Even so, they were only found in seven of them, a fairly small proportion of the total. Two niches (in courtyard O of the Casa di Iulius Polybius and *atriolum* 41 of the Casa del Menandro) have also been referred to as *lararia*. Such niches occur in a variety of locations throughout Pompeii and Pompeian houses. It has yet to be demonstrated that they all had a religious purpose. They very probably served a variety of domestic functions.

---

[3] Room nos. largely follow Bragantini *et al.* (1981–6). For fuller list see Allison (1992*b*: figs. 2–31).

[4] Tables 1 and 2 in Allison (1993) have been incorrectly laid out. For correct groupings see Allison (1992*b*: 42–6). For a summary of the furnishings of this room type, see also Allison (1993: 4–8).

Fixed bases, in or near the catchment pool, possibly for supporting tables, statuary, and fountain fittings, were found in the forecourts of only two houses in the sample. However, there were another ten houses from which the remains of luxury furniture (e.g. marble tables, statuary, basins) were reported. These bases, household shrines, and luxury furnishings seem quite commonplace in these forecourts (e.g. in the forecourt of the Casa di Obellius Firmus: Sogliano 1905: figs. 2 and 6), but they were not a prerequisite. It is illogical to ascribe the lack of marble furniture, in *atria* with a plethora of other finds (e.g. Casa del Sacello Iliaco, Casa dei Quadretti teatrali; and House VI 15, 5), to post-eruption disturbance. The latter house in particular seems to have been a substantial establishment which might well have been expected to have had such fittings.

Puteals, or cistern head covers, were found in the forecourts of five houses in the sample, one in each of the forecourts of the Casa di Iulius Polybius. Of the thirty-one puteals in the sample, then, only six were recorded in these forecourts. Thus, like the above marble furnishings, these were not as prolific here as they were in other parts of the house.

By far the most frequent furnishings in these forecourts were wooden cupboards and chests, of which there could be at least four pieces in one forecourt (cf. Casa dei Quadretti teatrali: Maiuri 1929: 401 fig. 26; 404 fig. 29; de Vos 1990: 371 fig. 19*b*). Evidence of such furniture was reported in a forecourt of at least eighteen of the sampled houses. These cupboards were mainly used for domestic storage, of fairly utilitarian quality. A few contained luxury items, and some seemed to contain both domestic and industrial/commercial material. The majority of these containers can be shown to be cupboards, with upright doors, or small wooden chests. Strongboxes, such as those in the Casa dei Vettii, are a rarity.

Weaving also seems to have been an activity associated with these forecourts, with evidence for it (predominantly in the form of loomweights) recorded in six forecourts in the sample. The remains of storage amphorae were found in eleven forecourts in this sample, a number of which did not include domestic storage.

Thus, the most pronounced pattern for the furnishings of these forecourts demonstrates that they were cluttered with domestic storage in wooden cupboards, with little evidence of elaborate containers for household valuables. A smaller proportion had display furniture in the central area. This lack of display furniture indicates that in most cases in Pompeian houses the forecourt generally had a fairly utilitarian function, acting as a service court around which the mundane household activities revolved.

If service areas can be identified by their lack of painted decoration, then the above conclusion is also borne out in the wall finishes of some of these forecourts. At the time of excavation, only about 30 per cent of forecourts in the sample had any remains of extant wall-painting. The others were either decorated with a simple red socle and white upper zone or were only coarsely plastered or completed undecorated. While one might attempt to argue that coarsely plastered or undecorated forecourts were in the process of redecoration, it has been observed that at least half of them also contained cupboards and quantities of domestic apparatus, implying that they functioned as part of a domestic establishment in this condition. Others seem to have been used for more industrial/commercial activities rather than to be in the course of refurbishing.

4. Small closed room off covered forecourt (*atrium-cubiculum*). This is one of the largest groups of room types in Pompeian houses, consisting of 129 examples in this sample. For this analysis they have been divided into two categories—decorated and undecorated.

(*a*) Decorated: of the sixty-six decorated examples, thirty-seven had reported contents. About two-thirds of the decorated rooms from the houses in Regions I and IX, the most recently excavated of the sample, had some finds at least. Only half the rooms in houses from Regions V and VI had finds, and finds were reported from only five of the fifteen rooms from the older excavations in Region VIII. It is very probable that the lack of material, in the latter two groups, is due to poor recording and that decorated rooms of this type more usually had some contents. The exceptions are those in the Casa dei Quadretti teatrali where four out of five such rooms were empty, despite the wealth of finds from the forecourt itself and despite the fact that the latter had more evidence of post-eruption disturbance than these surrounding rooms.

Cupboards or large chests with a range of domestic contents, both utilitarian and of finer quality, were found in only four rooms of this type. This suggests that the type of domestic storage and activity witnessed in the forecourt was not usually carried out in the surrounding decorated rooms.

More common were assemblages which consisted variously of the remains of small chests and caskets; a variety of bronze serving, pouring, and storage vessels; pottery vessels which were usually small and of fine quality, but occasionally included large amphorae; and items related to dress, toilet, needlework, and lighting. These were found, generally in small quantities, in twelve to fourteen such rooms in the sample.

The consistent pattern of limited quantities of this material suggests that the items were used in these locations rather than stored. From their character they seem to be related to personal domestic activities. For example, objects associated with more communal domestic activities, such as cooking, eating, and drinking, are apparently not represented.

Of all the decorated rooms of this type, four had so-called bed recesses but no other finds. On the other hand, six other rooms of this type contained evidence of bedding but only one room with bedding evidence had an associated recess. In three, possibly four, rooms which contained the types of personal items mentioned above, evidence of beds or couches was also found. It is probable that evidence of bedding went unrecorded in the earlier excavations but this is unlikely for many of those of the twentieth century. Thus, while some of these rooms have direct evidence of permanent or semi-permanent sleeping activity during the final occupation phase, a higher proportion of them do not. No direct relationship between evidence of bedding and recesses can be established (cf. Allison 1995*b*).

The prevailing pattern among the small, closed, decorated rooms off the forecourt suggests that the usual activities in these rooms were related to seemingly private activities. However it should be noted that actual evidence of permanent bedding is relatively rare.

(*b*) Undecorated: of forty-eight rooms of this type, which were undecorated or had only the white plaster or the simplest painted decoration, contents were recorded in thirty-four. Another fifteen had only fixtures and no loose finds: two had recesses; eight had evidence of shelving, one being one of those with a recess, and six had other fixtures, such as stairways and niches.

The lack of finds in rooms with shelving, presumably intended for storage, in four houses in Region VIII may be the result of bad recording. However this lack is noteworthy in the Casa degli Amanti where the decorated rooms 4 and 7 around this forecourt did contain finds. This is in opposition to the more usual pattern.

In two rooms the recorded finds were door-fittings, implying that the excavators were unlikely to have overlooked any contents, and, therefore, that these rooms were probably devoid of contents.

Thus, only eighteen rooms of this type had contents necessarily related to their final occupation phase. Four such rooms had evidence of shelving with copious, often various, domestic utensils, and six had shelving but with more utilitarian/industrial storage.

Rooms with shelving, off the forecourt, were, therefore, used for both domestic and industrial storage. The difference in storage type would not seem to be dependent on the size of the house but more probably on its overall condition prior to the eruption. One room of this type had a recess and a domestic assemblage, comparable to tha*ı* usually found in decorated rooms of this type.

5. Open room off covered forecourt (*ala*). Twenty-five rooms have been categorized as this type with contents recorded in ten. In two of them, these contents consisted of door-fittings and isolated coins, implying that the lack of other recorded contents was not a result of bad reporting but more probably an indication that these rooms were indeed empty.

Storage vessels, usually of glass but also of pottery, were found in three such rooms in the sample. A built-in cupboard with shelving was recorded in another and building or industrial material and lamps were found in two others. While considerable quantities of lamps were found in two such rooms, one of these also contained fragmentary sculptural pieces, implying disrupted circumstances. A small casket was found in one such room and another had a bed.

Thus, there is no clear pattern, but in two of the houses the type of storage found in the forecourts appeared to continue in these rooms. Also, room F in the Casa della Ara Massima may have replaced the forecourt in this role and the cupboard in room h of the Casa di Giuseppe II might be for a similar activity.

The presence of building material in two of the rooms of this type indicates that they were not performing their usual function. The bed in room r of House I 7, 19 may also have been placed in makeshift conditions during repair work.

6. Medium-sized/large room off corner of covered forecourt (*triclinium*). Rooms categorized under this type are generally long, narrow, and closed, usually with a narrow doorway in the end of one long wall. They do not occur in all houses and some houses could have two. In many cases they appear to have been converted to open on to the garden. In such instances, therefore, they have been categorized as room type 10 (see below).

Of the thirty-four rooms in this category, twenty-four had contents. In three, these consisted of recesses but with no other finds to demonstrate how these recesses may have been used. Other types of fixtures—e.g. a small oven (*fornello*), understair cupboards, shelving, niches—were found in eight such rooms. With one possible exception, the fixtures indicate that these rooms had fairly utilitarian functions. As some rooms with these fixtures also had wall-decoration it might be implied that the use of this room type was not static throughout the life of these houses. Shelving with storage was witnessed in two such rooms, while one contained a mixed assemblage with building material. In another, building material alone was reported. Finds of bone hinges, jewellery, and toilet and weighing items were reported from three such rooms but it is not certain that these did not fall from the upper floor. Evidence of weaving and cupboards or chests containing glass and pottery storage vessels, bronze pouring vessels, toilet and needlework items, and marble fragments were variously recorded in four such rooms. A similar assemblage, but including fishing and weighing equipment and evidence of food, was found in room G in the Casa della Ara Massima. Fragments of furniture and cooking and storage vessels were found in two such rooms, one of which had been decorated in Fourth Style.

It is difficult to find a prevalent pattern in this room type but the combination of decoration and utilitarian fixtures, cooking vessels, and building material suggests that many of them were in a deteriorated state prior to the eruption. This state seems more pronounced in this room type than in the others so far studied in this part of the house. If any pattern is discernible at all, it is that these rooms contained chests or cupboards and a mixture of domestic paraphernalia.

7. Open room leading to garden, or open-sided room opposite main entranceway (*tablinum*). Of the thirty-three rooms of this type, sixteen were recorded with contents. Evidence of storage cupboards and chests were found in eight of them, but it is notable that four of these were undecorated and that, in five of the eight examples, these cupboards/chests included apparently haphazard storage (i.e. combinations of domestic and luxury items with furniture and marble fragments and building material). It might be argued that such rooms, when decorated, were not normally used for storage activity but had a formal function. However the frequent occurrence of storage in rooms which were decorated, some in Fourth Style, implies that this was not necessarily an activity under makeshift conditions, at least in the final occupation phase. One such room contained both built-in cupboards, a wooden chest, and an assemblage consisting of glass and pottery storage vessels, and statuary. In another the assemblage in a cupboard was also more domestic, consisting of items concerned with toilet, gaming, fishing, needlework, and dress. Another such room had finds of a similar character.

In three rooms of this type the contents included a bed or couch. This is not a significant number, but it is proportionately similar to the occurrence of beds in closed rooms off the forecourt. In one room a brazier, bronze vessels for cooking over a hearth, and bronze jars were found. In another were found two chests full of pottery bowls and lamps, in quantities and in a state of preservation which might be considered commercial. Weights and loomweights were found in one such room and building material was found in another. These latter three might be seen to have had a more utilitarian/industrial function as witnessed in the other rooms of these three houses.

The prevailing pattern for this type of room is that it contained cupboards and chests for domestic storage. However these contents may only have been placed here in the later life of the city and may not usually have been found here in earlier periods. The presence of beds or couches is noteworthy although not significantly representative to indicate that these rooms were used for sleeping or dining, under normal conditions. The presence of a brazier in one such room might seem to echo the evidence for cooking (cf. Salza Prina Ricotti 1978–80: 240–1) in the peristyle area, as indicated below.

8. Long, narrow internal corridor. There are fifty-seven examples of this room type in the sample. Twelve had fixtures (e.g. stairways and understair cupboards—one containing an oven—cisterns, hearths, latrines, recesses, niches, shelves, masonry tubs) which indicated that they served another function as well as that of a passageway. Loose finds were reported from fifteen, in two of which these consisted of door-fittings and losable finds only. The understair cupboard in corridor 3 in the Casa dei Vettii contained horse harness. Other finds made in these corridors included a bronze basin, a chest containing a variety of mainly fine domestic items and building material. Storage amphorae were found in three such corridors.

These corridors would, no doubt, normally be clear for access. Nevertheless, storage vessels seem to have been habitually left in these corridors, particularly in service or industrial/commercial parts of the house. It is highly improbable that the recesses in corridor 14 of House I 10, 8 and in corridor K of House VI 16, 26 (Allison 1995*b*: fig. 6) had been used for beds. The finds associated with the latter imply that they were used for storage.

9. Main garden or peristyle (also terraces). At least one movable find was reported from each garden area in the twenty-three most recently excavated houses in the sample which had a garden. Lack of such finds in the houses in Region VIII is more than likely attributable to poor recording methods.

The garden is divided into two areas—the colonnaded ambulatory and the open garden or terrace. Eleven of the gardens in the sample had fixtures such as a pool and fountain, statue-bases, and a dining area, either a masonry or wooden structure, e.g. Casa del'Efebo (Maiuri 1927: pl. V; Jashemski 1979: fig. 145), while sculpture or marble furniture possibly was recorded in either the garden or the ambulatory of nine, possibly ten, houses, e.g. in Casa degli Amorini

Dorati (Seiler 1992: figs. 205–8); Casa dei Vettii (Warscher 1948: 4 nos. 213–14). These types of furnishings, found in a total of fourteen, possibly fifteen, such gardens, suggest the role of the garden as a display and possibly an entertainment area. It is notable that the fixtures tend to be found in the larger, often fully peristyle gardens. Sculpture and marble furnishings can also be found in the gardens of smaller, presumably less affluent houses. Other garden fixtures include *aediculae*, found in either ambulatory or garden areas of four houses, e.g. Casa di Prinicipe di Napoli (Strocka 1984: fig. 126); Casa degli Amorini Dorati (Seiler 1992: fig. 292), and smaller niches found in the garden areas of seven houses. Puteals were reported in fourteen garden areas and are thus more frequently found in here than in forecourts. Only one sundial, in garden F in Casa degli Amorini Dorati, was definitely found in a garden context.

Stairways are recorded in gardens and ambulatories of five houses, none of which had the more formal furnishings discussed above. Amphorae were common in both gardens and ambulatories, being found in these areas in twelve to thirteen houses in the sample. While these amphorae were not generally found in the gardens which had formal furnishings, they could be found in the ambulatories of such gardens. Large storage jars (*dolii*) were also present in four garden areas, but generally in those which seem to have been converted for a commercial/industrial purpose, rather than in those with formal furnishings, e.g. House I 7, 19 (Maiuri 1929: 369 fig. 8). Fragmentary furniture, industrial and building material were found in the garden areas of six houses. In two garden areas the skeletons of tortoises were found. One of these gardens also had a fruit-picking ladder (Jashemski 1979: fig. 42). Apparently a kennel was built in the garden of another house (Maiuri 1929: 394). Scattered domestic utensils (e.g. bronze vessels, lighting, toilet, etc.) were recorded from five gardens in the sample. They seem to be dislocated items but it is difficult to ascertain whether this was a pre- or post-eruption condition. Eight, possibly ten, ambulatories contained chests and cupboards, usually with domestic contents, but sometimes also with tools, weaving implements, etc. This type of furnishing seems quite normal, particularly as the houses in which it occurs sometimes had formal garden furniture as well. This is reminiscent of the kind of domestic multi-activity seen in the forecourt area. Braziers and other cooking evidence were also found in the ambulatory areas of five houses in the sample. This type of outdoor cooking might have been a normal activity as braziers were also recorded in rooms off the garden area. Large terracotta basins, possibly for washing, were found in two garden areas, e.g. Casa degli Amanti (Jashemski 1979: fig. 88).

In summary, while many garden areas have a formal display or entertainment fixtures and were furbished with luxury furniture and statuary, the accompanying ambulatories bear witness (as in the forecourts) to busy daily domestic activities being carried out in this area. It is also notable that many of these gardens, especially those which have little or no formal furnishings, appear to have been under repair or converted for a more industrial/commercial use. There appears to be a general correspondence between gardens which had amphorae, *dolii*, and building/industrial material. The most obvious exception is the Casa degli Amorini Dorati, perhaps demonstrating overlaying of different activities. Cooking with braziers in this area, in either situation, seems not uncommon.

10. Large/medium-sized closed room off garden/terrace but without good view (*triclinium*). There are twenty rooms of this type. Of those in the twenty-three most recently excavated houses, all but five such rooms had contents. Five, possibly six, of those which did have contents seemed to contain the remains of a chest, or possibly even a cupboard. Where these pieces of furniture also had contents they appear to have consisted of utilitarian items (e.g. cooking pots, storage vessels, and scales) or to be related to toilet and dress. With the one possible exception, all these rooms are decorated in Fourth Style. Therefore this kind of storage is either normal for a room so decorated, or relates to a phase subsequent to its Fourth Style decoration.

Possible couch remains were found in two rooms of this type and lamps were found in another two. Evidence of a hearth and a brazier were found in one room and there may also have been the remains of a brazier in another. This is commensurate with the number of braziers already recorded in peristyle areas and, possibly, may be a further indication of cooking in this area. Other fixtures in such rooms included a stairway, a high recess (height 1.3m.), and shelving.

A precise architectural distinction between this room type and the following (room type 11) is not always clear in Pompeian houses and particularly in the published plans. Therefore, the contents patterns of both types will be assessed together.

11. Medium-sized/large open-fronted room, either off garden/ terrace with window or wide entranceway giving view of garden, or on lower floor (*oecus/exedra*). Fifty-three rooms have been categorized as this type. They include the spacious rooms on the lower floor of the houses of Region VIII which must have commanded a view over the Sarno River and the Bay of Naples. Contents were recorded in twenty-four of them and another seven had fixtures which help identify their function.

A fountain is located in one such room and recesses, both short (c.37cm.–1.47m.) and long (c.2.2–2.4m.), were found in six. Thus there would appear to be proportionately many more recesses in this room type than there were in the small closed rooms around the forecourt. Other fixtures found in rooms of this type include a niche, shelving, and a structure, reputedly a table. If these latter two rooms had once had a formal function then these fixtures indicate that they had subsequently been downgraded.

Evidence of couches or beds and tables was found in eight such rooms and bronze vessels and bronze lamps were found in six. A close correspondence between the rooms which contained these two classes of material, which might have been dining equipment, was noted. Remains of chests, cupboards, and utilitarian domestic and/or industrial utensils were found in seven, possibly eleven, such rooms. This is reminiscent of the predominant pattern observed in the medium-sized/large closed rooms off the garden. The high proportion of such contents, including some overlap with rooms which also contained dining equipment, suggests that the storage of this material in such rooms may have been normal. However some overlay of activity might have occurred during later disruption.

Pottery vessels and other utilitarian contents were found in seven rooms of this type. The presence of these finds might be taken to suggest downgrading of the room's use if it were not for the above observation that chests of such material were common in this room type. Personal and toilet items were found in two such rooms, but both of these rooms seem to have been downgraded. Fragmentary statuary and other marble fragments were found in four of these rooms. The location of this material might suggest salvaging either before or during the final eruption (Allison 1993). Building material was found in three rooms of this type indicating that these rooms were also not performing their normal function at the time of the eruption.

There is more evidence of a relationship between recesses and the presence of dining couches or beds in this room type than in the closed rooms around the forecourt. Given the potential lack of evidence for such furnishings, their occurrence in at least eight of the rooms of this type implies the use of the latter as a dining room.

From this study there would seem sufficient evidence to confirm that rooms of this type, and type 10, were used for dining. In room type 10 there is also evidence of cooking having been carried out. However the most predominant pattern is that these dining rooms were also used for the storage of equipment which is not necessarily fine tableware. The persistence of this pattern suggests that this was probably not just an activity during disrupted circumstances.

12. Small closed room either off garden/terrace or on lower floor. As with the small closed rooms off the forecourt, these rooms have been divided into those which have painted decoration and those which do not. There are fourteen examples, in the houses in Region VIII, for which no documentation of the decoration is available.

(*a*) Decorated: of the thirty-four rooms of this type which have documented painted decoration, contents were reported in only eleven: household shrines are found in two; recesses in three; the remains of possible beds and wooden objects were recorded in one; cupboards and chests were found in two; tools were found in two; luxury furniture, statuary, bronze, glass, and pottery (serving?) vessels and lighting equipment were found in two such rooms; bronze or pottery vessels (including cooking), an altar, lamps, tools, and marble fragments were found in two; utilitarian material such as amphorae, pottery vessels, stone basins and mortars, spinning and weaving implements, and tools were reported in four such decorated rooms; a mixture of items related to washing and weaving and luxury activities were found in two others; shelving was found attached to, and therefore defacing, the decoration of two, possibly three such rooms; and building material was found in one.

In general, therefore, it is very difficult to find a predominant assemblage pattern for the decorated examples of this room type. There is a considerable mixture of material, much of a utilitarian type which might seem strange for small decorated rooms off a formal garden area.

(*b*) Undecorated: thirty-six rooms of this type have been recorded as having no painted decoration. A number of these had function-related fixtures: a stairway is located in five such rooms; latrines are found in two; small niches were located in another two; high cupboard recesses (*c*.1–2m. in height) were recorded in two such rooms; and shelving is located in nine such rooms. The niches were likely to have been used for storage rather than to have had religious significance (see above). The same might also apply to the niche in the decorated room s in the Casa di Trebius Valens.

Utilitarian domestic contents (i.e. large weights and amphorae) were found in two of these rooms and similar utilitarian material (weights, scales, harness(?), weaving equipment, amphorae, and mortars) were found in eight, possibly nine, such rooms, none of which had shelving. However, in three of these, marble fragments or fragments of sculpture were included, implying disrupted circumstances. One room with shelving had finer quality material, while another included a mixture of both utilitarian and luxury finds. Contents seemingly related to bathing and toilet activities, sometimes with an associated chest, were found in three, possibly four, such rooms. A chest was possibly recorded in one room, and a casket of jewellery in another, the latter perhaps dropped during the final eruption.

In these undecorated rooms, there are no recesses of the type found in decorated rooms and no evidence of beds was recorded. As might be expected, the undecorated examples of this type had more fixtures related to utilitarian functions, such as stairway, latrines, and shelving. While shelving also occurs in the decorated rooms, there is a predominance of storage evidence, mainly fairly utilitarian and sometimes in chests, in the undecorated examples. Where storage in decorated rooms is reported, it tends to be luxury storage but mixed storage could occur in both decorated and undecorated rooms. There was also a notable presence of contents seemingly related to bathing or washing, toilet activities, and weaving.

The number and use of these types of rooms will obviously vary according to the size and status of the house. Consequently they are likely to be more sensitive to changed living conditions than other room types. Some of the anomalies in this study are no doubt related to the proposed deteriorated circumstances prior to the final eruption. The predominant pattern is that the undecorated rooms were storage areas of a variety of material, not excluding utilitarian and bulk storage in this garden area. While bed evidence is rare, the contents of some undecorated as well as decorated rooms imply that both could be used for private activities.

13. Small open room, either off garden/terrace or on lower floor. Fourteen rooms have been categorized as this type. Eight of them had recorded finds. Of these: a household shrine with associated statuary was found in one; braziers and chests were found in three; pottery vessels and lamps were found in another; and bathing and toilet material was found in another. Building material was also found in two of these rooms. The sample is admittedly small but rooms of this type appear to repeat assemblages found either in the ambulatories of the peristyles, e.g. braziers (cf. Maiuri 1933: fig. 45) and chests, or in the small closed rooms—i.e. private activities. The shrine and statuary in area 25 of the Casa del Menandro (Maiuri 1933: figs. 48–9) seem in keeping with the religious evidence noted in the main garden areas of other houses.

14. Room with cooking hearth, or associated room ('kitchen' area). By definition, rooms of this type have a built-in hearth, e.g. the Casa dei Vettii (Sogliano 1898: 266 fig. 13), or are dependent on a room so furbished. They are not restricted to a particular location within the house-plan. At least one such room is documented in each of the houses in the sample, with three exceptions.

The downgraded condition of the Casa di Stallius Eros and the presence of a circular hearth in the forecourt may explain the lack of such a room in this house. In House I 10, 8 there appears to be a cooking hearth in corridor 9 (Elia 1934: 315 fig. 27) but in the Casa della Ara Massima the lack of a seemingly necessary fixture is noteworthy.

Seven houses had more than one room which apparently served as a 'kitchen'. The inclusion of more than one 'kitchen' is not directly related to the size of the establishment. It may be an indication of a house having been divided into separate apartments. Other possibilities are that these 'kitchens' may have had different functions or that one may have replaced another chronologically.

In fifteen, possibly seventeen, cases latrines are found in, or immediately off, these rooms. Basins or sinks were also located in nine, possibly ten, of them. Niches and paintings for household shrines were found in or near seven such rooms. Niches with no painted evidence to indicate a religious significance were found in two. Other fixtures such as stairways, seats, tables, platforms, podia, and baking ovens were found in eleven. A high recess (height 1.65m.) is located in room xi, off the 'kitchen' of the Casa dei Vettii and room 7 in the Casa dell'Efebo has two long low recesses (one 2.2m. long and 65cm. high, and one 3.68m. long and 45cm. high).

Tripods, marble vessel supports, bronze and pottery food-preparing vessels, grinding stones, and weights were found in eighteen, possibly twenty, rooms of this type. Truncated amphorae, presumed by the excavators to have been used as vessel supports or for cooking, were found in four. Tools, lamps, fragments of sculpture, and puteals were variously included with the cooking material in eight, possibly nine, such rooms. Other bronze and glass vessels, unrelated to food preparation, and perhaps a chest, were found in three, possibly four, such rooms.

Thus, the fixtures of a 'kitchen' area frequently included a latrine and a sink, as well as a cooking hearth. A variety of other fixtures such as tables, seats, and ovens was common. While household shrines were found in this area they were only recorded in seven of the thirty-six examples in the sample. Utensils which might be expected in such an area (tripods, vessel stands, bronze cooking pots, and other bronze and pottery food preparation vessels) were reported in some sixteen of these areas. Truncated amphorae were found in four of them.

15. Latrine as entire room. As noted above, latrines were frequently located in 'kitchens'. Of the ten cases in the sample where it was a separate room, six are next to the kitchen. This was no

346 *Artefacts and Spatial Function in Pompeii*

doubt related to the drainage system (cf. Jansen 1991). Besides the obvious fixture (cf. Jansen 1991: 155–6), the only other recorded finds were a basin and tap in one such room and tools and spinning and needlework implements in another. The latter assemblage seems out of place and may have fallen from the upper floor.

16. Other service areas outside the *atrium*-peristyle complex. Seventy-seven spaces are categorized as this type. They do not occur in all the houses in the sample and tend to be concentrated in the larger houses which have suites of rooms outside the *atrium*-peristyle complex. For example, seventeen of this room type are in the Casa del Menandro.

Contents were found in twenty-six of the rooms of this type. In five a latrine was located. With the possible exception of room C in the Casa del Menandro, these latrines were not near the kitchen area, but most of these five houses also have other latrines which were. Niches were recorded in five rooms of this type, most of which seem utilitarian rather than of religious significance. An oven, either a large domed oven or a small closed hearth (*fornello*), was located in four, possibly five, such rooms. The precise function, or functions, of the *fornelli* is by no means established, either by its location or associations, and warrants further investigation. In two such rooms a table was recorded. Both of these are in the vicinity of a large oven and may have been involved in breadmaking, as suggested by Mau (1887: 133).

Low recesses are located in two underground rooms in this category. The lack of ventilation in these rooms suggests that these may have been utility recesses rather than for sleeping. Shelving and cupboards were found in two, possibly five such rooms. It is notable how much less frequent these are in this room type than in undecorated rooms in the *atrium*-peristyle complex, despite the fact that these rooms are presumed to have been service rooms. Nails driven into the walls of two of these were possibly for the suspension of items. Other fixtures such as cistern-mouths and stairways were recorded in five areas of this type. A manger was recorded in room 29 of the Casa del Menandro, indicating that it was a stable. The skeleton of a horse reported in room 4 in the Casa dei Vettii implies that this room was also a stable.

Amphorae were recorded in nine rooms of this type, suggesting that they were used for bulk storage. Utilitarian domestic contents, including glass and pottery vessels, lamps, spinning and weaving material, and animal bones were recorded in ten rooms of this type and similar assemblages, which included tools and more industrial quality material, were found in three. Thus a variety of mainly utilitarian/domestic storage seems normally to have occurred in rooms of this type. However, objects related to bathing and personal items were recorded in three, possibly four, such rooms. The evidence is slight but it may be possible to envisage that these rooms, attached to service areas of the house, were servants' quarters. Luxury quality material in the form of decorated furniture, silver and bronze tableware vessels, sculpture (fragmentary), jewellery, toilet items, and coins occurred in six rooms of this type. These, a brazier and further marble fragments, found in two such rooms may be the result of a similar disruption.

In summary, the contents show that rooms of this type were mainly used for utilitarian and bulk storage or for animal, and possible servants', quarters. Some might also have been used for breadmaking. The few more luxurious finds in these areas perhaps relate to the disruption of normal living conditions.

17. Stairway. The areas categorized here are those completely taken up with stairways. Their obvious function as access to an upper or lower floor needs no further discussion. There are twenty-three such areas in the sample. Many of them have a cupboard or storage area underneath. Amphorae were found under two stairways, in one case filled with hazelnuts. Building material was found under another stairway and bronze rings and a cistern-mouth under another. Amphorae and other terracotta vessels were found on the stairs themselves, in four cases on the landing. Amphorae were similarly found on the stairway in room o of House VIII 5, 9, in a kitchen area. Thus, it might seem normal to leave vessels on the landing, presumably while in transit to and from the upper floor. On one stairway were also found two bronze jugs, possibly indicating a similar activity, although an associated brazier seems a less normal utensil to be moving to and from the upper floor.

18. Back entrance/service court or secondary non-colonnaded gardens. There are twenty-one examples of this type in the sample. Most of them appear to have been utility courtyard areas as well as back entranceways. However, at least three appear to have been formal garden areas, with no direct access to the street. Another three with fixtures—a water catchment area (*impluuium*); and a stairway and a recess—appeared more utilitarian but also had no street access. The occurrence of a recess in an open courtyard seems to be another example of one which could not have been used for a bed. From the recorded planting evidence, courtyard 50 in the Casa del Menandro has been identified as a produce garden (Maiuri 1933: 216). A small oven (*fornello*) was found in two such courtyards; basins or troughs were located in two and amphorae and other pottery vessels were

recorded in seven, e.g. in the Casa del Menandro (Maiuri 1933: fig. 90). Only a puteal was located in area B of the Casa delle Nozze d'Argento but it should be noted that thirty-four amphorae were found in the entrance of adjoining room E. All these areas have direct access to the street and may have been used for either distributing, or storing, materials in bulk. A cart and harness were found in court-yard 34 of the Casa del Menandro (Maiuri 1933: figs. 88–9). The quantities of amphorae in many of these areas suggest commercial activity.

19. Room at front of house open to street (shop). There are twelve areas of this type in the sample, six of which have contents, while two others have fixtures only. A wooden bench and two *dolii* set in the ground were recorded in one example of this room type and podia, of indeterminate use, are found in two other examples (cf. Maiuri 1929: 392 fig. 21). In one such space, a *lararium* paint-ing and a few pottery vessels were recorded. Another had building material, presumably indicating that this area was not functioning normally at the time of the eruption. Small glass and pottery vessels and coins were recorded in two such spaces. In neither case does there seem to have been commercial activity during the final occu-pancy. Amphorae and pottery jugs were found in four such spaces, one of which also contained scales, lanterns, and other vessels, and another of which also contained loomweights, buckles, and a marble vessel support. Thus, there is a hint of commercial activity in these spaces, but generally there is little evidence to give information on retail activity being carried out at the time of the eruption.

20. Bath area. Areas in six houses in the sample have been con-vincingly identified as bath areas. In one, the evidence consisted of a bronze basin on a podium only (Maiuri 1927: 38 fig. 14), whereas in the other houses it consisted of a suite of two to five rooms with hypocaust flooring and a recess or apse. In one such area a metal tub was found. In two rooms in this area amphorae were found. While such vessels might well have been used to carry water to the bath area, those filled with lime suggest other activities not associ-ated with bathing, possibly repair work. No other contents were recorded from these areas. The lack of baths and bathing equip-ment, despite the fact that the latter has been reported in other areas of the houses in this sample, and the presence of lime-filled amphorae suggest that these baths may have been inoperative at the time of the eruption.

21. Upper storey. Objects, not definitively recorded as from the ground floor, possibly formed part of upper-floor assemblages. While, in many cases, these objects may have been moved from ground-floor

contexts during post-eruption disturbance, there are a few assemblages which can be safely attributed to upper-floor areas and which assist in the identification of the types of assemblages likely to have been from an upper-floor context, rather than from a disturbed context.

Two assemblages were found in the upper rooms of the Casa del Fabbro. Above room 9 the assemblage consisted of bronze vessels, conceivably washing vessels, toilet objects, remains of a stool, and lighting equipment. Above room 7 it consisted of chests containing a variety of bronze vessels, glass storage jars, toilet or pharmaceutical instruments, and a few larger tools. A third possible assemblage, above room 10 in House I 10, 8, was made up of pottery vessels, lighting equipment, fragments of terracotta sculpture and weaving equipment. Amphorae were stored in a room above room 18 in the Casa degli Amanti.

Thus, most of the assemblages ascribed to the upper floor consisted of pottery vessels, items which appear to have been related to toilet or pharmaceutical activities, jewellery, and lighting equipment. Sometimes gaming pieces, weights, scales, or needlework and weaving equipment are included. Amphorae were also a frequent find in these upper levels, sometimes with the other finer material, sometimes alone or with other pottery vessels. This latter situation recalls the amphorae and vessels found on stairways in a number of houses. Rooms in the upper levels seem generally to have been used either for private activities or for storage. Precisely how these areas were used would depend very much on how the rest of the house was functioning during its final phase of occupation. For example, the upper rooms in the front area of the Casa di Iulius Polybius show predominantly storage activity, whereas the assemblage above room 7 in the Casa del Fabbro is comparable to those in the ground-floor rooms of this house.

SUMMARY

As there is much information in these lists which is not readily digestible it is appropriate to summarize briefly the activities which might seem to be represented by the assemblages in each of the main areas of the house: the forecourt area, the garden/peristyle area, and other areas outside these first two.

Forecourt (*atrium*) area. The distribution patterns in this area suggest that the forecourt (*atrium*) itself, while some formal display and religious activities were noted, was predominantly the centre around which many of the household activities revolved, with such activities also carried out in the open rooms (*alae*) to either side.

The contents of the small closed decorated rooms off this area implied that they were used for personal domestic activities, the lack of definitive sleeping evidence implying these might have acted more as a boudoir than as a bedroom in the modern sense. The rooms to either side of the main entranceway had a fairly utilitarian function as did the small undecorated rooms off the forecourt. The frequent occurrence of shelving in such rooms implies that they were for storage, which could be both domestic and industrial. No clear pattern of activity was discernible in room type 6 (*triclinium*), suggesting that it lacked a distinctive function at least at the time of the eruption. The prevalent pattern for the rooms leading from the forecourt to the garden (*tablina*) was that they had storage furniture, with domestic storage, similar to the forecourt itself.

Thus, there is ample evidence that the front area of the house was used for general domestic activities, both seemingly public and private, as well as for a certain amount of more commercial activities. However, notable domestic activities for which evidence is lacking in this area are food preparation and eating.

Garden/peristyle area. The garden/peristyle area, in general, seems to have been the most ostentatious area of the house, particularly in the larger houses. However, many of the small households seem to have given over this display area for more utilitarian purposes, at least during the final occupation of the town. But even in the houses with a wealth of display in the garden area and spacious and richly decorated banqueting rooms, utilitarian and everyday domestic activities were not excluded from this area. The garden itself seems often to have performed the function of a produce garden (cf. Jashemski 1979: 31) in combination with the formal type as reconstructed in the Casa dei Vettii (cf. Sogliano 1898: pl. 8). It seems that it was not improper to have latrines in this area, or domestic storage, weaving, and other household activities in the ambulatories of the entertainment areas, or even in the dining-rooms themselves. Bulk storage could be found side-by-side with banqueting halls and food preparation could be carried out in this area, possibly in front of the diners.

Other areas. The assemblages in the so-called 'kitchens' indicate food preparation activities but, as noted above, it is very probable that some cooking, perhaps formal cooking, was carried out much closer to the formal dining areas. It is, therefore, perhaps not quite accurate to assume that these 'kitchen' areas would have functioned as their counterparts in large nineteenth- and early twentieth-century European domestic establishments.

Other areas outside the main *atrium*-peristyle complex seem predominantly utilitarian. However, in some of them personal and more luxury assemblages were recorded, and hence the activities witnessed in these areas vary considerably across the sample. Where many of these areas include back entranceways and rear courtyards, the goods which seemed to have passed through them do not necessarily seem related to the domestic activities of the household but either to repair work or to the commercial/industrial activities of the establishment, emphasizing the multiple character of such residential establishments in a pre-industrialized society. This sample showed a marked lack of evidence of commercial activity in the supposed 'shops'.

Upper floors. What little evidence there is for upper-floor activity indicates personal activities but also storage. Objects which were probably destined for the upper floor, particularly amphorae which perhaps carried water, were deposited on the stairway.

ARCHAEOLOGICAL EVIDENCE FOR THE ROMAN FAMILY IN POMPEII

How can all these assemblages, and the activities to which they seem to be related, inform us about the inhabitants of these houses? Can they be used to differentiate between the spaces used by members of the household or by visitors, or to differentiate between spaces used by different household members? Can we assign particular assemblages to particular individuals or groups of individuals? Can we isolate activity areas which are gender, age, or status specific?

If we assume that visitors entered places which had display furnishings, both the forecourt and the formal gardens of these houses would seem to have been open to them. Only the fact that the peristyle garden is usually further inside the house implies that it might have been more secluded. Ostentatious furnishings, however, were more prevalent in the garden than the forecourt. It is impossible to determine whether this meant that it was a more public area or that the householders reserved their most luxurious vistas for their most valued visitors. Bath suites are usually in the peristyle area but again it is not possible to ascertain whether or not visitors were invited to use them.

These courtyard areas, however, do not appear to have been reserved for public activity. Rather they appear to have been centres around which routine domestic activities revolved. There would appear to have been little concern among Pompeian householders for hiding their domestic activity from outsiders. Perhaps only the smaller rooms to the sides of these main circulation areas were more private and out of bounds for visitors. Or perhaps we should be more critical of our seemingly culturally and gender-biased assumptions concerning the meanings, or even existence, of public and private domestic spaces in Roman houses.

Contact with visitors involved with the commercial or industrial enterprises of the establishment would appear to have been carried out through back entranceways and service courts but commercial material has been noted in the forecourt areas of houses which also had back entranceways. It would, therefore, seem inaccurate to apply the analogy of a main entranceway and separate 'tradesmen's' entrance, as in large houses of this and last century, to Pompeian houses.

If we take the members of the household to be the family and slaves, then we should perhaps look for differentiations first between family and slave and then between different members of the family, according to age, gender, and status. The greatest problem in using archaeological data to make such distinctions is that it is practically impossible to relate any particular material, class of material, or assemblages to any of these groups. While it is probably justifiable to assume that many of the service activities were usually carried out by slaves, and hence that the utilitarian assemblages might be used to identify the spaces which they frequented, it cannot be assumed that it was exclusively so. And if it was, the occurrence of utilitarian assemblages throughout the diverse areas of the house, with the exception perhaps of the small decorated rooms off the forecourt and perhaps the large rooms off the peristyle-garden, suggests that slaves did not have restricted access in certain areas of the house. One might wish to argue that they did not enter the small decorated rooms off the forecourt or frequent the upper floors. However, the kinds of personal assemblages found in these former rooms and in the upper floors are also known to occur in what were considered the service areas of the house. One cannot use artefact assemblages to isolate slave activity unless one brings in external assumptions about what slaves did in a Pompeian household.

Differentiation between members of the household is also difficult. As no recorded artefacts can, as yet, be attributed to children, artefact assemblages cannot be used to trace their activities. Likewise it is difficult to find any gender distinctions in the assemblages, without in-built assumptions about the gender roles. For example, only if one assumes that spinning, weaving, and needlework were carried out by women, whether freed or slave, can one perhaps identify areas frequented by women. Evidence for spinning and weaving was recorded in forecourts, in small undecorated rooms, and large corner rooms off the forecourt, in the ambulatories of peristyle-gardens, in small closed rooms off the garden, in rooms outside the *atrium-*peristyle complex, and possibly on the upper floor. Evidence for needlework was reported in both types of small closed room off the forecourt, in storage containers in the larger corner rooms of the forecourt and large rooms opening off the garden, and in the upper floors.

Likewise, many toiletry items might be assumed to be women's objects. These were found predominantly in the small decorated rooms off the forecourt but also occurred in the undecorated rooms of this type, and were found stored in the large corner rooms off the forecourt, the open room (*tablinum*) leading to the garden and both types of large rooms off the garden. They also occurred in different types of small rooms off the garden, in the rooms away from the *atrium*-peristyle complex and on the upper floor. Thus, even if these activities can be shown to be women's activities, there is no evidence to suggest that they might have been restricted to specific areas of the house.

Seemingly high-status public and religious artefacts are most prominent in the two main courtyards. However, high-status domestic material (e.g. silver and decorated bronze vessels) can be found in a variety of locations around the house, including in what are assumed to be service areas. A differentiation between place of use and place of storage is needed. While some of the public and religious artefacts were undoubtedly discovered at their place of use it would seem that many other such artefacts were discovered in their storage locations.

In general, this analysis does not find support for stratification by status, gender, or age (or any other of the supposed 'hierarchies of power') as being a significant element in living patterns (cf. also Wallace-Hadrill 1991*b*: 227). Any suggestion of status is borne out by the architecture rather than the distribution of artefacts (cf. Wallace-Hadrill 1988: 167). A discussion on the reasons for this is beyond the aims of this paper.

CONCLUSIONS

This chapter has outlined the kinds of contents discovered in a sample of houses, of one particular architectural type, from one Roman town in southern Italy. The patterns isolated here are specifically relevant to this group of houses, this town, and the circumstances under which the artefacts were deposited. Further, similar investigations of other house types in this town and of houses at other Roman sites may throw more light on the potential universality of some of these patterns, as will a more rigorous assessment of the relationship of these patterns to patterns of activity known from Roman texts.

The degree of correspondence between these assemblages and the activities seen to be ascribed, by use of the traditional nomenclature, to these rooms has not been dealt with here. While some correspondence can be found, any lack of it should not be seen to invalidate the conclusions reached here (cf. Allison 1992*b*: 40–85). Rather, it should be taken to emphasize the need to reinvestigate the validity of the ascription of such nomenclature to these precise spaces and, at the same time, to assess more critically the interpretations of ancient texts which are seen to designate activities to spaces in Roman houses. It should also highlight that the kind of information which we can glean from archaeological data is often in a very different form from that which we can glean from written texts. Neither is more valid than the other. They are just different and the relationship between them is often very difficult to grasp.

References

Adams, B. (1964), *Paramoné und verwandte Texte: Studien zum Dienst-vertrag im Rechte der Papyri*. Berlin.

Albertini, A. (1971), 'Un patrono di Verona del secondo secolo d. C.: G. Erennio Ceciliano', in *Il territorio veronese in età romana*. Verona. 439–57.

Alföldy, G. (1984), *Römische Statuen in Venetia et Histria. Epigraphische Quellen* (Abhandlungen der Heidelberger Akademie der Wissenschaften 3). Heidelberg.

—— (1992), *Studi sull'epigraphia augustea e tiberiana di Roma*. Rome.

—— (1995), 'Bericht der Schweigsame sein Schweigen? Eine Grabinschrift aus Rom', *Mitteilungen des Deutschen Archäologischen Instituts. Römische Abteilung* 102: 251–68.

Alföldy, G., and Halfmann, H. (1973), 'M. Cornelius Nigrinus Curiatius Maternus, General Domitians und Rivale Traians', *Chiron* 3: 331–73.

Allison, P. M. (1991), ' "Workshops" and "Patternbooks" ', *Kölner Jahrbuch für Vor- und Frühgeschichte* 24: 79–84.

—— (1992a), 'Artefact Assemblages: Not "The Pompeii Premise" ', in E. Herring, R. Whitehouse, and J. Wilkins (edd.), *Papers of the Fourth Conference of Italian Archaeology: New Developments in Italian Archaeology*. London. Part 1, 49–56.

—— (1992b), *The Distribution of Pompeian House Contents and its Significance* (Ph.D. thesis, Sydney), UMI, Ann Arbor 1994.

—— (1993), 'How Do we Identify the Use of Space in Roman Housing?', in E. M. Moorman (ed.), *Functional and Spatial Analysis of Wall Painting: Proceedings of the Fifth International Congress on Ancient Wall Painting*. Leiden. 1–8.

—— (1995a), 'On-Going Seismic Activity and its Effect on Living Conditions in Pompeii in the Last Decades', in *Archäologie und Seismologie*. Munich.

—— (1995b), 'House Contents in Pompeii: Data Collection and Interpretative Procedures for a Reappraisal of Roman Domestic Life and Site Formation Processes', *Journal of European Archaeology* (forthcoming).

Amedick, R. (1991), *Vita Privata* (*Die antike Sarkophagreliefs*, i. 4). Berlin.

Ameling, W. (1983), *Herodes Atticus*. 2 vols. Hildesheim.

Andreau, J. (1973), 'Remarques sur la société pompéienne', *Dialoghi di Archeologia* 7: 213–54.

Ariès, P. (1960), *L'enfant et la vie familiale sous l'Ancien Régime*. Paris.

—— (1962), *Centuries of Childhood*. Harmondsworth, rev. 1973.

Balil, A. (1974), *Casa y Urbanismo en la España antigua* IV (Studia archaeologica 28).Valladolid.

Balland, A. (1981), *Fouilles de Xanthos VII: Inscriptions d'époque impériale de Létoön*. Paris.

Barbet, A., and Allag, C. (1972), 'Techniques de préparations des parois dans la peinture romaine', *Mélanges de l'École française de Rome* 84: 935–1069.

Becatti, G. (1948), 'Case Ostiensi del Tardo Impero', *Bollettino d'Arte* 24: 102–28, 197–224.

Beekes, R. S. P. (1976), 'Uncle and Nephew', *Journal of Indo-European Studies* 4: 43–63.

Bek, L. (1980), 'Towards a Paradise on Earth: Modern Space Conception in Architecture, a Creation of Renaissance Humanism', *Analecta Romana Instituti Danici. Suppl.* 9.

—— (1983), 'Quaestiones Conviviales: The Idea of the *Triclinium* and the Staging of Convivial Ceremony from Rome to Byzantium', *Analecta Romana Instituti Danici* 12: 81–107.

Bellemore, J., and Rawson, B. (1990), '*Alumni*: The Italian Evidence', *Zeitschrift für Papyrologie und Epigraphik* 83: 1–19.

Berczelly, L. (1978), 'A Sepulchral Monument from Via Portuense and the Origin of the Roman Biographical Cycle', *Acta ad Archaeologiam et Artium Historiam Pertinentia* 8: 49–74, pls. I–XI.

Bergemann, J. (1990), *Römische Reiterstatuen: Ehrendenkmäler im öffentlichen Bereich*. Mainz.

Bettini, M. (1991), *Anthropology and Roman Culture: Kinship, Time, Images of the Soul*. Baltimore.

Biondi, B. (1954), *Il diritto romano cristiano*. 3 vols. Milan.

Birley, A. R., and Eck, W. (1993), 'M. Petronius Umbrinus, Legat von Cilicia, nicht von Lycia-Pamphylia', *Epigraphica Anatolica* 21: 45–54.

Bisel, S. (1986), 'The People of Herculaneum AD 79', *Helmantica* 37: 11–23.

Bloch, M. (1971), 'The Moral and Tactical Meaning of Kinship Terms', *Man* 6: 79–87.

Boersma, J. (1985), *Amoenissima Civitas: Block V. ii at Ostia*. Assen.

Bonfante, L. (1984), 'Dedicated Mothers', *Visible Religion* 3: 1–17.

—— (1985), 'Votive Terracotta Figures of Mothers and Children', in *Italian Iron Age Artefacts in the British Museum*. London. 195–203.

Bonner, S. F. (1969), *Roman Declamation in the Late Republic and Early Empire*. Liverpool.

Bormann, E. (1896), 'Inschriften aus Umbrien', *Archäologische-epigraphische Mitteilungen* 19: 120–3.

Boschung, D. (1987), *Antike Grabaltäre aus den Nekropolen Roms*. Berne.

Bourdieu, P. (1973), 'The Barber House', in *Rules and Meanings: The Anthropology of Everyday Knowledge*, ed. M. Douglas. Harmondsworth. 98–100.

Bowersock, G. W. (1982), 'Roman Senators from the Near East: Syria, Judaea, Arabia, Mesopotamia', *Epigrafia e Ordine Senatorio II* (Tituli 5). Rome. 651–68.

Bradley, K. R. (1984), *Slaves and Masters in the Roman Empire*. Brussels.

—— (1987), 'Dislocation in the Roman Family', *Historical Reflections* 14: 33–62.

—— (1991), *Discovering the Roman Family*. Oxford.

—— (1994), *Slavery and Society at Rome*. Cambridge.

Bragantini, I., de Vos, M., and Parise-Badoni, F. (1981, 1983, 1986), *Pitture e Pavimenti di Pompeii*, i (1981), ii (1983), iii (1986). Rome.

Bremmer, J. (1976), 'Avunculate and Fosterage', *Journal of Indo-European Studies* 4: 65–78.

Brilliant, R. (1984), *Visual Narratives*. Ithaca, NY.

Brown, P. (1988), *The Body and Society: Men, Women and Sexual Renunciation in Early Christianity*. New York.

Brunt, P. A. (1971), *Italian Manpower 225 B.C.–A.D. 14*. Oxford.

Buckland, W. W. (1908), *The Roman Law of Slavery*. Cambridge.

—— (1963; repr. 1966), *A Text-Book of Roman Law: from Augustus to Justinian*. 3rd edn., rev. P. Stein. Cambridge.

Burrow, J. W. (1966), *Evolution and Society. A Study in Victorian Social Theory*. Cambridge.

Burton, A. (1989), 'Looking Forward from Ariès? Pictorial and Material Evidence for the History of Childhood and Family Life', *Continuity and Change* 4: 203–29.

Bush, B. (1990), *Slave Women in Caribbean Society 1650–1838*. Bloomington, Ind.

Butler, H. E., and Owen, A. S. (1917), *Apulei Apologia sive Pro Se de Magia Liber*. Oxford.

Byrne, B. (1979), *Sons of God, Seed of Abraham: A Study of the Idea of the Sonship of God of all Christians in Paul against the Jewish Background*. Rome.

Camodeca, G. (1979), 'Curatores rei publicae I', *Zeitschrift für Papyrologie und Epigraphik* 35: 225–36.

Cannon, A. (1989), 'The Historical Dimension in Mortuary Expressions of Status and Sentiment', *Current Anthropology* 30: 437–58.

Capitanio, M. (1974), 'La necropoli romana di Portorecanati', *Notizie degli Scavi di Antichità* ser. 8, 28: 142–445.

Carandini, A. (1988), *Schiavi in Italia—Gli strumenti pensanti dei Romani fra tarda Repubblica e medio Impero*. Rome. 359–87.

—— (ed.) (1985), *Settefinestre: Una villa schiavistica nell'Etruria romana*. Modena.

Carrington, R. C. (1933), 'The Ancient Italian Town House', *Antiquity* 7: 133–52.

Champlin, E. (1980), *Fronto and Antonine Rome*. Cambridge, Mass.

—— (1991), *Final Judgments: Duty and Emotion in Roman Wills*. Berkeley.

Chastagnol, A. (1977), 'Le Problème du domicile légal des sénateurs romains à l'époque impériale', *Mélanges offerts à Léopold S. Senghor*. Dakar.

—— (1992), *Le sénat romain à l'époque impériale*. Paris.

Cherry, D. (1990), 'The Minician Law: Marriage and the Roman Citizenship', *Phoenix* 44: 244–66.

Clark, M. E. (1983), 'Spes in the Early Imperial Cult: "The Hope of Augustus"', *Numen* 30: 80–105.

Clarke, J. R. (1991), 'The Decor of the House of Jupiter and Ganymede at Ostia Antica: Private Residence Turned Gay Hotel?', in Gazda (ed.), *Roman Art in the Private Sphere*. Ann Arbor. 89–104.

—— (1992), *The Houses of Roman Italy, 100 BC–AD 250: Ritual, Space and Decoration*. Berkeley.

Clarke, S. (1990), 'The Social Significance of Villa Architecture in Celtic Northwest Europe', *Oxford Journal of Archaeology* 9: 337–53.

Clauss, M. (1973), 'Probleme der Lebensalterstatistiken aufgrund römischen Grabinschriften', *Chiron* 3: 395–417.

Coarelli, F. (1978), 'La statue de Cornélie, mère des Gracches, et la crise politique à Rome au temps du Saturninus', in *Le dernier siècle de la république romaine et l'époque augustéenne*. Strasburg. 13–28.

—— (1983), 'Architettura sacra e architettura privata nella tarda Repubblica', in *Architecture et Société de l'archaïsme grec à la fin de la république romaine*. Rome. 191–217.

Comaroff, J. L., and Roberts, S. (1981), *Rules and Processes: The Cultural Logic of Dispute in an African Context*. Chicago.

Corbier, M. (1991), 'Constructing Kinship in Rome: Marriage and Divorce, Filiation and Adoption', in Kertzer and Saller (1991), 127–44.

Corcoran, G. (1985), *St. Augustine on Slavery*. Rome.

Cox, C. A. (1988), 'Sibling Relationships in Classical Athens: Brother–Sister Ties', *Journal of Family History* 13: 377–95.

Crawford, M. (1974), *Roman Republican Coinage*. 2 vols. London.

Crema, L. (1959), *L'architettura romana* (*Enciclopedia Classica* III. 12. 1). Turin.

Crifo, G. (1988), 'Romanizzazione e Christianizzazione: certezze e dubbi in tema di rapporto tra Cristiani e istituzioni', in G. Bonamente and A. Nestori (edd.), *I Cristiani e l'Impero nel IV secolo: Colloquio sul Cristianesimo nel mondo antico*, Macerata. 75–106.

Crook, J. A. (1967), 'Patria Potestas', *Classical Quarterly* 17: 113–22.

Currie, S. (1993), 'Childhood and Christianity from Paul to the Council of Chalcedon'. Ph.D. thesis. Cambridge.

—— (1996), 'The Empire of Adults: The Representation of Children on Trajan's Arch at Benevento', in J. Elsner (ed.). Cambridge. 153–81.

Dalla, D. (1987), 'Aspetti della patria potestas e dei rapporti tra genitori e figli nell'epoca postclassica', *Atti dell'Accademia Romanistica Costantiniana. VII Convegno Internazionale*. Perugia. 89–109.

Daube, D. (1947), 'Did Macedo Murder his Father?', *Zeitschrift der Savigny-Stiftung für Rechtsgeschichte* 65: 261–311.

—— (1950), 'Actions between *Paterfamilias* and *Filiusfamilias* with *Peculium Castrense*', *Studi in memoria di Emilio Albertario*. Milan. 435–74.

—— (1969), *Roman Law: Linguistic, Social and Philosophical Aspects*. Edinburgh.

Davey, N., and Ling, R. (1982), *Wall-Painting in Roman Britain*. Gloucester.

de Alarcão, J., and Étienne, R. (1981), 'Les Jardins à Conimbriga (Portugal)', in *Ancient Roman Gardens*, E. B. Macdougall and W. F. Jashemski (edd.). Washington. 67–80.

De Albentiis, E. (1990), *La casa dei Romani*. Milan.

Delaval, E., and Savay-Guerraz, H. (1992), *La Maison des Dieux Oceans*. Vienne.

Delplace, C. (1990), 'Evergétisme et construction publique dans la Regio V (Picenum). A propos du théatre d'Urbs Salvia', *Picus* 10: 101–6.

de Ste Croix, G. E. M. (1981), *The Class Struggle in the Ancient Greek World*. London.

Devijver, H. (1989), 'Equestrian Officers and their Monuments', in H. Devijver (ed.), *The Equestrian Officers of the Roman Imperial Army* (Mavors 6). Amsterdam. 416–49.

Devijver, H., and van Wonterghem, F. (1992), 'The Funerary Monuments of Equestrian Officers of the Late Republic and Early Empire in Italy', in H. Devijver (ed.), *The Equestrian Officers of the Roman Imperial Army II* (Mavors 9). Amsterdam. 180–4.

de Vos, A., and de Vos, M. (1982), *Pompei Ercolano Stabia*. Rome/Bari.

de Vos, M. (1990), 'Casa dei Quadretti teatrali', in *Pompei, Pitture e Mosaici*. Roma. 361–96.

de Zulueta, F. (1953), *The Institutes of Gaius*. 2 vols. Oxford.

Dixon, S. (1984), 'Family Finances: Tullia and Terentia', *Antichthon* 18: 78–101.

—— (1988), *The Roman Mother*. London.

—— (1992), *The Roman Family*. Baltimore.

Dondin-Payre, M. (1994), 'Choix et contraites dans l'expression de la parenté dans le monde romain', *Cahier Glotz* 5: 127–63.

Donzelot, J. (1979), *The Policing of Families*. New York.

Downey, G. (1946), 'On Some Post-Classical Greek Architectural Terms', *Transactions of the American Philological Association* 77: 22–34.

Drerup, H. (1959), 'Bildraum und Realraum in der römischen Architektur', *Rheinisches Museum* 66: 145–74.

Drew-Bear, T., and Eck, W. (1976), 'Kaiser- Militär- und Steinbruchin-schriften aus Phrygien', *Chiron* 6: 289–318.

Drummer, A. (n.d.), 'Villa: Untersuchungen zum Bedeutungswandel eines Motivs in römischer Bildkunst und Literatur, Republik bis mittlere Kaiserzeit' (unpubl. thesis, Munich 1994).

Dulière, C. (1979), *Lupa Romana*. Brussels.

Dunbabin, K. M. D. (1991), '*Triclinium* and *Stibadium*', in Slater (1991), 121–48.

—— (1995), 'The Use of Private Space', in *Proceedings of the XIV Congreso Internacional de Arqueología Clàsica, Tarragona, 1993*, 165–76.

Dwyer, E. (1979), 'Sculpture and its Display in the Roman House', in *Pompeii and the Vesuvian Landscape: Papers of a Symposium Sponsored by the Archaeological Institute of America and the Smithsonian Institute*. Washington, DC. 59–77.

—— (1982), *Pompeian Domestic Sculpture*. Rome.

—— (1991), 'The Pompeian *Atrium* House in Theory and in Practice', in Gazda (1991), 25–48.

Eberle, A. F. (1990), 'Un sarcophage d'enfant au J. Paul Getty Museum', in *Roman Funerary Monuments in the J. Paul Getty Museum*. Malibu, Calif. i. 47–58.

Eck, W. (1972), 'Die Familie der Volusii Saturnini in neuen Inschriften aus Lucus Feroniae', *Hermes* 100: 461–84.

—— (1973), 'Berichtigung' (von *Hermes* 100), *Hermes* 101: 128.

—— (1977) (with T. Drew-Bear and P. Hermann), 'Sacrae Litterae', *Chiron* 7: 355–83.

—— (1980), 'Die Präsenz senatorischer Familien in den Städten des Imperium Romanum bis zum späten 3. Jahrhundert', in *Studien zur antiken Sozialgeschichte: Festschrift Fr. Vittinghoff*, ed. W. Eck, H. Galsterer, H. Wolff. Cologne. 283–322.

—— (1981*a*), 'Miscellanea prosopographica', *Zeitschrift für Papyrologie und Epigraphik* 42: 227–56.

—— (1981*b*), 'Altersangaben in senatorischen Grabinschriften: Standeserwartungen und ihre Kompensation', *Zeitschrift für Papyrologie und Epigraphik* 43: 127–34.

—— (1982), 'Die fistulae aquariae der Stadt Rom: Zum Einfluss des sozialen Status auf administratives Handeln', in *Epigrafia e Ordine Senatorio II* (Tituli 4). Rome. 197–225.

—— (1984*a*), 'Senatorial Self-representation: Developments in the Augustan Period', in *Caesar Augustus: Seven Aspects*, ed. F. Millar and E. Segal. Oxford. 129–67.

—— (1984*b*), 'CIL VI 1508 (Moretti, IGUR 71) und die Gestaltung senatorischer Ehrenmonumente', *Chiron* 14: 201–17.

—— (1986), 'Inschriften aus der Nekropole unter St. Peter', *Zeitschrift für Papyrologie und Epigraphik* 65: 245–93.

—— (1991*a*), 'Die Struktur der Städte in den nordwestlichen Provinzen und ihr Beitrag zur Administration des Reiches', in *Die Stadt in Oberitalien und den nordwestlichen Provinzen des römischen Reiches* (Kölner Forschungen 4), 73–84.

—— (1991*b*), 'L. Marcius Celer M. Calpurnius Longus Prokonsul von Achaia und Suffektkonsul unter Hadrian', *Zeitschrift für Papyrologie und Epigraphik* 86: 97–106.

—— (1992), 'Ehrungen für Personen hohen sozio-politischen Ranges im öffentlichen und privaten Bereich', in *Die römische Stadt im 2. Jahrhundert n. Chr. Der Funktionswandel des öffentliches Raumes*, ed. H.-J. Schalles, H. v. Hesberg, P. Zanker. Cologne. 359–76.

—— (1992/3), 'Urbs Salvia und seine führenden Familien in der römischen Zeit', *Picus* 12/13: 79–108.

—— (ed.) (1993), *Prosopographie und Sozialgeschichte*. Cologne.

—— (1994), 'Grundbesitz der senatorischen Roscii auf Sizilien', in *Catania antica*. Rome.

—— (1995), 'Rang oder Alter: Die Kompensation von Standeserwartungen in öffentlichen Ehrungen in Volubilis', in *Festschrift J. Fitz = Tra Epigrafia, Prosopografia ed Archeologia*. Rome.

Eisner, M. (1986), *Zur Typologie der Grabbauten im Suburbium Roms*. Mainz.

Elia, O. (1934), 'Pompei—Relazione sullo scavo dell'Insula X della Regio I', *Notizie degli Scavi di Antichità* 17: 264–344.

Ellis, S. (1991), 'Power, Architecture, and Decor: How the Late Roman Aristocrat Appeared to His Guests', in Gazda (1991), 117–34.

Elsner, J. R. (1995), *Art and the Roman Viewer*. Cambridge.

—— (ed.) (1996), *Art and Text in Roman Culture*. Cambridge.

Engels, F. (1884), *The Origins of the Family, Private Property and the State*. Chicago.

Étienne, R. (1960), *Le Quartier Nord-Est de Volubilis*. Paris.

Evans, E. M. (1984), 'The Atrium Complex in the Houses in Pompeii'. Ph.D. thesis, Birmingham. British Library Microfilms.

Evans, J. K. (1991), *War, Women and Children in Ancient Rome*. London/New York.

Evans-Grubbs, J. (1993*a*), 'Constantine and Imperial Legislation on the Family', in J. Harries, I. Wood (edd.), *The Theodosian Code: Studies in the Imperial Law of Late Antiquity*. London. 120–42.

—— (1993*b*), '"Marriage more Shameful than Adultery": Slave–Mistress Relationships, "Mixed Marriages", and Late Roman Law', *Phoenix* 47: 125–54.

Evans-Pritchard, E. C. (1929), 'The Study of Kinship in Primitive Societies', *Man* 29: 190–3.

Eyben, E. (1991), 'Fathers and Sons', in Rawson (1991), 114–43.

—— (1993), *Restless Youth in Ancient Rome*. London.

Fear, A. T. (1990), '*Cives Latini, servi publici* and the *Lex Irnitana*', *Revue Internationale des Droits de l'Antiquité* 37: 149–66.

Felleti Maj, B. M. (1960), 'Ostia, la casa delle volte dipinti', *Bolletino d'Arte* 45: 45–65.

Finley, M. I. (1977), *Aspects of Antiquity*. 2nd edn. Harmondsworth.

—— (1981), 'The Elderly in Classical Antiquity,' *Greece and Rome* 28: 156–71.

Flory, M. B. (1984), 'Where Women Precede Men: Factors Influencing the Order of Names in Roman Epitaphs', *Classical Journal* 79: 216–24.

Fora, M. (1992), 'Ummidia Quadratilla ed il restauro del teatro di Cassino (Per una nuova lettura di AE 1936, 174)', *Zeitschrift für Papyrologie und Epigraphik* 94: 269–73.

Fortes, M. (1957), 'Malinowski and the Study of Kinship', in R. Firth (ed.), *Man and Culture*. London.

—— (1970), *Time and Social Structure and Other Essays*. London/New York.

Fox, R. (1967), *Kinship and Marriage*. London.

Frenz, H. G. (1985), *Römischer Grabreliefs in Mittel- und Suditalien*. Rome.

Friedrich, P. (1979), *Language, Context, and the Imagination*. Stanford, Calif.

Frier, B. (1982), 'Roman Life Expectancy: Ulpian's Evidence', *Harvard Studies in Classical Philology* 86: 213–51.

—— (1983), 'Roman Life Expectancy: The Pannonian Evidence', *Phoenix* 37: 328–44.

Fröhlich, T. (1991), *Lararien- und Fassadenbilder in den Vesuvstädten*. Mainz.

Fustel de Coulanges, N. D. (1980), *The Ancient City*. Baltimore. (Orig. pub. 1864.)

Gardner, J. F. (1986a), *Women in Roman Law and Society*. London.

—— (1986b), 'Proofs of Status in the Roman World', *Bulletin of the Institute of Classical Studies of the University of London* 33: 11–14.

—— (1989), 'The Adoption of Roman Freedmen', *Phoenix* 43: 236–57.

—— (1991), 'The Purpose of the lex Fufia Caninia', *Echos du Monde Classique/Classical Views* 35, NS 10: 21–39.

—— (1993), *Being a Roman Citizen*. London.

—— (forthcoming), 'Status, Sentiment and Strategy in Roman Adoption', in *Adoption et Fosterage: Proceedings of C.N.R.S. Colloquium 1993*, ed. M. Corbier. Paris.

Gardner, J. F., and Wiedemann, T. (1991), *The Roman Household: A Sourcebook*. London.

Garland, R. (1985), *The Greek Way of Death*. London.

Garnsey, P. (1975), 'Descendants of Freedmen in Local Politics: Some Criteria', in *The Ancient Historian and his Materials*, in Levick (1975), 167–80.

—— (1981), 'Independent Freedmen and the Economy of Roman Italy under the Principate', *Klio* 63: 359–71.

—— (1994), 'Philo Judaeus and Slave Theory', *Scripta Classica Israelica* 13.

Garnsey, P., and Saller, R. P. (1987), *The Roman Empire: Economy, Society and Culture*. London.

Garzetti, A. (1977), 'I Nonii di Brescia', *Athenaeum* 55: 175–85.

Gaudemet, J. (1959), *L'Église dans l'empire romain*. Paris.

—— (1962), 'Les Transformations dans la vie familiale au Bas-Empire et l'influence du Christianisme', *Romanitas* 5: 58–85.

—— (1975), *Le Droit romain dans la littérature chrétienne occidentale*. Paris.

Gazda, E. (ed.) (1991), *Roman Art in the Private Sphere*. Ann Arbor.

George, M. (1996), '*Servus* and *domus*: The Slave in the Roman House', suppl. to *Journal of Roman Archaeology*, ed. A. Wallace-Hadrill and R. Laurence.

Gercke, W. B. (1968), 'Untersuchungen zum römischen Kinderporträt von den Anfängen bis in hadrianische Zeit.' Ph.D. thesis. Hamburg.

Goette, H. R. (1989), 'Beobachtungen zu römischen Kinderporträts', *Archäologischer Anzeiger, Deutsches Archäologisches Institut*, 453–71.

Golden, M. (1988), 'Did the Ancients Care when their Children Died?', *Greece and Rome* 35: 152–63.

González, J. (1986), 'The Lex Irnitana: A New Copy of the Flavian Municipal Law', *Journal of Roman Studies* 76: 147–243.

Goode, W. (1963), *World Revolution and Family Patterns*. Glencoe, Ill.

—— (1964), *The Family*. Englewood Cliffs, NJ.

—— (1971), 'Force and Violence in the Family', *Journal of Marriage and the Family* 33: 624–36.

Goody, J. (ed.) (1973), *The Character of Kinship*. Cambridge.

—— (1990), *The Oriental, the Ancient and the Primitive*. Cambridge.

Gore, R. (1984), 'The Dead Do Tell Tales at Vesuvius (After 2000 Years of Silence)', *National Geographic*, 556–614.

Goudineau, C. (1979), *Les Fouilles de la Maison au Dauphin, Gallia,* suppl. 37, Paris.

Gozlan, S. (1994), 'Les mosaïques de la maison d'Asinius Rufinus à Acholla (Tunisie)', in *Fifth International Colloquium on Ancient Mosaics, Bath 1987, Journal of Roman Archaeology* suppl. 9, ed. P. Johnson, R. Ling, D. J. Smith. Ann Arbor. 163–72.

Gozlan, S., and Bourgeois, A. (1992), *La Maison de Neptune à Acholla (Botria, Tunisie)* i. *Les mosaïques.* Rome.

Graham, J. W. (1966), 'Origins and Interrelations of the Greek House and the Roman House', *Phoenix* 20: 3–31.

Grant, M. (1971), *Cities of Vesuvius.* Harmondsworth.

Gray-Fow, M. (1988), 'The Wicked Stepmother in Roman Literature and History: An Evaluation', *Latomus* 47: 741–57.

Green, J. R., and Rawson, B. (1981), *Antiquities.* Canberra.

Groag, E. (1939), *Die römischen Reichsbeamten von Achaia bis auf Diokletian.* Vienna.

Guadagno, G. (1977), 'Frammenti inediti di Albi degli Augustali', *Cronache Ercolanesi* 7: 114–23.

Habicht, C. (1969), *Altertümer von Pergamon VIII,* iii. *Die Inschriften des Asklepieions.* Berlin.

Halfmann, H. (1979), *Die Senatoren aus dem östlichen Teil des Imperium Romanum bis zum Ende des 2. Jahrhunderts n. Chr.* Göttingen.

—— (1982), 'Die Senatoren aus den kleinasiatischen Provinzen des römischen Reiches vom 1. bis zum 3. Jahrhundert (Asia, Pontus-Bithynien, Lycien-Pamphylien, Galatien, Cappadocien, Cilicien)', in *Epigrafia e Ordine Senatorio II,* ed. S. Panciera. Rome. 603–50.

Hallett, J. P. (1984), *Fathers and Daughters in Roman Society.* Princeton.

Harris, C. C. (1990), *Kinship.* Minneapolis.

Harrison, A. R. W. (1968), *The Law of Athens,* i. *The Family and Property.* Oxford.

Harrod, S. G. (1909), *Latin Terms of Endearment and Family Relationships.* Princeton.

Harsh, P. (1935), 'The Origins of the Insulae at Ostia', *Memoirs of the American Academy at Rome* 12: 7–66.

Helbig, W. (1963–72), *Führer durch die öffentlichen Sammlungen klassischer Altertümer in Rom*[4], 4 vols. Tübingen.

Hermansen, G. (1981), *Ostia: Aspects of City Life.* Edmonton.

Herrmann, E. (1980), *Ecclesia in Republica: Die Entwicklung der Kirche von pseudostaatlicher zu staatlich inkorporierter Existenz.* Frankfurt.

Herzfeld, M. (1980), 'Social Tension and Inheritance by Lot in Three Greek Villages', *Anthropological Quarterly* 53: 91–100.

Hopkins, K. (1966), 'On the Probable Age Structure of the Roman Population', *Population Studies* 20: 245–64.

—— (1978), *Conquerors and Slaves.* Cambridge.

—— (1983), *Death and Renewal.* Cambridge.

Humbert, M. (1972), *Le Remariage à Rome: Étude d'histoire juridique et sociale.* Milan.

Hunter, V. J. (1994), *Policing Athens: Social Control in the Attic Law-suits*. Princeton.

Huskinson, J. (1996), *Roman Children's Sarcophagi: Their Decoration and its Social Significance*. Oxford.

Husselmann, E. M. (1957), 'Donationes mortis causa from Tebtunis', *Transactions of the American Philological Association* 88: 135–54.

Jansen, G. C. M. (1991), 'Water Systems and Sanitation in the Houses of Herculaneum', *Mededelingen van het Nederlands Instituut te Rome* 50: 145–72.

Jashemski, W. F. (1979), *The Gardens of Pompeii, Herculaneum and the Villas Destroyed by Vesuvius*. New York.

Johansson, S. R. (1987), 'Centuries of Childhood/Centuries of Parenting: Philippe Ariès and the Modernization of Privileged Infancy', *Journal of Family History* 12: 343–65.

Jones, C. P. (1970), 'Sura and Senecio', *Journal of Roman Studies* 60: 98–104.

Kampen, N. (1981), 'Biographical Narration in Roman Funerary Art', *American Journal of Archaeology* 85: 47–58 + pls. 7–12.

Kaser, M. (1966), *Das römische Zivilprozessrecht*. Munich.

—— (1971), *Das römische Privatrecht*. 2nd edn. 2 vols. Munich.

Kellum, B. A. (1985), 'Sculptural Programs and Propaganda in Augustan Rome: The Temple of Apollo on the Palatine', in Winkes (1985), 169–76.

—— (1990), 'The City Adorned: Programmatic Display at the *Aedes Concordiae Augustae*', in K. A. Raaflaub and M. Toher (eds.), *Between Republic and Empire: Interpretations of Augustus and his Principate*. Berkeley. 276–307.

Kent, S. (ed.) (1990), *Domestic Architecture and the Use of Space*. Cambridge.

Kepartová, J. (1984), 'Kinder in Pompeji: Eine epigraphische Untersuchung', *Klio* 66: 192–209.

Kertzer, D. I., and Saller, R. P. (edd.) (1991), *The Family in Italy from Antiquity to the Present*. New Haven.

Klein, R. (1988), *Die Sklaverei in der Sicht der Bischofe Ambrosius und Augustinus*. Stuttgart.

Kleiner, D. (1977), *Roman Group Portraiture: The Funerary Reliefs of the Late Republic and Early Empire*. New York.

—— (1978), 'The Great Friezes of the Ara Pacis Augustae: Greek Sources, Roman Derivatives and Augustan Social Policy', *Mélanges de l'École Française de Rome: Antiquité* 90: 753–84.

—— (1983), *The Monument of Philopappus in Athens*. Rome.

—— (1985), 'Private Portraiture in the Age of Augustus', in Winkes (1985), 107–35.

—— (1986), review of Frenz (1985), *American Journal of Archaeology* 90: 369–70.

—— (1987a), *Roman Imperial Funerary Altars with Portraits*. Rome.

—— (1987b), 'Women and Family Life on Roman Imperial Funerary Altars', *Latomus*, 46: 545–54.

—— (1988), 'Roman Funerary Art and Architecture: Observations on the Significance of Recent Studies', *Journal of Roman Archaeology* 1: 115–19.

—— (1989*a*), review of S. Diebner, 'Reperti funerari in Umbria', *American Journal of Archaeology* 93: 155–6.

—— (1989*b*), review of Boschung (1987), *American Journal of Archaeology* 93: 306–7.

—— (1992), *Roman Sculpture*. New Haven/London.

Kockel, V. (1993), *Porträtreliefs stadtrömischer Grabbauten: Ein Beitrag zur Geschichte und zum Verstandnis des spätrepublikanisch-frühkaiserzeitlichen Privatporträts*. Mainz.

Kolb, A. (1993), *Die kaiserliche Bauverwaltung in der Stadt Rom*. Stuttgart.

Kuper, A. (1983), *Anthropology and Anthropologists*. London.

—— (1985), 'Ancestors: Henry Maine and the Constitution of Primitive Society', *History and Anthropology* 1: 265–86.

La Torre, G. (1988), 'Gli impianti commerciali ed artigiani nel tessuto urbano di Pompei', *Pompei, L'informatica al servizio di una città antica*. Rome. 75–102.

Lacey, W. K. (1968), *The Family in Classical Greece*. Ithaca, NY.

Lahusen, G. (1983), *Untersuchungen zur Ehrenstatue in Rom. Literarische und epigraphische Zeugnisse*. Rome.

Lahusen, G., and Formigli, E. (1990), 'L. Cornelius Piso. Kommandant der XVI. Legion in Neuss', *Bonner Jahrbücher* 190: 65–77.

Laing, J. D. (1971), *The Politics of the Family and Other Essays*. London.

Langham, I. (1981), *The Building of British Social Anthropology: W. H. R. Rivers and his Cambridge Disciples in the Development of Kinship Studies 1898–1931*. Dordrecht.

Laslett, P. (1977), *Family Life and Illicit Love in Earlier Generations: Essays in Historical Sociology*. Cambridge.

—— (1983), The World We Have Lost[3]. London.

—— (1988), 'La Parenté en chiffres', *Annales ESC* 43: 5–25.

Lattimore, R. (1962), *Themes in Greek and Latin Epitaphs*. Urbana, Ill.

Lauter, H. (1975), 'Zur Siedlungsstruktur Pompejis in samnitischen Zeit', in *Neue Forschungen in Pompeji und den anderen vom Vesuvausbruch 79 n. Chr. verschütterten Städten*, ed. B. Andreae and H. Kyrieleis. Recklinghausen. 147–54.

Lawrence, D., and Low, S. M. (1990), 'The Built Environment and Spatial Form', *Annual Review of Anthropology* 19: 453–505.

Le Glay, M. (1981), 'Les Jardins à Vienne', in *Ancient Roman Gardens*, ed. E. B. Macdougall and W. F. Jashemski. Washington. 49–65.

Letta, C., and d'Amato, S. (1975), *Epigraphia della regione dei Marsi*. Milan.

Lévi-Strauss, C. (1969), *The Elementary Structures of Kinship*, trans. J. H. Bell and J. R. von Sturmer; ed. R. Needham. Boston. (Orig. pub. 1947.)

Levick, B. (1975), *The Ancient Historian and His Materials*. Oxford.

Lexicon Topographicum Urbis Romae, ed. E. M. Steinby. Rome 1993– .

Libertini, G. (1926), *Centuripe*. Catania.

Linke, U. (1992), 'Manhood, Femaleness, and Power: A Cultural Analysis of Prehistoric Images of Reproduction', *Comparative Studies in Society and History* 34: 579–620.

Lopez Baria de Quiroga, P. (1986), 'Latinus iunianus: una aproximación', *Studia Historica* (Salamanca) 4/5: 125–36.

Lund, C. (1971), *The Family: Revolutionary or Oppressive Force?* New York.

Lyall, F. (1984), *Slaves, Citizens, Sons: Legal Metaphors in the Epistles.* Grand Rapids, Mich.

McAlindon, J. (1957), 'The Senator's Retiring Age: 65 or 60?', *Classical Review* 71: 108.

McKay, A. G. (1977), *Houses, Villas and Palaces in the Roman World.* Southampton.

MacMullen, R. (1982), 'The Epigraphic Habit in the Roman Empire', *American Journal of Philology* 103: 233–46.

—— (1990), 'What Difference did Christianity Make?', *Changes in the Roman Empire: Essays in the Ordinary.* Princeton. Ch. 13.

McWilliam, J. C. (1990), 'Children in Rome and Italy in the Early Empire'. Honours thesis. Canberra.

—— (1994), 'The Commemoration of Children in Rome and Italy in the Early Empire'. MA thesis. Canberra.

Maine, H. (1931), *Ancient Law.* London. (Orig. pub. 1861.)

Maiuri, A. (1927), 'Pompei—Relazione sui lavori di scavo dal marzo 1924 al marzo 1926', *Notizie degli Scavi di Antichità* ser. 6, 3: 1–83.

—— (1929), 'Pompei—Relazione sui lavori di scavo dall'aprile 1926 al dicembre 1927', *Notizie degli Scavi di Antichità* ser. 6, 5: 354–438.

—— (1933), *La Casa del Menandro e il suo Tesoro di Argenteria.* Rome.

—— (1954), 'Gineceo e Hospitium nella casa pompeiana', *Memorie dell'Accademia dei Lincei* 449–67.

Malinowski, B. (1932), *The Sexual Life of Savages in North-Western Melanesia.* 3rd edn. London.

Manganaro, G. (1989), 'Iscrizioni latine nuove e vecchie della Sicilia', *Epigraphica* 51: 161–209.

Mansuelli, G. A. (1981), *Roma e il mondo Romano.* Turin.

Marquardt, J., and Mau, A. (1886), *Das Privatleben der Römer.* Leipzig.

Martin, D. L. (1990), *Slavery as Salvation: The Metaphor in Slavery in Pauline Christianity.* New Haven.

Mau, A. (1887), 'Scavi di Pompei, Reg. 8 ins. 2 n. 38: Casa di Giuseppe II', *Mitteilungen des Deutschen Archäologischen Instituts, Römische Abteilungen* 2: 110–38.

—— (1908), *Pompeji in Leben und Kunst.* Leipzig.

Meiggs, R. (1973), *Roman Ostia.* Oxford.

Meinhart, M. (1967), *Die Senatusconsulta Tertullianum und Orfitianum in ihrer Bedeutung für das klassische römische Erbrecht.* Graz.

Meyer, E. (1990), 'Explaining the Epigraphic Habit in the Roman Empire: The Evidence of Epitaphs', *Journal of Roman Studies* 80: 74–96.

Michel, D. (1990), *Casa dei Cei (Häuser in Pompeji 3.)* Munich.

Millar, F. (1977), *The Emperor in the Roman World.* London.

—— (1993), *The Roman Near East 31 BC–AD 337*. Cambridge, Mass.

Mitterauer, M., and Sieder, R. (1982), *The European Family*, trans. K. Oosterveen and M. Hörzinger. Oxford.

Momigliano, A. (1989), 'The Origins of Rome', in *Cambridge Ancient History*², vii. 2, 52–112.

Morgan, L. H. (1877; repr. 1964), *Ancient Society*. New York.

Mount, F. (1982), *The Subversive Family: An Alternative History of Love and Marriage*. London.

Mouritsen, H. (1988), *Elections, Magistrates and the Municipal Élite*. Rome.

Mylonas, G. (1946), *Excavations at Olynthus*, xii. *Domestic and Public Architecture*. Baltimore.

Nardi, E. (1983), *Squilibrio e deficienza mentale in diritto romano*. Milan.

Nash, E. (1961–2), *Pictorial Dictionary of Ancient Rome*. 2 vols. London.

Néraudau, J. P. (1984), *Être enfant à Rome*. Paris.

Nevett, L. (1994), 'Separation or Seclusion? Towards an Archaeological Approach to Investigating Women in the Greek Household in the 5th to 3rd centuries BC', in *Architecture and Order: Approaches to Social Space*, ed. M. Parker Pearson and C. Richards. London/New York. 98–112.

Noy, D. (1991), 'Wicked Stepmothers in Roman Society and Imagination', *Journal of Family History* 16: 345–61.

Oliva, M. (n.d.), 'Giornali degli scavi' of the Casa di Iulius Polibius, vols. I–IX (unpub.).

Otterbein, K. F., and Otterbein, C. S. (1965), 'An Eye for an Eye, a Tooth for a Tooth: A Cross-Cultural Study of Feuding', *American Anthropologist* 67: 1470–82.

Overbeck, J., and Mau, A. (1884), *Pompeji in seinen Gebäuden, Alterthümern und Kunstwerken*. Leipzig.

Packer, J. (1971), 'The Insulae of Imperial Ostia', *Memoirs of the American Academy at Rome* 31. Rome.

Parkin, T. (1992), *Demography and Roman Society*. Baltimore.

Pflaum, H.-G. (1966), *Les Sodales Antoniniani de l'époque de Marc-Aurèle*. Paris.

Phillips, J. E. (1978), 'Roman Mothers and the Lives of Their Adult Daughters', *Helios* 6: 69–80.

Pietrangeli, C. (1951), 'Fistule aquarie della collezione Gorga', *Epigraphica* 13: 17–32.

Pinon, P., *et al.* (1982), *La Laurentine et l'invention de la Villa Romaine*. Paris.

Poque, S. (1984), *Le Langage symbolique dans la prédication d'Augustin d'Hippone: Images héroïques*. Paris.

Radcliffe-Brown, A. R. (1952), 'The Mother's Brother in South Africa', in *Structure and Function in Primitive Society*. London. (Orig. pub. 1924.)

Rapoport, A. (1990), 'Systems of Activities and Systems of Settings', in *Domestic Architecture and the Use of Space*, ed. S. Kent. Cambridge. 9–20.

Rapp, R., Ross, E., and Bridenthal, R. (1979), 'Examining Family History', *Feminist Studies* 5: 174–200.

Rawson, B. (1966), 'Family Life Among the Lower Classes at Rome in the First Two Centuries of the Empire', *Classical Philology* 61: 71–83.

—— (1986a), 'Children in the Roman *Familia*', in Rawson (1986b), 170–200.

—— (ed.) (1986b), *The Family in Ancient Rome: New Perspectives*. London/Sydney/Ithaca, NY.

—— (1989), '*Spurii* and the Roman View of Illegitimacy', *Antichthon* 23: 10–41.

—— (ed.) (1991), *Marriage, Divorce and Children in Ancient Rome*. Oxford.

Rebuffat, R. (1969/71), 'Maisons à péristyle d'Afrique du nord–répertoire de plans publiés', *Mélanges d'Archéologie et d'Histoire de l'École française de Rome* (1969), ii. 659–721; (1971), i. 445–99.

Reed, E. (1975), *Woman's Evolution from Matriarchal Clan to Patriarchal Family*. New York.

Reinach, S. (1912), *Répertoire de reliefs grecs et romains*. 3 vols. Paris.

Richardson, L. (1988), *Pompeii: An Architectural History*. Baltimore.

Roberti, M. (1935), ' "Patria potestas" e "paterna pietas": contributo allo studio dell'influenza del cristianesimo sul diritto romano', in P. Ciapessoni (ed.), *Studi in memoria di A. Albertoni I: Diritto romano e bizantino*. Padua. 257–70.

Ronke, J. (1987), *Magistratische Repräsentation im römischen Relief: Studien zu standes- und statusbezeichnenden Szenen*. London.

Rose, C. B. (1990), ' "Princes" and Barbarians on the Ara Pacis', *American Journal of Archaeology* 94: 453–67.

Rose, H. J. (1923), 'Nocturnal Funerals in Rome', *Classical Quarterly* 17: 191–4.

Ross, A. (1982), 'Absence of Evidence: Reply to Keryn Kefous', *Archaeology in Oceania* 17: 99.

Rossiter, J. J. (1978), *Roman Farm Buildings in Italy*. Oxford.

Russell, J. C. (1948), *British Medieval Population*. Albuquerque, N. Mex.

Sachers, E. (1951), 'Das Recht auf Unterhalt in der römischen Familie der klassischen Zeit', *Festschrift Fritz Schulz*, i. 310–63.

Saller, R. P. (1982), *Personal Patronage in the Early Empire*. Cambridge.

—— (1984), '*Familia, Domus* and the Roman Concept of the Family', *Phoenix* 38: 336–55.

—— (1986a), '*Patria Potestas* and the Stereotype of the Roman Family', *Continuity and Change* 1: 7–22.

—— (1986b), Review of Hallett (1984), *Classical Philology* 81: 354.

—— (1987a), 'Men's Age at Marriage and its Consequences in the Roman Family', *Classical Philology* 82: 20–35.

—— (1987b), 'Slavery and the Roman Family', in M. Finley (ed.), *Classical Slavery*. London.

—— (1988), '*Pietas*, Obligation and Authority in the Roman Family', in P. Kneiss and V. Lasemann (eds.), *Alte Geschichte und Wissenschaftsgeschichte: Festschrift für Karl Christ*. Darmstadt. 393–410.

—— (1991), 'Corporal Punishment, Authority, and Obedience in the Roman Household', in Rawson (1991), 144–65.

—— (1993), 'The Social Dynamics of Consent to Marriage and Sexual Relations: The Evidence of Roman Comedy', in A. E. Laiou (ed.), *Consent and Coercion to Sex and Marriage in Ancient and Medieval Societies*. Washington. 83–104.

—— (1994), *Patriarchy, Property and Death in the Roman Family*. Cambridge.

Saller, R. P., and Shaw, B. D. (1984a), 'Tombstones and Roman Family Relations in the Principate: Civilians, Soldiers and Slaves', *Journal of Roman Studies* 74, 124–56.

—— (1984b), 'Close-Kin Marriage in Roman Society', *Man* 19: 432–44.

Salza Prina Ricotti, E. (1978/80), 'Cucine e quartieri servili in epoca romana,' *Rendiconti: Atti della Pontificia accademia romana d'archeologia* 51/2: 237–94.

Sasel, A., and Sasel, J. (1986), *Inscriptiones Latinae quae in Iugoslavia inter annos MCMII et MCMXL repertae et editae sunt*. Ljubljiana.

Schäfer, T. (1989), *Imperii insignia: Sella curulis und fasces: Zur Repräsentation römischer Magistrate*. Mainz.

Schaps, D. M. (1979), *Economic Rights of Women in Ancient Greece*. Edinburgh.

Schiffer, M. (1985), 'Is there a Pompeii Premise?', *Journal of Anthropological Research* 41: 18–41.

Schneider, D. M. (1984), *A Critique of the Study of Kinship*. Chicago.

Schumacher, L. (1976), 'Das Ehrendekret für M. Nonius Balbus aus Herculaneum (AE 1947, 53)', *Chiron* 6: 165–84.

Schwarte, K.-H. (1979), 'Traians Regierungsbeginn und der Agricola des Tacitus', *Bonner Jahrbücher* 179: 139–75.

Scott Barchy, S. (1973), *First-Century Slavery and 1 Corinthians 7: 21* (Society of Biblical Literature Diss. Series 11). Montana.

Scullard, H. H. (1981), *Festivals and Ceremonies of the Roman Republic*. Ithaca, NY.

Seiler, F. (1992), *Casa degli Amorini Dorati (VI 16.7) (Häuser in Pompeji 5)*. Munich.

Shackleton Bailey, D. R. (1965–70), *Cicero's Letters to Atticus*. 4 vols. Cambridge.

—— (1971), *Cicero*. London.

Shaw, B. (1984), 'Latin Funerary Epigraphy and Family Relationships in the Later Empire', *Historia* 33: 457–97.

—— (1987a), 'The Family in Late Antiquity: The Experience of Augustine', *Past and Present* 115: 3–51.

—— (1987b), 'The Age of Roman Girls at Marriage: Some Reconsiderations', *Journal of Roman Studies* 77: 30–46.

—— (1991), 'The Cultural Meaning of Death: Age and Gender in the Roman Family', in Kertzer and Saller (1991), 66–90.

Sherwin-White, A. N. (1966), *The Letters of Pliny. A Historical and Social Commentary*. Oxford.

Sherwin-White, A. N. (1973), *The Roman Citizenship*. 2nd edn. Oxford.

Sigismund Nielsen, H. (1987), '*Alumnus*: A Term of Relation denoting Quasi-adoption', *Classica et Mediaevalia* 38: 141–88.

Sigismund Nielsen, H. (1990), '*Delicia* in Roman Literature and in the Urban Inscriptions', *Analecta Romana Instituti Danici* 19: 79–88.

—— (1991), '*Ditis examen domus*', *Classica et Mediaevalia* 42: 221–40.

—— (1995), 'Recreating the Physical Context: Roman Epitaphs and their Original Setting', *Analecta Romana Instituti Danici* (forthcoming).

—— (1996), 'Quasi-kin, Quasi-adoption and the Roman Family', in *Adoption et Fosterage: Proceedings of CNRS Colloquium 1993*, ed. M. Corbier. Paris.

Silvestrini, F. (1987), *Sepulcrum Marci Artori Gemini. La Tomba detta dei Platorini nel Museo Nazionale Romano*. Rome.

Sinn, F. (1987), *Städtrömische Marmorurnen*. Mainz.

Sirks, A. J. B. (1981), 'Informal Manumission and the Lex Junia', *Revue Internationale des Droits de l'Antiquité* 28: 247–76.

—— (1983), 'The Lex Junia and the Effects of Informal Manumission and Iteration', *Revue Internationale des Droits de l'Antiquité* 30: 211–92.

Skolnick, A. (1975), 'The Family Revisited: Themes in Recent Social Science Research', *Journal of Interdisciplinary History* 5: 703–19.

Slater, W. J. (ed.) (1991), *Dining in a Classical Context*. Ann Arbor.

Smith, J. E., and Oeppen, J. (1993), 'Estimating Numbers of Kin in Historical England using Demographic Microsimulation', in R. Schofield and D. Reher (edd.), *Old and New Methods in Historical Demography*. Oxford.

Smith, J. T. (1987), 'The Social Structure of Roman Villas', *Oxford Journal of Archaeology* 6: 243–55.

Sogliano, A. (1898), 'La Casa dei Vettii in Pompei', *Monumenti Antichi* 8: 233–416.

—— (1905), 'Pompei: Relazione degli scavi fatti dal dicember 1902 a tutto marzo 1905', *Notizie degli Scavi di Antichità* 2: 245–57.

Sprey, J. (1988), 'Sociobiology and the Study of Family Conflict', in E. Filsinger (ed.), *Biosocial Perspectives on the Family*. Boulder, Colo. 137–58.

Strocka, V. M. (1984), *Casa di Principe di Napoli (Häuser in Pompeji 1)*. Tübingen.

—— (1991), *Casa del labirinto (VI 8.10) (Häuser in Pompeji 5)*. Munich.

Stupperich, R. (1991), 'Das Grabmal eines Konsularen in Attaleia', *Istanbul. Mitteilungen* 41: 417–22.

Sutherland, I. (1989), 'Colonnaded Cenacula in Pompeian Domestic Architecture', Ph.D. thesis. Duke University.

Syme, R. (1988), *Roman Papers IV*. Oxford.

—— (1991), *Roman Papers VII*. Oxford.

Talbert, R. J. A. (1984), *The Senate of Imperial Rome*. Princeton.

Taubenschlag, R. (1932), 'Die Alimentationspflicht im Rechte der Papyri', *Studi in onore di S. Riccobono* 1: 507–18.

—— (1955), *The Law of Greco-Roman Egypt in the Light of the Papyri, 332 BC–AD 640*. Warsaw.

—— (1956), 'La γηροκομία dans le droit des papyrus', *Revue Internationale des Droits de l'Antiquité* 3: 173–9.

Taylor, L. R. (1961), 'Freedmen and Freeborn in the Epitaphs of Imperial Rome', *American Journal of Philology* 82: 113–32.

Tellegen, J. W. (1982), *The Roman Law of Succession in the Letters of Pliny the Younger*. Zutphen.

Thébert, Y. (1987), 'Private Life and Domestic Architecture in Roman Africa', in P. Veyne (ed.), *A History of Private Life*: i. *From Pagan Rome to Byzantium*. Cambridge, Mass. 313–409.

Thomson, D. (1991), 'The Welfare of the Elderly in the Past: A Family or Community Responsibility?', in M. Pelling and R. M. Smith (eds.), *Life, Death, and the Elderly*. London.

Thompson, D'A. W. (1936), *A Glossary of Greek Birds*. London.

Trautmann, T. R. (1987), *Lewis Henry Morgan and the Invention of Kinship*. Berkeley/Los Angeles.

Treggiari, S. (1969), *Roman Freedmen during the Late Republic*. Oxford.

—— (1975), 'Family Life among the Staff of the Volusii', *Transactions of the American Philological Association* 105: 393–401.

—— (1981), '*Contubernales* in *CIL* 6', *Phoenix* 35: 42–69.

—— (1991), *Roman Marriage*: Iusti Coniuges *from the time of Cicero to the time of Ulpian*. Oxford.

van Aken, A. R. A. (1949), 'Late Roman Domus Architecture', *Mnemosyne* ser. 4, 2: 242–51.

Walker, S. (1985), *Memorials to the Roman Dead*. London.

Wall, R. *et al.* (edd.) (1983), *Family Forms in Historic Europe*. Cambridge.

Wallace, S. L. (1938), *Taxation in Egypt from Augustus to Diocletian*. Princeton.

Wallace-Hadrill, A. (1988), 'The Social Structure of the Roman House', *Papers of the British School at Rome* 56: 43–97.

—— (ed.) (1989), *Patronage in Ancient Society*. London.

—— (1990), 'The Social Spread of Roman Luxury: Sampling Pompeii and Herculaneum', *Papers of the British School at Rome* 58: 145–92.

—— (1991*a*), 'Élites and Trade in the Roman Town', in J. Rich and A. Wallace-Hadrill (edd.), *City and Country in the Roman World*. London. 241–72.

—— (1991*b*), 'Houses and Households: Sampling Pompeii and Herculaneum', in Rawson (1991), 191–227.

—— (1994), *Houses and Society in Pompeii and Herculaneum*. Princeton.

Warscher, T. (1948), 'I Marmi di Pompei' (unpublished, Swedish Institute in Rome).

Watson, A. (1967), *The Law of Persons in the Later Roman Republic*. Oxford.

—— (1968), *The Law of Property in the Later Roman Republic*. Oxford.

Watson, P. A. (1995), *Ancient Stepmothers: Myth, Misogyny and Reality*. Leiden.

Weaver, P. R. C. (1986), 'The Status of Children in Mixed Marriages', in Rawson (1986), 145–69.

—— (1990), 'Where have all the Junian Latins gone? Nomenclature and Status in the Roman Empire', *Chiron* 20: 275–305.

Weaver, P. R. C. (1991), 'Children of Freedmen (and Freedwomen)', in Rawson (1991), 66–90.

Weiskittel, S. F. (1979), 'Vitruvius and Domestic Architecture at Pompeii', in *Pompeii and the Vesuvian Landscape: Papers of a Symposium sponsored by the Archaeological Institute of America and the Smithsonian Institute*. Washington DC. 25–38.

Whittaker, C. R. (1985), 'Trade and the Aristocracy in the Roman Empire', *Opus* 4: 49–75.

Widdicombe, P. (1994), *The Fatherhood of God from Origen to Athanasius*. Oxford.

Wiedemann, T. (1989), *Adults and Children in the Roman Empire*. London.

Will, E. L. (1979), 'Women in Pompeii', *Archaeology* 32/5: 34–43.

Wilson, A. (1980), 'The Infancy of the History of Childhood: an Appraisal of Philippe Ariès', *History and Theory* 19: 132–53.

Winkes, R. (ed.) (1985), *The Age of Augustus: Interdisciplinary Conference held at Brown University 1982*. Providence, RI./Louvain-la-Neuve, Belgium.

Wiseman, T. P. (1987), '*Conspicui postes tectaque digna deo*: The Public Image of Aristocratic and Imperial Houses in the Late Republic and Early Empire', in *L'Urbs: Espace urbain et histoire*. Rome. 393–413.

Wistrand, E. (1970), 'Das altrömische Haus nach den literarischen Quellen', *Eranos* 68: 191–223.

Yanagisako, S. J. (1979), 'Family and Household: The Analysis of Domestic Groups', *Annual Review of Anthropology* 8: 161–205.

—— (1991), 'Capital and Gendered Interest in Italian Family Firms', in Kertzer and Saller (1991), 321–39.

Yaron, R. (1960), *Gifts in Contemplation of Death*. Oxford.

Zanker, P. (1975), 'Grabreliefs römischer Freigelassener', *Jahrbuch des Deutschen Archäologischen Instituts* 90: 267–315.

Zanker, P. (1988), *The Power of Images in the Age of Augustus*. Ann Arbor.

Index

Emperors' names are given in their common English form in *italic*.

actio 42, 43
adoption 36, 37, 40, 45, 46, 202
adrogation 40–1
Aelius Aurelius Antoninus, M. (*Marcus Aurelius*) 77, 186–7, 225, 227
Aelius Aurelius Antoninus, T. (*Antoninus Pius*) 77, 225, 227
Aelius Hadrianus, P. (*Hadrian*) 225, 226
age distribution 173–5, 184–5, 191–2, 197–8
age indication 174–5, 177, 191, 192, 197
agnation 12
Agrippina the Elder 217
Agrippa (M. Vipsanius Agrippa) 212
alae 289, 305, 329, 337, 350
album Augustalium 68, 71–2
alimenta 132, 211, 224
alumni, see foster-children
Ambrose, bishop of Milan 101
amita 8, 9, 21, 22, 24
amphorae 335, 340, 341, 345, 346, 347, 348, 351
angels 112, 113
anniculi (causae) probatio 57, 59, 60, 66, 68, 70
anthropology 7, 8, 10
Antoninus Pius, see Aelius Aurelius Antoninus, T.
apartments, *see* multiple dwellings
apotheosis 208, 223, 231
Apuleius 155, 161, 162–3
Ara Pacis Augustae 207, 211, 213–14, 216, 235, 237
Arch of the Sergii, Pola 85
Arch of Trajan, Beneventum 225
Ariès, Philippe 205
Aristophanes 127–8
art:
  Christian 233
  Hellenistic 208
  Imperial 212–17, 217–20, 220–4, 224–31
  Republican 206, 207–12
atrium 286, 290, 292, 297, 300, 305–6, 306–10, 311, 313, 314, 323, 329, 333–5, 349–50, 353
atrium houses 281, 283, 289, 295, 296, 303–6, 325–8

Attia Viriola 161, 162
Atticus (Q. Caecilius Pomponius Atticus) 155–61
Augustales 68, 72
Augustine, St, of Hippo 104–5, 112–19, 120, 121
Augustus (C. Iulius Caesar Octauianus) 78, 206, 207, 210, 211, 212, 213, 214, 215, 217
auunculus 15, 19–23, 25, 26, 27, 29, 33
auus 19, 25

beds 336, 337, 338, 339, 342, 343, 344
beneficium 66, 67, 69
Bettini, Maurizio 8, 9, 22, 23, 25
braziers 338, 339, 340, 341, 344, 347
Britannicus, son of Claudius 217, 219
bulla 211

Caecilia Metella 86, 210
Caesar, *see under* Iulius
Calatoria Themis 69–71
Calpurnia, wife of Pliny the Younger 136
Calpurnius Dexter, Ser. 87
Calpurnius Piso, Cn. 75
Campus Martius, Rome 209
captatores (legacy-hunters) 13
carmen saeculare (Horace) 213
cenaculum 294, 323
Cestius 86, 210
childhood:
  in art 233
  concept 205
  iconography ch. 9 *passim*, 233–8
children:
  age-portrayal 237
  artistic representations 205, 206, 209, 217, 231, 233, 234, 236, 238
  commemoration 192, 211, 231–2, 235; of parents 200, 245, 246, 248–50, 265–6
  dedicands 273–9
  in epitaphs 273–9
  epithets used 189, 190
  freeborn 49, 60, 61, 203
  gender ratio 242
  in law 206, 207
  in literature 206, 207

children (*cont.*):
  maintenance 224, 227
  missing parents 240, 254–5
  mythological images 235
  property rights 227
  rearing 28, 200
  social context 234, 236
  status 38, 39, 55, 63, 67, 225–7, 233, 237
  visibility 206, 207, 235
Christ 107, 117
Christianity 2, 3, 5, ch. 5 *passim*
Cicero, *see under* Tullius
citizenship 3, 35, 39, 40, 50, 51, 52, 56, 59, 60, 62, 63, 64, 66, 68–9, 70, 72
Claudius Drusus Caesar Germanicus *Nero* 219
clientela, see patronage
Cluuius Maximus Paullinus, P. 87
coinage 208, 214, 217, 223, 224, 272
commemoration:
  age distribution 173–5
  class differences 224
  gender differences 224
  patterns 170
  regional variations 255
commercium 57
concubinage 38, 39
Constitutio Antoniniana 50, 57, 67
contubernia 197
conubium 35, 38, 39, 50, 69
cooking vessels 338, 343, 345
Cornelius Pusio, L. 78–9
cubiculum 283, 290–1, 292, 294, 297, 300, 302, 318, 323, 329
cupids, *see* Erotes
cura furiosi et prodigi 146, 147
curator, see guardianship

daughters 129, 190, 192, 196–7, 202, 204, 243–7
death, premature (*mors immatura, mors acerba*) 174–5, 193, 198–202, 235
death and burial 208–9, 229
Didius Seuerus Iulianus, M. 79
divorce 136, 150, 153
domestic space, *see* household space
Domitian (T. Flauius Domitianus) 223
domus, see houses
donatio mortis causa 129–30
door-fittings 333, 336, 337, 339
dowry 44, 46, 150, 167
Drusus the Younger (Drusus Iulius Caesar) 217

education 223
elderly people 4, 148, ch. 6 *passim*

dependency 148
  maintenance 132, 134, 139
  welfare 134
emancipation 36, 37, 43, 133
epitaphs 4, 169–71, 173
epithets 4
  bene merens 179–85
  carus/carissimus 185–92
  dulcis/dulcissimus 185–94
  family relationships 175–6, 177–9
  friendships 186
  interpretation ch. 8 *passim*
  pius/piissimus/pientissimus 193–8
  used by poets 188, 195, 196
equestrians 76, 77
equity (*aequabilitas*) 111
Erotes 231, 236
exedra 291, 294, 341–2
extended family 134

familia, see family structure
family conflict 4, 139–40, ch. 7 *passim*
family law 3, 7, ch. 2 *passim*, 216
family life 149, 151, 153, 204, 224, 281, 300, 301, 322, 323
family members 149–50, 152, 167
  abuse 149–50, 152, 167
  changing roles 153
  commemoration 2, 196–7, 211, 216, 240, 244–8, 249, 255, 264, 265–6
  conflicting interests 150, 165
  maintenance ch. 6 *passim*
  status ch. 2 *passim*, 204, 211, 216
  see also under the names of family members, e.g. sons
family obligations, *see pietas*
family relationships 164, 171–3, 176–7, 190, 192, 194, 203, 204, 239
family size 240, 241–2, 249, 250, 255, 258, 259, 262–3, 278–9
family structure 1, 2, 4–5, 12, ch. 2 *passim*, 169
  gender balance 240, 242–3, 244, 246–7, 254, 255, 260–4
  generations 250–1, 267
  see also extended family; nuclear family
farms, working 286, 293, 295–6
father–son conflict 117, 140, 143, 145
father–son relationships 103, 113, 121
fathers 244, 245, 246, 249
fecunditas 224, 225
fideicommissum 46, 57, 71
fistulae aquariae 76–7
fixtures 328, 334, 336, 337–8, 339, 340, 341, 343, 345
forecourts, see *atrium*
Forum of Augustus 215

foster-children 70, 183, 190, 193, 197, 203, 240, 251, 253–4, 255, 270
foster-parents 253–4, 255
fosterage 173, 202
freedmen 41, 45, 203–4, 216, 219, 232, 234, 248, 249
  location in houses 316–17
  status 65, 203, 211
freedom, see *libertas*
freedwomen 48, 52–3
friendship 27, 186
Fronto, M. Cornelius 77, 186–7, 188
funerary altars 207, 210, 219–20, 235, 237–8
funerary foundations 211
funerary inscriptions 30, 211, 216, 231–2
funerary monuments (*sepulchra*) 4, 79, 81, 84, 207, 208–10, 211, 216
funerary reliefs 207, 210, 219
funerary urns 210, 238
furniture 297, 302, 331, 333, 334, 337, 338, 339, 340, 341, 342, 343, 347
Fustel de Coulanges, N.D. 7, 10, 11, 12

Gaius Caesar 212, 213, 214–15
gardens 77, 339–41, 347, 351, 353
generational conflict, see family conflict
genius 27
Germanicus (Germanicus Iulius Caesar) 217
gifts 44–5, 71
Graeco-Roman society 102, 103, 111
grandchildren 240, 250–2, 267, 268
grandparents 126, 250–2, 267, 268
gratia 110, 181, 182
great-grandparents 126, 251
guardianship 28, 32, 46, 57, 106, 136–7, 146, 148, 227

Hadrian, see Aelius Hadrianus, P.
hearths 289, 293, 329, 344–5
Herennius Caecilianus, C. 97–8
Herodes Atticus, Ti. Claudius 92
hibernaculum 289, 293
household 2, 31
  metaphor 3, 104, 108, 109–10, 115
household organization 281, 282, 286, 287, 288, 296, 301
  seasonal changes 289, 291–3
household space 2, 5, ch. 11 *passim*, 299, 301, 302, 303, 305, 309, 315, 316, 317, 318, 319, ch. 13 *passim*
houses:
  activities 5, 282, 283, 297, 306, 310, 324, 334, 335–6, 340, 350–2, 353, 354

artefacts 302, 319, ch. 13 *passim*
back entrances 347–8, 351, 352
bath areas 329, 344, 347, 348, 351
Campania 287, 289
corridors 314, 339
decoration 282, 283, 297, 301–2, 305, 310, 319, 329, 335–6, 338, 341, 342, 344, 350
excavation reports 326–7
Gaul 315
industrial areas 29, 326, 333, 339, 340, 341, 348, 349, 350–1, 352
inhabitants ch. 12 *passim*, 351–3
North Africa 311–16
Ostia 281, 315
Pompeii 281, 284, 305, 306–11, 313–16, ch. 13 *passim*
private areas 283, 300
public areas 283, 300
service areas 346–7, 352
social status 299, 319
symbolism 289
upper storeys 338, 346, 348–9, 351, 353
visitors 290, 291, 295, 297, 299, 303, 305–6, 308, 309, 310, 318, 319, 351, 352
women's quarters 307–9, 353
see also *atrium* houses; gardens; rooms; town houses; villas

illegitimacy 36, 47–9, 50, 225–6, 252
impluuium 333, 347
infants 207
  exposure 199
  lack of commemoration 174
ingenui 245, 248, 252, 255
inheritance 29, 45, 49, 50, 52, 58, 69, 71, 120, 153, 167
inheritance rights 19, 36, 37, 40, 57
inscriptions 30, 81, 84, 85, 169, 179, 202, 209, 211, 216, 231–2, 239
intestacy 42, 47
Iulius Antiochus Philopappus, C. 90–1
Iulius Caesar, C. 157, 158, 159, 160, 161, 166, 215
Iulius Celsus Polemaeanus, Ti. 89–90
Iulius Geminius Marcianus, P. 97
Iulius Marinus Caecilius Simplex, L. 82–3
Iulius Quadratus Bassus, C. 90
ius commercii 64, 65, 69
ius conubii 59, 64
ius gentium 35, 64
ius Latii 61, 63, 66, 67
ius liberorum 46, 47, 48, 49
ius naturale 35

Julia, daughter of Augustus 212, 214
Julia Livia, *see* Livilla (Claudia Livia Julia)
Junian Latins 3, 38, 40, 46, 50, ch. 3
    passim
Justa, *see* Petronia Justa

kinship 7, 14, 18, 26, 27, 31
kinship terminology 2, 13, 16, 17, 18–19,
    20, 30, 34
kitchens (*culinae*) 283, 289, 293, 316–17,
    344–5, 346, 350
kline monuments ii, 227
knights, *see* equestrians

Lactantius 104–5, 106, 108–12, 119, 120,
    121
lararium 316–17, 333, 348
Latini coloniarii 58, 63, 64, 66, 71, 72
latrines 329, 339, 343, 345–6, 350
legitimacy 40, 41, 42, 44, 45, 47–9, 51,
    57
lex Aelia Sentia 38, 39, 49, 51, 56, 58,
    60, 62, 64, 65, 70
lex Irnitana 64, 65
lex Iunia 38, 57, 58, 59, 60, 62, 63, 64,
    65
lex Minicia 38, 39
lex Papia Poppaea 42, 45, 46
libertas 56, 57, 59
Livia, wife of Augustus 214
Livilla (Claudia Livia Julia) 217
Lucius Caesar 212, 213, 214–15
Lucius Verus 186–7

Maine, Henry 8, 10, 11, 33
manumission 51, 55, 61, 62, 64, 65, 102,
    121, 245, 249, 252, 278
    formal 56, 59, 60, 62, 70
    informal 56, 57, 61, 62
    testamentary 66
manus marriage 35, 41, 42, 48, 50
Marcus, son of Cicero, *see under* Tullius
Marcus Aurelius, *see* Aelius Aurelius
    Antoninus, M.
Marius Maximus 79
marriage 29, 35, 39, 46, 50, 51, 59, 136
marriage legislation 41, 45, 46, 49, 213,
    252
martyrs 112–13
master–slave relationships 7, 102, 103,
    109, 113, 115, 117, 118
matertera 8, 9, 21, 22, 24, 29, 30
matrimonium iustum, *see* marriage
mental disabilities 141, 142–3, 147–8
Minicia Marcella Fundani f. 86, 224
Minicius Fundanus, C. 73, 86, 224
Morgan, Lewis 8, 10, 11, 33

mors acerba/immatura, *see* death,
    premature
mothers 47–50, 207, 244, 245, 246, 249
multiple dwellings 294, 295, 296
municipium 64, 65, 67

needlework 335, 338, 349, 352, 353
nepos 19–20
Nero, *see* Claudius Drusus Caesar
    Germanicus Nero
Nerva (Cocceius Nerva, M.) 224
niches, *see* recesses
Nigrinus Curiatius Maternus, M. Cornelius
    91–2
nomenclature 26, 56, 72, 216, 248, 252,
    274–5, 276
Nonii family 93–5, 96
North Africa 104, 113, 117, 311–16
nuclear family 35, 172, 240
Numicius Pica Caesianus, P. 78
Nummii family 95, 96

obsequium 24, 33
oecus 329, 341–2
oikos 143, 144
old age 128, 137, 140, 143
orphans 251
ovens 293, 337, 339, 345, 346, 347

parents:
    commemoration of children 171, 197–8,
        240, 244–8, 265
    expectations 199, 200–1
    transfer of responsibilities 153–4
    treatment by children ch. 6 *passim*
paterfamilias 4, 32, 35, 108–9, 110, 114,
    131, 133, 134, 135, 144, 146, 150,
    152, 154, 166, 194, 290, 299, 301,
    305, 307, 319
patria potestas 11, 12, 13, 14, 24, 30, 36,
    41, 43, 50, 51, 106, 131, 134, 135,
    144, 145, 148, 150, 152, 167
patronage 7, 283, 290, 299, 323
patrons 31, 36, 42, 45, 48, 50, 62, 65,
    67, 173, 183, 190, 204
patruus 8, 9, 21, 22, 23, 24, 30, 31, 32, 33
Paul, St 101, 102, 104–8, 119, 120, 121
peculium 63, 145, 225–6
Penates 289, 293
peregrinus 40, 245, 248, 255
peristyles 289, 292, 300, 310–16, 326,
    329, 339–41, 350
Petronia Justa 69–71
Petronia Vitalis 69–71
Petronius Stephanus, C. 69–71
Philopappus, C. Iulius Antiochus, *see* Julius
    Antiochus Philopappus, C.

pietas 16, 21, 24, 25, 33, 35, 36, 40, 43,
    45, 124, 131, 132, 133, 134, 151,
    165, 172, 194, 195, 198, 204, 207,
    213, 216, 224, 236, 246
Pinarius Cornelius Clemens, Cn. 84
Plautii family 81, 87
Plautius Siluanus Aelianus, Ti. 81–2
Plautus 21
Pliny the Younger (C. Plinius L. f.
    Secundus) 21, 28, 73, 98–9, 136, 162,
    187, 188, 223, 317–18
Pompeius Falco, Q. 97
Pompeius Sosius Priscus, Q. 97
Pompeius Vopiscus C. Arruntius Catellius
    Celer Allius Sabinus 83
Pompey (Cn. Pompeius Magnus) 157, 158,
    159
Pomponia 155–61, 182
portraiture 211, 234
Postumii family 95, 96
potestas, see *patria potestas*
poverty 137, 138
privacy 285, 287, 297, 300, 310, 317–18
property 25–6, 42, 43, 48, 69, 145, 146,
    153
public monuments 78, 85, 212
Pudentilla of Oea 161, 163, 166
puellae Faustinianae 225
punishment 25, 108, 110, 114–15, 116,
    117, 120, 121

Quadratus, C. Antius A. Iulius 95–6
querela de inofficioso testamento 162, 165
Quintus, brother of Cicero, *see under*
    Tullius
Quintus, nephew of Cicero, *see under*
    Tullius

Radcliffe-Brown, A. R. 8, 9, 14, 15, 24,
    33
recesses 333, 336, 337, 339, 341, 342,
    343, 344, 345, 346
Regulus, M. Aquilius 223
remarriage 136, 165, 252
Roman law 11, 13, 106, 108, 132
rooms:
    finds 297
    functions 284–5, 297, 302, 311, 328,
        329, 333–54 *passim*
    relationships 287
    use 328, 329, 330, 354
    *see also under the names of specific
    rooms* e.g. *alae*; kitchens

salutatio 303, 305
sarcophagi 207, 208, 210, 227, 229, 231,
    233, 235–6, 237–8

Scipiones 209
Secular Games 207, 213, 219, 223
self-commemorations 175, 184, 191, 203,
    204
senators 3, 74, 75, ch. 4 *passim*
    funerary inscriptions 3, 75, 85
    funerary monuments 80, 81
    honours 78, 79, 84, 94
    houses in Rome 77, 78
    tombs 75, 86, 87–8, 91, 210
senatus consultum Claudianum 225
senatus consultum Orphitianum 48, 226
senatus consultum Tertullianum 47, 48
Seneca (L. Annaeus Seneca) 199, 200
senility 139–48
Seruilii relief 211
shrines 343, 344
siblings 196–7, 240, 248, 251, 254–5, 271
Sicinii family 162–3, 166
slave-owners 55, 59
slaves 3, 37, 38, 55, 60, ch. 5 *passim*,
    203–4, 216, 225, 245, 248, 249, 306,
    352
    family relationships 60, 317
    location in houses 316–17
    status 3, 63, 211
social organization 7, 11, 12, 13, 16, 17,
    316, 319
social relationships 7, 22, 282, 283, 288,
    299
social welfare 123, 139
soldiers 225–6
Solon 126, 135
sons 3, ch. 5 *passim*, 129, 145, 148, 190,
    192, 196–7, 202, 204, 243, 244, 245,
    246
Sosius Senecio, Q. 73, 97
space, *see* household space
spinning 346, 352, 353
spouses:
    age difference 247, 252
    commemoration 184, 197, 247
    dedications 171, 179
    epithets used 190–1
    maintenance 136–7
stairways 329, 336, 339, 340, 341, 343,
    345, 346, 347
Statius (freedman of Quintus) 156, 157, 158
Statoria M. f. Marcella 86, 224
statues 208, 212, 223, 334, 338, 339,
    341, 342, 343, 344
status 2, 3, 37, 38, 53
    Augustales 72
    freeborn 70, 203–4
    freedmen 203–4
    indication 203–4
    Junian Latins 70, 71, 203–4

stepchildren 240, 252–3, 255, 269
stepfathers 152, 155
stepmothers 152, 155, 162, 167
stepparents 161, 162–3, 164–5, 252, 255
Stoicism 101, 102
storage 297, 334–42 *passim*, 344, 346–7,
    350, 351
storage vessels 335, 337, 338, 339, 340,
    341, 347, 348
Sulpicius Maximus, Q. 223, 237
Sulpicius Platorinus 86, 210

tablinum 289, 290, 305, 306, 329, 338–9,
    350
toga uirilis ceremony 215
tombs 170, 208, 210, 211, 216
town houses 281, 288–92, 295, 298
Trajan (M. Ulpius Traianus) 187, 224, 227
triclinium 289, 291, 292, 300, 302, 303,
    329, 337–8, 341, 350
Trojan Games 215
Tullia 157, 200, 208
Tullius Cicero, M. 21, 23, 24, 27–8,
    155–61, 166, 167, 181, 182, 187,
    199, 200, 208

Tullius Cicero, M., junior 157, 159
Tullius Cicero, Q. 155–61, 166, 167, 182
Tullius Cicero, Q., junior 155–61, 166
tutela, see guardianship

Ummidius Durmius Quadratus, C. 92–3
uncles 8, 16, 24, 33, 250

Venidius Ennychus, L. 68–9, 72
uerna 227
Vespasian (T. Flauius Vespasianus) 220
vessels 335, 342, 343, 345, 347, 348
    see also cooking vessels; storage vessels
vestibules (*fauces*) 289, 300, 307, 313,
    314, 329, 333
Vibii relief 211
Villa Doria Pamphili relief 217, 235
villas 292–3, 295, 296, 317–18
Volusii family 82
votive figures, Italian 207–8

water-pipes, see *fistulae aquariae*
weaving 334, 338, 343, 344, 346, 349,
    350, 352, 353
wills 29, 36, 42, 45, 47, 57, 71